Sons of
the Soil

SONS OF THE SOIL

Migration and Ethnic Conflict in India

MYRON WEINER

PRINCETON
UNIVERSITY
PRESS

Copyright © 1978 by Princeton University Press
Published by Princeton University Press,
Princeton, New Jersey
In the United Kingdom:
Princeton University Press, Guildford, Surrey

All Rights Reserved

Library of Congress Cataloging in Publication Data
will be found on the last printed page of this book

Publication of this book has been aided by a grant
from the Paul Mellon Fund of Princeton University Press

This book has been composed in Linotype Times Roman

Printed in the United States of America by Princeton
University Press, Princeton, New Jersey

IN MEMORY OF

Hyman Weiner

Labanoras, Lithuania, circa 1897
Van Nuys, California, 1965

There is much talk these days about the "Sons of the Soil." The advocates and opponents of this theory do not seem to agree among themselves. Perhaps, the following classification might solve the problem of those involved in the controversy.

First, we must not accept the present division of states and districts as they are political and man-made. When we swear by the soil, we must adhere to the natural, geological division. Our earth has been clearly divided into different kinds of soil regions: alluvial, volcanic, etc. It is but natural that sons should work only in their respective mother soils. For example, only those born in the alluvial soil can work in the alluvial region. They may call themselves "alluvians" and proclaim "Alluvial soil for alluvians only." People of other soil regions may form similar groups. People may be given identity cards with the name of soil clearly printed on it.

To solve the problem of babies born in the air (planes), they should be employed as pilots and air hostesses. Nobody except the sons and daughters of the air should get these air jobs. They should be allowed to stay on earth in a non-classified soil region when they are off-duty.

S. Pushparaman
Tiruchirapalli
Letter to the *Times of India*,
January 28, 1973

PREFACE

For financial support for this study I am grateful to the Behavioral Sciences Research Branch of the National Institute of Mental Health, which provided me with a grant to study the socio-political consequences of interethnic migrations in India, and to the Rockefeller-Ford Program for Population Research and the National Institute of Child Health and Human Development, which provided me with grants to study governmental policies toward ethnic migrations within India. Permission to engage in field research in India was granted by the Ministry of Education and by the Indian Council for Social Science Research. In 1970-1971, when the initial field research was undertaken, and on subsequent visits to India in 1973 and 1976 I enjoyed the hospitality of the Institute of Economic Growth at Delhi University, where I was a visiting research scholar. I am most grateful to its various directors, Professors P. N. Dhar, Ali Khusru, and P. B. Desai, and to my colleague Professor Ashish Bose, for their support. I am also particularly grateful to the Registrars General of the Indian Census, Mr. Chandrasekhar and Mr. Chowri, and to the staff of the census offices in New Delhi and in the various state capitals. In the states in which I worked I also received the support of many local institutions, scholars, and government officials, without whose assistance this study would not have been possible. I have enumerated many of these individuals and institutions in the relevant chapters. To all those cited there and to many others whom I have no doubt inadvertently omitted, I am most appreciative.

At M.I.T. I had the assistance of several graduate students, including Mary Fainsod Katzenstein, whose own research on nativist movements in Bombay was of great help to me, and Kartikeya Sarabhai, John Satorius, Ijas Gilani, Colin Mc-Andrews, Robert Berrier, Martin Slater, John McDougall, Jessie White, and Carrie Hunter, and, among the staff, Jessie Janjigian, Frances Powell and Gail Morchower, who painstakingly typed innumerable drafts. Some of the statistical calculations were performed by my daughter, Beth Weiner. A variety of administrative supports was provided by the Center for International Studies.

Some of the arguments presented in this book were honed in discussions with my colleagues in the Migration and Development Study Group at M.I.T.: Jagdish Bhagwati, Nazli Choucri, Wayne A. Cornelius, John R. Harris, Michael J. Piore and Rosemarie S. Rogers.

I also profited from the comments of Paul Brass, Carolyn M. Elliot, Marcus Franda, Sidney Goldstein, Waheeduddin Khan, Nirmal Minz, Lucian W. Pye, K. V. Narayana Rao, P. Satyanarayana, Jyoti Sen, Amar Kumar Singh, M. N. Srinivas and L. P. Vidyarthi.

Portions of this study were published in the following journals or books: "When Migrants Succeed and Natives Fail," in the *Proceedings* of the International Union for the Scientific Study of Population, Liège, Belgium, 1973; "Socio-Political Consequences of Interstate Migration in India" in W. Howard Wriggins and James F. Guyot, editors, *Population, Politics, and the Future of Southern Asia*, New York: Columbia University Press, 1973; and "Assam and Its Migrants," *Demography India*, Vol. ii, No. 2, 1973.

The research for this study was conducted during an eventful period in India's history: popular elections for Mrs. Gandhi's Congress in 1971, civil war in Pakistan and a massive influx of refugees to northeastern India from East Pakistan, war between India and Pakistan over Bangladesh, the subsequent electoral triumph of Mrs. Gandhi's Congress in the 1972 state assembly elections, the growing centralization of authority culminating in the declaration of a national emergency and the suspension of the democratic process, nineteen months of authoritarian rule, and free elections in 1977 that restored the democratic process and brought a new government to power. These events were an important backdrop for both the demographic and political processes described in this book.

Throughout this entire period I was freely permitted to conduct research in India and to travel with almost no restrictions. Mahatma Gandhi spoke of India's many open windows, windows that allow those on the inside to look out, but also those on the outside to look in. India remains one of the small number of free, self-assured societies—alas, dwindling in number—that permit foreign scholars and journalists to study and report what is taking place within its walls, warts and all.

Though the dedication reveals where my deepest personal sympathies lie, this book seeks to take a balanced look at some of the costs and benefits of migrations to the local inhabitants of places to which migrants move. While working on this study it was apparent that India is faced with a genuine dilemma—dilemma in the precise sense of a situation requiring a choice between two evils; for to provide special protection for one ethnic group is to deny equal opportunities to others, while not to act is to permit the resentment of local people to fester. Not too long ago linguistic and tribal groups in India might have accepted their unequal economic positions, as India's castes did. But today the desire to move ahead has become pervasive among virtually all ethnic groups. To be discontent, not to accept things as they are, is, I suppose, what makes a people modern. Increasingly, in multiethnic societies gross inequalities between ethnic groups have become even less acceptable than gross inequalities between social classes. To find a way in which local people belonging to one ethnic group can obtain greater equality in the employment market without at the same time restricting the opportunities of migrants and their descendants belonging to other ethnic groups may prove to be as intractable in India as in other multiethnic societies. We know remarkably little about how one can best achieve greater equality among ethnic groups; and we know even less about how to go about reducing ethnic conflict. Social scientists are not likely to find solutions to what ultimately are political issues; at best we can only point to the likely consequences of different courses of action. This book states the problems. Finding solutions I leave to wiser minds.

CONTENTS

PREFACE   ix
LIST OF TABLES   xvii
LIST OF MAPS   xviii

ONE
INTRODUCTION   3

TWO
MIGRATION AND THE GROWTH OF ETHNIC
DIVERSITY   19
  Introduction: Why Study the Exceptions?   19
  The Ethnic Context of Migration   27
  Types and Magnitudes of Migration   31
  Ethnicity: Barrier or Incentive to Migration?   42
  The Impact of Migration on Linguistic Diversity   49
  Recent Trends in Interstate Migration   59
  Appendix: India's Migrating Peoples, a
    Statistical Note   65

THREE
WHEN MIGRANTS SUCCEED AND NATIVES
FAIL: ASSAM AND ITS MIGRANTS   75
  The Problem   75
  The State of Assam   79
  The Political Geography of Migrant Settlements   82
  The Assamese Response to Migration: Collective
    and Political   104
  Conclusion: Migrants as Determinants of Conflict
    and Change   130
  Appendix: Estimates of Religio-Linguistic-Tribal
    Communities in the Brahmaputra Valley, 1961   136
  Bibliography: Nineteenth and Twentieth-Century
    Assam   139

FOUR

TRIBAL ENCOUNTERS: TRIBALS AND MIGRANTS IN CHOTA NAGPUR, BIHAR   145

Regional Development—Solution or Problem?   145
The Problem and the Argument   149
Who Are the Tribals?   151
How the Tribals Lost Their Lands   157
Notes from a Tour of Tribal Chota Nagpur   167
The Tribal Encounter with the Cities   175
Schisms in the Tribes: The Encounter with
  Christianity and Hinduism   184
Tribal Responses: The Argument Recapitulated   200
Bibliography   210

FIVE

MIDDLE-CLASS PROTECTIONISM: MULKIS AGAINST MIGRANTS IN HYDERABAD   217

Introduction   217
Historical Roots   221
Hyderabad City: Periphery Controlling the Center   223
The Social Base of the Telangana Praja Samiti   231
Creating a Telangana Identity   236
Explaining the Movement   244
The End of the Telangana Movement?   248
Appendix: Hyderabad Student Survey   255
Bibliography   259

SIX

MIGRATION AND THE RISE OF NATIVISM   265

Overview   265
Theories of Nativism   269
Conditions for Nativist Movements in India   274
Social Mobility versus Spatial Mobility   293
Nativism as a Variety of Ethnic Politics   294

SEVEN

WHO IS LOCAL? TERRITORIAL VERSUS ETHNIC IDENTITIES   299

Territorial Identities   300
Identities in India's Northeast   303
Migrant Constituencies   308

CONTENTS

The Survey   309
Who Is "Local"?   311
Employment for Locals and Nonlocals   315
Investment in Business and Land   318
Education for Locals and Nonlocals   319
Assimilation and Integration   320
Why the Differences?   321

EIGHT

CITIZENSHIP AND INTERNAL
MIGRATION LAWS   325
Citizenship and National Identity   325
Citizenship and Freedom of Internal Movement   327
Ethnic Groups as Legal Entities   329
Clashing Claims: Cities and States as Homogeneous
   or Heterogeneous Cultures   332
The Origin and Development of Protected Labor
   Markets   335
Legal Trends: Equality of Opportunity versus
   Protection   339
Conclusion: Common or Dual Citizenship?   344

NINE

CONCLUSION: TRENDS AND CONSEQUENCES   349
Costs and Benefits, Winners and Losers   350
The Effects of Nativist Politics and Policies   356
The Future of Protectionist Policies   366

INDEX   373

LIST OF TABLES

2.1   All-India Migration (1971)   32
2.2   Interstate Migration and Intrastate Migration
        (1971)   33
2.3   Migrants by State of Birth (1961, 1971)   38
2.4   Migrants by State of Residence (1961)   39
2.5   State Languages (1961)   50
2.6   Linguistic Dispersal (1961)   51
2.7   Bengalis in Districts of Assam (1961)   52
2.8   Languages of Bombay (1911-1961)   54
2.9   Languages of Bangalore (1911-1951)   54
2.10 Languages of Ahmadabad (1911-1961)   55
2.11 Bilingualism within Linguistic States and Outside
        (1961)   57
4.1   Tribal and Nontribal Population, Chota Nagpur
        (1971)   153
4.2   Immigration and Emigration, Chota Nagpur and
        Santal Parganas (1891-1961)   161
4.3   Migrants in Chota Nagpur and Santal Parganas
        (1961)   166
4.4   Population Growth, Ranchi and Singhbhum
        Districts (1961-1971)   172
4.5   Population Growth, Chota Nagpur (1961-1971)   172
5.1   Intraregional Migration in Telangana (1961)   226
5.2   Migrants from Coastal Andhra to Hyderabad
        District (1961, 1971)   227
5.3   Net Decadal Migration by Regions of Andhra
        Pradesh (1931-1971)   245
6.1   Educational Enrollment in Mysore   291

LIST OF MAPS

States of India   2
India's Urban Linguistic Groups, 1961   20
Assam: Ethnic Composition, 1961   76
Bihar, Chota Nagpur and Santal Parganas,
    Tribal and Nontribal Composition, 1971   144
Andhra Pradesh, Administrative Divisions   216

Sons of
the Soil

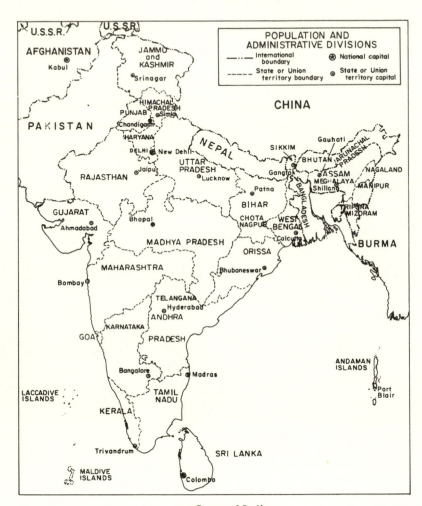

States of India

ONE

INTRODUCTION

THIS book examines the social and political consequences of internal migration in a multiethnic low-income society. The study begins with two simple hypotheses: 1. that the process of modernization, by providing incentives and opportunities for mobility, creates the conditions for increasing internal migration; and 2. that the modernization process nurtures the growth of ethnic identification and ethnic cohesion. These two processes are often antagonistic, since in a multiethnic society the one encourages the movement of individuals across cultural, linguistic, and ethnic regions, thereby changing the "mix" of ethnic groups within a given space, while the other often generates antimigrant sentiments among "local" people. Economic and demographic tendencies thus conflict with social, cultural, and political tendencies.

Interethnic relations in the multiethnic societies of the developing world are in a fluid state because of both these processes: migration is critical because it changes both the demographic and economic balance of groups within a given space. Hence, the "protection" of space and the economic opportunities that exist within it are often central objectives of the local population, while the expansion of opportunities within that space is a central objective of migrants. Migration within a multiethnic society, therefore, frequently has destabilizing effects and tends to arouse intense conflicts.

This book is a contribution to the study of ethnic demography, a field that brings together the concepts and tools of demographers and the concerns of social scientists with the study of ethnicity. Ethnic demography is a branch of political demography—a field of study that examines the size, composition, and distribution of population in relation to both government and politics, and deals with the political determinants and political consequences of population change.[1]

In this study of ethnic demography, three concepts have proven to be particularly useful. The first is the notion of territorial ethnicity—the notion that certain ethnic groups are "rooted" in space. Whether a people see themselves as having an exclusive proprietary right over what takes place within that space, or whether they envisage sharing that space with others is a critical element in the patterns of integration within a political system.

The second is the notion of a dual labor market, with its conception of two types of jobs: those in what have been called "traditional," "marginal," "unorganized," or "informal" sectors, employing low-skilled manpower at low wages; as against the more "modern," "developed," "organized," and "formal" sectors that employ the skilled at higher wages. One scholar has distinguished between a "core" region, where centralized authority makes its appearance and industrial development becomes more advanced, and a "peripheral" region that is less developed and is usually at the "geographical extremities of the state," with the core region recruiting its low-skilled, low-wage labor from the peripheral region.[2] Migrants from the periphery move to the core region to pursue low-paying jobs that the indigenous population does not want. Such a pattern can be found in much of Western Europe, where low-income migrants are imported from the "periphery" countries of the Mediterranean, or in the United States in areas where Mexicans, Puerto Ricans, or Blacks are employed in low-skilled, low-wage occupations.

Third is the idea of an ethnic division of labor. The dual labor market may be ethnically stratified, that is, each occu-

[1] See "Political Demography: An Inquiry into the Political Consequences of Population Change," by Myron Weiner, in National Academy of Sciences, *Rapid Population Growth: Consequences and Policy Implications* (Baltimore: The Johns Hopkins Press, 1971).

[2] Michael Hecter, "Ethnicity and Industrialization: On the Proliferation of the Cultural Division of Labor," *Ethnicity*, 3 (1976), 214-224.

pation in the system of occupational stratification recruits primarily from a single ethnic group. In the classical conception of an ethnic division of labor, migrants belonging to one ethnic group move from the periphery to work in subordinate positions to the ethnic group predominating in the core. The migrants settle into their own communities, where they develop culturally distinct ethnic associations that both strengthen their identity and provide them with social support; the migrants thus become separated from the local population in employment, housing, and in social, cultural, and even political organization. In a multiethnic society, or in a society that imports portions of its labor force, migration is often ethnically selective and a dual labor market is generally accompanied by an ethnic division of labor.[3] Uneven development can thus take place between peoples as well as between places.

But it does not follow that migrants need be at the bottom of the labor market. In developing countries, as in advanced industrial societies, migrants can be engaged in a variety of occupations up and down the occupational hierarchy, and their education level can range from little or no education to the most advanced degrees. This simple and obvious observation about migration is often overlooked in much of the discussion of migration to the crowded cities of Asia, Africa,

---

[3] See Edna Bonacich, "A Theory of Ethnic Antagonism: The Split Labor Market," *American Sociological Review*, 37 (1972), 547-559; Paul R. Brass and Pierre L. van den Berghe, "Ethnicity in World Perspective," *Ethnicity*, 3 (September 1976), 197-201; Milton Esman, "Communal Conflict in Southeast Asia," in Nathan Glazer and Patrick Moynihan, ed., *Ethnicity: Theory and Experience* (Cambridge: Harvard University Press, 1975), pp. 391-416; C. Hirschman, *Ethnic and Social Stratification in Peninsular Malaysia* (Washington, D.C.: American Sociological Association, 1975); R. E. Kranem, ed., *Manpower Mobility across Cultural Boundaries* (Leiden: E. J. Brill, 1975); Helen I. Safa and Brian M. Du Toit, ed., *Migration and Development* (The Hague: Mouton, 1975); Michael Hecter, "Towards a Theory of Ethnic Change," *Politics and Society*, 2 (Fall 1971), 21-43; and Donald L. Horowitz, "Three Dimensions of Ethnic Politics," *World Politics*, 23 (1971), 232-244.

and Latin America, where it is all too often assumed that migrants are necessarily illiterate, unskilled, poor, and dwellers in slums and squatter settlements. Though in most developing countries this is the largest single group of migrants, there are other types of migrants whose characteristics—and therefore whose place in the ethnic division of labor—are quite different.

Migrants may be entrepreneurs, shopkeepers, traders, and moneylenders, generating new economic activities either in the "core" or in the "periphery." They may be self-employed professionals or employees who by virtue of their advanced education, their skills, and their drive are able to take positions that the local population are either unable or unwilling to take or, in some instances, from which they have been excluded.

The reasons for this particular ethnic division of labor are not easy to describe briefly. It may have resulted from policies adopted by the colonial government to provide facilities or preferences to some ethnic groups over others; it may have resulted from the character of the local economy, which made the new positions in the labor market less attractive to local people than to migrants; or it may have resulted from differences in the social structures and cultures of the various ethnic groups. Observers—and more importantly, participants—are likely to offer very divergent explanations: some (usually local people) will emphasize the political element that made it possible for one ethnic group to "exploit" another; others (usually migrants) will emphasize the "cultural" differences that led one ethnic group to take advantage of opportunities more successfully than others. But whatever the explanation, the result may be the emergence of another sector, while "locals" remain in the traditional sector or in the marginal parts of the emerging economy.

An ethnic division of labor—even one with the migrants on top of the occupational hierarchy—does not necessarily result in ethnic strife. In multiethnic plural societies diverse

6

ethnic groups may interact in the marketplace, but maintain their cultural diversity, all under the control of a state system dominated by a single ethnic group. Under these circumstances there may be relatively little conflict among ethnic groups. This level of "integration" also seems likely when each group maintains its spatial exclusiveness, when there is little in the way of social mobility, and when there are few new resources over which ethnic groups may compete.

It is not inequalities between ethnic groups that generate conflicts, but competition. Inequalities, real or perceived, are a necessary but not a sufficient condition for ethnic conflict; there must also be competition for control over or access to economic wealth, political power, or social status. There are a number of conditions under which such competition takes place; under each of these the existing ethnic division of labor may become questioned by one or more ethnic groups.

First, when the ethnic division of labor between migrants (and their descendants) and nonmigrants parallels class relationships that ordinarily have a high conflictual potential, as between industrial managers and workers, landlords and peasants, grain merchants and agricultural producers, the police and the public, shopkeepers and consumers, and so on, competition may occur. For whatever reasons—and there may be many—these exchange relationships become conflictual, and when the groups in the exchange belong to different ethnic communities, there is a high potential for ethnic conflict.

In other words, conflicts that ordinarily take place in any society that is modernizing can become defined as an ethnic problem because of the ethnic division of labor. Marxists often dismiss these ethnic conflicts as a form of "false consciousness," that disguises the "real" class tensions. What is "real" and what is "false" in human relationships is a deep epistemological issue that will not be resolved by mere empirical facts; here we can only note the empirical facts themselves—that when there is a close fit between the class di-

7

vision and ethnic division, conflicts generally take on an ethnic character that often transcends whatever class differences exist within each of the ethnic groups.

Second, when the local population seeks access to occupations that they previously did not seek or from which they were once excluded, conflict may ensue. In short, the ethnic division of labor may no longer be acceptable because there is increasing mobility, or aspirations for increasing mobility, on the part of the indigenous population. Such aspirations may be stimulated by a variety of factors—an expansion of the educational system to provide new opportunities for local children, a decline in agricultural income or employment that leads agriculturalists or their children to try to enter urban occupations, or the stimulant to change provided by the growth of the mass media.

To anticipate a central proposition of this book, middle-class nativist movements in opposition to migrants tend to emerge in those communities where the local population has recently produced its own educated class that aspires to move into jobs held by migrants—in the civil service, as teachers in the local schools, as clerks, managers, and technicians. In a situation in which the employment market in the modern sector is not expanding as fast as the number of entrants, local middle-class aspirants may view migrants as blocks to their mobility.

Third, conflict may occur when a change in the power structure stimulates competition by giving one group the political resources for modifying or transforming the ethnic division of labor. Hence, the movement into political power of an indigenous population that is economically and socially in subordinate positions typically stimulates efforts on the part of the new power group to change the occupational structure. The example of the Burmans in relation to Indians, Malays in relation to Chinese, and Ugandans in relation to Asians all come to mind. In India, examples are the Marathis in relation to Tamils and the Assamese in relation to Bengalis.

Much of the discussion of core-periphery relationships and "internal colonialism" has focused on the ways in which the dominant "core" population dominates the migrants from the periphery—the English in relation to the Welsh and Irish, the French in relation to Brittany, and so on. What this analysis neglects are those situations in which population flows are in the other direction, and it is the migrants who become dominant. In the post-colonial phase those who come to exercise governmental authority often belong to the subordinate economic group in the ethnic division of labor, especially when power shifts to those who are the most numerous. To put it another way, the ethnic division of labor and the political division of labor may become divergent. In this situation, governmental authority is likely to be directed toward restructuring the ethnic divisions of labor—a situation fraught with conflict.

An additional potentially explosive situation exists when the new power elite is economically and socially subordinate to the ethnic group that dominates the urban center in which the capital is located, that is, when the geographic "core" and the political "core" are held by different ethnic groups. This is what made the cities of Rangoon (with its Indian population), Kuala Lumpur (Chinese migrants), Gauhati in Assam (Bengali and Marwari migrants), and Bombay (Tamil migrants, and others) particularly explosive centers. One can find similar parallels in the post-Ottoman, post-Hapsburg urban centers of eastern and southeastern Europe in the 1920s and 1930s, when the governments were dominated by nationalist elites representing the ethnic majority, while the urban centers were predominantly dominated by ethnic minorities.

Perhaps, ultimately, it is the development process itself that undermines the existing ethnic division of labor by opening up new avenues for educational, social, economic, and political advancement. There may be new opportunities in the industrial sector as a result of industrial expansion. Or on the land, because government has "opened" up new lands through irrigation works, land clearance, and rural colonization schemes. Or in education, which has been opened to ethnic groups that had hitherto been excluded. There may be new opportunities in administration, either because the bureaucracy has expanded its size, or because it has become more open and less ethnically restrictive. And finally, the political process itself may create new opportunities by permitting competition for public office. Tensions are most often produced when modernization opens some sphere more than others—when, for example, local people are given new access to political power, but not to education or to employment, or to education, but not to employment, or to employment in the public sphere, but not in the private.

The arenas within which migrants and locals compete are thus defined by what the development process and the political process have opened, for a critical dimension of ethnic conflict is the extent to which groups battle over access to and control over new resources. Moreover, to the extent that group interactions lead to a sharpening of ethnic distinctions, then an adversary relationship emerges that, in turn, further strengthens ethnic identities, promotes ethnic solidarity, and intensifies ethnic exclusiveness. An adversary relationship between ethnic groups also undermines the growth of class-based relationships, for it inhibits the development of class conflicts within ethnic groups even when there are growing economic and social inequalities within the ethnic group.

In this struggle for access to resources, ethnic groups also create their own resources. Most important is the development of various ethnic infrastructures:[4] ethnic restaurants, religious institutions, newspapers, neighborhood associations, charitable organizations, welfare institutions, medical facilities, burial associations, and educational centers. These institutions also become centers for the emergence of ethnic

---

[4] For an analysis of the role of ethnic infrastructures as an incentive to migration see Oli Hawrylyshyn, *Is Ethnicity a Barrier to Migration? The Yugoslav Experience* (Cambridge: Migration and Development Series, Center for International Studies, M.I.T., 1976).

leaders who try to speak on behalf of the community: news-paper editors, heads of ethnic associations, the clergy, and elected political leaders.

Not only migrants but local groups also organize new re-sources in this struggle. Indeed, to the extent that local groups seek to restructure the ethnic division of labor, they must build political resources—new journals to articulate the claims of the local people, literary associations to attract the emerging intelligentsia and, ultimately, political organizations to press nativist claims upon government.

In this study we view policy not as an attempt by govern-ment to find a solution to the tension between natives and migrants, but rather as an instrument by one group or an-other in the struggle to maintain or transform the ethnic division of labor. Indeed, government may be willing to tolerate and even generate ethnic strife if it serves to reduce migration or reverse the flow, or to bring about compliance with policies intended to change the ethnic division of labor.

This book examines the political consequences of inter-ethnic migrations in India. It explores the arenas for compe-tition between migrants and locals in selected regions of the country, the struggle for access to and control over new re-sources in these regions, the role that policies play in the struggle for restructuring the ethnic division of labor, and the kinds of consequences that have resulted from these various state and central government interventions. By fo-cusing on a single country we have an opportunity to explore in depth how these processes operate, and to consider some of the alternative ways in which government policy makers—if they chose to—might attempt to restructure the ethnic di-vision of labor so as to achieve greater equality among ethnic groups, without at the same time restricting the spatial and social mobility of some of its own people.

India provides an ideal case for such a study. Ethnicity, at least insofar as language and tribe are concerned, has a ter-ritorial base; the ethnic homogeneity of some areas of the country have long since been eroded by population move-

11

ments, and these migrations continue at a rapid and growing pace; there exist ethnic divisions of labor in several regions that have experienced continuous migrations; and in recent years, antimigrant political movements have emerged, demanding governmental intervention to restructure the ethnic divisions of labor.[5]

These antimigrant political movements first became prominant in the late 1960s. They were most active in the northeastern state of Assam, the western portion of the southern state of Andhra, the southernmost districts of Bihar, and in the cities of Bombay and Bangalore. These political movements all shared the aim of restricting the flow of "outside" migrants into their region and increasing the access of local people to jobs held by migrants or by their descendants. In at least three instances, in the states of Assam, Andhra, and Maharashtra, the state governments responded to these demands by imposing restrictions on migrants through a system of preferences for local people in employment, education and, sometimes, housing. Even Prime Minister Indira Gandhi and many officials of the central government declared that in employment, preferences should be given to local people or, as they are called in India, "sons of the soil."

These demands were intensified by an acutely competitive labor market in which there has been large-scale and increasing unemployment, especially among the educated. The country's rapid population growth, which accelerated in the

[5] While there is no single comprehensive account of India's complex ethnic demography, the following specialized studies are of considerable use: *Economic and Socio-Cultural Dimensions of Regionalisation: An Indo-U.S.S.R. Collaborative Study*, Census of India, 1971, Census Centenary Monograph No. 7 (Delhi, 1972), especially the paper by I. V. Sakharov, "Ethnolinguistic Geography of India: Facts and Problems"; also by Dr. Sakharov (in Russian) *West Bengal: Ethnic Demography and Ethnic Geography* (Leningrad: Nauka Publishing House, 1977) (summary translation in English made available by author); and "Ethnic Community, Class, and Occupation," *Journal of Social Research* (Ranchi), 18:1 (1975).

12

years immediately after independence; the rapid expansion of education, especially at the secondary school, college, and university levels, and the capital-intensive, urban-oriented emphasis of the early development plans combined to generate the unemployment crisis of the late 1960s and 1970s.

After India's states were reorganized along linguistic lines so as to create a closer fit between ethnicity, territoriality, and political power, the numerically dominant linguistic group in each state made a special claim to the territory it occupied and to any economic and educational activities that took place within it.

In this respect, of course, the Assamese who claimed that they should be preferred over Bengali migrants and their descendants, and the Marathis who claimed that they should be given employment in preference to Tamils were reacting no differently than the Ugandans, or Burmans, or Sinhalese who sought to expel Indian settlers, or to the Malays, Indonesians, and Filipinos who were anti-Chinese. What made the Indian situation different is that these sentiments were expressed by one Indian linguistic community toward another within the same country. Should such preferences be granted, should jobs be reserved for "local" people in each state or section of a state, and should migrants from other regions be encouraged to leave, then what would be left of the concept of a nation in which all Indians shared a common citizenship? Would a time come when, in the words of the *Illustrated Weekly*, a widely read Indian magazine, "an Indian will need a passport, or at least a permit, to go from one state to another"?

At issue was a fundamental clash between the claims of individual citizens to equal access and the collective claims of ethnic groups to equality. Do people who "belong" to a given territory have a special claim to educational facilities, housing, and employment within that territory? Does "belonging" to the place of one's birth imply a kind of proprietary claim on behalf of the specific ethnic group to the

13

territory it occupies? The phrase "sons of the soil" and its variants in many languages convey this special collective right of an ethnic group over a territory.

We shall selectively examine those regions of India that have a high rate and level of in-migration from other regions, and where an ethnic division of labor has emerged in which the migrants dominate the modern sector of the economy. In each instance, the following issues will be explored:

1. How have local communities responded to the ethnic division of labor resulting from the presence of migrants from other cultural-linguistic regions? Why have the reactions to migrants been more acutely hostile and nativist in some regions than in others, and toward some but not all migrants? Who are the nativists and against whom is their hostility directed?

2. How have local, state, and national governments responded to nativist demands for restructuring the ethnic division of labor by proposing protectionist policies against migrants and their descendants? What policies have been adopted, especially in the areas of education and employment, and what has been the relationship between these state government policies and the constitutional provisions of equal rights for all Indian citizens in a multiethnic state?

3. Finally, what have been the effects of the nativist politics and policies on the migrants themselves? Has there been a restructuring of the ethnic division of labor? Has migration diminished? Have local people taken on the positions once held by migrants? And have the migrants themselves linguistically assimilated into the area into which they have moved? Is it now expected that individuals will integrate—or assimilate—into the region where they settle as distinct from, or in addition to, their integration into national life?

These issues are, of course, in no sense unique to India. The movement of people from one linguistic or cultural region to another within the same country is quite characteristic of multiethnic societies; in Nigeria, for example, Ibo move northward to create businesses and find employment in the

14

areas where Fulani and Hausa reside; in Indonesia the Javanese move from their densely packed island to nearby Sumatra; in Pakistan Punjabis move to Karachi in the province of Sind; in Malaysia the Malays move to Chinese-dominated urban settlements and, in turn, Chinese move into the Malay countryside; in the Philippines the Christians from the northern islands have settled in the Muslim-occupied Mindanao region of the south.[6] In much of southern Asia and Africa the process of culturally diversifying towns and cities, and even sometimes the countryside, through internal population movements is well under way.[7] To the extent that

[6] Among the handful of studies that deal with the interaction between migration, ethnicity, and political conflict in developing countries are: Kenneth Little, *Urbanization as a Social Process: An Essay on Movement and Change in Contemporary Africa* (London: Routledge and Kegan Paul, 1974); Abner Cohen, ed., *Urban Ethnicity* (London: Tavistock, 1974); Edward M. Bruner, "Urbanization and Ethnic Identity in North Sumatra," *American Anthropologist*, 63 (April 1961), 508-521; G. K. Gillion, *Fiji's Indian Migrants* (Melbourne: Oxford University Press, 1962); Shahid Javed Burki, "Migration, Urbanization and Politics in Pakistan" in Howard Wriggins and James Guyot, ed., *Population, Politics, and the Future of Southern Asia* (New York: Columbia University Press, 1973); Frederick L. Wernstedt and Paul D. Simkins, "Migration and the Settlement of Mindanao," *Journal of Asian Studies*, 25 (November 1965), 83-103; M. S. Gore, *Immigrants and Neighborhoods* (Bombay: Tata Institute of Social Sciences, 1971); Lela Garner Noble, "The Moro National Liberation Front in the Philippines," *Pacific Affairs*, 49 (April 1976), 405-424; Kenneth Little, *West African Urbanization: A Study of Voluntary Associations in Social Change* (Cambridge: Cambridge University Press, 1965).

[7] On Africa the following studies are particularly useful for exploring the diversifying effects of ethnic migrations: W. J. Hanna and J. L. Hanna, "Polyethnicity and Political Integration in Umuahia and Mbala," in R. T. Daland, ed., *Comparative Urban Research: The Administration and Politics of Cities* (Beverly Hills: Sage, 1969); J. C. Caldwell, *African Rural-Urban Migration: The Movement to Ghana's Towns* (New York: Columbia University Press, 1969); M. A. Cohen, *Urban Policy and Political Conflict in Africa: A Study of the Ivory Coast* (Chicago: University of Chicago Press, 1974); W. A. Hance, *Population, Migration and Urbanization in Africa* (New York:

15

individuals are free to move, the process is likely to continue. Only governmental intervention, aroused by political demands, is likely to slow or arrest this process.

In other developing countries opposition to culturally "alien" migration has also arisen, along with demands that government intervene to halt or regulate internal migration. In Nigeria the tensions that arose between Ibo migrants and the local population were no small element in the strife that led to the civil war. In Malaysia the Malays speak of themselves as *bhumiputra*, or "sons of the soil," in opposition to migrant Chinese, demanding that they be given special rights to employment, education, and land. In the Mindanao region of the Philippines the indigenous Moros have violently turned against the Christian settlers, demanded their expulsion, and called for the creation of a separate independent Muslim country.

The pattern is a familiar one. The development process is uneven. Some ethnic groups move ahead more rapidly than others. History and culture combine to give some ethnic groups a head start, leaving others fearful that they will lose out in the race for education and employment, in the struggle to enter the modern urban industrial sector, and in some instances, even in the effort to maintain the dominance of their culture within a region that constitutes a historic homeland.

Columbia University Press, 1970); W. J. Hanna and J. L. Hanna, *Urban Dynamics in Black Africa* (Chicago: Aldine-Atherton, 1971); H. Heisler, *Urbanization and the Government of Migration: The Interrelation of Urban and Rural Life in Zambia* (New York: St. Martin's Press, 1974); H. Kuper, ed., *Urbanization and Migration in West Africa* (Berkeley and Los Angeles: University of California Press, 1965); W. A. Shack, "Urban Ethnicity and Cultural Process or Urbanization in Ethiopia," in A. Southall, ed., *Urban Anthropology* (New York: Oxford University Press, 1973); E. W. Soja, *The Geography and Modernization in Kenya: A Spatial Analysis of Social, Economic and Political Change* (Syracuse: Syracuse University Press, 1968); Howard Wolpe, *Urban Politics in Nigeria: A Study of Port Harcourt* (Berkeley and Los Angeles: University of California Press, 1974).

The issue is not why the differentials exist—successes and failures have a thousand causes—but how people and their governments respond to these differences and the fears and demands that accompany them. This book provides an account of how indigenous ethnic groups attempt to use political power to overcome their fears of economic defeat and cultural subordination by more enterprising, more skilled, better educated migrant communities; it is an account of how the backward but socially mobile sectors seek to protect themselves against those who are more advanced.

The following chapter describes the population flows in India, exploring where (and why) there are movements across cultural boundaries and the different types of migration. A primary concern of this chapter is to examine the extent to which migrants have changed the ethnic composition of selected urban areas and regions. In Chapters Three, Four, and Five we look at three areas where migrants have crossed cultural boundaries. These three chapters are intended to provide the reader with a concrete appreciation of the social and political conflicts and cleavages that have emerged as a result of the response of the indigenous population who have, in each case, moved into middle-class employment and sought to displace the migrant communities.

In Chapters Six, Seven, and Eight we analyze the effects of intercultural migrations in three spheres: on politics, group identities, and government policies. Chapter Six examines nativist movements in five regions in an effort to ascertain the conditions under which local populations have become hostile to migrants, and why in recent years these hostilities have grown. Particular attention is given to examining the changes experienced by the local population and how these changes have shaped their reactions to migrants and to the existing ethnic division of labor. Chapter Seven is concerned with the ways in which communities have sought to define who is "local" and to clarify the differences between territorial and ethnic identities. Following an analysis of linguistic usage, we report on a survey of members of

17

parliament from a sample of multiethnic districts in which the MPs talk about their attitudes toward their own constituents, both native and migrant, and their conceptions of group identities and group rights. Chapter Eight, on citizenship and internal migration laws, describes the policy responses of local, state, and national authorities to conflicts between local people and migrants, and explores the implications of these policies for concepts of citizenship in a multiethnic society.

The last chapter, on trends and consequences, starts with an assessment of the costs and benefits of migration to the local population, as distinct from migrants, and then turns to an examination of the impact of nativist politics and policies on both the local and migrant populations. This chapter suggests a number of ways in which policy interventions can be assessed: demographic, political, economic, social, and cultural, focusing particularly on the question of whether controls over internal migration through preferential policies actually contribute to ethnic equality. Given the persistence of competing ethnic claims in a society where the migration of people from one region to another takes place in an economy of acute job scarcity, the chapter concludes that there would appear to be little prospect of avoiding confrontations among ethnic groups.

I discuss some alternative policies that the Indian government might pursue to respond to the concerns of the local population without imposing restrictions on the mobility of its citizens and creating policies that protect the local population against competition. It seems unlikely that state and local governments, faced with the demands of local groups, would find such policies as attractive as might the central government, concerned with the larger issues of creating a single citizenship and a single nationality in a diverse society. Whether such alternatives are politically feasible, therefore, will depend primarily on the balance of forces between central and state governments.

TWO

MIGRATION AND THE GROWTH OF ETHNIC DIVERSITY

INTRODUCTION: WHY STUDY THE EXCEPTIONS?

INDIA can, alternatively, be described as a land of nearly infinite ethnic diversity or a land of largely homogeneous territorial units. Looking at India as a whole, it is certainly the heterogeneity that is striking, but from the vantage point of any single region, rural community, or town, it is the homogeneity that captures one's attention. Though dozens of languages are spoken in India, and Indians belong to diverse religions, sects, and tribes, most Indians live in the familiar world of their own people, sharing a common language, cuisine, and dress with their neighbors, participating in the same religious and cultural festivals, and living in similar types of dwellings. How homogeneous the surroundings are —at least linguistically—is revealed by a few simple statistics.

Eight of every ten Indians speak the dominant language of the state in which they reside. Madras, Kanpur, Ahmadabad, and Delhi are cities overwhelmingly populated by people who share the same language. In the state of Kerala, 95 percent of the population speaks Malayalam; in Gujarat 90 percent of the population is Gujarati; and in Uttar Pradesh, India's most populous state, 85 percent of the population is Hindi-speaking and another 10 percent speaks the closely related language of Urdu.

The homogeneity of India's states is reinforced by the lack of mobility. Nearly 95 percent of all Indians live in the state in which they were born, and most have never lived outside their own district. It is largely India's women who move

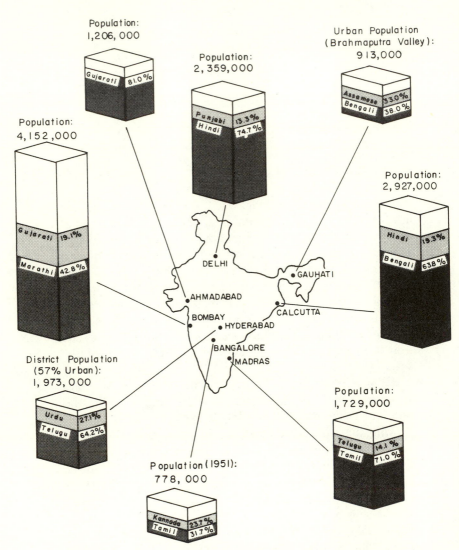

Population:
1,206,000

Gujarati 81.0%

Population:
2,359,000

Punjabi 13.3%
Hindi 74.7%

Urban Population
(Brahmaputra Valley):
913,000

Assamese 33.0%
Bengali 38.0%

Population:
4,152,000

Gujarati 19.1%
Marathi 42.8%

Population:
2,927,000

Hindi 19.3%
Bengali 63.8%

DELHI

GAUHATI

AHMADABAD

BOMBAY
HYDERABAD
CALCUTTA

BANGALORE
MADRAS

District Population
(57% Urban):
1,973,000

Urdu 27.1%
Telugu 64.2%

Population:
1,729,000

Telugu 14.1%
Tamil 71.0%

Population (1951):
778,000

Kannada 23.7%
Tamil 31.7%

India's Urban Linguistic Groups, 1961

within or across districts, for reasons of marriage, but this movement reinforces cultural bonds, rather than creating cultural diversity. The bulk of the rural-to-rural migration across state boundaries consists of women, undeterred when state boundaries traverse areas in which no cultural-linguistic boundaries exist. In 1971, when India's population was 548 million, only 19.4 million Indians resided outside of the state of their birth, plus another 9 million who originated from neighboring Pakistan, Bangladesh, Nepal, and other countries.[1] Even when a community contains migrants from another state, the result need not be cultural heterogeneity. Migrants who move between the Hindi-speaking states of Rajasthan, Madhya Pradesh, Uttar Pradesh, Bihar, and Haryana generally speak the same language and share similar customs and cultural outlook.

India is, then, by and large a land of native peoples. Men and women live among friends and relatives. Men are born, go to school (if they do go to school), work, marry, and die in the same community. Their wives come from nearby villages, mainly within the district, some from villages in nearby districts, fewer still from villages in neighboring states.

This book is about the exceptions. It deals with those places in India that are culturally and linguistically heterogeneous, where men and women, originating from different parts of the country, reside in a rural or urban settlement containing communities each speaking different languages,

---

[1] All 1971 migration figures provided in this study are computed from the one percent sample data provided by the Census of India, Series I, Part II, *All India Census Tables, 1971.* The one percent table provides national and state, but not district or city data. I have, therefore, made use of the 1961 tables when more detailed data have been necessary and seemed appropriate. The national data for 1961 are taken from Volume I (India), Part II-C (iii) and Part II-C (iv) of the *Census of India 1961,* and the district data from the state volumes. In the state series these volumes are generally published as Part II-C and are titled "Cultural and Migration Tables," which contain both language and migration data.

21

subscribing to different customs and beliefs, and identifying with different cultures.

Why study these exceptions?

One reason is that the exceptions include some of the most important commercial and industrial centers in India: the industrial belt around Calcutta, the industrial complex in and around Bangalore; the Bombay region; southern Bihar with its coal mines, steel mills, and heavy engineering plants; and the tea and coffee plantation areas of Kerala, Mysore, and Assam. It includes a substantial number of Indian cities, particularly those that are growing rapidly as a consequence of industrial expansion.

A second reason is that in many areas cultural heterogeneity, or at least linguistic heterogeneity, has been increasing. Migration has been a decisive determinant of the heterogeneity of a number of urban centers and regions. Linguistic diversity has increased in Bombay, Bangalore, Delhi, and Ahmadabad. In Bombay the indigenous Marathi-speaking population is only a plurality, and in Assam only a third of the urban population is now Assamese. In the tribal region of southern Bihar the indigenous tribal population forms less than a majority in every town in the region with a population above 20,000, for the urban population is almost entirely migrant or descended from migrants. Between 1961 and 1971, migration from one state to another, typically across cultural zones, increased by 33 percent. While there are political forces at work to discourage such population movements, there are evidently strong economic forces that point toward their continued increase.

A third reason is that interstate migration in India has created a new tension in the complex relationship that exists between modernization and integration. So long as the sense of regional identity was not well articulated, Indians were generally disposed to be tolerant toward or, more often, indifferent to those individuals speaking other languages and subscribing to other cultural traditions who entered their

22

state to work and settle. The cultural encapsulation of minorities within a social order based upon cultural pluralism, social hierarchy, and group solidarity was the framework within which interstate migrants settled in the past. Prior to independence, the number of such migrants was, moreover, small, and the oft-repeated statements that Indians, like most preindustrial people, were attached to their land seemed valid. In 1931, only twelve million persons in all of what is now India, Pakistan, and Bangladesh, or 3.6 percent of the population, lived in states other than the one in which they were born.[2]

In recent years there has been a growing nativist reaction to migrants and the descendants of migrants who have moved from other cultural-linguistic regions. The number of such persons, while still proportionately small, has increased since independence.[3] But more important than the change in numbers is the change in attitudes that people in each cultural-linguistic region have toward themselves and toward "outsiders." In recent years there has been growing opposition to the unrestricted right of Indians to move and to maintain their own regional traditions after they move. Many Indians now believe that the local population, speaking the local

[2] K. C. Zachariah, *A Historical Study of Internal Migration in the Indian Sub-Continent 1901-1931* (Bombay: Asia Publishing House, 1964), p. 2. Comparisons of interstate migration from one decennial census to another are made difficult by the frequent redrawing of state boundaries since independence. Persons who migrated from one district to another when the districts were within the same state are classified as interstate migrants if the district in which they were born or to which they moved has been transferred to another state. Similarly, individuals who moved from one state to another are classified as intrastate migrants if the districts concerned are subsequently located in the same state. Comparisons since 1961 are somewhat more meaningful, since there have been fewer redrawings of state boundaries compared to the period between 1951 and 1961.

[3] In 1971 the census reports 19.4 million interstate migrants, as compared with 14.6 million in 1961, an increase of 32.9 percent as against a population increase during the decade of 24.7 percent.

23

regional language, ought to have a prior claim to employment and housing, that "outsiders" are not loyal to the culture and traditions of the region, that all too often they tend to "exploit" local people and are "clannish," and that if they or their children remain they must be assimilated to the local language and culture and identify themselves with the region in which they now live.

These nativist sentiments have grown since independence with the establishment of linguistic states, the mushrooming of regional nationalism, and an increase in popular political participation. Regional languages are now growing in usage with an expansion of regional networks of communication and the growth of a middle class more deeply rooted in the local culture and economy. Today, to an extent unknown a generation ago, the people within each region are increasingly aware of their own regional identity.

As a result, in state after state, especially in places such as Assam and Maharashtra, where the proportion of migrants is high, there are demands for ordinances and legislation to restrict the opportunities and cultural position of the migrants: domicile regulations in employment and housing, domicile rules for admission into universities, medical schools, and engineering colleges, language or residence requirements for employment in the universities and in state bureaucracies, restrictions on the use of other regional languages as the medium of instruction in schools to which migrant children are sent, and limitations on the granting of licenses to "alien" entrepreneurs.

But while some features of the development process increase regional identities and engender nativist antagonisms toward out-of-state migrants, still other features of the development process encourage greater migrations. Economic development in India has been accompanied by (one might even say, partially caused by) increased internal migration. The industries of Bombay, Calcutta, Delhi, Madras, Hyderabad, and Bangalore were started by entrepreneurs from all over India and their laborers, office help, and technical personnel were often widely recruited. The tea and coffee plantations started by the British recruited their labor force from across linguistic regions; tribal laborers from Bihar went to Assam, Nepalis to Darjeeling and Jalpaiguri in Bengal, and Kerala labor to Mysore. India's most modern institutions— her industrial enterprises, the national civil service, the military, universities, research institutions, and the courts—recruited nationally. Indeed, historically, the migration of skilled people in India—bureaucrats, educators, professionals, entrepreneurs and technical personnel—has played an important role in India's modernization. And as the country continues to modernize and social mobility increases, we can expect skilled people, as in other modern societies, to seek opportunities wherever they are available. The expansion of the professions, the requirements of modern industry, the growth of a national market, the establishment of national educational institutions all contribute to the making of a society in which there is mobility of persons, not simply from rural to urban areas, but from one part of India to another.

The right to migrate within India is, moreover, guaranteed by the Indian constitution, which specifies that all citizens "shall have the right to move freely throughout the territory of India" and "to reside and settle in any part of the territory of India."[4] The constitution also provides that those who move can retain their regional identity by permitting them to send their children to schools conducted in their own regional language.[5]

[4] Constitution of India, Article 19.

[5] Article 29 of the constitution specifies that "any section of the citizens residing in the territory of India or any part thereof having a distinct language, script or culture of its own shall have the right to conserve the same"; Article 30 says that "all minorities, whether based on religion or language, shall have the right to establish and administer educational institutions of their choice," and "the State shall not, in granting aid to educational institutions, discriminate

There are thus two sets of principles in growing opposition to one another, each supported by different sets of people, each strengthened by different elements of the modernization process. One principle builds on the notion of a common Indian citizenship made up of diverse cultures whose members freely intermingle; the other assumes more autonomous regional cultures and a national political system based not only on dual identities but even dual citizenship with special rights and privileges accruing to citizens within each state.

In a multiethnic society internal migration has both an integrative and disintegrative potential. It can lead to a sense of national awareness and of the benefits of a larger national polity and economy; or it can lead to civil strife, as it did in Nigeria and Malaysia. The political and policy reactions of localities and states with substantial numbers of alien migrants can have far-reaching consequences for the country as a whole, for those localities will define the parameters within which population movements in India take place in the future, affect the relationship between native majorities and migrant minorities, and define the rights of citizens to work, study, reside, and buy and sell land anywhere in the country. How these localities and their governments respond to the problems and conflicts associated with cultural-linguistic heterogeneity will determine whether India will consist of relatively homogeneous regions bound together in a single political system, or whether there will also exist culturally

---

against any educational institution on the ground that it is under the management of a minority, whether based on religion or language." Article 350A stipulates that "it shall be the endeavor of every State and every local authority within the State to provide adequate facilities for instruction in the mother tongue at the primary state of education to children belonging to linguistic minority groups; and the President may issue such directions to any State as he considers necessary or proper for securing the provision of such facilities." Article 350B creates a Special Officer to be appointed by the President of India to ensure the protection of linguistic minorities.

26

heterogeneous pockets that are vital, expanding centers where people, cultures, and ideas can intermingle.

THE ETHNIC CONTEXT OF MIGRATION

Indians live in twenty-two states and several union territories, each of which typically contains one majority linguistic community. State boundaries roughly coincide with linguistic boundaries, though several states of northern and central India share Hindi as a common language.[6]

There are four categories of linguistic minorities in India, of which interstate migrants are only one.

There are several linguistic groups straddling state boundaries that do not have a "home" state. At least seven of these languages are spoken (1971 figures) by more than a million persons each—Urdu (28.6 million), Santali (3.7 million), Bhili (1.2 million), Gondi (1.5 million), Konkani (1.5 million), Kurukh Oraon (1.2 million), and Pahari (1.3 million). Two non-Indian languages, Sindhi (1.2 million) and Nepali (1.3 million), are also widely dispersed. English, of course, is a widely dispersed language as well, but except for the small Anglo-Indian community it is not a mother tongue but a second language.

In addition, there are other languages that are indigenous to a single state and whose speakers constitute a minority within that state, though they may constitute a majority of the people living within a single district or several districts. Examples of these are the many languages spoken by India's

[6] Hindi is the majority language of Bihar, Delhi, Madhya Pradesh, Haryana, Rajasthan, Uttar Pradesh, and Himachal Pradesh. There are substantial movements across state lines within the Hindi-speaking states. The 1961 census reported that a total of 4,280,000 persons within these six states came from one of the other states. Of these, slightly over a million came from the Punjab, a substantial proportion of which is Punjabi-speaking. Many of the other migrants within the Hindi-speaking belt also belong to non-Hindi-speaking communities, including Marwaris, Rajasthanis, and some of the tribal communities.

27

thirty-eight million tribals (some of which, like Santali and Bhili, straddle state boundaries). There are also many variants of Hindi (such as Awadhi, Baghelkandi, Pahari, Chhattisgarhi, and Khariboli), some of which are quite distinct, that are spoken in regions of the Hindi-speaking states; and there are several subregional languages whose independent status as a language is sometimes disputed, such as Bhojpuri, Maithili, Magadhi, Kamauni, Rajasthani, Marwari, and Coorgi.

A third category of linguistic minorities includes those who speak the language of a contiguous neighboring state and who are a minority by virtue of the way in which state boundaries have been drawn. When India's state boundaries were redrawn in the mid-1950s to create linguistic states, many villages, towns, even substantial parts of districts were left on the "wrong" side of the border, creating pockets of linguistic "minorities." Some of these people have demanded that their localities be transferred to the neighboring state so that their minority status could be ended, but there are often complex geographic, administrative, and political reasons why such transfers have not taken place.

Interstate migrants are the fourth major category of linguistic minorities. Of course, interstate migrants need not become a minority. Those who move from the Hindi-speaking state of Uttar Pradesh to the neighboring state of Bihar remain part of the linguistic majority. But movement outside of the Hindi-speaking states generally means exchanging a majority for a minority status. What distinguishes this category of linguistic minorities from the others is that it is the most changeable, since the number of migrants from one region to another can substantially increase or decrease from year to year.

In any study of the relationship between migration and cultural regions in India, we must also note the present fluidity of cultural identities. India is a society where individuals have a variety of identities simultaneously—caste, religion, language, tribe, and territory—and which of these

28

becomes salient at any particular time is often a function of political circumstances. In recent years, cultural groups that are part of a larger political identity have been asserting the autonomy of their own culture. There are now nascent movements for more cultural, and in some instances even political, autonomy among the Kumauni, Konkani, Bhojpuri, and Maithili-speaking peoples and among many tribes in northeastern and central India, and there are substantial sentiments in Andhra, Maharashtra, Madhya Pradesh, Assam, and Bihar for the creation of smaller states based upon the cultural and historic affinities of people who live within regions of these states. The growth of such identities has an important bearing on whether migrants to a given city, district, or region are considered by local people to be outsiders or fellow members of a common cultural identity.

It was in the early 1920s that several linguistic groups, each divided by state boundaries, demanded that states be reorganized so that each of the larger languages could have states of their own. This linguistic demand was incorporated into the program of the Indian National Congress with the promise that such states would be created once the country became independent. After independence the central government was initially reluctant to carry out its promise, for the government quickly recognized how formidable a task the reorganization of state boundaries would be; moreover, they feared the possible divisive consequences of linguistically homogeneous states each making demands upon the center and upon one another. Delaying at first, the government changed its mind after a number of major violent upheavals shook several states. A commission was appointed by the government, which recommended that the states be organized along linguistic lines.

Subsequently, but reluctantly, the central government also acceded to the demands for statehood by one religious and several tribal communities. In the Punjab the Sikhs, a religious community that asserted its claim was linguistic and not religious, were given a state of their own called the Pun-

29

jab; the residual territory became Haryana. In the hill areas of India's northeast, the Naga tribes were given their own state, Nagaland; the Khasis and Garos were given the state of Meghalaya; the Mizos formed Mizoram; and the various hill tribes of the northeast frontier formed Arunachal Pradesh.

The demand for still more states persists. In recent years several former princely areas or geographic regions of states that have some historical identity have become the focal point for new claims. A separate political identity has been claimed for the portion of Andhra known as Telangana, a region that had once been part of the former princely state of Hyderabad. In both Madhya Pradesh and Maharashtra there are demands from several of the backward regions that they be allowed to create their own states. In southern Bihar a transtribal political party has called for the creation of a state for the tribals of the region.

Attention should be called to two features of these territorial identities in India. The first is that those who assert their territorial identification—invariably individuals with a wide variety of other identities who have coalesced around territorial sentiments—believe that their identity can be legitimized only if they achieve statehood; the second is the notion of exclusiveness, that is, that the territory with which they identify "belongs" to those who are indigenous to it.

The first assertion is a byproduct of the linguistic agitation. The decision of the government to create linguistic states precipitated similar demands by smaller linguistic groups and by a variety of other social identities, for each ethnic group perceived that statehood was the most effective means of legitimizing its claim for a separate cultural identity. Thus, the tribes of India's northeastern state of Assam concluded that so long as they remained within Assam they would be under pressure to assimilate to the Assamese language and culture and to the Hindu religion, while if they had a state of their own they could assert their own identity.

Moreover, many minorities believe that those who hold power within states tend to use the state administrative ap-

30

paratus and fiscal resources to benefit the majority group, so that minorities, especially when their income and education is below the state average, tend to be neglected by the state governments. Hence, the relatively backward regions of states often demand statehood.

Territorial exclusiveness is a relatively new phenomena in India; those who hold this view assert that the indigenous population has a special claim to the region: a first claim on employment, schools, housing, positions in the administrative services, and even control over the state political system. Thus, newcomers are only entitled to benefits after these benefits have been adequately distributed to the indigenous population. Outsiders, it is asserted, do not have an equal claim on jobs, housing, education, and the like, though they are as Indian as the local population.

Paradoxically, the assertion of an ethnic identity may itself be triggered by the migration process. A given social group may not be aware of the extent to which it differs from others who live elsewhere in the state until migrants enter their area. Migration may precipitate self-awareness both on the part of the migrant and on the part of the indigenous population. Ethnic self-awareness is made possible when individuals are able to contrast their cultural characteristics with those of others.

TYPES AND MAGNITUDES OF MIGRATION

In 1971 India had a population of 548 million, of whom 170 million, or about a third of the Indian population, lived in a village or town other than the place in which they were born (Tables 2.1 and 2.2). Of these migrants, 117 million were women, 53 million were men. Most of the migrant women, 96 out of 117 million, lived in rural areas, while a majority of the male migrants, 31 out of 53 million, lived in cities and towns.

Most of the migrants moved within their own state: 141.6 million migrants (of the 170), as against 19.4 million who

31

TABLE 2.1
All-India Migration (1971)

	Number* (thousands)	Percent
Born within place of enumeration	375,397	68.8
Migrants		
Born elsewhere in district of enumeration	106,274	19.5
Born in other districts of state	35,393	6.5
Born in other states of India	19,423	3.6
Born in Pakistan & Bangladesh	8,113	1.5
Born in Nepal	486	0.1
Born in other countries	391	
Total population	545,477	100.0

* These figures based on the one percent sample data provided in the *All India Census Tables of 1971*, Series I, India, Part II. India's actual 1971 population based on the full census was 547,949,000.

moved from other states, and 9 million who migrated to India from Pakistan, Bangladesh, Nepal, and other countries. The intrastate migrants were largely women—103 million— and most had merely changed residence within their own district. The proportion of male migrants to total migrants increases as one moves from within the district, to other districts in the same state, to movement across state boundaries; while the proportion of male migrants to total migrants is greater in the urban than in rural areas. The reverse, of course, is the pattern for females.

This pattern reflects the large female marriage migration. Though we have no statistical information as to what proportion of India's female migrants moved either to get married or to accompany their migrant husbands, the tradition of caste endogamy combined with village exogamy in rural India leads us to conclude that a substantial proportion moved for marital reasons. One striking feature of the mar-

32

TABLE 2.2
Interstate Migration (1971)
(THOUSANDS)

Place of birth	Place of Residence	
	Rural	Urban
Rural	6,197	5,639
Urban	1,266	4,982
Undesignated	909	430
Total	8,372	11,051
Population Movement	Male	Female
Rural to rural	2,284	3,913
Rural to urban	3,597	2,042
Urban to rural	573	694
Urban to urban	2,670	2,311
Undesignated	514	826
Total	9,538	9,786

Intrastate Migration (1971)
(THOUSANDS)

Place of Birth	Place of Residence	
	Rural	Urban
Rural	106,850	18,158
Urban	6,535	9,011
Undesignated	860	254
Total	114,245	27,423
Population Movement	Male	Female
Rural to rural	23,066	83,784
Rural to urban	8,793	9,365
Urban to rural	2,324	4,211
Urban to urban	4,129	4,882
Undesignated	307	808
Total	38,619	103,050

riage network in India, one that calls for more detailed knowledge than can be derived from the census, is the large and expanding territorial network for the marriage market. There is some evidence to suggest that Indians choose their mates over longer distances than in the past. Between 1961 and 1971, the intradistrict migration of women had increased by 17.9 percent, interdistrict migration within the same state had increased by 24.8 percent, and interstate migration had increased by 44.1 percent.

Since a given caste can range over a large territory encompassing several districts, the territorial network of marriage can expand within the framework of caste endogamy. Thus, the Kamma caste in Andhra predominates in the eastern districts, but Kammas can be found all over the state. Moreover, the movement of male migrants across the state and across linguistic boundaries further expands the territorial marriage network. For male migrants marriage within the caste is a barrier to interlinguistic (hence, intercaste) marriages, a factor that leads male migrants to seek their wives from their state of origin.

The use of the classified advertisements in India's newspapers by members of the educated classes represents an effort on the part of the middle classes to maintain both class and caste relationships by searching for brides and grooms over long distances. One illustration is the case of my research assistant on this study. A Sikh by religion and a member of the Arora caste, she held a master's degree in sociology from Delhi University. One day she informed me that her parents had arranged her marriage with another Sikh Arora, a graduate engineer employed in Chicago. He had gone, unmarried, to Chicago to study and upon the completion of his degree found a job and arranged to remain in the United States permanently. His parents in Delhi advertised for an educated Arora girl and were soon in touch with the parents of my research assistant. After some investigation by each family of the status and background of the other family and the respective educational achievements (and employment)

34

of their children, arrangments were made for the two to meet when the engineer made a one-month trip from Chicago to Delhi. The prospective bride and groom agreed to the marriage proposals of their families, and after a few meetings during the month the marriage was arranged, a dowry provided, and the couple flew to Chicago.

Here we have all the ingredients of the traditional marriage market—prearranged marriage by the family, marriage within the caste, a concern for the status of the respective families (now measured by education, however, rather than by land), a dowry, a traditional (and elaborate) wedding ceremony—but with an expansion of the marriage market that went beyond district, state, and even national boundaries.

Though most of India's rural-to-rural migration consists of female migrants—88 out of 113 million—a substantial number of males, about 25 million, move from one rural area to another. Much of this migration consists of agricultural laborers, plantation workers in tea and coffee, rural construction workers (the large irrigation schemes often employ hundreds of thousands of construction workers, both male and female), and some agricultural colonization of new lands. Only a small proportion of India's rural-to-rural migration consists of male migrants moving from one state to another—only 2.3 million out of the 113 million rural migrants.

A majority of the interstate migration consists of migration to urban areas. Of the 19.4 million interstate migrants (exclusive of those who have moved across international boundaries), 11 million live in urban and 8.4 million in rural areas. Among migrants from Pakistan and Bangladesh slightly more live in rural than in urban areas—4.3 million as against 3.8 million. Nepali migrants are substantially more rural (358,000) than urban (128,000).

In 1971, one out of every thirteen Indians was a migrant to a city or town—42.6 million—forming nearly 40 percent of the country's total urban population of 108.6 million. More than a third of these migrants, 15.2 million, were born outside of the state (including more than 11 million from other states and about 4 million from other countries), and 27.4 million from elsewhere in the same state. One out of every seven urban dwellers now comes from another state or from outside of India. Among those who come from other states, 55 percent come from rural areas, 45 percent from other urban areas.[7] Those who migrate long distances in India are more likely to move from one urban area to another, while those who move short distances are more likely to be moving from a rural to an urban area.

City-wide breakdowns of migration data by urban area for the 1971 census are not available, so we are unable to report where interstate migrants currently reside. But according to the 1961 census, the cities with the largest proportion of interstate migrants were Bombay, Calcutta, Delhi, Madras, Ahmadabad, and Bangalore, where they constituted approximately one-fourth of the combined population of these cities. Of India's 107 cities (in 1961) with populations exceeding 100,000, interstate migrants were more than 10 percent of the population in 30. More than a third (38 percent) of the interstate migrant urban dwellers lived in the 6 large cities listed above.

Still, it is striking how widely dispersed rather than how narrowly concentrated are the interstate migrants. About 40 percent of India's interstate migrants live in 26 districts and another 26 cities outside of these districts; the remaining millions are scattered throughout the country, with scarcely

[7] Much of the migration to India's cities is from other urban areas. Of the 14 million migrants to urban areas from other districts of the same state, 6 million come from urban and 8 million from rural areas. Within districts, urban migration is predominantly rural to urban, 10.3 out of the 13 million. This suggests that there is considerable step-wise migration from rural areas to district towns, and from the towns to other towns or cities elsewhere within or outside the state boundaries, often with a generation intervening. In short, a large part of the growth of India's larger urban centers is due to migration from other cities and towns, not exclusively from rural India.

36

a district in the country with fewer than ten thousand persons who had migrated from another state (about 1 percent of the district population, on the average).

Where do interstate migrants come from, and to what states do they move? In terms of numbers of people, the largest exporting states, according to the 1971 census (Table 2.3), are Uttar Pradesh (3.5 million), Bihar (2.1 million), Rajasthan (1.4 million), Punjab (1.2 million), and Madhya Pradesh (1 million), all in the north; with four other states, Maharashtra, Mysore, Andhra, and Tamil Nadu exporting about 1.1 million persons each. In terms of the percentage of population of each state that has emigrated, Punjab is first, with 8.8 percent, followed closely by Haryana (8.4), then Delhi (6.8), Rajasthan (5.2), Kerala (4.4), Uttar Pradesh (3.9), Mysore and Bihar (both 3.7). West Bengal, with only 1.7 percent of its residents outside, is well below the national average of 3.5 percent, but if East Bengal migrants to India are included, then in absolute numbers the Bengalis appear high on a list of migrant communities in India.

To what states do migrants move? According to the 1961 census, the major flows have been to West Bengal (especially the industrial belts in the Hooghly and Damodar valley regions), Maharashtra (greater Bombay and Poona), Punjab (the industrial towns along the railway lines between Amritsar and Delhi), Assam (the tea plantation), Mysore (the industrial complex around Bangalore and the gold fields at Kolar), and Madhya Pradesh (with the heavy electrical industries at Bhopal).[8]

In terms of proportion of immigrants to total population (Table 2.4), West Bengal and Punjab, with 15.7 percent and 14.2 percent, respectively, are the highest states; though the centrally administered areas, Delhi (with 56.4 percent) and Tripura (with 37.2 percent) have an even higher proportion.

[8] For a mapping of migration flows see the Census Atlas, part IX of Volume I of the *Census of India, 1961*, edited by Dr. P. Sen Gupta, especially maps 60, 61, and 62.

TABLE 2.3

Migrants by State of Birth (1961, 1971)

	1961		1971	
	Number		*Number*	
State	*(thousands)*	*% **	*(thousands)*	*% **
Assam	116	1.0	183	1.2
West Bengal	505	1.5	783	1.7
Jammu & Kashmir	78	2.0	79	1.7
Maharashtra	867	2.2	1,141	2.3
Madhya Pradesh	824	2.5	1,017	2.4
Orissa	471	2.7	434	2.0
Andhra Pradesh	870	2.7	1,065	2.4
Gujarat	734	3.0	858	3.2
Tamil Nadu	1,095	3.5	1,092	2.7
Uttar Pradesh	2,583	3.5	3,463	3.9
Kerala	624	3.4	928	4.4
Mysore	794	3.4	1,094	3.7
Bihar	2,041	4.5	2,114	3.7
Rajasthan	1,132	5.6	1,399	5.2
Punjab	1,318	6.5	1,192	8.8
Haryana			843	8.4
Delhi	183	7.0	275	6.8
Unclassified			908	
Other states & territories	406		555	
India	14,641	3.3	19,475	3.5

* Percentage represents proportion of the total population born in each state residing outside of the state.

SOURCE: 1971 data based on estimates from one percent sample data, *All India Census Tables of 1971*, Series I, India, Part II. Note that in the cases of Assam and Punjab the percentile increases partly reflect the redrawing of state boundaries; the 1961 and 1971 figures, therefore, are not comparable.

TABLE 2.4

Migrants by State of Residence (1961)

State	Number (thousands)	Percent of state population
Kerala	244	1.5
Andhra Pradesh	601	1.7
Tamil Nadu	667	2.1
Orissa	347	2.2
Uttar Pradesh	1,563	2.2
Bihar	1,063	2.4
Jammu & Kashmir	83	2.5
Gujarat	696	3.4
Mysore	1,055	4.7
Rajasthan	954	4.9
Madhya Pradesh	1,669	5.2
Maharashtra	2,865	7.4
Assam	1,352	11.4
Punjab	2,859	14.2
West Bengal	5,438	15.7
Tripura	415	36.3
Delhi	1,490	56.4
India*	23,705	5.4

* Includes immigrants from other countries (such as Pakistan, Bangladesh, and Nepal) as well as other states of India.

Assam comes next, with 11.4 percent of its population migrants—though with illegal migration from East Pakistan (now Bangladesh) it is probably higher—followed by Maharashtra, with 7.3 percent, and the hill state of Himachal with 6.6 percent.

Who are the migrants who move across state boundaries, what do they do, and why have they migrated? Why have millions of Indians moved, sometimes over long distances and often to states in which alien languages are spoken? One can distinguish among different social categories of migrants, each characterized by a different set of motivations:

1. The largest group, as we have noted, consists of women who cross district or state borders to marry or to join their husbands.

2. Students seeking a college education move from the countryside to a nearby district college, or to one of the state universities, usually in one of the larger cities in the state. In some instances, young people move across state boundaries to enter the national universities or one of the national technological institutes. It is not simply the size of this migration—the number of college and university students increased from 360,000 in 1950 to 2.9 million in 1972, from 0.8 percent in the age group 17 to 23, to 4.0 percent—that makes it significant, but the role such migration plays in permanently moving many young people out of their community of origin.

3. There is a substantial low-income, low-skilled labor force moving from the countryside to the city or from one urban area to another. Parts of this labor force are permanent, but a very substantial portion consists of short-term migrants whose number may be larger than is revealed by the decennial census. Much of this migration, particularly the temporary sojourners, consists of males without their wives and children. An important feature of this migration is that while it may be short-term, the settlements into which these migrants move are well established; thus, the slums of Delhi, Bombay, Calcutta, and Madras are permanent features of the landscape, though the individual slum dwellers are often temporary residents.

4. There are many migrants moving from one rural area to another, some as seasonal workers during the harvest season; but others are more prosperous peasants who have moved into newly colonized lands or lands that have been transformed from dry to wet cultivation. The migration of the former—like that of many low-income movers from the countryside to the city—is often indicative of considerable

economic duress; but the latter migrations are often a mark of substantial social mobility, as peasants move into locales where they can increase their incomes and generally improve the well-being of their families. Though India has not had any large frontier (compared to, say, Brazil), there are areas that improved technology has opened—waste lands made arable, dry lands that have become irrigated, and malarial areas opened through the elimination of mosquitos. Large hydroelectric dams and irrigation works have attracted migrants to Ganganagar district in Rajasthan and Nizamabad district in Andhra; malarial reduction and reclamation projects have opened districts in Uttar Pradesh along the terrai; and in Assam large-scale jumming or deforestation (often illegally) has made it possible for Bengalis and Nepalis to settle lands in the hills along the Brahmaputra valley.

5. Members of the middle class often move from one urban center to another in search of employment. This broad social category includes high school and district college graduates who move to larger towns and cities in search of employment, and it also includes the technical and professional classes in search of better jobs with higher salaries. In this category one should also include those "migrants"—they would not call themselves "migrants" for the term itself has lower-class overtones—who have been transferred or assigned by their employers to another location. These migrants are often central and state government officials who belong to administrative cadres in which there is a well-established tradition of transferring personnel from one locale to another. Among the large public and private sector firms, from the Indian Airline Corporation to Tata Industries, transfers of personnel are also not uncommon.

6. Entrepreneurs, a loose term that includes traders, small merchants, and moneylenders, as well as large industrial investors, avail themselves of the opportunity created by a national government and a common market to move and invest freely throughout the country. Since these classes are not equally found among all ethnic groups in the coun-

41

try, the expansion of the private sector has invariably meant a wider diffusion of entrepreneurial migrants throughout the country.

This diversified list should remind us that individuals move for a variety of reasons that are closely tied to the major decisions they make throughout their lives: what (and where) to study, who (and where) to marry, what kind of job to seek (and where to work), and what kind of investment one should make (and where).

ETHNICITY: BARRIER OR INCENTIVE TO MIGRATION?

There is probably a natural preference on the part of most people to live in a locality where they share the same language and culture with their neighbors, where their children can readily marry within their own ethnic community, where they can buy familiar food, read newspapers in their own mother tongue, attend a familiar temple, send their children to a school conducted in their own language, and in general avoid the discomfort—and the hostility—that so often accompanies living as a stranger in an alien culture.

It is generally assumed that only force of circumstances, such as the need for a job, the search for a higher salary, the drive for a more profitable place to invest, or the desire for a better education, leads individuals to put aside these natural preferences. In this section we shall suggest that ethnic considerations are not only not a barrier, but that there are circumstances under which they may actually be an incentive to migration.

One way in which ethnicity is an incentive to migration in India is the existence of ethnic enclaves that make it possible for migrants to move into localities in which people of their own language and culture already reside. Some border districts have large spill-over populations from earlier migrations, while in some instances state boundaries arbitrarily cut through cultural-linguistic communities. Many border districts are occupied by people who speak the language of the neighboring state. Thus, Kolar district in Mysore, a gold mining region, is 53 percent Telugu (rather than Kannada, the state language); Cachar district in Assam is 79 percent Bengali; Ganganagar district in Rajasthan is 28 percent Punjabi; Bangalore district in Mysore is 17 percent Telugu and 16 percent Tamil; and Nilgiris district in Tamil Nadu is 31 percent Kannada and 20 percent Malayalam.

Moreover, there are well-established migration streams from one state to another. For several decades there has been a movement of Munda, Oraon, and Ho tribesmen (and women) from districts of Chota Nagpur in southern Bihar and districts of northern Orissa to the tea plantations in the hill areas of Assam; a stream of migrants from western Andhra to the Kolar mines in Mysore; a stream of Malayalees from northern Kerala to the coffee plantations of Coorg; Bangalore and Bombay have had small streams of educated migrants from Tamil Nadu taking jobs as clerks, typists, stenographers, and administrators in private firms. Some districts of northern Bihar regularly export their surplus agricultural laborers to the factories of Calcutta and Howrah, and Nepalis from the hill districts of eastern Nepal regularly trek across the mountain ranges to Darjeeling and Jalpaiguri districts in West Bengal to work in the tea gardens. In many towns and villages from which migrants come, it is quite common for one or more sons in a family to join a relative who had previously migrated. These migration patterns are, of course, quite familiar to other societies; the added dimension in India, as in some other multiethnic societies, is that the first wave of migrants generally plays a role in creating the ethnic infrastructures that make it possible for a migrant to move from one cultural region to another without having to give up those features of his culture life that require community support, such as schools, newspapers, temples, and restaurants. Moreover, these institutions themselves provide a source of employment for potential migrants, as schoolmasters and teachers, editors and compositors, priests, cooks, and waiters. In short, once a migrant beachhead is established in another culture, the boundaries that divide states (and cultures) become less of a barrier to migration.

A second factor that makes ethnicity itself a determinant of migration is the self-perceived skills, resources, and motivations that lead members of an ethnic group residing in one locality to believe that they can successfully compete for employment in the locality where other ethnic groups reside. Differentials in wages and employment opportunities between Place A and Place B may not in itself be an adequate incentive to move, for there may be many places with lower wages or fewer job opportunities than Place A; but the belief on the part of the people who reside in Place A that they can effectively compete with the native population in Place B or migrants from other localities is an important element in the decision to move.

At the micro (individual) level, migration is an instrument of social mobility; at the macro (economic) level, migration is an instrument for the movement of skilled persons to areas in which such skills are in short supply. At one level migration is thus affected by the varied capacities of individuals to work, invest, acquire an education, use skills, be ambitious; at another level, migration is affected by patterns of regional investment and regional development. The matching of these two elements, the micro-individual and the macro-economic are important determinants of selectivity in migration.

The more differentiated the division of labor, the less likely it is that all the relevant skills for a new economic activity can be found locally. The opening of an aluminum factory in Belgaum or a new steel mill at Roorkela necessitates the employment of metallurgists from outside these two towns, and even outside the state. The Heavy Engineering Corporation in Ranchi, the Atomic Energy Laboratories in Bombay, and Hindustan Aeronautics in Bangalore are all magnets for engineers, professional managers, computer programmers, scientists, and economists from all over the country. Members of these modern professions tend to be occupation-oriented, like their counterparts in the developed countries,

44

rather than place-oriented, and they are often willing to change their residence if they can improve their status, income, or work satisfaction.

For a variety of complex and often idiosyncratic reasons, some related to the culture of the community, others to opportunities created under particular historical circumstances, some ethnic groups contain larger numbers of people who have acquired the skills, resources, and motivations that lead them to avail themselves of the opportunities resulting from variations in regional economic development. Several examples from the Indian scene will illustrate the point:

The establishment of a common national government and a common internal market provided, as we noted earlier, investment opportunities throughout the country for India's entrepreneurs. The Marwaris, a trading community from Rajasthan, is a self-chosen business community that has established banking and trading facilities in every state and in virtually every major town in India. In all, 460,000 Marwari speakers, or 7.4 percent of all Marwaris, lived outside their home state in 1961. Though the largest number lived in the nearby Hindi-speaking states, as many as 21,000 could be found in a handful of towns in far-off Assam in India's northeast. Similarly, the Punjabi Sikhs, many of whom served in India's armed forces, have developed India's transport industry, plying taxis, trucks, and busses, manufacturing and repairing automotive parts, tractors, and related agricultural equipment and bicycles. Two hundred thousand Punjabis live in Assam, Andhra, Bihar, Gujarat, Kerala, Tamil Nadu, Maharashtra, Mysore, Orissa, and West Bengal, all states a good distance from the Punjab. In Maharashtra alone (in 1961) there were 64,000 Punjabis, while West Bengal had 54,000.

In India's largest cities, the major industrial enterprises are almost all owned by "outsiders," not Europeans, but Marwaris from Rajasthan, Parsis from Bombay, and Gujaratis, Punjabis, and Sindhis. It is a rare large city—Ahmadabad is one of the few exceptions—in which the major industries are owned by individuals who belong linguistically to the state. The fact that such a large part of India's trading, banking, and industrial classes are aliens in the area in which they work is no doubt a significant element in the widespread anti-business, socialist attitude of so many Indians.

Every city and town in India is dotted with ethnic enclaves of migrant origin with specialized economic functions. In Madurai, the weavers originate from Saurashtra; in Bombay, the city's milk is delivered by migrants from Uttar Pradesh, the port laborers are from Andhra, the clerical personnel are from Tamil Nadu, and construction workers are from Rajasthan; in the famous Chandi Chauk bazar of old Delhi each specialized section of the bazar (one selling gold jewelry, another Banaras silks, a third brassware, a fourth wedding ornaments, a fifth leathergoods) is run by a caste whose members come from and continue to be linked to other bazars in towns of northern India.

Even the unskilled labor force is often organized along ethnic lines. Many of India's dams, irrigation schemes, office buildings, and roads have been constructed by migrants from among the lower-caste landless laborers from Andhra and Rajasthan. These are often organized by local *sardars* or bosses who move their workers from one project to another as contracts become available. Agricultural laborers may also move seasonally after the harvest to nearby urban centers in search of daily employment: Bihari agricultural laborers find employment plying rickshaws in Gauhati, Rajasthani agricultural laborers engage in construction work in Hyderabad, and Telugu agriculturalists find day labor jobs in Bangalore.

A striking feature of occupational specialization by ethnic community in India is the way in which so many Indians view such specialization as an immutable "given," almost as if ethnic groups were programmed to behave in a particular way. Thus, it is widely asserted that the "opening" of tribal areas to outsiders without restrictions would result in their "invasion" by Marwari, Punjabi, and other mercantile com-

46

munities who would establish lucrative (and in the minds of many, almost by definition, "exploitative") businesses that the tribals themselves are incapable of creating, even if they had or were given the financial resources to do so.

Many local communities assert that some migrant ethnic groups are so superior in skills or motivation that local people would not be able to compete for employment in a wholly free labor market; it is this belief—to anticipate a proposition that will be developed at greater length in another chapter—that underscores the political argument for a protected labor market in many regions of India. In this context, competition is not viewed as a stimulus for change, but as a force for growing inequality among ethnic groups.

It should be noted, however, that there are also some kinds of jobs that the local population does not seek and for which migrant laborers must be imported. Some jobs, as we have indicated, are thought to *belong* to certain ethnic groups. Other jobs are rejected because the wages are too low or their status makes them undesirable. In the nineteenth century, Assamese peasants, almost all landowning cultivators, had no desire to give up self-employment for low-paying proletarian jobs in the tea plantations. They therefore left this expanding labor market to migrant workers from tribal Bihar. Nor do Bengalis ordinarily take jobs as rickshaw pullers, a beast-of-burden occupation they readily turn over to Bihari migrants. Similarly, construction work, accepted by Telugu and Rajasthani low-caste landless laborers, is not often sought by most local urban dwellers, even when there is unemployment.

This leads us to a third way in which ethnicity has facilitated interregional migrations: the role of employer preferences.

For specific occupations many entrepreneurs prefer to hire particular ethnic communities. Tea plantation managers in Assam and northern Bengal have historically employed tribals from Bihar and Orissa; similarly, port managers, construction contractors, and many industrialists prefer to re-

47

cruit their unskilled labor force from a specific ethnic group, often from a considerable distance. Employers often find a particular ethnic group suitable because of such traditional virtues as their honesty, good temperament, obedience, willingness to work hard, reliability, and so on. Moreover, managers often prefer a migrant labor force to a local labor force since it is less likely to be influenced by local politics, and less likely to be unionized. There are also some benefits in recruiting workers from a single community speaking a single language: communication is easier, and there is less likely to be the tensions that often exist in a multicultural labor force.

In the preindependence era, the British civil servants also had their preferences among ethnic groups—for appointments in the military, the civil service, the railroads, and the police. The early establishment of colleges and universities in the areas where Tamils and Bengalis lived also gave these communities an advantage for employment in the civil service. The British soon concluded that the Bengalis and Tamils were particularly well suited for the administrative services.

In the presidencies of Bengal and Madras, the Bengalis and Tamils were recruited for positions in state administrations whose writ then extended far beyond the Bengali and Tamil-speaking regions. Bengalis were sent to Assam, Bihar, and Orissa in the nineteenth century, when these provinces were under the administrative jurisdiction of Calcutta, and Bengali (along with English) was the administrative *lingua franca* throughout northeastern India. Similarly, Tamils were posted in Andhra and in portions of what is now Mysore and Kerala, then governed under Madras.

Even now we continue to find Bengalis manning the post offices and railways in Ranchi, working as clerks in the tea plantations in Assam, and teaching at the university in Cuttack; and we find Tamils at the universities in Andhra and in the state secretariat in Bangalore. When the linguistic regions of Madras and Bengal presidency each became separate

48

states, the new employers—the state politicians, the university vice chancellors, the state ministers of education—no longer preferred Bengalis and Tamils, though both communities continued to have some competitive advantages in the national civil service examinations. With the establishment of a wholly new system of employment preferences for local people, many of the older linkages of ethnic groups to specific jobs began to come to an end.

But the managers of private firms continue to prefer some ethnic groups over others in the expectation that those who belong to a particular community are likely to excel: Tamils as accountants, Nepalis as guards, Malayalees as clerk-typists, and so on; stereotypes are deeply engrained, though who is to say that the employers' preferences are not supported by experience?

To summarize, then, individuals may move from one cultural-linguistic region to another because of: 1. decisions they themselves have made, based on the availability of opportunities for which they believe they can successfully compete, and the existence of ethnic enclaves into which they can move; 2. decisions by local people that there are certain jobs that they do not want, or for which they cannot qualify; and 3. decisions by employers to give preference to one ethnic group over another in hiring.

THE IMPACT OF MIGRATION ON LINGUISTIC DIVERSITY

How does the flow of migrants across state boundaries contribute to the linguistic diversity of India's states? As noted earlier, nearly one out of every five Indians belongs to a linguistic minority, that is, does not speak the regional language of the state as a mother tongue (Table 2.5). Those who speak a minority language range from only five percent in Kerala to a third or more of the population in a half-dozen states. However, as we have noted earlier, the minority language may be a local language, that is, one indigenous to the state; it may be Urdu, the language of nearly half of

49

TABLE 2.5

State Languages (1961)

State	Regional language	Percent speaking regional language
Kerala	Malayalam	95.0
Gujarat	Gujarati	90.5
Rajasthan	Rajasthani, Hindi	89.9
Andhra	Telugu	86.0
Uttar Pradesh	Hindi	84.7
West Bengal	Bengali	84.2
Haryana	Hindi	83.3
Tamil Nadu	Tamil	83.2
Orissa	Oriya	82.3
Bihari	Bihari, Hindi	79.7
Delhi	Hindi	77.4
Maharashtra	Marathi	76.4
Madhya Pradesh	Hindi	67.0
Punjab	Punjabi	65.6
Tripura	Bengali	65.2
Mysore	Kannada	65.1
Assam	Assamese	62.3
Jammu & Kashmir	Kashmiri	53.2
India		80.9

India's sixty million Muslims; it may be a language that originates outside of India, such as Nepali or Sindhi; or it may be the regional language of another state.

One way of ascertaining how many people speak migrant languages, that is, languages that are the mother tongues commonly used in other states, is to consider how many Indians speaking a regional language live in another state (Table 2.6).

In 1961 there were 26 million Indians speaking one of India's official languages, residing in a state in which they

TABLE 2.6
Linguistic Dispersal (1961)

Language[a]	Number of speakers not residing in home state	Percent speakers in home state	Percent speakers in other states
Assamese	19,000	99.7	0.3
Kashmiri	18,000	99.0	1.0
Bihari[b]	364,000	97.8	2.3
Hindi[c]	4,187,000	96.6	3.4
Malayalam	929,000	94.5	5.5
Tamil[d]	2,129,000	93.0	7.0
Gujarati	1,434,000	92.9	7.1
Marwari	460,000	92.6	7.4
Oriya	1,175,000	92.5	7.4
Marathi	2,534,000	92.3	7.7
Bengali[e]	3,624,000	89.2	10.8
Kannada	1,944,000	88.8	11.2
Punjabi	1,531,000	84.5	15.5
Telugu	6,710,000	82.2	17.8
Rajasthani	3,547,000	76.2	23.8
Total	30,605,000		

[a] Several other major languages do not have a "home" state and are widely dispersed. These include Urdu (23,323,000), Santali (3,247,000), Bhili (2,439,000), Gondi (1,501,000), Konkani (1,352,-000), Kurukh/Oraon (1,141,000), and Pahari (1,004,000). One other language with more than a million speakers, Kumauni, is confined to Uttar Pradesh. Two non-Indian languages, Sindhi (1,371,000) and Nepali (1,021,000), are widely dispersed.

[b] Bihari includes Bhojpuri, Maithili, and Magadhi, including their variant forms.

[c] The major variants of Hindi—Awadhi, Baghelkhandi, Chhattisgarhi, and Khariboli—are not included here, but in each instance more than 99 percent of these languages are spoken in their home state. The home states of Hindi are here defined to include Delhi, Bihar, Madhya Pradesh, Punjab, Rajasthan, Uttar Pradesh, and Himachal Pradesh.

[d] The home states of Tamil include Tamil Nadu and Pondicherry.

[e] The home states of Bengali are West Bengal and Tripura.

were a linguistic minority. To this figure we have added 3.5 million Rajasthani speakers and nearly a half million Marwaris who live outside of Rajasthan, bringing the total to 30.6 million. There is no reliable method of ascertaining how many of these are themselves indigenous peoples who happen to be located on the "wrong" side of the state border—the situation of many Telugu speakers in southern Orissa and parts of northern Tamil Nadu, Marathi speakers in northern Mysore, and Kannada speakers in western Andhra—and how many are migrants or their descendants. The number of actual migrants and their descendants speaking these languages is surely below 30.6 million, but it is also surely higher than the number of interstate migrants reported in the census, since there is considerable evidence to suggest that second and third generations of migrants (and beyond) continue to speak the mother tongue of the original settlers. Consider, for example, how many more Bengali speakers there are in the districts of Assam than migrants from either West Bengal or Bangladesh (Table 2.7).

Similarly, for each of these districts, the Oriya-speaking population is generally twice that of the number of migrants from Orissa, while the Hindi-speaking population is sub-

TABLE 2.7

Bengalis in Districts of Assam (1961)

Districts of Assam	Percent of population migrants from West Bengal & Bangladesh	Percent speaking Bengali
Goalpara	10.5	12.0
Kamrup	7.0	9.9
Darrang	7.7	9.9
Lakhimpur	4.2	8.2
Nowgong	11.8	17.3
Sibsagar	2.6	3.1

stantially larger than those who come from the Hindi-speaking states.

A similar pattern can be found in other districts, including those that do not border on the states from which migrants come: in Hyderabad, the Marathi-speaking population is twice that of the number of migrants from Maharashtra; in Poona district, Telugu speakers are twice that of migrants from Andhra; less than 2 percent of the population of Bangalore district comes from Andhra, but 17 percent speak Telugu; 11 percent of Bombay's population comes from Gujarat, but 19 percent speak Gujarati; and 3 percent of Indore's people come from Maharashtra, while 8 percent speak Marathi.

These figures suggest that some of the linguistic diversity of India's districts is the consequence of earlier settlement patterns, and that within each of these districts an ambiance exists that encourages migrants not only to retain their mother tongue but to transmit it to their children.

Some linguistic assimilation has taken place, and later we shall suggest that in some regions it has been quite substantial, but the main point is that there has been a widespread presumption in India that while migrants may acquire a second language, neither they nor their children need give up their first language. Under law, linguistic minorities are entitled to have primary schools provided by the government in their mother tongue if requested by parents.

In Mysore, to provide one example, more than a quarter million children attend primary schools in which Telugu, Tamil, Hindi, Marathi, Gujarati, and English (not Kannada, the regional language) are the medium of instruction: 128,000 in Marathi, 59,000 in Tamil, and 19,000 each in Telugu and English.

Migration thus has a cumulative effect on the linguistic heterogeneity of a region. This is illustrated by the effect that migration has had on the linguistic composition of Bombay city (Table 2.8).

TABLE 2.8

Languages of Bombay (1911-1961)

	1911	1931	1961
Marathi	53.7%	47.6%	42.8%
Gujarati	21.0	20.8	19.1
Hindustani	14.8	17.3	8.0 (Hindi)
			9.7 (Urdu)
Other	10.5	14.3	20.4

The number of Bombay residents speaking Marathi as their mother tongue has been declining continuously since 1911, while there has been a persistent increase in the number of people speaking a variety of other languages. In 1961 the other languages included Konkani (4.6%), Tamil (2.5%), Sindhi (2.3%), Kannada (2.0%), Telugu (2.4%), Malayalam (1.6%), and Punjabi (1.3%). The number speaking Hindi and Urdu has also increased over these fifty years. Since the natural population increase of Marathis is no less than that of other linguistic groups, the declining proportion of Marathi speakers in Bombay clearly reflects the increase in the number of migrants from non-Marathi-speaking regions.

Bangalore, the largest city located in Kannada-speaking Mysore state reveals a similar pattern. Unfortunately, language data for Bangalore are not available after 1951, but we have such data for earlier years (Table 2.9).

TABLE 2.9

Languages of Bangalore (1911-1951)

	1911	1921	1931	1951
Kannada	33.3%	33.6%	32.5%	23.7%
Telugu	23.5	25.6	23.0	17.8
Tamil	—	21.1	22.6	31.7
Hindustani	12.4	11.6	11.5	15.8

There has been a decline in the number of Kannada and Telugu speakers, a rise in the number of Tamils and, after 1931, in the number speaking Hindustani, that is, Hindi and Urdu, reflecting the increasing migration into Bangalore of workers from Tamil Nadu and from northern India.

Historically, Delhi has been an Urdu and Hindi-speaking center. The 1911 census reported that 97.6 percent of the population spoke Urdu, Hindi, or Hindustani. With the partition of India, and the partition of the Punjab, there was an influx of Punjabi-speaking refugees. In 1911 less than 1 percent of the city was Punjabi speaking; in 1931 it was 3.7 percent; but in 1961 Punjabi speakers constituted 13.3 percent of the city, or more than one out of every eight persons.

There was also a sharp decline in the number of Urdu speakers, reflecting the Muslim emigration to Pakistan.

Ahmadabad, another predominantly homogeneous city, continues to be overwhelmingly Gujarati speaking, but here, too, migrations from other states have reduced the proportion of Gujaratis (Table 2.10).

TABLE 2.10

Languages of Ahmadabad (1911-1961)

	1911	1921	1931	1951	1961
Gujarati	92.5%	91.7%	89.4%	83.5%	81.0%
Sindhi	4.3	3.8	3.8	2.8	2.4
Urdu	0.7	0.6	—	2.4	2.9
Other	2.5	3.9	6.8	11.3	13.7

In contrast, India's two other large cities, Calcutta and Madras, have experienced increases in the proportion of people speaking the regional language. In Calcutta the proportion of Bengali speakers changed only slightly from 1911 (53.4 percent) to 1931 (54.9 percent), but there was a sharp increase in 1951 (65.9 percent) as a result of the movement of Bengali refugees from East Pakistan. In 1961,

Bengali was spoken by 63.8 percent of the population of Calcutta. Hindi is the second language of the city, with nearly one out of every five speaking the language. The proportion of people speaking other languages has been rising almost continuously from 1911 (9.2 percent) to 1961 (16.9 percent), reflecting the attraction to the city of migrants from all over the country.

Language data for Madras are available only for 1951 and 1961, when there was a slight increase in the proportion of Tamil speakers (from 68 to 71 percent) and a decline in the Telugu-speaking population (from 16.5 to 14.1 percent), probably the consequence of carving out of Madras the Telugu-speaking state of Andhra with its own capital at Hyderabad. (The Hyderabad census revealed a 4 percent increase in the proportion of Telugu speakers in the decade it became the capital of Andhra.)

The linguistic heterogeneity of some Indian cities has thus increased as a result of a more rapid growth in interstate than intrastate migration, and the low rate of linguistic assimilation. It is also noteworthy that bilingualism in these cities is quite common. Though India is a linguistically heterogeneous country, most Indians are monolingual. Only 8.3 percent or 28.7 million of the 346 million Indians speaking one of the regional languages in 1961 were bilingual (Table 2.11), but 40 percent of these bilinguals resided outside of their own linguistic state. It is evident that migrants and their descendants are far more bilingual than those who reside in the state in which their mother tongue is the official language. Bilingualism is highest among south Indians residing outside of their home state—Malayalees (49 percent), Kannadas (56 percent) and Telugus (56 percent)—and comparatively low among Hindi-speaking minorities outside the Hindi-speaking region (30 percent bilinguals).

The second language of bilinguals is ordinarily the regional language of the state in which they reside. In Andhra, the second language of bilingual minorities is Telugu; in Mysore it is Kannada. But there are some striking exceptions. In

56

Table 2.11
Bilingualism within Linguistic States and Outside (1961)
(THOUSANDS)

Mother tongue	Number speakers	Number bilingual	Percent bilingual	Bilinguals in linguistic states		Bilinguals outside linguistic states	
				Number	Percent	Number	Percent
Assamese	6,803	610	9.0	602	8.9	8	44.1
Bengali[a]	33,754	2,922	8.7	1,681	5.6	1,241	34.3
Gujarati	20,105	1,470	7.3	799	4.3	671	46.8
Hindi[b]	123,025	6,280	5.1	5,032	4.2	1,248	29.8
Kannada	17,305	2,498	14.4	1,403	9.1	1,095	56.3
Kashmiri	1,914	204	10.7	198	10.5	6	33.1
Malayalam	16,994	1,209	7.1	754	4.7	455	49.0
Marathi	32,767	3,431	10.5	2,419	8.0	1,012	40.0
Oriya	15,610	898	5.8	451	3.1	447	38.0
Punjabi	9,868	1,397	14.2	818	9.8	579	37.8
Tamil[c]	30,465	2,470	8.1	1,608	5.7	862	40.5
Telugu	37,642	5,284	14.0	1,534	5.0	3,750	55.9
	346,252	28,673	8.3	17,299[d]	5.4	11,374[e]	43.7

[a] Spoken in West Bengal and Tripura.
[b] Spoken in Bihar, Madhya Pradesh, Punjab, Rajasthan, Uttar Pradesh, Delhi, Himachal Pradesh.
[c] Spoken in Tamil Nadu and Pondicherry.
[d] The regional languages are spoken as the mother tongue by 321,015,000 persons in their own linguistic states.
[e] The regional languages are spoken as the mother tongue by 26,232,000 persons residing outside of their own linguistic states.

Maharashtra, bilingual Telugu and Kannada speakers tend to speak Marathi as their second language, but Tamils speak English and Hindi. Hindi also appears to be a second language of an unusually high proportion of migrant groups in some states, even when Hindi is not the regional language: 11 percent of the Nepalis in Assam speak Hindi, 9 percent of the Sindhis in Gujarat, and in Maharashtra Hindi is spoken by 20 percent of the Gujaratis, 38 percent of the Punjabis, 23 percent of the Tamils, 27 percent of the Sindhis, and 15 percent of the Konkanis. The data also reveal that interstate migrants are more likely than nonmigrants to know Hindi or English as a second language.

But the most remarkable feature of India's bilingualism is that in the districts and cities with large ethnic minorities, even the population speaking the regional language is far more bilingual than people elsewhere in the state. In Andhra, for example, only 5 percent of the Telugus speak a second language, but in Hyderabad district 16 percent of the Telugus are bilingual. In Bangalore district, Kannada speakers are twice as bilingual (18 percent) than Kannadas in the state as a whole (9 percent). And in Bombay 29 percent of Marathi speakers are bilingual as against 8 percent in the state. Nor is the second language necessarily English; in all three instances cited, the Hindi and Urdu speakers far exceed those who speak English. In a few instances some of those who speak the regional language as their mother tongue also speak the language of the linguistic minorities.

India's migrant cities are neither melting pots for linguistic minorities merging into the indigenous linguistic majority, nor cultural-linguistic enclaves of people who live in isolation from one another; they are polyglot centers in which substantial numbers of both migrants and natives have acquired each other's language or learned to communicate through a third tongue. The migration process has thus not only transformed the ethnic makeup of cities; it has also transformed the linguistic makeup of the individuals who live there.

But what of the future? Will the flow of interstate migration decline, thereby reducing the diversity of India's cities? We turn to this question in the remaining section of this chapter.

RECENT TRENDS IN INTERSTATE MIGRATION

There are many reasons to expect India's urban centers to become less linguistically diverse in the future. Simply to retain the present linguistic composition of these cities, the proportion of new migrants belonging to each linguistic group must be the same as the proportion of each linguistic group currently residing in the city—assuming, moreover, that each linguistic group has the same rate of natural population increase. Since migrants often have a lower rate of natural population increase, because the proportion of females among migrants is generally less than in the population as a whole, to retain the existing linguistic distribution, therefore, the proportion of interstate migrants must actually be somewhat larger.

There are a number of reasons why interstate population movements ought not to increase as rapidly as intrastate movements. The growth of nativist movements and policies should slow the pace of interstate migration. The switch to regional languages in secondary schools and colleges has diminished opportunities for the employment of outsiders as teachers; state governments give preferences to local people in employment; even the employment of outsiders by the private sector is generally discouraged. And in some areas there have been violent attacks against outsiders: the burning of Marwari bazars and the beating of Bengalis in Assam, attacks against Tamils in Bombay, and threats against outsiders in pro-Kannada demonstrations in Bangalore.

The recent growth of India's widely dispersed middle-sized cities should also serve to encourage rural-to-urban migration within the states rather than across state lines. Between 1961 and 1971 there has been a substantial growth in cities whose populations range between 100,000 and 250,000. Of India's 91 cities in this size range, 31 had growth rates that were at least twice that of the natural population increase of the state in which they are located. The cities in the 250,000 to 500,000 range were also high-growth cities: 13 out of 32 cities in this range grew at least twice the rate of population increase. These include Surat and Baroda in Gujarat; Dhanbad, Ranchi, and Jamshedpur in Bihar; Cochin, Trivandrum, and Calicut in Kerala; Vijayawada, Guntur, and Visakhapatnam in Andhra; Hubli-Dharwar in Mysore; and Bhopal in Madhya Pradesh. Growth among the larger cities, that is, those with populations exceeding half a million, as a result of migration has been slower; only 4 of India's 18 large cities have had migrations equal to the natural growth of population: Madras, Hyderabad, Bangalore, and Jaipur.

In view of these considerations, it is all the more surprising to find that for many of the regional languages the proportion of speakers now residing outside the home region actually increased between 1961 and 1971. For five large linguistic groups the percentage increase of speakers residing outside the home region well exceeded natural population growth: 39 percent for Hindi-speakers, 44 percent for Malayalees, 34 percent for Gujaratis, 34 percent for Marathis, and 58 percent for Bengalis. For three other groups the increases were below population growth, suggesting a return migration: Oriya speakers 18 percent, Tamils 11 percent, and Telugus only 1 percent. The Kannada percentage, 21 percent, is commensurate with the natural population increase. Figures for Kashmiris, Assamese, Rajasthanis, and Punjabis were either too small or, for technical reasons, not comparable.

These figures on the redistribution of language groups are reflected by the provisional 1971 interstate migration tables (Table 2.3), which show high increases in outmigration from West Bengal (55%), Maharashtra (31%), Uttar Pradesh (34%), Kerala (49%), and Mysore (38%). Figures on emigration from East Pakistan (now Bangladesh) to

India are not available, but the greater increase in the percentage of Bengali spoken outside of West Bengal and Tripura than the percentage of outmigration from those two states suggests that there may have been a substantial unreported migration of Bengalis from East Pakistan into India in the 1961-1971 decade.

The 1971 figures also revealed a substantial drop in the percentage of migrants from Orissa (−8 percent), and no growth at all in migration from Tamil Nadu. The growth in outmigration from Andhra (22 percent), with almost no increase in the number of Telugu speakers outside of Andhra, suggests that many of the Andhra migrants were not Telugu speakers.

If detailed language and migration data become available by district and city, we shall need to take a closer look at whether nativist politics and policies have had an impact on migration into and out of some areas. The absolute decline in the number of Tamil migrants and the slowdown in Telugu-speaking migrations suggest that it could be a factor for these groups (though it could also reflect the reorganization of these two states), but the evidence elsewhere suggests that the movement of people across linguistic-cultural regions continues, and for some groups and some localities the movement may actually be accelerating. But only a microanalysis of local data will clarify these questions. In any event, in the country as a whole, interstate migrants increased from 14.6 million in 1961 to 19.4 million in 1971, a growth of 33 percent.

One other feature of the 1971 census should be noted. For the country as a whole, interstate migration to urban areas has been increasing slightly more rapidly than intrastate migration, 22.6 percent as against 21.3 percent. In 1971, there were 19.6 million male migrants living in India's cities (exclusive of foreign-born migrants), 13.1 million of whom came from within the state, while a third, 6.5 million, came from other states. The comparable figures for the previous decade were 10.8 million intrastate and 5.3 million interstate male migrants. A striking feature of this migration is that a substantially larger part of the interstate male migration to urban areas, nearly one-half originates from urban areas of other states, while only a third of the intrastate male migration is urban-to-urban.

Hazardous as it is to forecast long-term interstate migration trends in India, several features of past and present trends are suggestive of factors currently at work.

One feature of the earlier migrations, particularly those that commenced in the mid-nineteenth century, is the extent to which interstate migrations were so closely associated with governmental actions: the British created the coastal cities that became magnets for migrants; the British created the tea and coffee plantations; the British created the system of indentured labor that pulled Indians out of the subcontinent into Africa, Latin America, the Caribbean, and Southeast Asia; the British established canals and canal colonies in the Punjab; and the British recruited Indians from all over the country into the administrative services.

Not until the latter part of the nineteenth century did interstate migration begin to become more closely related to India's industrial development and less directly linked to British colonial policies.

The older migrations have more or less come to an end. The plantations no longer recruit in large numbers; their period of expansion has ended and many have reduced their labor force. The system of indentured labor, both abroad and within India, no longer exists. Little in the way of new lands is now available to migrants. And with the expansion of higher education all over India and the intensity of regional sentiments, both state and central governments now recruit civil servants more nearly in proportion to population.

Moreover, there has even been a return migration of Indians from former British colonies. People of Gujarati origin have migrated from East Africa, especially from Uganda, to Gujarat, where they are beginning to play a notable role in the economic growth of that state. Similarly, there has been a movement of Tamils back from both Burma and Sri Lanka, the former to the city of Madras (where there is now a large "Burma Bazar"), and the latter scattered throughout Tamil Nadu, and to a lesser extent to Kerala and Mysore.

The new interstate migrations are more closely related to industrial expansion and to urban growth. Administrative centers no longer attract interstate migrants as in the past, unless they have also become industrial centers. The more educated continue to migrate from state to state, but now no longer for administrative posts in the state government alone, but for positions in the private sector or in the nationalized industrial enterprises that recruit nationally. In spite of the growth of intense regional loyalties, the language barriers continue to be broken, both by the agrarian poor and by the urban middle classes as they move long distances in search of employment.

Disparities in regional income, regional growth rates, and regional levels of education remain important incentives for the movement of people from one cultural-linguistic region to another. The 1971 census, for example, reports a continued outpouring of Malayalees to other states—a 49 percent increase in emigration over the decade—reflecting the high educational level and high unemployment rate of that state; and the census also reports high migration to rapidly industrializing towns like Dhanbad (a coal mining center in Bihar), Ludhiana (a center for small industries in the Punjab), Visakhapatnam (an expanding seaport in Andhra), Bhopal (an industrial center in Madhya Pradesh), and the cities of Bombay, Madras, Hyderabad, and Bangalore.

Differentials between countryside and city as well as between regions will stimulate migration. Some landless laborers will be driven by rural poverty and others will be pulled by the higher wages paid in the cities as against the countryside. Some rural people will be attracted by the availability of employment opportunities in the city, limited as these may be, when so few jobs are available in their own community. Should the Indian countryside stagnate while its population

63

grows, there will be a movement outward as men and their families seek to escape hunger and starvation; and if the economy prospers and the industrial and service sectors grow, then the drive for higher income will also lead migrants into the city.

More difficult to measure, and therefore easy to underestimate, is the impact that many aspects of the development process have on liberating individuals from an exclusive attachment to their place of birth. The monetization of land makes it possible for peasants to buy and sell land. The establishment of a cash nexus between peasants and artisans, and between peasants and agricultural laborers makes it possible for those who do not own land to move more freely to places where they can increase their income. The breakdown of the old *jajmani* (traditional exchange of services) system therefore creates new opportunities (and compulsions!) for spatial mobility. The growth of nonagricultural occupations has opened up new occupational possibilities for the children of those who work on the land. The growth of education and exposure to newspapers, radio, and the cinema have made individuals aware of new employment opportunities away from their homes. And the improvement of transportation makes it possible for individuals to go long distances—and still be able to return home—at a reasonable cost. To the extent that modernization means an increase in the opportunities for widening choice of spouse, education, and employment, spatial mobility seems likely to increase.

The trends point to the growth of heterogeneous urban centers in India,[9] for it is evident that forces are at work that

[9] There is a large and growing literature on urbanization in India, but little of it gives attention to the impact of migration on the creation of ethnically heterogeneous urban centers. For an unusually thorough survey of both the secondary literature and sources on urban growth in India, see Ashish Bose, *Urbanization in India: An Inventory of Source Materials* (New Delhi: Academic Books, 1970). For a history of urban growth in India incorporating 1971 data, see Ashish Bose, *Studies in India's Urbanization 1901-1971* (New Delhi: Tata McGraw Hill, 1973).

encourage or propel migrants to move across the invisible boundaries that divide linguistic communities. The cities of Bombay and Bangalore and the regions of southern Bihar and the Brahmaputra valley of Assam will remain or even become more multilingual and multicultural, while the linguistic minorities of many of India's rapidly growing towns and cities are likely to increase. These exceptions to India's pattern of linguistically homogeneous settlements are not merely legacies of the past, but pointers to the future.

APPENDIX:
INDIA'S MIGRATING PEOPLES, A STATISTICAL NOTE

Who are the people who migrate from one cultural-linguistic region to another? This note explores the migrating propensities of India's major linguistic communities. For each of twelve regional languages I shall report how many people live outside their home region and where they reside.

There are at least three measures that can be used for analyzing the tendencies of specific ethnic groups to migrate outside their home region: one is the simple measure of how many people (and what proportion) live in another linguistic area; the second is distance—how far migrants move; and the third is dispersal—do the migrants tend to settle in a small number of places or do they widely disperse over large areas of the country?

Assamese

Among the major linguistic communities, the Assamese are India's least mobile people. In 1961, 99.7 percent of all Assamese resided in Assam. More than half of the nineteen thousand Assamese who lived outside the state resided in West Bengal, mainly in Calcutta and the hill districts of Jalpaiguri and Darjeeling, both bordering on Assam. A small number of Assamese also lived in the Punjab, mainly serving in the army.

The Assamese, incidentally, do not move much within their

65

own state, either. The Assamese constitute a minority within most of their own urban centers, since there is little Assamese rural-to-urban migration.

Bengali

One out of every eight Bengalis in India—4.3 million—lives outside of the state of West Bengal. The largest number reside in Assam—a million in Cachar district alone, but the bulk of these residents are not of migrant descent, since Cachar district was once part of Bengal and is fundamentally an extension of the Bengali-speaking region. This is not so for those who live elsewhere in Assam. The million residents of the Brahmaputra valley districts of Assam are mainly of migrant origin; the Bengali-speaking rural dwellers are predominantly Muslims, while the Bengali urban dwellers are predominantly Hindus, both having come from districts that are now part of Bangladesh.

Another three-quarters of a million Bengalis live in the state of Tripura, a region bordering on Bangladesh with a spillover of migrants from Bangladesh, most of whom came as refugees after partition.

More than a million Bengalis (1.2 million) live in the neighboring state of Bihar, largely in the border districts of Singhbhum, Dhanbad, Santal Parganas, and Purnea, which together contain 1.06 million Bengalis.

To the south of West Bengal, the state of Orissa has 125,000 Bengalis, with more than half (70,000) residing in the four districts that border on West Bengal.

In other words, while many Bengalis reside outside of West Bengal, the vast majority are in states and districts in close proximity. Only a small number of Bengalis live in more distant states. There are only 8,000 Bengalis in all of south India, 14,000 in Bombay, and a few thousand in Gujarat and the Punjab. A substantial number of Bengalis have settled in Uttar Pradesh, about a hundred thousand, mainly in the cities of Allahabad, Nainital, Kanpur, and Lucknow.

There is also a substantial Bengali settlement in the capital city, Delhi: some 28,000.

Bengalis, then, migrate, but they tend to stay close to home in India's northeastern region, largely in the states of Orissa, Assam, and Bihar, which had been part of the presidency of what was once a Greater Bengal.

Gujarati

The Gujaratis are homebodies. Ninety-eight percent of all Gujaratis live in their own state (92.9 percent) or in neighboring Maharashtra (5.3 percent), which until the early sixties had been joined together in a single state. Fewer than 400,000 Gujaratis live elsewhere in the country, but then they are remarkably dispersed. More than half, 230,000, live in the four southern states: Tamil Nadu, Kerala, Mysore, and Andhra. Indeed, there is not a single district in south India that does not have a resident Gujarati population, reflecting the willingness of Gujarati merchants and businessmen to settle in far places wherever there are business opportunities.

Hindi

The vast bulk of Hindi migrants move from one state to another within the large Hindi-speaking belt of northern India. In percentage terms, only a small proportion, 3.5 percent, live outside the Hindi-speaking states, but given the size of India's Hindi-speaking population this constitutes a formidable number—over 4 million people. The largest number reside in two states: West Bengal with 1.9 million Hindi-speakers, largely in the Calcutta industrial region, and Maharashtra with 1.1 million, half of whom live in and around the two principal cities of Bombay and Nagpur. Outside the Hindi region, Hindi speakers constitute a substantial part of India's industrial labor force or are engaged in a great variety of urban services, from delivering milk to plying rickshaws. A half-million Hindi speakers can also be found in

67

Assam—a small proportion of India's Hindi-speaking population, but a large portion of the population of Assam. Many work in the tea plantations, some work as agricultural laborers, and a considerable number find employment in the towns.

There is hardly a large city in India that does not have Hindi-speaking laborers; in Ahmadabad district there are nearly 100,000 Hindi speakers, in Hyderabad 77,000, Bangalore 18,000, Madras 16,000.

Punjabi

The Punjabis, surrounded by the Hindi-speaking heartland, can be found in substantial numbers in all Hindi states. Nearly a quarter of the population of the Punjab (including Haryana, which was part of the Punjab during the 1961 census), live outside the state—2.5 million, of whom 2.3 million live in the Hindi-speaking states, especially in the southern part of Kashmir (Jammu), Delhi, Ganganagar district in Rajasthan, and the western districts of Uttar Pradesh. The vast majority of the Punjabis outside of their home state are cultivators, among the more enterprising and successful in northern India, but many are in transport-related activities (running buses, taxis, automotive repair shops, bicycle shops, and so on) in urban centers. Of the remaining 175,000 Punjabis outside the Hindi-speaking region, 100,000 live in Maharashtra and the remainder are widely dispersed throughout the towns of India. As with the Gujaratis, there is hardly a district in India that does not have Punjabis in its towns, usually engaged in a transport-related occupation.

Marathi

At first look it appears as if Marathis move outside their state—as many as 2.5 million, or 7.7 percent of Marathi speakers reside outside of Maharashtra—but the bulk live in districts that border on the state. More than three-quarters of a million Marathi speakers live in border districts of Mysore state, 150,000 in neighboring districts of Andhra,

68

200,000 in Gujarat, and nearly a million in border districts of Madhya Pradesh. Far from Maharashtra—in the states of Assam, Bihar, Delhi, Jammu and Kashmir, Orissa, Uttar Pradesh, and West Bengal, one hardly finds any Marathi speakers at all.

Oriya

The Oriyas have primarily migrated to factories in the Calcutta metropolitan region. Of the Oriya-speaking population, 7.5 percent, or 1.2 million, live outside of Orissa, but apart from the 170,000 migrants to the Calcutta region, the bulk reside in districts neighboring Orissa and are not migrants. Three-quarters of a million Oriyas live in Visakhapatnam and Srikakulam districts of Andhra, Bastar, Raigarh, and Raipur districts of Madhya Pradesh, and Singhbhum district in Bihar, all on the Orissa border. Outside of the Calcutta region the only other area of India with Oriya migrants is Assam, especially in the districts of Lakhimpur, Sibsager, and Darrang; 145,000 Oriyas reside in Assam, most of whom work as laborers in the tea gardens.

Rajasthani and Marwari

Considering the many languages and dialects spoken in Rajasthan that are shared with neighboring Hindi-speaking states, it is difficult to ascertain how many people of Rajasthani origin reside elsewhere in India. But the census reports that a substantial number of migrants in other states were born in Rajasthan—1.1 million persons, or 5.6 percent of the Rajasthan population, making the Rajasthanis more mobile than most other linguistic groups.

I have singled out the two largest linguistic communities of Rajasthan with speakers residing in other states: those who report Marwari or Rajasthani as their mother tongues. There are 5.8 million Marwaris in Rajasthan and 461,000 persons speaking Marwari outside of Rajasthan, or 7.4 percent of all Marwaris. A mercantile trading community, the Marwaris are scattered throughout the country. Three-quar-

69

ters of the Marwaris outside of Rajasthan live in states that do not even border on Rajasthan. The largest number, about half, are in Maharashtra, but there is hardly a district in northern and central India without Marwaris, and there is a scattering of Marwaris in the southern states as well.

The census reports that 24 percent of those who speak Rajasthani live outside of Rajasthan—3.5 million, with the largest number in neighboring Madhya Pradesh. Rajasthani landless laborers seek employment as agricultural laborers and construction workers in distant districts and states. Nearly 900,000 Rajasthanis work in the southern states of Andhra and Mysore, and another 600,000 in Maharashtra. It should be noted that even in these relatively long-distance migrations, the proportion of females to males is the same as in Rajasthan, indicating that male migrants are accompanied by their wives and/or that the women are themselves a part of the labor force. Both are true.

Telugu

We turn now to the largest of the south Indian communities, the Telugus. Nearly 18 percent of all Telugus lived outside of Andhra—6.7 million people—but almost all, 6.4 million, live in bordering states, with 3.4 million in Tamil Nadu alone. Since most of Andhra was once part of Madras presidency, Telugus freely settled throughout the region, not simply in the border districts. The districts of Tirunelveli, Madurai, and Ramanathapuram near the southern tip of Tamil Nadu, far from the Andhra borders, have three-quarters of a million Telugus. Telugu speakers are also scattered throughout Mysore, though the border districts do have the largest share of the two million Telugus living in the state.

Telugus work in the gold fields in Kolar and in plantations throughout Mysore, as agricultural workers in Tamil Nadu, and in the ports of Bombay. Along with the Rajasthanis and Hindi-speaking Biharis, they do much of the earth-moving work that is required for the construction of bridges, roads, and dams all over India.

70

The Telugus are by no means confined to south India. Many live in states in northern and central India—37,000 in Bihar, 58,000 in Madhya Pradesh, 623,000 in Maharashtra, and 80,000 in West Bengal.

Tamil

The Tamils have a reputation of being a highly mobile community, since 7 percent of Tamil speakers reside outside of Tamil Nadu and Pondicherry. But most of these 2.1 million Tamils actually live in neighboring districts: 330,000 in border districts of Andhra, 600,000 in border districts of Mysore, and 460,000 in border districts of Kerala. Of the remaining 710,000 Tamils living outside of Tamil Nadu, 460,000 live in other districts of the three southern states. The Tamils are thus in a position similar to the Bengalis; they tend to migrate within the region rather than throughout the country.

Nonetheless, the number of Tamils living in northern and central India is by no means trivial—a quarter of a million— and since a substantial proportion of these are relatively well-educated migrants holding middle-class positions, they are readily noticeable in the cities. There are 104,000 Tamils in Bombay, 22,000 in Delhi, and 15,000 in Calcutta.

Malayalam

The Malayalis, like the Tamils, are widely dispersed throughout south India. Of the Malayalam-speakers, 5.5 percent reside outside of Kerala, or 929,000, with 400,000 in Tamil Nadu, and 300,000 in Mysore. Many of these simply spill over into border districts, but quite a few are migrants or of migrant origin working in plantations or as agricultural laborers. Many also hold middle-class jobs, for a large number of Malayalis—a proportionately greater number than among the Tamils—are graduates of secondary schools and colleges.

There are many Malayalis scattered in cities throughout the country: 65,000 in Bombay, nearly 10,000 in Delhi, and

71

a small number, 5,000 in Calcutta. But in all, only 165,000 Malayalis live outside of south India, or about 1 percent of all Malayalam speakers; similarly, only 306,000 Tamils or 1 percent of all Tamil speakers reside outside of south India. A substantially larger proportion of Telugu speakers live outside the south; even if we exclude those districts of north and central India bordering on Andhra, 692,000 Telugus live in northern and central India, or 1.8 percent of all Telugus.

Kannada

Among the south Indians, the Kannadas are the least likely to leave south India. Though 1.9 million Kannada speakers live outside of Mysore—11.2 percent of the Kannada speakers—all but 156,000 live in south India or in districts of Maharashtra bordering on Mysore, or only 0.9 percent of those who speak Kannada. Moreover, the bulk of these live in neighboring Maharashtra, more than half (82,000) in Bombay city alone. In many states—Assam, Bihar, Punjab, Orissa, Rajasthan, Uttar Pradesh, Delhi, and West Bengal, Kannada speakers number only in the hundreds.

But more Kannada speakers, proportionate to their population, live in the other three states of south India (8.2 percent), than do the Tamils (5.9 percent) or the Malayalees (4.3 percent), though substantially fewer than the Telugus (14.5 percent), who are more ubiquitous outside their home state than any other south Indian community.

Indians Abroad

The overseas migrants can be divided into three major social classes: 1. educated Indians who have migrated abroad into professional occupations as doctors, academics, engineers, and so on. These Indians appear to be recruited from all over India, though the numbers are highest from those states with developed institutions of higher learning. Their largest settlements are in Britain, Canada, the United States, and Australia, and until recently in East Africa; 2. businessmen who

72

have settled in East Africa, South Africa, Sri Lanka, Burma, and Malaysia. These came predominantly from Gujarat and Tamil Nadu—the Gujaratis went westward to Africa, while the Tamils went south and eastward to Sri Lanka, Burma, Malaysia, and Singapore. Several hundred thousand expelled from Burma have resettled in Tamil Nadu; many businessmen and professionals expelled from East Africa have resettled in various Commonwealth countries, though some have returned to Gujarat; 3. unskilled workers recruited for tea, coffee, and rubber plantations in Sri Lanka, Malaysia, parts of Latin America, and South Africa, and the islands of Mauritius and Fiji. These unskilled laborers were recruited from among the tribals of Orissa and the Chota Nagpur region of Bihar, the Hindi region of Bihar and eastern Uttar Pradesh, and among the landless of Tamil Nadu. Many were recruited throughout the nineteenth and early twentieth centuries through the indenture system, which remained in operation until its abolition in 1920. Most of these emigrants settled abroad permanently, though in the past decade there has been a return migration from the tea plantations in Sri Lanka under an agreement between the two governments. Most of these migrants are resettling in Tamil Nadu, from which they originated.[10]

Though precise data on place of origin within India is not available, it would appear that the Tamils, Punjabis, Gu-

[10] The most comprehensive account of Indian emigration in the nineteenth and early twentieth centuries is Hugh Tinker, *A New System of Slavery: The Export of Indian Labour Overseas 1830-1920* (London: Oxford University Press, 1974). Chapter 3 provides some account of the place of origin of migrants within India, a list of districts from which emigrants were recruited (p. 40), data on emigration to Assam from Chota Nagpur and Santal Parganas in Bihar (p. 50)— a source for overseas emigration as well—and data on emigration from Madras to Mauritius, Natal, the Straits Settlements, Burma, and Ceylon at the end of the century (p. 57). The Institute of Race Relations in London, which published Tinker's excellent book, has also published a number of useful studies on Indian emigration to Trinidad, Jamaica, Malaysia, Singapore, and Burma, collectively providing a picture of the substantial Indian diaspora.

73

jaratis, Oriya and Bihari tribals, and Bihari and U.P. Hindus, have constituted a very substantial proportion of India's overseas migrants—the Gujaratis as traders and businessmen; the Punjabis in trade, transport and, in recent years, the professions; the Tamils in the trades, professions, and plantations; and the tribals and Bihari and U.P. Hindus as unskilled laborers in plantations and construction.

The former British colonies are no longer magnets for Indian migrants; nationalist sentiments in several of these countries have forced families of Indian descent, some of whom have lived in these areas for many generations, to return to India or settle in Britain. The industrial countries are the new magnets for Indian migrants, but while the educational level of these new "brain drain" migrants is high, their number remains small. Most recently there has also been a growth in short-term migration of Indians to the countries along the Persian Gulf.

THREE

WHEN MIGRANTS SUCCEED
AND NATIVES FAIL:
ASSAM AND ITS MIGRANTS

THE PROBLEM[1]

CLASHES between migrants and the indigenous population have been a prominent feature of postindependence politics within multiethnic developing countries. In Nigeria violent attacks against Ibo settlers in the north precipitated the events that subsequently led to the civil war. In Malaysia, where many Chinese have lived as long as the Malays, Malay antagonisms toward the Chinese have been defined in terms of a conflict between indigenous residents (known locally as the "Bhumiputra," or sons of the soil) and the Chinese migrants. African countries have readily violated the spirit of Pan-Africanism by expelling migrant residents from neighboring African states. In Sri Lanka, Burma, Kenya, and Uganda, Indian and Pakistani residents, often of long standing, have been forcefully ejected. Violent clashes between

[1] For the statistical data provided in this chapter I am grateful to the Director of Census Operations in Assam, Mr. A. K. Saikia. I should also like to take this opportunity to express my appreciation to Mr. B. K. Nehru, Governor of Assam, Professor Naren Bhagavati of the Department of Anthropology of the University of Gauhati, Mr. Pulin Behari Bharthakur, chief information officer of the Governor of Assam, and Mr. D. C. Bhuyan, former director of the Publicity Department. Both for statistical documentation and interviews I am also grateful to the officials of the Ministry of Education, the Labour Commission, the Director of Industries, the Employment Exchange, the Department of Public Instruction, the Ministry of Refugees and Rehabilitation, the Directorate of the Department of Economics and Statistics, and to two newspapers and their staffs, the *Assam Tribune* and *Amrita Bazar Patrika*.

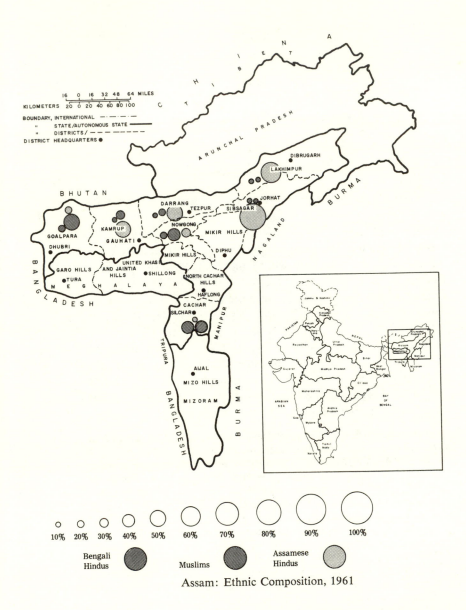

Assam: Ethnic Composition, 1961

76

native Bengalis and migrant Biharis have occurred in Bangladesh. In Cambodia hostilities have been directed against the Vietnamese. Within India tensions have erupted between migrants and the local population in the states of Assam, Maharashtra, Bihar, and Andhra.

The earlier hope that migration would be "an instrument of cultural diffusion and social integration," to use Donald Bogue's optimistic phrase,[2] has hardly been borne out by the events and conflicts of the past decade in the developing areas. Nor can the tensions be attributed to recent migratory flows, since most of these movements are of long duration— the consequences of various systems of international contract labor established by the imperial European powers, new opportunities to move from one cultural region to another as a result of the creation of multinational empires, and long-standing differentials of both regional development and the skills and motivations of various ethnic groups.

The focus of this and the following two chapters is on one dimension of ethnic conflict and migration in India: the problems that arise when migrants of one or more ethnic communities are economically successful, in apparent contrast to the lack of success among the native population of another ethnic group. The focus, therefore, is on those situations in which first, the migrant is able to achieve higher income and occupational levels than the natives, and second, the native population perceives those differences with resentment.

While ordinarily migrants earn lower incomes than do the native inhabitants of the area to which they move, there are some situations in which the income of migrants is higher. First, the new jobs created in a region may be attractive to both local people and to migrants, but the migrants may have superior skills or patterns of work behavior that make them more desirable to employers. Regional development in

---

[2] Donald J. Bogue, "Internal Migration" in Philip Hauser and Otis Duncan, *The Study of Population: An Inventory and Appraisal* (Chicago: University of Chicago Press, 1969), p. 487.

an area with low-skilled manpower will therefore attract skilled individuals from outside. Second, outside entrepreneurs may see opportunities for investment that local people do not perceive or do not have the skills or capital to exploit. Indeed, the local community may not have entrepreneurs capable of responding to new economic opportunities. Third, new employment opportunities may not be initially as attractive to local people as to migrants. The wage differentials, for example, may be greater for the migrants than for local agriculturalists. In a few years, however, the jobs held by migrants may be paying higher salaries than those earned by local people, either as a result of a rise in industrial wages or of a decline in agricultural income.

Finally, we should note that at the time migrations began, whatever the differences were between the wages received by migrants and the local population, or the respective skills and motivations of the two groups, once a chain migration is established the flows may persist even when the circumstances have substantially changed. Thus, although local people may be willing or able to compete for jobs that at an earlier time they did not seek, these jobs are no longer easily accessible to them, for migrant employers and job holders are likely to help provide employment to their own friends and relatives.

How are these patterns established? Why do population flows across ethnic lines continue in spite of clashes among ethnic groups? And most importantly, why are clashes occurring now, often several generations after the process of migration began?

We shall first discuss these questions with respect to the state of Assam, in northeastern India, an area where the conditions described above exist. Migrant communities belonging to "alien" ethnic groups earn higher wages and have the preferred jobs—a situation that has engendered intense hostility on the part of the native population toward migrants and their descendants.

The State of Assam

Assam has been the fastest growing area in the subcontinent for the past seventy years. Its population has grown more than fourfold: from 3.3 million in 1901 to nearly 15 million in 1971, as compared with an increase of 130 percent for India as a whole. Approximately 11.4 percent[3] of the state's population comes from outside the state,[4] but in both the 1920s and 1930s the migrant population exceeded 20 percent.

The major indigenous language of Assam is Assamese, an Indo-Aryan language closely related to, but different from, Bengali. The state also has a substantial indigenous tribal population. Part of that population has recently been granted a state of its own, carved out of the southern hill portions of Assam. As a result of the long-term migratory flows into Assam, it is now linguistically and ethnically the most diversified state in India. Only 57 percent of the state's population speaks Assamese; another 16 percent speaks one of the local tribal languages. Bengali, the language of Bangladesh and the neighboring Indian state of West Bengal, is the mother tongue of 17.4 percent of the population. Hindi, the language of migrants from Bihar, Uttar Pradesh, and Rajasthan, is spoken by 4.3 percent of the population. In all, 27 percent of the population (2.9 million persons) in 1961 spoke the languages of other states or neighboring countries, mainly Bengali and Hindi, but also Nepali, Santali, Oraon, and Munda (tribal languages spoken in the states of Bihar and

[3] Here, as elsewhere in this chapter unless otherwise noted, figures are from the 1961 census. Population totals are available from the 1971 census, but migration and language data have not yet been published.

[4] Exceeded only by West Bengal, with 15.7 percent migrants, and Punjab, with 14.2 percent migrants, but in both instances a large proportion of the migrants come from linguistically similar areas of neighboring East Bengal (now Bangladesh) and West Punjab (now Pakistan). Assam thus has the highest proportion of migrants from dissimilar linguistic regions of any state in India.

79

Orissa). There is reason to believe that the 27 percent figure is low and the figure for Assamese speakers high, since Bengali Muslims report Assamese to the census enumerators as their mother tongue for reasons we shall soon explain. Moreover, many descendants of tea plantation laborers who came to Assam decades ago are now Assamese-speaking, or at least report themselves as Assamese to the census enumerators. The controversies between migrants and the native population have been so intense that census figures with respect to both language and migration must be viewed as only crude approximations that really underestimate the numbers of migrants and of non-Assamese speakers.

For more than a century Assam has been India's frontier area, not simply in the literal sense as a border state touching Burma, Tibet, Bhutan, and Bangladesh, but also as a new land attracting millions of settlers from other regions of the subcontinent. This was not an empty land, for it contained the Assamese, an Indo-Aryan agricultural people living in the plains of the Brahmaputra valley, and a variety of tribal peoples in the surrounding hills, all of whom had lived for six centuries under the rule of the independent Ahom kings, a people of Shan origin who had become culturally absorbed as Hindus by those whom they had conquered. Under the Ahoms, Assam had a heterogeneous social order whose central principle of social organization was one of maintaining stability through a social hierarchy that had at the top the Ahom aristocracy and monarchy.

Ahom rule was brought to an end, after a short-lived Burmese conquest, by British conquest in the 1820s. For the first time in six centuries Assam was politically a part of India. Into this low-density region came millions of settlers from Rajasthan, Bihar, Punjab, Nepal, and, most of all, from Bengal, occupying land, moving into tea plantations, entering the bureaucracy, starting new businesses and trade, taking up the modern professions of teaching, law, medicine, and journalism. Since the turn of the twentieth century, nearly six and a half million migrants and their descendants have settled in

Assam. The population in 1971 was slightly under 15 million.[5]

The presence of these migrants has shaken the foundations of Assamese social structure and created solidarity among the Assamese even while generating cleavages between the indigenous Assamese and the indigenous tribals. It has influenced the educational, social, and economic aspirations of countless Assamese, determined their central political concerns, and become a decisive factor in the periodic restructuring of the state's boundaries. Migration to Assam has also given rise to powerful assimilationist and nativist sentiments and backlash separatist agitations, to massive conflicts over language, education, and employment policy, and to political cleavages that have not only led to the intervention of India's central government and the use of the Indian army, but have also affected Assam's relationship to neighboring Bangladesh, formerly East Bengal, and hence India's relationship to Pakistan. In short, migration has been a force for social, cultural, economic, and political change in Assam. The process by which these changes have been brought about is examined in this chapter.

Assam is by no means a "typical" area for studying the relationship between local populations and migrants from which one can generalize to other regions of India. On the contrary, it is an extreme case, since it has had and, even now,[6] continues to have the highest in-migration rate of any

[5] The population of Assam (present boundaries) in 1901 was 3.3 million. Had Assam's population increased at the same rate as the rest of India from 1901 to 1971 (130 percent) her population would now be 7.6 million rather than 15 million, a difference of 7.4 million. Actually, the proportion of migrants and descendants is substantially greater since large-scale migrations into the state commenced in the middle of the nineteenth century. If we accept the 1891 census estimate that one-fourth of the population of the Brahmaputra valley was then of migrant origin, we can estimate that the migrant population (and its descendants) in 1971 was more like 8.5 million, as against an "indigenous" population of 6.5 million.

[6] Between 1961 and 1971 the population of Assam increased by

state in India. But as such, it provides us with an opportunity to see the problems that arise from interstate migration in a low-income region with greater clarity than elsewhere; for here varied ethnic groups and the state and central governments have had to face issues that few other areas in India have encountered in such acute form. Moreover, precisely because it is the state that has had the highest rate of in-migration, an examination of Assam's experiences may lead us to understand what problems and policy choices may arise elsewhere in India, if and when in-migration grows.

Finally, the Assam case itself is intrinsically interesting and an important one for India because of the strategic importance of a state that borders on several countries. Assam has, in recent years, felt the brunt of an invading Chinese army; experienced the influx of refugees from Bangladesh; and, a generation ago, was a staging area for British and American troops flying the hump to Chungking and fighting Japanese forces on the Burmese border.

THE POLITICAL GEOGRAPHY OF MIGRANT SETTLEMENTS

Contemporary Assam is only a small portion of what was termed "Assam" only a few decades ago. Today, Assam

---

34.7 percent, as against 24.6 percent for India as a whole. Assam's growth rate was exceeded only by the union territories of Delhi, Chandigarh, and the Andaman and Nicobar Islands, and by several small states surrounding Assam that had until recently been union territories, Manipur and Nagaland. The percentage variation of population of India and Assam has been as follows:

	Assam	India
1901-1911	16.8	5.7
1911-1921	20.2	-0.3
1921-1931	20.1	11.0
1931-1941	20.5	14.2
1941-1951	20.1	13.3
1951-1961	35.0	21.6
1961-1971	34.7	24.6

consists of nine districts containing 30,408 square miles. Most of the population lives in two valleys: the Brahmaputra valley, predominantly Assamese-speaking, with about 12.5 million people, and the Surma valley, predominantly Bengali-speaking, with 1.7 million persons. Between the two valleys are the Khasi and Garo hills, once part of Assam, but now in the newly created state of Meghalaya. To the north is Tibet and a sparsely inhabited mountain region known formerly as NEFA (North East Frontier Agency) and now as Arunachal Pradesh. In the northwest, Assam touches the independent kingdom of Bhutan, and to the southwest is Bangladesh. A small tip of western Assam touches a narrow corridor of West Bengal that constitutes Assam's only physical link with the rest of India. Eastward lies Burma, the state of Nagaland (previously a part of Assam), and the state of Manipur. To the south lies the Union territory of Mizoram (until recently a district of Assam) and the predominantly Bengali state of Tripura.

The Brahmaputra valley contains, in addition to the Assamese-speaking inhabitants, a large migrant tea plantation population that came largely from the state of Bihar, and a substantial migrant population from what is now Bangladesh. The Surma valley consists of the single district of Cachar with a Bengali-speaking population.

The Assamese often think of themselves as a "forgotten" and "neglected" state within the Indian union, and as a neglected people in danger of being overwhelmed by migrant peoples and absorbed by neighboring states. This sense of being apart has long historic roots, beginning with the six hundred years they lived under the rule of the Ahoms. The Ahoms entered Assam from Burma in the thirteenth century, and gave the province its present name of Assam, or as it was called earlier, Aham or Asam. During this period, the Ahoms were absorbed by the Assamese-speaking Hindus who lived in the Brahmaputra valley. The Ahoms spread their control from the valley to the surrounding hill areas, and soon asserted their domination over the various hill peoples such as the Nagas, the Mikirs, the Kacharis, Khasis, and Jaintias.

Though Mughal power spread across northern India, following the path of the Ganges and Brahmaputra rivers into Bengal, the Ahoms successfully resisted incorporation into the Mughal empire. To this day the Assamese speak with great pride of their resistance to "Muslim aggression," and to the successful spread of Hindu Vaishnavaism throughout Assam's Brahmaputra valley in the sixteenth century, under the influence of the great Hindu sage Sankaradeva, at a time when Muslim influence elsewhere was at its zenith.

In India's middle ages, therefore, Assam held a distinctive place. It was not part of the Mughal empire. It had a substantial Tibeto-Burman speaking population linking it to regions both to the north and east. And its cultural links with the rest of India remained tenuous, even with the growth of Vaishnavism and the spread of Aryan speech of the Assamese to the governing Ahoms.[7]

British rule came late to Assam. The British did not move into Assam until 1826, when they dislodged the Burmese invaders who had conquered the province in 1819. They extended their control over the northeast region slowly, and did not incorporate some of the hill areas of Assam until the 1870s. But even under British rule, Assam remained a peripheral region. After the British occupied Assam they incorporated the area into the province of Bengal. It was not until 1874 that Assam was separated from Bengal and was administered by a chief commissioner, and not until the last decade of the nineteenth century was the area given the status of a self-contained state responsible directly to the viceroy.

At the turn of the century, in 1905, a new reorganization

[7] For an account of Assam's connections with the rest of India from the thirteenth to nineteenth centuries, see Suniti Kumar Chatterji, *The Place of Assam in the History and Civilisation of India* (Gauhati: University of Gauhati, 1955). The standard history is E. A. Gait, *History of Assam* (rev. ed.; Calcutta: Thacker and Spink, 1963).

took place that was to have a lasting influence on the attitude of Assamese toward migrants from the neighboring areas of East Bengal. At that time the British partitioned the sprawling, densely populated province of Bengal into a predominantly Bengali Muslim province in the east, which incorporated Assam, and a predominantly Bengali Hindu province in the west. There followed bitter hostility from the Bengali Hindus, who resented the partition of their province, and from the Assamese, who resented incorporation into a portion of Bengal. In 1912 the British annulled partition, reunited East and West Bengal, and reestablished Assam as a separate chief commissioner's province that now included the predominantly Bengali Muslim district of Sylhet and the predominantly Bengali Hindu district of Cachar. These new boundaries were to remain intact until the partition of India, and of Assam, in 1947. Prepartition Assam thus consisted of the two valleys, the Garo, Khasi, and Jaintia hills, the Naga hills, Mizo hills, and Sylhet district.

With the inclusion of Sylhet district, Assam was demographically and politically balanced precariously between the Assamese Hindus and the Bengali Muslims. The 1937 elections produced a minority Muslim League government under Mohammad Saadulla which, except for a one-year interlude of Congress rule, governed the state until the close of World War II. The Saadulla ministry had aroused fears among Assamese that the entire province might be incorporated into the Muslim state of Pakistan, a fear made more credible by the increasing influx of Bengali Muslim migrants into the state in the late thirties and early forties.

In the elections of early 1946, the Congress party won an absolute majority in the state Legislative Assembly. A British Cabinet Mission proposal to create a predominantly Muslim zone in eastern India that would include Assam was rejected by the Congress party ministry. When the British put into effect the partition scheme creating the Muslim-majority state of Pakistan with its eastern and western provinces, Assam

85

remained with India, but the Muslim majority district of Sylhet was transferred to East Pakistan, following a referendum in the district.

Even without Sylhet, Assam after 1947 remained one of the most diverse cultural regions in the subcontinent. It included three groups of native peoples: the Assamese-speaking Hindu population residing primarily in the Brahmaputra valley; the hill tribes—the Garo, Khasi, Naga, Mikir, and Mizo—speaking diverse languages and of Mongoloid stock, racially and culturally akin to the tribal peoples of Southeast Asia; and the indigenous plains tribals believed to predate the Assamese Indo-Aryans, known as the Bodo or Kachari.

The migrant communities included: tribal laborers from the Chota Nagpur region of Bihar and Orissa, mainly belonging to the Santal, Oraon, and Munda tribes, who were employed in the British-owned tea gardens; Bengali Muslims, mainly from the East Bengal district of Mymensingh (hence, their name, the Mymensinghias), who settled on land along the Brahmaputra valley and, to a lesser extent, in the Surma valley; Bengali Hindus, originating in East Bengal and especially from Sylhet district, who settled in Cachar district and throughout the towns of the Brahmaputra valley, where they held middle-class jobs; Marwaris, an entrepreneurial community from Rajasthan, engaged in trade, commerce, and moneylending, and, more recently, in a few industries and many tea plantations purchased from the British; a scattering of other migrant communities, such as Nepalis, who have settled in the low-lying hills around the Brahmaputra valley, tending cattle; Bihari males, who work as seasonal migrants in construction projects and in the towns; and a small but economically significant number of Punjabis working in the transport industry, and more recently in their own businesses.

This mosaic was partially taken apart by the Indian government after 1961. The rebellious Naga tribes were given their own state, Nagaland, in 1963. The Garo, Khasi, and Jaintia tribes were given autonomous status as Meghalaya, which was subsequently (in 1972) made into a separate state. The Mizo district was separated from Assam in 1971 and constituted as the union territory of Mizoram. The North East Frontier Agency (NEFA) was converted into a union territory and, in 1972, declared the state of Arunachal Pradesh. The two remaining hill districts, the Mikir hills and North Cachar district, decided to remain in Assam rather than join Meghalaya; the Bengali Cachar district also remained in Assam, though there were serious proposals to merge Cachar with the predominantly Bengali state of Tripura.

While the creation of separate tribal states has reduced some of the cultural heterogeneity of Assam, it has also brought the tensions between the indigenous Assamese and the migrant communities into sharper relief. Both are now proportionately larger. In the Brahmaputra valley, 73 percent of the population is reported by the census as Assamese speakers, but this figure includes the large Muslim population of Bengali origin.[8] Another 9.8 percent of the population is Bengali, and 9.4 percent speak other migrant languages (Hindi, Nepali, Oriya, Santali, Oraon, and Munda). Finally, 10.2 percent belong to scheduled tribes, though only 7.3 percent report they speak tribal languages; a large number of plains tribals (Bodo or Plain Kachari) report Assamese as their mother tongue.

What, then, has been, and continues to be, the response of the indigenous Assamese to the migrant populations? We shall focus on four migrant communities—the tea plantation

---

[8] Twenty-six percent of Assam's population is Muslim, making it second only to Kashmir as India's major Muslim state. The Muslims of the Brahmaputra valley (2.2 million) report their mother tongue as Assamese, though most are Bengalis, while the half million Muslims of Cachar district report Bengali as their mother tongue. If we reallocate the Muslims of the Brahmaputra valley, the Assamese speakers are reduced to 49.3 percent and the Bengali speakers increased to 33.8 percent, figures likely to attract a violent (literally!) reaction from some Assamese.

87

migrants, the Bengali Hindus, the Bengali Muslims, and, finally, the small but economically influential Marwari community.

Tea Plantation Migrants: The Incorporation of Assam into the World Tea Market

Failure, like success, can have many causes. A man may succeed because of his skill, his appearance, his drive, his luck, and the opportunities available to him. In a stable hierarchical social order it is ordained that boys will do more or less what their fathers and uncles did. Until the middle of the nineteenth century, the Assamese social order was stable. There were higher castes and lower castes, and men with power and wealth, and men without, but there were few, if any, who moved from one category to another. Few men sought to change their social status by seeking new occupations, for apart from living in a tradition that discouraged upward mobility, there were few opportunities to move up.

The British created new opportunities. The steamy verdant hills, hitherto ignored by Assamese peasants, were converted by the British into rich tea plantations, whose products were soon to reach out to markets across the seas. In 1821 tea was discovered by an Englishman, and in the 1830s the governor general, Lord William Bentinck, took steps to create a tea industry in Assam. Within a few decades tea became a booming business, with gardens in Lakhimpur, Darrang, Kamrup, and Cachar districts.

In the beginning, the one major obstacle to creating a tea industry in Assam was the lack of an adequate local labor supply. Diseases, civil conflict, and the Burmese invasions had depopulated much of the province. For the local Assamese cultivators there was little incentive to work as low-income wage laborers in unhealthy jungle terrain; they were comparatively prosperous, for there was much land.

The British first thought of solving their labor problem by importing Chinese coolies from Singapore; it was assumed by the British that the Chinese, whatever their background, knew how to cultivate and prepare tea. Several hundred Chinese coolies were brought from Singapore to the port at Calcutta, then sent upland to Assam. En route the Chinese apparently engaged in a brawl with some Indians. Sixty were arrested and jailed by a local magistrate and the remainder refused to go on alone to Assam until their compatriots were released. The entire group, their contracts cancelled, were returned to Calcutta where, in their anger, they proceeded to be a nuisance to the local police. The Assam Tea Company, reporting to the London office, noted that "these men turned out to be of a very bad character; they were turbulent, obstinate and rapacious. Indeed they committed excess which on occasions endangered the lives of the people among whom we had sent them and it was found almost impossible to govern them. So injurious did they seem likely to prove that their contracts were cancelled and the whole gang with the exception of the most expert tea makers dismissed."[9] Thus ended the project to colonize the tea plantations with overseas Chinese!

Finding an alternative labor supply proved not to be an easy task. Laborers were imported from other parts of India, first from the Chittagong region of East Bengal, then later from the hill areas of southern Bihar, but the mortality rate was apparently appallingly high. Cholera was rampant, and few escaped the fever. One historian, describing the attitudes of the young English officers shortly after they arrived in the unhealthy jungle, wrote, "we could hardly expect anything but despair, irritability, illness and often a speedy death."[10]

A system of contract labor was established. The British employers recruited indigent tribesmen from the hill areas of southern Bihar, a region known as Chota Nagpur, paid

---

[9] Quoted by Harold H. Mann, "The Early History of the Tea Industry in North-East India," *The Assam Review* (September 1934), p. 10.

[10] *Ibid.*, p. 12.

their transportation and provided them with housing and medical care in return for a contract that indentured the laborers to their employers. By the turn of the century there were 764 tea gardens in Assam, employing 400,000 persons, and producing 145 million pounds of tea per year. The number of migrants to the plantations soared even higher between 1911 and 1921, when the tea industry imported 769,000 laborers. Another 422,000 came during the following decade.

Migration rose again during the Second World War, when Assam tea garden laborers were employed by the American and British armies to build roads and aerodromes to defend Assam against a possible Japanese invasion from Burma.[11]

A considerable amount of assimilation has taken place. The children of migrants attend schools conducted in Assamese. Many of the tribals now observe Assamese Hindu rituals, especially the Bihu festivals that are so central to Assamese cultural life.[12] According to the 1961 census, only 204,000 persons reported that they speak a tribal language of Bihar and Orissa (Santali, Oraon, Munda, or Sadan/ Sadri) as their mother tongue, though clearly the number of persons who are tribal migrants is considerably larger. The 1921 census estimated that migrants to tea gardens and their descendants numbered a million and a third, one-sixth of the total population of the province.[13]

A substantial number of the tea garden laborers have now become ex-tea garden laborers. Some have settled as cultivators, either as landholders or tenants in land provided by

[11] The large number of airports now scattered throughout the Brahmaputra valley is a legacy of this early construction boom.

[12] For a contemporary account of the economic and social conditions of the tea plantation workers see "Social and Economic Processes in Tea Plantations with Special Reference to Tribal Labourers," *Census of India 1961*, Vol. I, Part VII-A (New Delhi, 1970). See especially Part II, an account of the Dejoo Tea estate in Lakhimpur District (pp. 32-71). For a historical account of the development of the tea industry in Assam, see E. A. Gait, *History of Assam*, chapter 23, pp. 404-414.

[13] Gait, *History of Assam*, p. 414.

the government. Others have found employment in construction industries. Of the 38,000 construction workers in Assam, 21,000 are migrants. Almost all the remaining construction workers in Assam are Khasi tribesmen, a non-Assamese speaking ethnic group from the Khasi and Garo hill districts that are now part of the state of Meghalaya. Technically, therefore, even the Khasis working in Assam as construction laborers are migrants.

The tea plantation migrants have never been nor are they now economic, cultural, or political threats to the Assamese. The jobs they hold are not those sought by the Assamese. Their tendency to assimilate linguistically makes them model migrants to the Assamese. And though there are trade unions among the tea plantation laborers, they play no significant role in the politics of the state. Nor are the tribal migrants in day-to-day social contact with the Assamese, for those who live on or near the tea plantations are physically removed from contact with the local population. A number of laws and rules—the Plantations Labour Act of 1951, and the Assam Plantation Labour Rules of 1956—require plantation owners to provide housing accommodations, dispensaries and hospitals, crèches for the children of women workers, and schools for children who work on the plantations. Canteens for meals and recreational facilities must also be provided by employers. The effect of these provisions is to limit routine contacts between tea garden workers and the Assamese.

Bengali Hindu Migrants:
The Incorporation of Assam into
the Imperial Bureaucratic Structure

Early in their administration, the British sought to make use of high-ranking officials from the Ahom government, especially in revenue administration and the judiciary. But these officials did not fit into the Anglo-Mughal administrative structure created by the British in Assam. They had never kept written records; even judicial proceedings were

91

conducted without recording the statements of witnesses, complainants, or defendants. Moreover, the new administrative offices and titles created by the British, such as *tahsildar* or district revenue collector, were not based on indigenous Ahom administrative structures, but were adapted from British governance in Bengal. It was no wonder, therefore, that the British increasingly imported trained Bengali officers to work in Assam. David Scott, the agent of the East India Company in Assam, expressed his concern that Ahom and Assamese functionaries were rapidly losing their position of wealth and power as more and more Bengalis came in, but he "was equally aware of the extreme difficulty of finding local officials competent to serve the company."[14] Scott proposed that a system of indirect rule be established that would provide positions for the nobility and the low-ranking officials of Assam; but the East India Company doubted the capacity of a native government to maintain order among the various tribes on the frontier, and had no intention of permitting a weak and possibly hostile state to stand between itself and this frontier. Once the government rejected Scott's proposal, the British officer in upper Assam, Captain J. B. Neufville, proceeded to remove from his administration the many Assamese nobles that Scott had employed.

The indolence and incapacity of the nobility, the impossibility of making them account for the revenues they collected without the use of duress, led Neufville to introduce *tahsildars*, who were all native of Bengal. Neufville also removed from office not less than a hundred *kheldars* who were in charge of revenue collection, and in their place employed various foreigners or Assamese clerks of inferior rank who, he thought, would be real "men of business." Neufville declared that he could find no nobleman in the country capable of conducting the business of a

[14] Nirode K. Barooah, *David Scott in North-East India: A Study in British Paternalism* (Delhi: Munshiram Manoharlal, 1970), p. 137.

tahsildar entrusted with the task of collecting and regularly accounting for even 30,000 rupees.[15]

And so the Bengalis came. First they moved into administrative positions. Then, since the Bengali Hindus were among the first social group in India to study at the British-created missionary and government colleges, they entered the modern professions. By the beginning of the twentieth century the doctors, lawyers, teachers, journalists, clerks, railway and post office officials, as well as officers of the state government were Bengali Hindu migrants.

Since the Bengali and Assamese languages and the scripts are similar, the Bengalis were able to persuade the British government that Assamese was only a corrupt and vulgar dialect of Bengali, "a patois bearing to it the same relation which Yorkshire bears to the literary English, and that it ought in no way to be encouraged, but to be crushed out as quickly as possible, by using Bengali as the official tongue and teaching it in schools."[16] For more than a half century of British rule this viewpoint was dominant. It was not until 1871 that the Assamese, with the support of American missionaries settled at Sibsagar, persuaded the government to recognize Assamese as a separate language and to use it as the medium of instruction in schools throughout the Brahmaputra valley.[17] By the 1880s it was used in the primary schools, but the middle schools were still conducted in Bengali. Teaching materials for that level were not yet available.[18] So long as Bengali was a medium of instruction, Ben-

[15] *Ibid.*, p. 149.

[16] E. A. Gait, in *Census of India, Assam, 1891*, Vol. I, *Report* (Shillong, 1892), p. 157, describes not his own views but those of other government officials.

[17] Bengali was made the language of the courts and schools in Assam as early as 1837. After an extensive period of controversy in the late 1860s, Assamese was officially restored in 1871 by an order of the lieutenant governor of Bengal, Sir George Campbell.

[18] Gait, *Census of India*, p. 157.

gali young men flocked into the expanding educational system to teach, and continued to move into the expanding administrative system. Soon, the Assamese perceived themselves as having two sets of alien rulers.

Educated Assamese in the late nineteenth century were resentful not only of Bengali domination in the administrative services, but of the efforts of Bengalis to treat them as culturally inferior provincial cousins. It is true that leading Bengali intellectuals "discovered" Assamese classical literature, Boranjis or chronicles, Assamese translations of Sanskrit poems, and many other indigenous Assamese literary works, but the legacy of this early effort at "Bengalization" of the Assamese remained.

The rise of an Assamese middle class in the twentieth century into positions that were previously the monopoly of the Bengalis did not stop the Bengali Hindu influx. Migration continued even after the separation of Assam from Bengal. At the same time, Bengali Hindus from Sylhet and Cachar districts in Assam freely took jobs in the Brahmaputra valley.

In 1961 nearly a million of the seven million people living in the Brahmaputra districts were Bengalis. Fifty-seven percent, or 43,000 out of 75,000 persons employed in transport, storage, and communications (census categories that include railways, post, and telegraphs), were migrants, and one-third of all persons listed by the census as having other "service" occupations (139,000 out of 424,000) were migrants. Neither of these sets of numbers includes the descendants of Bengali Hindu migrants, nor does either reveal the extent to which the high-paying positions were held by Bengali Hindus.

The persistently dominant position of Bengalis in middle-class occupations in Assam is further indicated by their concentration in urban areas, especially in the Brahmaputra valley towns. Of 913,000 urban dwellers in Assam, 350,000 are Bengali, whereas only 304,000 are Assamese. Assamese speakers constitute 33.4 percent of the urban population. Some 37.9 percent are Bengali speakers, and 13 percent Hindi speakers. In some towns in Goalpara, Darrang, and

Nowgong districts, Bengalis constitute over 40 percent of the population. Another way of looking at it is that only 5 percent of the Assamese in the Brahmaputra valley live in urban areas, as compared with 40 percent of the Bengalis. The Assamese still remain a predominantly rural people living off the land.

Bengali Muslim Migrants:
The Incorporation of Assam into
Bengal's Demographic and Agrarian Network

Throughout the nineteenth century Assam was regarded as an area with large virgin tracts, not only with forest lands to be cleared, but also with rich arable land along the Brahmaputra river. Considering how densely populated the nearby province of Bengal was, it is somewhat surprising that Assam remained an area of low density. One likely explanation is that Assam had a high mortality rate and a reputation for unhealthiness.

John Butler, an officer of the Assam Light Infantry for the East India Company in the middle of the nineteenth century, has given us an account of Assam in which he says that in portions of Goalpara district "the mortality both of Europeans and natives, equals, if it does not exceed, that of any district in Assam. . . . Unless endowed with great stamina, life is here frequently extinguished by jungle fever in the course of a few days."[19] Apart from disease, he said, "there is a painful sense of insecurity from the streams and rivers in many parts of Assam swarming with crocodiles. Natives, when bathing, are not infrequently seized by crocodiles, and I have heard that one of these amphibious monsters has been known to seize a paddler unsuspiciously sleeping in the front part of the board."[20] "Moreover," his account of the hazards of living in Assam continued, "an apothecary, who had long been attached to the Assam Light Infantry assured

[19] John Butler, *A Sketch of Assam: With Some Account of the Hill Tribes, by an Officer* (London: Smith, Elder, 1847), p. 3.
[20] *Ibid.*, p. 8.

95

me that pythons or boa-constrictors were very numerous in our vicinity, and of an immense size, some not being less than fifteen or eighteen feet in length."[21]

Malarial fevers and the plague continued to take a heavy toll of life in Assam well up to the end of the nineteenth century. A district officer in Nowgong district[22] reported that in his district the indigenous population decreased by 30 percent from 1891 to 1901. "Not a single British district in the whole of the Indian Empire lost so large a proportion of its population as the unfortunate district of Nowgong," he concluded.

With the gradual improvement of public health, Bengali Muslim cultivators began to move into the districts of Sylhet and Goalpara from the East Bengal districts of Mymensingh and Rangpur. But by the end of the century the migrations were still modest: the 1891 census reported that there were only 45,000 East Bengal migrants from those two districts in Assam out of the 510,000 migrants in the state, 83 percent of whom worked in the tea gardens.

The major influx of Bengali Muslims appears to have begun after 1900. While the growth rate of Goalpara district had only been 1.4 percent in the entire decade from 1881 to 1891, and only 2 percent from 1891 to 1900, it jumped to 30 percent between 1901 and 1911. By 1911 there were 118,000 migrants in the district of Goalpara alone. They constituted nearly 20 percent of the population. The 1911 census commissioner wrote, in a statement that has been quoted frequently by Assamese, that the migration was "likely to alter permanently the whole future of Assam and to

[21] *Ibid.*, p. 13.

[22] B. C. Allen, *Nowgong Assam District Gazetteer* (Calcutta, 1905), pp. 66-67. See also the *Imperial Gazetteer of Indian, Provincial Series: Eastern Bengal and Assam* (Calcutta, 1909), pp. 45-46, for estimates of population decreases in Nowgong, Kamrup, and portions of Darrang districts in the 1880s and 1890s, largely as a result of endemic malaria.

destroy more surely than did the Burmese invaders of 1820 the whole structure of Assamese culture and civilization."[23]

The following decade the census reported that the East Bengali settlers had moved up the Brahmaputra valley and formed 14 percent of the population of Nowgong district, and were rapidly taking up waste lands in Kamrup. "Almost every train and steamer," he wrote, "brings parties of the settlers and it seems likely that their march will extend further up the valley and away from the river before long."[24]

The 1931 census described the influx in military terms: "The second army corps which followed in the years 1921-31 has consolidated their position in that district and has also completed the conquest of Nowgong. The Barpeta subdivision of Kamrup has also fallen to their attack and Darrang is being invaded. Sibsagar has so far escaped completely but the few thousand Mymensinghias in North Lakhimpur is an outpost which may, during the next decade, prove to be a valuable basis of major operations.[25] The report went on,

Where there is waste land thither flock the Mymensinghias. In fact the way in which they have seized upon the vacant areas in the Assam Valley seems almost uncanny. Without fuss, without tumult, without undue trouble to the district revenue staffs, a population which must amount to over half a million has transplanted itself from Bengal to the Assam Valley during the last twenty-five years. It looks like a marvel of administrative organization on the part of Government, but it is nothing of the sort: the only thing I can compare it to is the mass movement of a large body of ants.[26]

The movements of Muslims into Assam continued through the 1930s and 1940s (abetted, many Assamese claim, by the

[23] Cited by R. B. Vaghaiwalla, *Census of India, 1951, Assam, Manipur and Tripura*, Vol. XII, Part I-A, *Report* (Shillong, 1954), p. 72.
[24] *Ibid.*, p. 72.   [25] *Ibid.*, p. 73.   [26] *Ibid.*

Muslim League government), reportedly rising during the Bengal famine of 1942. The migrations continued even after East Bengal (including Mymensingh) became part of Pakistan and an international border was interposed between Assam and East Bengal. In 1951 the census commissioner, Mr. Vaghaiwalla, wrote that though postindependence migration figures were not available, "I have personally seen hundreds of persons coming by trains during the first months I held the charge of Goalpara District. I had the same experience as the Deputy Commissioner in Cachar during 1948-1949 when hundreds of Muslim immigrants regularly traveled by the hill section railway from Badarpur to Lunding, in order to go to the Assam Valley for settlement."[27] In 1961 the Muslims of Goalpara constituted 43.3 percent of the population, 41.2 percent in Nowgong, 39.2 percent in Cachar, and 29.3 percent in Kamrup.

The impact of these Muslim migrants on land use in Assam has been considerable. Between 1930 and 1950, some 1,508,000 acres, mostly in the Brahmaputra valley, were settled by immigrants.[28] While some government officials, reflecting the political sentiment of many Assamese, feared the influx, others pointed to the contribution made by the migrants to the development of Assam's agriculture.

In 1921 Mr. Bentinck, deputy commissioner in Kamrup, wrote:

They have reclaimed and brought under permanent cultivation thousands of acres which the local cultivators had

[27] *Ibid.*, p. 75.

[28] *Annual Land Revenue Administration Reports of Assam*, cited *ibid.*, p. 81. In 1964 the net acreage sown in all of the two valleys was a little more than 5 million, of which 4.6 million was in the Brahmaputra valley. There is no reason to believe that many of the migrants were temporary sojourners, like many of the tea plantation laborers. They invariably brought their entire families, as far as we can ascertain from census data. The 1931 census reported that of the 338,000 migrants from Mymensingh then residing in Assam, nearly half, or 152,000, were women.

for generations past merely scratched with haphazard and intermittent crops or recognized as exigent of efforts beyond their inclination. The large undulating expanses of Char lands to be seen in late March or early April finely harrowed, weeded and newly sown are something to which the spectacle of ordinary Assamese cultivation is quite unaccustomed. They have, besides their industry, shown examples of new crops and improved methods.[29]

A decade later, P. G. Mukerji, the deputy commissioner of Nowgong (a district which was rapidly becoming the most Muslim district in the valley), wrote:

They have opened up vast tracts of dense jungle along the south bank of the Brahmaputra and have occupied nearly all the lands which are open for settlement in this tract. These people have brought in their wake wealth, industry and general prosperity of the whole district. They have improved the health of the countryside by clearing the jungles and converting the wilderness into prosperous villages. Their industry as agriculturalists has become almost proverbial and they extract from their fields the utmost that they can yield. Their care and love of cattle is also an object lesson to others. Government revenue has increased. Trade and commerce have prospered. The lakhs of rupees which annually pour into the district to buy their jute pass out of their pockets into those of the traders who sell them their foodstuffs and imported goods as well as into those of the lawyers and *mahajans* (money lenders) who look after their litigation and finance.[30]

But what was perceived as benefits by some was seen by Assamese as imposing costs. The census commissioner of 1951 wrote:

[29] *Ibid.*, p. 77. The citation is from the 1921 *Census of Assam*, p. 41.
[30] *Ibid.* The citation is from the 1931 *Census of Assam*, p. 51. Note that these two statements on the benefits of Muslim migrations are by an Englishman and a Bengali, respectively.

These benefits naturally were derived at a price. Their hunger for land was so great that in their eagerness to grasp as much land as they could cultivate, they not infrequently encroached on Government reserves and on lands belonging to the local people from which they could be evicted only with great difficulty. In the beginning they had their own way and there was some friction with the indigenous population who did not like their dealings as neighbors. Afterwards, when the land was not so abundant, their land hunger brought them into many conflicts and struggles in the economic sphere with the tribals and other indigenous people of Assam.[31]

Why did this massive settlement occur?

First, East Bengal, especially Mymensingh district, from which such a large proportion of the migrants came, was and continues to be one of the most densely populated rural areas of the world, with few industries or towns, a high rate of population growth accompanied by increased fragmentation of land holdings, and a growing number of landless laborers and marginal agriculturalists. In 1961, 51 million East Bengalis lived on 55,000 square miles, a density of 925 persons per square mile, while in Assam slightly under 12 million lived on 47,000 square miles, or a density of 252 persons per square mile.[32] In 1961, 4.4 percent of East Bengal's population lived in urban areas, as against 7.5 percent of Assam's.

Second, in contrast to East Bengal, Assam is a relatively low-density area which, in the past at least, had substantial virgin lands, some in easily flooded lowlands along the Brahmaputra valley that are similar to the deltaic areas of East Bengal. Moreover, Assam also has substantial forest reserves (unlike East Bengal) that can be exploited, often illegally, by land-hungry migrants.

Finally, population movement was facilitated by the con-

[31] *Ibid.*

[32] A more satisfactory comparison is with the Plains division of Assam, where density is (1961) 432, higher than the all-India average, but still half the density of East Bengal.

trasting land tenure of the two regions. East Bengal had (until shortly after independence) a landholding system in which large numbers of tillers were tenants or under-tenants to large landowners (known as *zamindars*), or to intermediary absentee rent collectors. Assam, by contrast, was a region of individual small landowner cultivators (*ryots*) who paid revenue directly to the state government.[33]

To these considerations several political factors should be added. Many Assamese claim that the Muslim League government, which controlled the state before and during the war, allowed—many say encouraged—Muslim migrants from Bengal to encroach on government lands and grazing and forest reserves, and that this came to a halt only in 1946, when the Congress party government began to enforce revenue laws and evict unauthorized trespassers. With partition in 1947, the flow of Muslims from East Bengal subsided, while the flow of Hindu refugees from East Bengal increased.[34]

The economic imbalances between East Bengal and Assam—at least insofar as opportunities for cultivating land are concerned—remained so great through the 1950s that even the existence of an international boundary, the imposition of a variety of legal restrictions, and the presence of an Assamese government failed to stem completely the flow of Bengali Muslims into Assam. In 1961 the census commissioner estimated that 221,000 Bengali Muslims had entered the state in the previous decade, almost all illegally.[35]

[33] For an account of the land system of Assam, see Narendra Chandra Dutta, *Land Problems and Land Reforms in Assam* (Delhi: S. Chand, 1968). Dutta reports that 10.5 percent of the total rural households in Assam belonged to the agricultural labor class in 1950, as compared to the all-India average of 30.4 percent (p. 119). In the last two decades there has been a substantial increase in the number and proportion of agricultural laborers in Assam, largely as a result of rapid population growth.

[34] The 1951 census reported 274,000 refugees, more than half of whom came in 1950. Virtually all of the Bengali Hindu migrants in Assam originate from East Bengal, where they constituted the gentry class in a Muslim agrarian society.

[35] Since illegal migrants obviously incorrectly reported their place

101

Finally, a statistical point warrants our attention: how many of the Muslims now residing in Assam are originally of "indigenous" Assamese origin, rather than Bengalis? Since there are no cross-tabulations for religion and migration, there is no way of knowing how many Muslims in Assam are migrants or of migrant origin. Presumably, the proportion of indigenous Muslims is small, since these consist of the descendants of Mughal prisoners of war who remained in Assam, and a small number who converted or migrated during Mughal times.[36] According to the 1891 census, 8 percent of the population of the Brahmaputra valley was Muslim, but a large portion of these were already Bengali Muslim migrants. In 1961 the corresponding figure was 24 percent, so it appears that approximately two-thirds of the Muslims are migrants or the descendants of migrants who settled in Assam after 1891.

Marwari Migrants: The Incorporation of Assam into the North Indian Trade Nexus

"The natives of Rajputana are the shrewd Marwari merchants who have succeeded in monopolizing practically the whole of the trade of the Assam valley." So wrote B. C. Allen, a British district officer, at the turn of the century.[37]

The number of Marwari migrants was not comparatively

---

of birth to census enumerators, this estimate was based upon the religious returns in the census. The difference between the expected and actual population increase of Muslims is assumed to represent illegal Muslim migration from Pakistan.

[36] According to H. K. Barpujari, the earliest known Muslim settlements in Assam date to 1662. Some Muslims were employed by the Ahom royal court to decipher Persian documents, carve inscriptions, mint coins, manufacture gun powder, and serve as tailors and silk weavers. Moghul works of art apparently found favor among members of the Ahom royal family and gentry. See his *Assam: In the Days of the Company 1826-1858* (Gauhati: Lawyer's Book Stall, 1963), pp. 264-265.

[37] B. C. Allen, *Assam District Gazetteers*, Vol. VII (Sibsagar, Allahabad: Pioneer Press, 1906), p. 75.

very large. The 1891 census reported only 4,877 migrants from Rajputana. But as north India's major traditional trading community, the Marwaris played an important role in opening up Assam to trade. They acted as moneychangers, bankers, and general agents to the managers of the tea gardens, especially in Sibsagar and Lakhimpur districts, operated the mustard trade in Kamrup and Goalpara districts, sold throughout the state hardware and other articles imported from other parts of India, and became dealers in rice and grains. The Marwaris served as bankers not only for agriculturalists, but for officers of the government as well. Though criticized and abused, as are traditional moneylenders everywhere, the Marwaris played an important economic role.

Though their numbers remain small,[38] the Marwaris are among the most visible of the migrant communities. Today, the Marwaris are the major business community in Assam, dominating trade, commerce, banking, and credit. In a drive through the main industrial area of Gauhati, one passes a flour mill, an automotive tire distributor, a bus transport company, a tea warehouse, a steel-iron works, a car distributor, an aluminum factory, and several petrol pumps, all Marwari owned. Though Marwaris can be found in the small towns in Assam, they are heavily concentrated in the larger towns, where they manage the major bazars. The Fancy Bazar[39] in Gauhati, probably the largest bazar in northeastern

[38] Marwaris originally came from Rajasthan, but they are found throughout northern India; the statistics on migration from Rajasthan into Assam grossly underestimate the number of Marwaris in Assam. The 1961 census reported 22,000 migrants from Rajasthan, with a sex ratio of 360 females to 1,000 males, suggesting that most of the migrants are not permanent settlers to Assam. However, one prominent leader of the Marwari community estimated that there may be as many as 20,000 Marwaris in the city of Gauhati.

[39] This is not an English name, but a corruption of the Hindi word, *fanshi*, meaning "hanging," since the jail where hangings took place was located near the bazar. The local post office is still called the Fanshi Bazar Post Office.

India, is run predominantly by Marwari merchants. The Marwaris have their own charitable organizations, hospitals, Hindi-language newspapers, and Hindi-medium schools; they are thus not only economically better off than most Assamese, but their institutions and bazars make them notably conspicuous and therefore vulnerable.

THE ASSAMESE RESPONSE TO MIGRATION: COLLECTIVE AND POLITICAL

The new opportunities created by the opening of Assam and the extension of British influence were thus exploited not by the Assamese, but by migrant communities. Tribals from Chota Nagpur became the labor force in the tea plantations. The British managed the gardens, and with the help of Marwaris established the tea trade. The Marwaris became the entrepreneurs, traders, and bankers of Assam. The Bengali Hindus dominated the administrative structure and constituted the professional classes in the cities, while the Marwaris became shopkeepers in the towns and larger villages. The Bengali Muslims developed the virgin lands and forests; and even some of the tea garden coolies, as the plantation workers were called, colonized land as independent cultivators. Others came too: Nepalis as herders, rubber tappers, and cultivators; artisans from the Punjab; peasants from U.P. and Bihar, who found jobs as carters and coolies; and Kavuli traders from as far west as Afghanistan.

For large numbers of people in northeastern India, especially in Bengal and Bihar, Assam was a land of opportunity where one could find a job, start a business, cultivate land, and do better than at home. But the question remains: why were the Assamese unable, or unwilling, to avail themselves of these opportunities?

One reason is that what was perceived as opportunity by others was not often seen as such by the Assamese. The Assamese were not blind to chances to improve themselves, but some of the new economic activities would not in fact have helped them. For an agricultural laborer or marginal cultivator in Bihar, a low wage in the tea industry represented a real opportunity, but not for the Assamese peasant. Similarly, a land-hungry Bengali peasant was prepared to clear forest lands or to cultivate crops on flood lands adjacent to the Brahmaputra, while the Assamese cultivator often had as much land as he or his sons could manage with the existing technology.

Second, the Assamese were largely unequipped to take advantage of some of these new opportunities. They lacked the education which the Bengalis had acquired, and it was a long time before many Assamese saw the benefits of going to secondary school and college. As for moving into entrepreneurial and banking activities, the Assamese lacked the skills and vast contacts that characterized the Marwaris, who for centuries had built up networks of trade and finance throughout northern India.

One could argue, of course, that a more enterprising people would have exploited these new opportunities. Moreover, even if enterprise and foresight were absent among the Assamese in the beginning of the nineteenth century, surely by the end of the century many Assamese should have learned from the experiences of the migrants and begun to compete with them successfully.

Such a view was widely held by British officials throughout the nineteenth century. In their blunt Victorian fashion, they wrote of "the utter want of an industrious, enterprising spirit, and the general degeneracy of the Assamese people."[40] Perhaps migrants, wrote a British officer of the Assam Light Infantry in a hopeful vein in 1847, might "stimulate the natives to increase exertions."

In many parts of the province, coal of a good quality is found; and indeed the soil of Assam generally may be considered extremely rich: it abounds in valuable products, such as rice, sugar-cane, moongah silk, pepper, mustard-

[40] John Butler, *A Sketch of Assam*, p. 34.

105

seed and cotton. But the bounty of nature is marred by the indolence and apathy of man: the cultivator seldom looks beyond his immediate wants, and makes no attempt to improve his condition. In fact, in agricultural, commercial and manufacturing industry, this country may be considered at least a century behind Bengal; and there seems little prospect of improvement, excepting by the introduction of a more active and industrious people, who might stimulate the native to increase exertions.[41]

This view is shared by some Assamese. Professor H. P. Das of Gauhati University, for example, has written of the "lethargic existence of the present-day population," which he attributes to the climate of Assam, it "being very damp and humid [and] not very congenial for continuous labor. Rather, it is extremely suitable for the growth of vegetation. So, while the people in Assam enjoyed great material prosperity, the ease of life depleted their physical and moral strength."[42]

It was, in any case, clear that the Assamese were unable— or unwilling—to compete effectively with either the Bengali Hindus or with the Marwaris, while they became increasingly fearful of the Bengali Muslim cultivators.

[41] *Ibid.*, p. 133.

[42] H. P. Das, *Geography of Assam* (New Delhi: National Book Trust, 1970), p. 12. Though Professor Das and Major Butler might agree that the "culture" of the Assamese accounts for their failures— though the Victorian English spoke of the "character" or "moral condition" of a people rather than their "culture"—they had different explanations on why the Assamese behaved as they did. For Professor Das, a geographer, it was a matter of climate (though the climate of East Bengal is surely as enervating as the climate of Assam). For Butler it was the widespread use of opium by the Assamese which, he said, accounted for their behavior by "depressing the industry and withering the physical energies of the people by limiting their desires to the gratification of the wants of the day" (*ibid.*, p. 134). Isolating the ingredients of the culture or environment that account for an achievement or nonachievement orientation continues to absorb the attention of contemporary scholars and remains as controversial an issue as ever.

The successful efforts of a small articulate Assamese middle class to persuade the government to drop Bengali as the medium of instruction in the schools in the 1860s was an important step toward improving the status of the Assamese. A decade later the restoration of Assamese in the schools and in the courts removed an important impediment to Assamese mobility. The establishment of Cotton College in Gauhati at the turn of the century provided new opportunities for Assamese young men, though it was as much of an attraction to Bengalis settled in Assam. Individual Assamese did, of course, move into higher education and into urban employment; but, by and large, few Assamese "made it." In the absence of large-scale individual achievement we begin to see, starting in the 1920s, and in a new form in the 1950s and 1960s, a collective political response on the part of the Assamese middle class.

By arguing that the response was collective and political rather than individual and economic, I am not suggesting that the choice was a conscious one. It was simply a response to what an increasing number of Assamese perceived as their humiliating status, their inability to remedy it through individual economic success, and their recognition of the potential uses of political power.

The Assamese and the Bengalis:
Defining Cultural Identity

Many politically articulate Assamese[43] explain their backwardness in relation to the migrant communities as a conse-

[43] The reader may wonder what my sources are when I refer to the views of "politically articulate Assamese." In this section I have relied heavily upon interviews I conducted with twenty-seven Assamese—members of parliament, the state Legislative Assembly, officials of the state government, journalists, and university professors—conducted in 1970-1971 and in 1973. In addition to these interviews, often of many hours' duration and sometimes involving two or three meetings, I had casual but informative conversations with dozens of Assamese in Gauhati and Shillong, and have made use of whatever

quence of political factors. They point to the success of the
Bengali Hindus and Bengali Muslims as a consequence of
political circumstances. The Bengali Hindus, it is argued,
took advantage of their dominant position in the British
administration. They not only moved into Assam with the
British, but they persuaded the British to establish Bengali
as the official language of Assam along with English, to
establish schools in Bengali, and to treat the Assamese as
culturally subordinate and inferior to the Bengalis. As for the
Bengali Muslims (though their large-scale migrations had
started shortly after the turn of the century), had not the
Muslim League government encouraged Muslim cultivators
to migrate to Assam to occupy illegally government reserve
forest lands? The Bengali Hindus, it is said, were intent upon
absorbing Assam into a "Greater Bengal"; and as the prospects for the creation of an Islamic Pakistan grew, the Bengali Muslims sought to incorporate Assam within it by increasing their numbers until they obtained a majority. Thus,
while the Bengali Hindus had sought to commit what some
Assamese perceived as "cultural genocide" through a process
of cultural absorption, the Bengali Muslims sought to assert
their domination through the force of their numbers. The one
had to be resisted by modifying the language and educational
policies of the government; and the other by restricting migration and by redrawing of state boundaries.

Fortunately for the Assamese, the Bengali Muslims and
Bengali Hindus were unable to come together politically; for

---

published sources I could find expressing an Assamese point of view.
From time to time I shall quote from these various sources, but I
am well aware of the methodological dictum, so well stated in the
Yiddish aphorism, "A for instance is not a proof." Readers will have
to accept on faith, as indeed I have had to, that the people I interviewed held views that are widely shared. How widely is, of course,
another matter, and for that reason I have refrained from indicating
what percentages of my respondents held to a particular view, since
such a number would suggest a degree of representativeness that these
interviews do not warrant.

their hostility to each other was far greater than their shared antagonisms to the Assamese. Ever since the British attempt to incorporate it into East Bengal, the Muslim leaders of East Bengal had looked covetously upon Assam. It was territorially larger than the Muslim majority districts of Bengal, and provided land for the demographically exploding, land-hungry Muslim peasants. The very existence of Assam made the idea of a Pakistani state attractive to many East Bengali Muslims.

But that idea came later. Even before the Muslim League proposed a separate Pakistan, the Assamese Hindus were fearful of the growing influx of Bengali Muslim migrants. For the Assamese there was a dual fear: that Assamese Hindus would be dominated by Muslims politically, and that Assamese culture and identity would be obliterated in a predominantly Bengali state.

The British attempted to restrict the flow of migrants into Assam by establishing the Line System in 1920, which prevented the settlement of migrants into selected, especially tribal, areas of Assam. The restrictions were tightened by the formal establishment of a Tribal Belt by the government of Assam in 1948 (through an amendment to the Assam Land and Revenue Regulations), but these restrictions probably had more impact on the distribution of Bengali Muslim settlers than in their numbers, for the Line System, restricting settlement in the hills, forced the migrants to seek land in the plains.

Assamese fears of the Muslims intensified when the Muslim League took control of the state government in 1936. The movement of Bengali Muslims into Assam when the League was in power was viewed not simply as the continuation of earlier chain migrations that reflected persistent economic differences between East Bengal and Assam, but as a deliberate act of the League to gain a solid majority through colonization. Clashes between Assamese Hindus and Bengali Muslims were common, and each side fought intensely for allies. Indeed, the political balance in the state legislature

109

was so precarious that for some time the small group of British tea plantation representatives held the balance.

The Congress party in Assam, as elsewhere in India, boycotted the government during the war, but with the end of the war and elections in 1946 the Congress party regained power in Assam. The Assamese Hindus were able to count upon the Bengali Hindus for support, since the Bengali Hindus were as fearful of being incorporated into a Pakistan state as were the Assamese. On the eve of partition it was agreed by virtually all the major parties that Assam would remain with India, but that a referendum would be held in Sylhet district. It was actually with some relief to the Assamese that Sylhet was removed from Assam and merged with East Pakistan.[44] With the creation of Pakistan, the Assamese no longer feared falling under Bengali Muslim domination. Moreover, Bengali Muslim leaders in Assam recognized that the partition was permanent. Some of their leaders, such as Maulana Bhashani, migrated back to East Bengal, while those who remained urged the Muslims to adapt themselves to living within a predominantly Hindu and Assamese-dominated political framework.

After independence there were a few communal clashes between Assamese Hindus and Bengali Muslims, but these were carryovers from the past.[45] The fear of Bengali Muslim domination had virtually ended. The new cleavage was now between the Assamese and the Bengali Hindus.

To appreciate fully the impact of Bengali Hindu migration on the Assamese, we must take a broader view of the kinds of

[44] As early as 1937, Nehru called for the transfer of Sylhet district to the province of Bengal in order to make Assam linguistically more homogeneous. See Jawaharlal Nehru, "The Brahmaputra Valley" in Satis Chandra Kakati, ed., *Discovery of Assam* (Calcutta, 1964).

[45] There were major communal disturbances in the state in early 1950. In February 1950 parliament passed the Immigrants (Expulsion from Assam) Act aimed at the removal of postindependence Muslim immigrants, technically known as "infiltrators." The act provides for the expulsion of any immigrant "whose stay was detrimental to the interest of the general public of India or of any scheduled tribes in Assam."

110

changes that the Assamese themselves have experienced in recent years, particularly since independence. The Assamese-dominated Congress party that took power with independence was committed not simply to the development of Assam, but more particularly to using state power to improve the position of the Assamese-speaking people. The new government devoted a considerable portion of the state's resources to expand educational institutions. The number of students in Assam increased from 934,000 in 1950 to 3,154,000 in 1965. There was a proportionately even larger educational explosion in the secondary schools and colleges. The number of students attending colleges and universities in Assam almost doubled every five years: from 8,601 in 1950 to 14,595 in 1955, 28,226 in 1960, and 45,387 in 1965.

There was now emerging in Assam, almost for the first time, a large middle class, "middle-class" by its educational attainment though not necessarily by its occupation and income. Indeed, the aspirations of this new class were middle-class long before it achieved any of the material standards of middle-class life.

For this aspiring Assamese middle class, it was the Bengali Hindus who stood as its obstacle to economic advancement. The new government sought to remedy this situation by quietly giving preference to Assamese over Bengalis in appointments to the state administrative services. Special attention was given to the appointment of Assamese young men in positions as teachers, since the teaching profession was the largest and most rapidly expanding single occupational category in government service. Between 1961 and 1965 alone, the number of teachers in Assam increased from 42,000 to 64,000. With the expansion of government services into health and community development, there was a similar expansion in public employment. In 1967, nearly 85,000 persons worked for the state government, apart from school teachers, as against only 81,000 factory workers.

As education expanded, language policy became the bone of contention between Bengali Hindus and the Assamese. The state government saw the establishment of Assamese as the exclusive language of the state, and the medium of instruction in the schools, as a measure benefiting young Assamese seeking government employment. Moreover, the Assamese increasingly demanded that Bengalis acknowledge the exclusive legitimacy of Assamese symbols in public life—not only the Assamese language, but Assamese cultural holidays, Assamese historic heroes, and recognition of the great events in Assamese history. Since it touched both upon the issue of employment and cultural identity, language policy became the focal point of controversy between the two communities. For the Bengalis, who favored the use of both languages, a dual language policy would give equal status to the Assamese and Bengalis, and would therefore mean equality of opportunity in employment and political and social status. The Assamese, however, viewed a dual language policy as a perpetuation of Bengali domination in both the cultural and employment spheres.

It is not easy to separate the issue of cultural identity from the struggle over access to jobs. While one could plausibly explain the conflict between Bengali Hindus and Assamese strictly in terms of competition for public employment on the part of their respective middle classes, the explanation would ignore the element of cultural conflict and the deep emotional content of this struggle. Certainly the Assamese would have developed a sense of their own cultural identity even in the absence of large "alien" migration, for regional identities have been emerging everywhere in India. What characterized the Assamese quest for a cultural identity was their need to distinguish themselves from the Bengalis in their midst; it is quite likely that the presence of large numbers of migrants from other states, especially from Bengal, sharpened the sense of Assamese identity and gave it what many outsiders perceived as its peculiarly aggressive character.

As one Assamese writer, referring to the immigrants of the past 100 years, observed in 1947, "If we cannot assimilate the major part of this population into our fold by giving them our language and culture, there is danger for us."[46] Twenty-five years later, another Assamese writer concurred: "How will this nationality [the Assamese] be able to keep its numerical position as the majority in Assam in the face of uncontrolled and *unassimilated* immigration. . . . In the absence of any arrangement in the form of assimilation of immigrants into its linguistic fold or of a constitutional provision for maintaining its majority position a weak nationality in the face of a ceaseless influx of people belonging to a strong linguistic national may face another eventuality."[47]

Three themes persistently emerged in my interviews with Assamese. The first is that the Assamese view the Bengali Hindus as cultural imperialists who, if given the opportunity, will assimilate the Assamese. The second is that the Assamese view their own nationality as weak; not only do the Assamese lag behind the Bengalis in education and employment, but the Bengali language itself is seen as more advanced, its literary traditions stronger, and its cultural institutions dominating. Finally, argued these Assamese, Bengali cultural imperialism can only be met by linguistic nationalism; the very weakness of the Assamese as a nationality makes it necessary for them to pursue an assimilationist policy if they are themselves to avoid being assimilated.

This sense of weakness is partially related to geography and numbers. Next door to Assam are West Bengal with 44 million people, Bangladesh with some 75 million people, and Tripura with 1.5 million. In all, there are 120 million Bengalis, one of the largest linguistic groups in the world, and in South Asia numerically second only to Hindi speakers.[48]

[46] Jyoti Prasad Agarwala, in an essay "Natun Dinar Kristi" written in 1947 and cited by Bhaben Barua, *Language and the National Question in North East India* (Gauhati, 1972), p. 5.

[47] *Ibid.*, p. 4.

[48] In 1961 the East Bengal district of Mymensingh, with a population of 7,019,000, had a density of 1,103 per square mile in a predominantly rural region; in 1971 the density is likely to approximate 1,400, as against a density of 493 for Assam. One cannot overestimate the extent to which these demographic differences are viewed

The Bengalis are not only numerous, but for the past 150 years they have overflowed from their original habitat. As an area with highly educated middle and upper classes and a high rural density, it has produced an overflow both of middle-class (Hindu) jobseekers and (Muslim) peasantry. From the middle of the nineteenth century, educated Bengalis moved across northern India to other parts of the Bengal Presidency, which then included Bihar, Orissa, and Assam, and to Uttar Pradesh. After partition, millions of Bengali Hindus fled from East Pakistan, not only to West Bengal, but also to Assam and to the small union territory of Tripura, where the Bengali population soon outnumbered the local tribal inhabitants.

Even before partition, most of the neighboring states took steps to curtail sharply the employment of Bengalis. In Bihar, for example, the state government in the late 1930s announced a policy of giving employment preference to local people, and though Bengalis continued to find employment in centrally administered services (such as post and telegraph and railways) they found it increasingly difficult to find jobs in the state government. In Bihar, as in most of the other states where Bengalis settled, the number of Bengalis was never great enough to threaten the cultural position of the Biharis, but in Assam the number of Bengalis was proportionately so large that the Assamese could genuinely fear that they might be numerically and hence culturally overwhelmed.

The large numbers of Bengalis settled in Assam provided a persistent attraction for Bengali friends and relatives who had not yet migrated, adding as elsewhere in the world an accelerating dimension to migration. If a Muslim cultivator in Mymensingh did not have enough land for all his children, he could send one or more to join his brother or cousin in Cachar district. If the Calcutta job market was tight, a man

---

with concern by Assamese, conditioning both their anxieties toward their Bengali neighbors, and affecting their attitudes toward population control policies for the Assamese.

could send his son to Gauhati, where his elder brother might find a job for him as a clerk in a bank or as an accountant in a tea plantation in Lakhimpur. And as the number of Bengali families settled in Assam increased, it no longer became necessary to send one's son "home" to find a bride, for now there were enough local Bengali girls available. Once Bengali Brahmans had settled, lower-caste Bengalis found it easier to migrate too, for priests would be available to perform weddings, conduct puja ceremonies, and perform the rites for the dead. Since Bengalis occupied high posts in the state administration as district magistrates, revenue collectors, and police officers, the Bengali middle class (or, as this class is called in Bengali, the *bhadralog* or "gentlefolk" as distinct from the *chotalog* or "little folk") felt some security in knowing that whenever needed, there was someone in the bureaucracy to whom they could turn for assistance.

Bengali migrants felt comfortable in Assam. They had their own Bengali schools, or they could send their children to English medium schools. They had their own Bengali newspapers. In their own localities, in their place of work, and in government offices, they could speak their own language. And their numbers were sufficiently large so that they could conduct the puja ceremonies that are at the core of Bengali cultural life, social identity, and religious expression.

These very elements, contributing to the Bengali migrant sense of security, made the local Assamese feel increasingly insecure. Would the Assamese have to speak Bengali when they spoke with a Bengali government official? Would their children find the Bengali pujas, with their colorful images, processions, and elaborate tents more exciting than the Assamese Bihu holidays? Would they and their children have to acquire Bengali while Bengalis remained ignorant of Assamese? Would Calcutta be the magnet for their young men seeking higher education, and would an extended stay in Calcutta destroy a student's Assamese identity, turn him into a Bengali in speech, manners, and feeling?

Everywhere he turned, the Assamese found the Bengali

in a superior, and himself in a subordinate, position. The teacher is Bengali, the pupil Assamese. The doctor is Bengali, the patient Assamese. The pleader is Bengali, the client Assamese. The shopkeeper is Bengali, the consumer Assamese. The government official is Bengali, the petitioner Assamese. One would hardly expect Bengalis not to look upon the Assamese as subordinate human beings and for the Assamese to feel the stare, the tone, the gestures of condescension.

Soon, every slight was magnified. Why had the great Bengali poet, Rabindranath Tagore, omitted Assam from the list of regions included in the poem that was to become India's national anthem? Did he omit Assam because, like other Bengalis, he considered it a part of Bengal?[49] Why do Bengalis use the word *Asami* to identify one who speaks Assamese, rather than the word preferred by the Assamese, *Ahomiya*? Is it because *asami* in Bengali means criminal?[50] And why is it that only a quarter of the Bengali population in Assam speaks Assamese as a second language, compared with half the Nepali, Oriya, and Hindi-speaking migrants?[51] Is it because the Bengalis do not accept the notion that Assam is the homeland of the Assamese?

In India the exercise of political power to "correct" a perceived status and economic imbalance must take place within a narrowly prescribed political framework. The Assamese cannot bar the province to migration, since the constitution guarantees freedom of movement. (Exceptions made for reserved tribal areas, as noted earlier, do not benefit the Assamese plains people of the Brahmaputra valley.) Under some conditions there can be restrictions on employment and

[49] No, said one of my witty, good-humored Bengali informants, who explained that he has told his Assamese friends that the poet omitted Assam because he was unable to find a rhyming word!

[50] More likely it is because the Assamese sound of *h* (which is close to the German *ch*) does not exist in Bengali.

[51] According to the 1961 census, 58 percent of the Oriyas speak Assamese, 54 percent of the Nepalis, and 44 percent of the Hindi speakers, as against 27 percent of the Bengalis.

on admissions into schools and colleges. In any event, such restrictions would not affect most of the Bengali Hindus in Assam, as they were born in Assam.[52]

Language policy, on the other hand, does affect the descendants of migrants as well as the migrants themselves, and it is a "legitimate" area of state intervention, justified on grounds other than the protection of a specific ethnic group.

Language controversies have taken a torturous course in Assam since the "Assam disturbances" of 1960, when rioting occurred over the passage of an act making Assamese the official language of the state. I shall here single out one controversy for description, since an analysis of a violent clash of interests provides a sharp picture of the major actors and their respective outlooks. This conflict occurred when I was in India, so that I was able to follow the newspaper accounts, pay a visit to Gauhati and Shillong, and conduct a number of interviews.

Anatomy of a Language Riot:
Cleavages and Coalitions

In the latter part of 1972, large-scale anti-Bengali riots erupted throughout the Brahmaputra valley. The dispute began in June, when the Academic Council of Gauhati University, with jurisdiction extending over the Brahmaputra valley as well as the predominantly Bengali Cachar district, passed a resolution calling for the introduction of Assamese as the medium of instruction, following a long-established trend in India's state universities to switch to the regional languages. The council made two concessions to the linguistic minorities in the state: 1. English was to be retained as the medium of instruction for a period of time; and 2. students would be permitted to answer their examination questions in English and Bengali, as well as in Assamese. Almost immedi-

[52] According to the 1961 census, the Bengali-speaking population of Assam (present boundaries) was 19 percent, while only 7 percent of the population reported Pakistan or West Bengal as the place of birth; in other words, 63 percent of the Bengali-speaking population was born in Assam.

117

ately, demonstrations by Assamese students broke out in Gauhati, demanding that the option of taking examinations in Bengali be withdrawn. Students boycotted classes and several were arrested for breach of peace.

As demonstrations, led by the All Assam Students Union, spread to other towns, the Academic Council met to reverse its decision. It withdrew the option of taking examinations in Bengali. The council said that its "partial modification" of the earlier decision was done after taking note of the "various representations from the public, teachers and students' organisations."[53]

Predictably, there was an uproar in Cachar district. The District Congress Committee, the Youth Congress, and a group of Bengali leaders agreed to seek legal remedies. One of the affiliate colleges of Gauhati University, Gurucharan College in the district town of Silchar, filed a petition with the Supreme Court arguing that the university's decision to restrict the medium of instruction to Assamese was in violation of Article 30 of the Indian constitution, which assured protection for linguistic minorities. The stay order was granted.

In September the state legislative assembly of Assam unanimously passed a resolution reaffirming the decisions of the academic councils of Gauhati University and Dibrugarh University, the state's only other university, but at the same time resolved that a separate university be established with territorial jurisdiction over Cachar district. Some members of the assembly saw this resolution as a compromise permitting the Assamese in the Brahmaputra valley to have their own universities, and assuring the Bengalis that they too would be entitled to educate their children through their mother tongue, while other members supported the resolution as a step toward the separation of Cachar district from Assam.

Opposition to the resolution came almost immediately from three important political groups in the Brahmaputra valley: the All Assam Students Union (AASU), the Action

[53] *Statesman*, July 1, 1972.

118

Committee of the Teachers of Gauhati University, and the Assam Sahitya Sabha, the state's paramount literary association, containing some of the state's most important Assamese leaders. The All Assam Students Union declared that the assembly had "failed to give due recognition to the Assamese language" and that their decision would "endanger the existence of Assam and the Assamese people." With an escalation in the rhetoric came an ultimatum to the chief minister that unless the Gauhati University Academic Council decision establishing Assamese as the sole medium of instruction was reinstated, the AASU would launch a "direct action" movement. Within a few days violence broke out in one town after another throughout the Brahmaputra valley. Nowgong district was hit hardest, with large-scale arson and looting. The government announced a curfew in Gauhati, Dibrugarh, and Nowgong, and as violence spread throughout the state, the government brought in the military to reestablish order.

At a public meeting in Gauhati in late October addressed by several former presidents of the powerful Assam Sahitya Sabha, a decision was made to broaden the student agitation into a "popular movement" to demand that the Assam assembly be called into special session to rescind its resolution. The president of the Gauhati University Teachers Association (GUTA) in a public letter to the *Statesman* that appeared on November 6, 1972, said that his organization opposed the establishment of a separate university in Cachar "since this would be detrimental to the accepted principle of linguistic states and regional languages as the medium of higher education."

As large-scale rioting and arson against Bengalis broke out throughout the valley in early November, officials of the central government sought to find ways to lower the tension. In a visit to Assam, Mrs. Gandhi met with a deputation from the All Assam Students Union to urge them to call off their movement. The chief minister subsequently issued a statement announcing that his government had no intention of implementing the assembly resolution since "it had proven

119

unacceptable to the people both in the Brahmaputra Valley
and in Cachar,"[54] and that the resolution would be recon-
sidered by the Assembly at its next regular session. The government, he said, would accept the recommendations of the
academic councils of the two universities on the question
of medium of instruction, and would also introduce Assamese
as a compulsory subject in all non-Assamese secondary
schools in the state. Almost immediately the AASU announced that the movement would be called off.

Just as the Assembly's decision was interpreted by Assamese militants as the first step toward a multilingual Assam,
in which the Assamese would lose their identity, so now the
chief minister's announcement was greeted by non-Assamese
as a major step toward forceful Assamization. One Bengali
expressed his fear that "the recurring disturbances are aimed
not at usurping the Bengali language but at driving out the
entire Bengali population from Assam."[55] Bengali leaders in
Cachar denounced what they called the cultural genocide
perpetrated on the linguistic minorities in Assam."[56] The
Assamese, complained another Bengali, "have developed an
irrational craze for cultural conquest."[57]

These fears were shared by many Bodos, the largest tribe
in the plains of Assam. The Bodo Sahitya Sabha, a leading
Bodo organization, announced that it would launch a movement to protest the government's decision to make Assamese
a compulsory subject in the Bodo-medium secondary schools.
The Plains Tribals Council of Assam announced that it
would press for the creation of a union territory of the Bodo
regions of the state. One tribal leader, "severely criticizing
the Assamization policy of the government," complained
that the tribal peoples "had been forced to learn through
the medium of Assamese in colleges and universities when
all along they had been demanding the retention of Eng-

[54] *National Herald*, November 12, 1972.
[55] Letter to the editor, *Amrita Bazar Patrika*, November 4, 1972.
[56] *Statesman*, December 23, 1972.
[57] *Amrita Bazar Patrika*, December 28, 1972.

lish."[58] The Bengalis of Cachar and the plains tribal leaders soon formed a coalition organization, the Minority Peoples Rights Committee, which called for a change in government language policy or, alternatively, the further division of Assam.

Behind the rhetoric and the political moves and countermoves clearly lay two divergent conceptions of what constitutes an appropriate social contract to guide the relationship between Assamese and non-Assamese in the state. The Assamese have been torn between two conflicting objectives. One has been to make Assam the land of the Assamese, in which Assamese language and culture would play the same dominant role that Bengali language and culture plays in West Bengal, Tamil language and culture in Tamil Nadu, and the other regional languages in their own states, and so to reject the notion that Assam is a "miniature India," a "patchwork quilt" of a variety of civilizations.[59] The second objective was to retain control over all those territories that the British had historically annexed to Assam, even though some of these are areas in which non-Assamese predominate.

These two objectives could only be achieved if the Assamese successfully persuaded or coerced the non-Assamese to adopt Assamese language and culture or, at a minimum, recognize their predominance. But the more the Assamese asserted the predominance of Assamese language and culture throughout the entire state, as it existed in 1947, the more the non-Assamese feared that their own languages and culture would be made subordinate, that the Assamese would

[58] *Indian Express*, December 3, 1972.

[59] "Aftab," a professor at Gauhati University, quotes approvingly Jawaharlal Nehru's rhetorical question posed at a public meeting in Gauhati in the wake of the 1960 language riots: "Where else but in Assam can Assamese be the official language?" And after a pause he is reported to have said derisively "In Bombay?" followed by thunderous applause. For the Assamese, writes "Aftab," Assam is the only state, indeed the only place in the world, in which the Assamese live. ("Aftab," "Assam: Behind the Trouble," *Frontier*, December 9, 1972.)

121

be given preferences in public and private employment, and that they would be second-class citizens in the power structure of the state. The result is that one by one each of the major non-Assamese groups pressed the central government for the creation of a separate political structure apart from Assam; the Nagas pressed for Nagaland, the NEFA tribes for Arunachal Pradesh, the Khasis and Caros for Meghalaya, and the Mizos for Mizoram. What remained was the thinly populated tribal areas of the Mikir hills and North Cachar hills, the predominantly Bengali district of Cachar, and the six districts of the Brahmaputra valley in which the Assamese predominate.

The Assamese efforts to assimilate non-Assamese into their political and cultural framework has thus largely resulted in the breakup of Assam into discrete cultural-political units. Many Assamese have advocated taking what they hope will be the last step in this process of creating a predominantly Assamese political system—the separation of Cachar. Still, some hope that they can impose Assamese upon Bengalis within Cachar as well as on others in the state. (Of the nearly 2 million Bengalis reported by the 1961 census, 1.1 million live in Cachar and 900,000 in the Brahmaputra valley.)

The Bengalis insist that even though Assamese is the official language of the state, Bengali should be retained as the administrative language of Cachar. They also insist that Bengalis be allowed to study in their own language, not only in Cachar, but throughout the state. They argue that cultural and linguistic minorities in India have the right to retain their language and culture wherever they reside, a principle enshrined in constitutional provisions that ensure the rights of minorities to establish their own educational institutions with state aid.

Moreover, the Bengalis—and earlier, the tribes that resided within what were then the boundaries of Assam—perceived Assam as a multicultural, multilingual state in which a variety of linguistic-cultural groups would share power,

122

and in which Assamese, Bengali, and English would be widely used (English is used by many tribals educated by British and American missionaries). Even with the breakup of Assam into several states, many Bengalis continue to argue that Assam remains a multilingual state. Much of their argument is based upon an attack against the census figures, which report the number of Assamese and Bengalis in the state, and particularly in the Brahmaputra valley. The enormous percentage increase in the number of Assamese speakers between 1941 and 1951, they argue, reflected a political move on the part of Bengali Muslims to side with the Assamese, and that Assamese speakers constitute barely 50 percent of the population, Bengalis another 30 percent, and tribals and others 20 percent.[60] "There is," concluded one Bengali leader, "only one way out of the crisis and that is recognition by the major linguistic group of the fact that Assam is a multilingual state."[61] To separate Cachar from Assam, therefore, would be to make the position of the Bengalis in the Brahmaputra valley even more vulnerable.

Some Assamese favor separation of Cachar district from Assam in order to match territory and language; now that Nagaland, Meghalaya, Arunachal Pradesh, and Mizoram have been separated from Assam, they argue, the process may as well be completed. There would then remain the predominantly Assamese Brahmaputra valley, though it would still retain substantial numbers of Bengali Hindus, Muslim peasants from East Bengal, tea plantation laborers, Marwari merchants, some Nepalis, and a substantial number of plains tribals. "One still hopes," wrote one Assamese, "that after all the cutting and chopping that has been done in Assam over the years, a more or less homogeneous political and cultural unit will emerge and whatever inner tensions may still remain (between "upper" and "lower" Assam, between

[60] Subodh Roy, "The Assam Happenings: Background and Way Out," *Amrita Bazar Patrika*, November 28, 1972. Roy is the former secretary of the Nikhil Assam Bangabhasabhasi Samiti (the All Assam Bengali Association).

[61] *Ibid.*

various castes of Assam, Ahom-caste Hindu, Plains Tribal-caste Hindu, etc.) will be more or less of the same kind of 'subregionalism' that 'plagues' every other state of the union."[62]

In closing this account of the cleavages between the Assamese and the Bengali Hindus, it is interesting to note the position of the Bengali Muslims, for they found themselves an unexpected beneficiary of the clash. After 1947 the Bengali Muslims became de facto allies of the Assamese in their conflict with the Bengali Hindus. Bengali Muslims have been willing to accept Assamese as the medium of instruction in their schools, and they have thrown their votes behind Assamese candidates for the state assembly and the national parliament. They have declared Assamese their mother tongue. In return, the state government has not attempted to eject Bengali Muslims from lands on which they have settled in the Brahmaputra valley, though earlier Assamese leaders had claimed that much of the settlement had taken place illegally. Moreover, Hindu-Muslim riots have virtually disappeared in Assam, a remarkable feat considering the long history of communal antagonism and the persistence of religious conflicts in other states where the proportion of Muslims to the population as a whole is smaller than in Assam (the percentage of Muslims in Assam, 23.3 percent, is the highest for any state in India except Jammu and Kashmir).

There is thus an unspoken coalition between the Assamese and the Bengali Muslims against the Bengali Hindus. It is not a wholly stable coalition, however, since it could be shattered if there were to be a new major influx of Bengali Muslims into Assam, or if Bengali Hindus and Bengali Muslims coalesce.

The Assamese and the Marwaris

Hostility to Marwari migrants and their descendants has turned many young Assamese into socialists, just as their

[62] M. S. Prabhakar, "The 'Bongal' Bogey," *Economic and Political Weekly*, October 21, 1972, p. 2142.

hostility to Bengali Hindus has turned them into cultural nationalists. To understand why, we must take a brief look at industrial development and employment in Assam.

Reliable data on per capita income, growth rates, and employment in India are not readily available; hence comparisons between Assam and other states must be made with great caution. Under Indian planning there is a tendency for state governments to underreport growth rates, since a low level of development strengthens claims for central resources. Assam state leaders regularly assert that Assam is a backward state neglected by the central government. Per capita annual income in the mid-sixties was Rs. 279, as against the all-India figure of Rs. 339, but Assam was still above Bihar, Orissa, and Uttar Pradesh—the states from which migrants come—and probably above most of Bangladesh. Literacy in Assam in 1971 was slightly lower than for India as a whole: 28.8 percent of the population could read and write, as against 29.3 percent in all of India, but again Assam was above Bihar, Orissa, and U.P., but well below more urbanized and industrialized West Bengal. Assam is considerably less urbanized than the rest of India: in 1971 only 8.4 percent of the population of Assam lived in urban areas, as against 19.9 percent for all of India. Orissa and Himachal were the only less urbanized states.

Economic growth in Assam[63] has been modest. Food grain products rose between 1950-1951 and 1967-1968 (base 1956-1957 = 100) from 81 to 110, while nonfood

[63] These and subsequent statistics on the economy of Assam are taken from the following reports: Department of Economics and Statistics, *Assam through the First Three Five-Year Plans—Selected Economic Indicators* (Shillong, 1970); Department of Economics and Statistics, *Estimates of State Income of Assam* (Shillong, 1970); Directorate of Economics and Statistics, *Report on the Sample Survey of Employment and Unemployment in Urban Areas of Assam* (Shillong, 1963); Department of Labour, Government of Assam, *Memorandum of the Government of Assam to the National Commission on Labour* (Shillong, 1968); Department of Economics and Statistics, *Statistical Abstract of Assam 1967-68* (Shillong, 1970).

agricultural production (such as jute, cotton, and tea) rose from 89 to 119 and industrial production from 100 to 135, with the largest increases in petroleum refinery products and the manufacturing of plywood and tea chests.

There has been a substantial increase in land utilization in Assam since 1951, so that much of the increase in agricultural production can be attributed not to increased productivity per acre, but to the extension of total cropped areas. In 1950, 1.6 million hectares of land were used for the cultivation of rice; in 1967, 2.0 million hectares were cultivated. During the same period, production increased from 1.4 million tons to 1.9 million tons.

The major economic changes in Assam from 1950 onward consisted of expansion of the supply of electricity, a doubling of road mileage, and an expansion in communications (post offices, telephones, and radio receiving sets).

The income of the state nearly doubled between 1950 and 1968, but population growth, both natural population increases and migration, made the per-capita income increases much smaller, only a 10 percent growth in an 18-year period.

Factory employment has hardly increased since 1951, when there were 65,000 factory workers; throughout the 1960s there were approximately 80,000 factory workers.

Two features of the employment market in Assam are striking. The first, as noted earlier, is the considerable expansion of school attendance in Assam, at all levels, but especially at the secondary school and college level, resulting in great increases in the number of applicants for clerical jobs registered at the employment exchanges.

The second is the expansion in the number of people employed in the public sector, either as school teachers or in the direct employ of the state government. Between 1961 and 1965, for example, the number of school teachers increased from 42,000 to 64,000. Between 1960 and 1966 the number of employees in the state government rose from 55,000 to 83,000. A persistent feature of the growing un-

126

employment in Assam has been the demand by students for greater access to employment in the state services and in the public sector, and demands by the state government to the central government for greater public sector investments.

In an effort to increase employment for Assamese, the state government asked all industrialists in Assam to hire only "local" people for jobs paying a salary of up to Rs. 500. In June 1972 there were demonstrations against a central-government-supported research laboratory at Jorhat, led by the opposition People's Democratic Party (PDP). The PDP demanded that all jobs in the laboratory carrying a salary of less than Rs. 500 a month be reserved for the Assamese. The agitation at Jorhat was one of a series of statewide demonstrations for pressuring the central government to locate industries in Assam that would process Assam's resources within the state.

An earlier agitation led the central government to locate a refinery and petrochemical complex in the state, although many economists and engineers doubted the wisdom of the decision. There were agitations by employees at the Oil Refinery at Gauhati against the policy of transferring senior engineers and administrators from other Indian oil plants, on the grounds that higher posts should be filled by promotions within the plant rather than by transfers. There was also agitation against the public-sector petrochemical complex at Bongaigaon for advertising posts in Bombay, Delhi, and Calcutta newspapers, and not in the Assam newspapers. The Indian Petrochemical Corporation at Bongaigaon then agreed to set up a local office to deal exclusively with hiring technicians and engineers from within Assam.

The state government also expressed its concern that the head office of public and private-sector industries located in Assam were outside the state. The head offices of the Fertilizer Corporation of India, the Indian Oil Corporation, and the Indian Petroleum Corporation are all outside of Assam, as are the headquarters for most of the tea agencies. As more

127

and more educated Assamese seek urban employment, they increasingly feel blocked by "foreign" domination of the commercial and industrial sectors.

In nonhousehold manufacturing industries, 50,000 out of 103,000 workers were migrants, and a large number of the remainder can be presumed to be the descendants of migrants rather than native Assamese. Similarly, there are 21,000 migrants employed in construction, out of a total labor force of 38,000, or 55 percent. In trade and commerce, 92,000 out of 183,000, or 50 percent, are migrants. In transport, storage, and communications, mainly in railways and post and telegraph, 43,000 out of 75,000 are migrants, or 57 percent; in other services, the migrants total 139,000 out of 424,000, or one-third. These statistics point to the conclusion that:

— in absolute numbers migrants are a majority or near majority in manufacturing, construction, trade and commerce, and transport and communications;
— Assamese are less likely to take positions as nonagricultural workers than are migrants;
— a very substantial proportion of employers in centrally controlled services—railroads, post and telegraph, and various centrally controlled departments—are non-Assamese, while employees in the state government are more likely "local," though one should include in the "local" category all those born in Assam, including a majority of the Bengali Hindus.

The Assamese middle classes, and most of the Assamese political leaders, attribute these conditions to the fact that most of the industries, trade and commerce, and tea plantations are owned by non-Assamese businessmen. The Marwaris have become a symbol of "foreign" domination, though increasingly the numbers of other entrepreneurs, especially Punjabis, have increased. Assamese complain that Marwari businessmen and shopkeepers do not employ sufficient numbers of Assamese. The charge is accepted by many

128

Marwaris, who claim that Assamese are lethargic, unwilling to work long hours, as do Marwaris, and are not reliable and "trustworthy" employees. In the mid-1960s local politicians and college students increasingly criticized Marwaris for their "failure" to provide employment to local Assamese. Violent clashes occurred in several urban centers, notably in Gauhati, where bands of young men smashed and burned shops throughout Fancy Bazar.

This so-called "foreign" domination has led many Assamese to press for an expansion of the public, as opposed to the private, sector. The state government of Assam continues to welcome private investment, but much of the effort of the state leadership has been directed toward pressing the central government to expand public-sector investment in the state, especially in petroleum and various raw-material-oriented industries, such as paper pulp and cement. It has also sought public-sector investment for the creation of fertilizer factories, the exploitation of natural gas, and the expansion of transport facilities.

State socialism, implying the expansion of public-sector investment, is supported by all Assamese political parties and by virtually all Assamese social groups, including the small Assamese business community. For in this context, socialist ideology represents not a demand for a fundamental restructuring of political and economic life, or a demand for greater income equality within Assamese society, but rather a desire to give employment preferences to natives as distinct from immigrant communities.

There are currently plans for creating a petrochemical complex and refinery at Bongaigaon, a paper mill at Jogighopa, a cement factory at Bokajan, a petrochemical complex at Namrup, and a sugar mill in Cachar—all of which, so the government hopes, will improve the employment situation in the state. The prospects on the employment front, however, are not favorable. Some of the public-sector investments (such as petrochemical) are capital, not labor; intensive industries. Moreover, public-sector investments that are cen-

129

trally controlled follow a national recruitment policy for highly skilled jobs, so that the establishment of more public sector plants will have a limited impact on employment for the Assamese. In any case, a policy of giving preferences to local people for certain posts in public or private firms does not assure positions for the Assamese, since locally born Bengalis are also eligible, and are often more qualified.

Nor have the Assamese sought employment outside their state. Of the major linguistic communities, the Assamese are among the least mobile in all of India. In 1961 only 19,000 Assamese-speaking persons, or 0.3 percent of the total Assamese-speaking population in India, lived outside of Assam, and nearly half of them lived in Nagaland, Manipur, and NEFA. By comparison, 5.5 percent of the Malayalum-speaking people, 7 percent of India's Tamils, and 15.5 percent of the Punjabis live outside of their "native" state.

CONCLUSION: MIGRANTS AS
DETERMINANTS OF CONFLICT AND CHANGE

Assam is but a single case, but it does help us understand some of the tensions and problems that arise when migrants move into superior economic positions, and the ways in which the local population attempts to exercise political power to redress the balance. We can summarize the process in a series of propositions.

1. The establishment of new economic opportunities did not necessarily benefit the local population. For the better part of the past century, it has been migrant rather than native populations that have taken advantage of new opportunities: the expansion of land use, the establishment of the tea industry, the growth of commerce and industry, and the expansion of employment in government and the professions.

2. The inability of the indigenous population to compete effectively with migrants was the result of a complex set of historical, social, demographic, and cultural circumstances. Features of the land system, combined with comparatively

130

low rural densities and a comparatively prosperous agricultural industry, slowed the pace of urbanization. British administrative policy favored the education and employment of Bengalis vis-à-vis Assamese, and Assamese culture and social structure has not produced an indigenous entrepreneurial community.

3. The indigenous population, especially the politically articulate and numerically expanding urban educated class, seeking middle-class employment, sees its failure to achieve equality of income as a consequence of political factors. The Assamese blame the British for giving the Bengalis a head start, Muslim politicians for encouraging Bengali Muslim migrations, and Bengali Hindus and Marwaris for using their superior economic positions to prevent Assamese from effectively moving up the occupational and income ladder.

4. The indigenous elite, on acquiring effective political control, attempted to use political instruments for equalizing the position of the Assamese. These instruments included the establishment of informal preferences for Assamese in employment, a language policy intended to improve the competitive position of the Assamese, and coercion or threats of coercion against both Bengali Hindus and Marwaris. For the Assamese government and political elites, the objective of policy and politics is the achievement of equality of income, occupation, and status—not equality of opportunity.

5. The indigenous leadership has not been adverse to forming coalitions with migrant communities prepared to support its political objectives. The Assamese have sought and won the support of the plantation workers and Bengali Muslims in their conflicts with Bengali Hindus and Marwaris. Cultural differences between the Assamese and the migrant tribals and Bengali Muslims have not proven to be an impediment to a political coalition.

6. In spite of government policies, there is no evidence that migrants have ceased to enter Assam or that migrants or their descendants have begun to leave. Neither ethnic differences nor government policies have thus far proven to be

131

a barrier to migration. For one thing, Assam continues to provide opportunities for outsiders; for another, the migration streams are so well established that residents from other states can turn to their friends and relatives within Assam to help them find employment and housing. Other things being equal, one assumes that migrants would prefer to seek employment in the linguistic region in which they live, but the persistently high migration rates into Assam suggest that for many people in neighboring states Assam continues to be a land of opportunity. Moreover, since Assam already has settled migrant communities, new migrants continue to be attracted to a region that has the infrastructures for preserving their ethnic group identity.

7. Finally, we have emphasized the ways in which contact with migrants have shaped the self-perceptions, the value preferences, and the ideological perspectives of the indigenous Assamese. The particular content given to socialist perspectives, the ways in which regional identities are asserted, and perceptions of what the Assamese can and cannot do are affected by the competitive relationship established by the presence of migrants. Moreover, the presence of competing aliens has reduced the competing claims that Assamese make upon one another. The low political salience of conflicts between Assamese landlords and their tenants and agricultural laborers, between large and small peasant proprietors, between Assamese bureaucrats and their clients, and between higher and lower-class Assamese further demonstrates the proposition that a politics that emphasizes ethnic solidarity in response to alien intruders tends to inhibit the emergence of class conflicts and class-defined issues.

The theme of this chapter has been the impact of migrants as an instrument of social change, not on the migrants themselves, but on the social and political order into which they move. There can be little doubt that migration has been an important factor in the economic development of Assam. Migrants have produced a tea industry with links to world markets; established a small industrial base in oil, petrochemicals, and forest products; developed trade with the rest of India, bringing to Assam consumer goods produced elsewhere in the country and the world; given Assam a legal and medical profession, and schools and colleges; opened new lands; and, to a small extent, improved the technology of agriculture.

To say all this is not to denigrate the role played by some Assamese entrepreneurs, educators, and bureaucrats in the development of the state. But in the main, the Assamese have not produced a class of people capable of producing work for others. Nor have they responded to the pressures of a contracting land-man ratio in agriculture with new agricultural technologies to increase productivity. The emerging middle class continues to remain dependent upon outside private entrepreneurs and central government bureaucrats to generate the productive activities on which to base a modern industrial economy.

Societies based upon status do not readily find a place for people who are not members of the local community. Strangers are more acceptable if they are subordinate to a privileged local class that provides protection in exchange for some required economic services. Just as a society giving importance to skills and a free choice of occupations implies spatial mobility, so does a system of status imply immobility.

In spite of the influx of migrants, the Assamese remain a predominantly nonmobile people in a status-based society. Not only have few Assamese left Assam, but there is remarkably little mobility within Assam itself. According to the 1961 census, only 3.5 percent of the population of Assam lives outside of the district in which it was born, and this figure also includes the non-Assamese-speaking people born in the state.

It is not surprising, then, that the assimilative powers of the Assamese are so limited. So long as the level of modernization among the Assamese remains low, economically successful migrants are likely not to be attracted to a culture practiced by a people largely out of tune with the modern

133

world.[64] There is here an elementary human response of successful people finding it disdainful to assimilate themselves linguistically and culturally to a local people, no matter how numerous, who are economically so unsuccessful and subordinate.

The migrant communities themselves, especially the Bengali Hindus, Marwaris, Punjabis, and Nepalis, believe they have the right to preserve their own cultural heritage wherever they reside, a "right" constitutionally legitimized through the Linguistic Minorities Commission, which has the responsibility of reporting to the president of India any violation of their right to preserve their own language in the school systems. Illiterate, less assured migrants are more likely to assimilate, and this we see among the tribals from Chota Nagpur and, for somewhat different reasons, some of the illiterate Muslim peasant migrants from what is now Bangladesh.

What of the future? Assam's economic growth is inextricably linked to that of India as a whole, but let us consider the social and political consequences of a low-growth (or stationary) economy versus a model of more rapid growth.

If the economy continues to grow at the same low rate as it has in the past few decades (only slightly above the rate of population growth), the unemployment among the Assamese is sure to increase. There may be a substantial expansion of investment in petroleum and natural gas in Assam as world prices of fossil fuels continue to rise, but these are capital-intensive investments not likely to provide substantial employment. And with growing unemployment (especially with a middle class expanding to incorporate the educated sons of the upper peasantry eager to move from agriculture to higher-status nonlaboring salaried occupations), the As-

[64] Among the more exotic sights in Shillong, until recently the capital of Assam, are long-haired Khasi young men playing rock music on electric guitars. For educated migrants, and for many educated natives, Calcutta is the cultural mecca less for its Bengali culture than for its links to the Western world.

samese political leadership is likely to seek political support by attacking the non-Assamese who in an economy of limited growth will be seen as a barrier to Assamese employment. It will also be politically attractive, though economically irrational, to attack alien entrepreneurs for the profits they extract, and in some instances, expatriate to other parts of India, while overlooking the wealth they produce. It may also become increasingly popular to attack the central government for its "neglect" of the region.

Should there be a substantial expansion of investment in Assam, either public or private (more likely the former than the latter), it does not follow that migration will decrease or that employment for the Assamese will substantially increase. To the contrary, new opportunities for employment in Assam, unless matched by rapid economic growth in the nearby states and in Bangladesh, will be a magnet to further migration, leading to increased competition between the Assamese and the migrants. Under such conditions it seems likely that the Assamese political leadership and the middle class from which it comes will press hard for preferential employment, as opposed to open competition, a position likely to generate conflicts between the state and central government over employment policies as well as between the Assamese and the migrants.

Migrant communities, and their descendants, have a limited capacity to fight back. The Marwaris and other business communities may choose to invest elsewhere in India; some migrants, no longer trusting the impartiality of the police, may meet force with force; Bengali Hindus in the Surma valley may press for the secession of Cachar district; Bengali Hindus in the Brahmaputra valley may attempt to build a broader coalition with non-Assamese communities or, if Cachar is removed, become a sullen minority.

The dual economy on which the social structure of Assam is based is no longer acceptable to the Assamese-speaking population; but while the Assamese have the political power to slow, arrest, or even reduce the role played by non-Assa-

135

mese, including those who now consider themselves permanent settlers in the state, they have yet to find a workable economic alternative. The Assamese are presently in a developmental cul-de-sac, in search of a strategy that will ensure them a greater share of the benefits of development than they have thus far received. The educational explosion among the Assamese, paralleling a period of rapid population growth that has substantially increased the number of Assamese joining the labor force each year, has created a new political imperative. But as long as economic growth remains low, protectionist and restrictive policies can provide only short-term benefits to a small number of Assamese, for such policies may slow the flow of investment from the private, and not inconceivably from the public, sector as well.

So long as the Assamese are unable to compete effectively in the employment and investment market against non-Assamese who remain culturally distinct, it seems likely that the Assamese will continue to remain nativists in their politics and protectionist in their policies. Regional antagonisms to the central government, socialist attacks against the alien business community, and aggressive cultural nationalism in relation to linguistic minorities are variant political orientations of a people who suffer from status deprivation, feel culturally threatened, and lack the skills and outlook to compete in the economic marketplace.

APPENDIX:
ESTIMATES OF RELIGIO-LINGUISTIC-TRIBAL COMMUNITIES IN THE BRAHMAPUTRA VALLEY, 1961

Estimates of the distribution of ethnic communities in the Brahmaputra valley of Assam have been made on the basis of the following assumptions and inferences:

1. Had the population of Assamese speakers increased at the same rate as the population of India as a whole from 1891 to 1961 (when population doubled), the 1961 Assamese-speaking population would have been 2,806,000. The

actual increase in the number of speakers of Assamese and other languages was as follows:

	1891	1961
Assamese	1,403,000 (57.3%)	6,730,000 (73.3%)
Indigenous languages other than Assamese	423,000 (17.3%)	680,000 (7.4%)
Migrant languages	624,000 (25.5%)	1,775,000 (19.3%)
	2,450,000	9,185,000

2. Since the actual population of Assamese speakers in 1961 was 6,730,000, there is a "surplus" of 3,924,000.

3. In 1961 the scheduled tribe population of the Brahmaputra valley was 939,000, of whom 680,000 spoke tribal languages indigenous to northeastern India and 259,000 spoke Assamese. This reduces the "surplus" to 3,665,000.

4. If we assume that all but a small fraction of Muslims are of Bengali origin, and that all of these now report Assamese as their language, we can account for another 2.2 million, leaving an unaccounted balance of 1,456,000.

5. This latter figure, therefore, represents the number of non-Bengali migrants and their descendants who now report Assamese as their mother tongue. Between 50 and 75 percent of this number probably are tea plantation and ex-tea plantation workers originating from tribal areas of Bihar and Orissa. In 1961 there were 439,000 tea plantation workers; with families their number exceeds a million, and may be as high as 1.5 million, but the 1961 census reports only 275,000 speakers of tribal languages (plus Oriya) of Bihar and Orissa. Even if we assume that a substantial proportion of Hindi speakers work in the tea plantations, it would appear that considerably more than half of those originating from the tribal areas of Orissa and Bihar report Assamese as their mother tongue.

6. Speakers of Assamese can, on the basis of these assumptions and inferences, be classified as follows:

137

Assamese-speaking Hindus native to Assam	2,806,000	30.5%
Bengali Muslims speaking Assamese	2,200,000	24.0
Migrants and descendants (exclusive of		
Bengali Muslims) speaking Assamese	1,465,000	15.9
Assamese tribals speaking Assamese	259,000	2.8
	6,730,000	73.2%

7. The 1961 census for Assam reports the following speakers of migrant languages in the Brahmaputra valley:

Bengali (probably Hindus)	900,000	9.8%
Hindi	350,000	3.8
Nepali	170,000	1.9
Oriya	133,000	1.4
Santali	65,000	.7
Oraon	42,000	.4
Munda	32,000	.3
Other migrant languages	83,000	.9
	1,775,000	19.4%

8. The 1961 census also reports that the following speak tribal languages indigenous to Assam: 680,000   7.4%

138

Nineteenth Century

Allen, B. C. *Assam District Gazetteers, 1905-1907*. Published in Allahabad and Calcutta.
Vol. IV, *Kamrup*. Allahabad: Pioneer Press, 1905.
Vol. V, *Darrang*. Allahabad: Pioneer Press, 1905.
Vol. VI, *Nowgong*. Calcutta: City Press, 1905.
Vol. VII, *Sibsagar*. Allahabad: Pioneer Press, 1906.

Barooah, Nirode K. *David Scott in North-East India: A Study in British Paternalism*. New Delhi: Munshiram Manoharlal, 1970.

Barpujari, H. K. *Assam: In the Days of the Company 1826-1858*. Gauhati: Lawyer's Book Stall, 1963.

Bhuyan, Suryya Kumar. *Studies in the History of Assam*. Gauhati, 1965.

Bora, Mahendra. *1857 in Assam*. Gauhati: Lawyer's Book Stall. 1957.

Butler, John. *A Sketch of Assam: With Some Account of the Hill Tribes, by an Officer*. London: Smith, Elder, 1847.

Butler, Major John. *Travels and Adventures in the Province of Assam*. London: Smith, Elder and Co., 1855.

Census of India, Assam, 1891. Vol. I: *Report*. Shillong, 1892.

Chatterji, Suniti Kumar. *The Place of Assam in the History and Civilisation of India*. Gauhati: University of Gauhati, 1955.

Cotton, Sir Henry. *Indian and Home Memories*. London, 1911.

Dutta, Kesav Narayan. *A Hand Book to the Old Records of the Assam Secretariat*. Shillong: Government Press, 1959.

Dutta, P. N. *Glimpses into the History of Assam*. Calcutta: Vidyodaya Library, 1964.

Gait, Sir Edward. *History of Assam.* Calcutta, 1906; rev. ed., Calcutta: Thacker and Spink, 1963.

Guha, Amalendu. "Colonisation of Assam: Second Phase (1840-1859)," *Indian Social and Economic History Review*, IV: 4 (December 1967), 289-371.

————. "Colonisation of Assam: Years of Transitional Crisis (1825-1840)," *Indian Economic and Social History Review*, V: 2 (June 1968), 125-148.

————. "A Big Push without a Take-off: A Case Study of Assam (1871-1901)," *Indian Economic and Social History Review*, V: 3 (September 1968), 199-221.

————. "Impact of Bengal Renaissance on Assam (1825-1875)," *Indian Economic and Social History Review*, IX: 3 (1972), 288-304.

Hamilton, Francis. *An Account of Assam.* Gauhati, Department of Historical and Antiquarian Studies, 1963.

Imperial Gazetteer of India Provincial Series: Eastern Bengal and Assam. Calcutta: Superintendent of Government Printing, 1909.

Robinson, William. *A Descriptive Account of Assam: With a Sketch of the Local Geography and a Concise History of the Tea Plant of Assam.* Calcutta: Ostell and Lepage, 1841.

Twentieth Century

GOVERNMENT OF ASSAM PUBLICATIONS (Shillong)

Assam Official Language Act, 1960 (As Amended up to 10th November, 1967), 1967.

Economics and Statistics, Department of.
Assam Through the First Three Five-Year Plans—Selected Economic Indicators, 1970.
Basic Statistics Relating to Assam's Economy, 1950-51 to 1961-62, 1963.
Basic Statistics Relating to Assam's Economy, 1955-56 to 1966-67, 1967.
Census of Assam Government Employees, 1967.
Economic Survey, Assam, 1969.

Estimates of State Income of Assam, 1950-51, 1955-56, and 1960-61 to 1968-69, 1970.

Report on the Sample Survey of Employment and Unemployment in Urban Areas of Assam, 1963.

Representation of Scheduled Caste/Tribe in State Government Services, 1967.

Statistical Abstract of Assam, 1967-68, 1970.

Gazetteer of India, Assam State, Sibsagar District, 1967.

Industrial Policy of the Government of Assam, 1969.

Labour, Department of. *Memorandum of the Government of Assam to the National Commission on Labour*, 1968.

Public Instruction, Director. *Progress of Education in Assam, 1947-65*, 1966.

Statistical Survey of Displaced Persons from East Pakistan in Assam, 1955-56, 1958.

Ali, Abu Nishar Md. Irshad, and Bhagabati, Annada Charan. "Hindu-Muslim Relations in an Assamese Village," *Bulletin of the Department of Anthropology*, I (1972), Gauhati University.

———. "Kinship and Marriage in a Rural Assamese Muslim Community," *The Journal of the Assam Science Society*, XIV (1971).

Assam Sahitya Sabha. *Assam's State Language*. Jorhat, 1960.

Barkataki, S. *Assam*. New Delhi: National Book Trust, 1969.

———. *The Grand Panjandrum*. Calcutta: Modern Book Depot, n.d.

Barthakur, Awani. "Present Political Situation in Assam and Language Disturbances," *Party Life* (monthly journal of the Communist Party of India), VIII: 12 (December 1972).

Barua, Hem. *The Red River and the Blue Hill*. Gauhati: Lawyer's Book Stall, 1962.

Barua, Harendra Nath. *A Glimpse of Assam Disturbances*. Gauhati: Assam State Language Convention, 1960.

Bhandar, Charu Chandra. *Thoughts on Assam Disturbances*. Rajghat, Kashi: A. B. Sarva Seva Sangh Prakashan, 1961.

Census of India

    1951, Assam, Manipur and Tripura. Vol. XII, Part I-A: *Report*. Shillong, 1954.

    1961, Social and Economic Processes in Tea Plantations with Special Reference to Tribal Labourers. Vol. I, Part VII-A, New Delhi, 1970.

    1961, Assam. Vol. VII, Part I-A: *General Report*.

    1971, Assam. Series 3, Part II-A: *General Population Tables*. Shillong, 1972.

Chaliha, B. P. *Infiltration and Deportation of Pakistanis*. Directorate of Information and Public Relations, Government of Assam, 1965.

Das, H. P. *Geography of Assam*. Delhi: National Book Trust, 1970.

Das, J. N. *An Introduction to the Land Laws of Assam*. Gauhati: Lawyer's Book Stall, 1968.

Dutta, K. N. *Landmarks of the Freedom Struggle in Assam*. Gauhati: Lawyer's Book Stall, 1958.

Dutta, Narendra Chandra. *Land Problems and Land Reforms in Assam*. Delhi: S. Chand, 1968.

Education and Youth Services, Ministry of, Government of India. *Educational Statistics District-Wise*. Vol. II: *Assam, 1965-66*. New Delhi, 1970.

Goswami, P. C. *The Economic Development of Assam*. Bombay: Asia Publishing House, 1963.

Goswami, Praphulladatta. *The Springtime Bihu of Assam*. Gauhati: Lawyer's Book Stall, 1966.

Home Affairs, Ministry of, Government of India. *Report on the Commission on the Hill Areas of Assam*. New Delhi, 1966.

Kakati, Satis Chandra, ed. *Discovery of Assam*. Calcutta: A. Guhar, 1964.

National Council of Applied Economic Research. *Industrial Programmes for the Fourth Plan for Assam*. New Delhi: NCAER, 1966.

Politicus. "Demand for a Probe into Assam Riots," *Amrita Bazar Patrika*, August 20, 1960.

Prabhakar, M. S. "Quick End to an Experiment," *Economic and Political Weekly*, December 19, 1970, pp. 199-205.

————. "Assam: Behind the Trouble," *Frontier*, December 9, 1972, pp. 5-7.

————. "Bongal Bogey," *Economic and Political Weekly*, October 21, 1972, pp. 2140-2142.

————. "Cool Behind the Noise and Fury," *Economic and Political Weekly*, Special Number, August 1972, pp. 1485-1488.

————. "East Bengal and Assam," *Frontier*, June 5, 1971, pp. 5-6.

————. "Not to be Deserted," *Economic and Political Weekly*, Annual Number, 1972, pp. 193-199.

Sociology of North Eastern Hill Areas. *Proceedings of the Third Summer School, Kohima* (April 1970). Department of Sociology and Center of Advanced Study in Sociology, University of Delhi, Delhi, 1970.

Spate, O.H.K. *India and Pakistan, A General and Regional Geography*. London: Methuen and Co., 1954. Chapter XX: "The Eastern Borderlands: Assam," pp. 551-562.

West Bengal State Council, Communist Party of India. *Recent Happenings in Assam: Who is Responsible, What is the Remedy*. Calcutta, 1960.

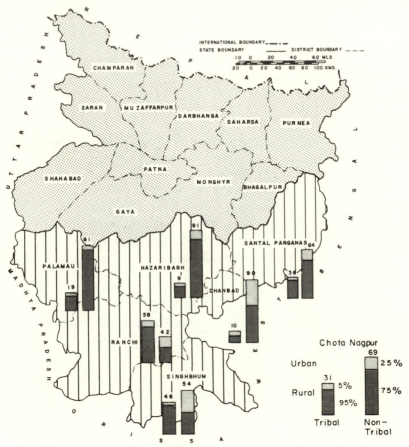

Bihar: Chota Nagpur and Santal Parganas, Tribal and Nontribal Composition, 1971

144

FOUR

TRIBAL ENCOUNTERS:
TRIBALS AND MIGRANTS
IN CHOTA NAGPUR, BIHAR

REGIONAL DEVELOPMENT—SOLUTION OR PROBLEM?[1]

THE textbook solution for regional backwardness is regional development.[2] The development of a backward region's

[1] The field research for this study was made possible through the kind assistance of Professor Amar Kumar Singh of the Department of Psychology and Professor L. P. Vidyarthi of the Department of Anthropology of Ranchi University. I also wish to express my appreciation to Dr. Jyoti Sen of the Anthropological Survey of India, to Reverend Nirmal Minz, principal of the G.E.L. Lutheran College in Ranchi, and to the late Professor Nirmal Kumar Bose, anthropologist, one-time Commissioner of Scheduled Tribes and Castes, a learned and humane scholar with a deep appreciation of the painful dilemmas faced by educated tribals.

For statistical data, reports, interviews, transportation, and hospitality I am grateful to many, including the principal of Tata College in Chaibasa, the Commissioner of Forests in Ranchi, the director and staff of the Bihar Tribal Welfare Research Institute, officials of the Ranchi Employment Exchange and the Government of Bihar Welfare Department, faculty members at St. Xavier's Institute of Social Service, the personnel director of the Heavy Engineering Corporation, faculty members of the A. N. Sinha Institute of Social Sciences in Patna, leaders of the Jharkhand party, the Birsa Seva Dal, the Congress party, the Adimjati Seva Mandal, officials of the Gossner E. L. Church, the Catholic Church, and the Church of India, members of parliament from Bihar and the Bihar state Legislative Assembly and Legislative Council, the superintendent of the Adivasi Hostel in Ranchi, and various faculty members and graduate students of Ranchi University. At M.I.T. I was assisted by John A. Satorius in the analysis of census data and a survey I conducted among tribal students at Ranchi.

[2] For an account of the way in which European governments have promoted development in their own backward regions, see James L.

145

transportation and communication, the establishment of mining and industries, the development of public power and irrigation, the promotion of education, including the development of institutions of higher learning, the expansion of government services in the fields of health, social welfare, and agricultural extension—all of these public and private programs promise to alleviate the distress of a backward region. The results of such efforts, we might anticipate, would be a substantial improvement in the health, education, and employment of the people within the backward region, a decline in outmigration, and a growing self-confidence among the local inhabitants that they, and their region, had at last become part of the national mainstream.

The story of Chota Nagpur, a historically backward region in the southern part of the state of Bihar, suggests that there is a less successful outcome to regional development. Here we have a region in which, in one sense, development was successful. An area of 25,600 square miles and a population in 1971 of eleven million, Chota Nagpur is a plateau, much of it covered by scrub jungle and forest. In large parts of the region the soil is poor, "badly leached and deficient in organic material, nitrogen and lime."[3] For centuries the region was occupied almost exclusively by various tribes—the Munda, Ho, Oraon, and others, subsisting on primitive agriculture, foraging and, in earlier times, on hunting. In the sixteenth century the local raja became a tributary of the Mughal emperor in Delhi. A landlord-peasant system was established, with the Hindu raja and non-

---

Sundquist, *Dispersing Population: What America Can Learn from Europe* (Washington, D.C.: The Brookings Institution, 1975).

[3] O.N.K. Spate, *India and Pakistan: A General and Regional Geography* (London: Methuen, 1954), p. 586. See also Enayat Ahmad, *Bihar: A Physical, Economic and Regional Geography* (Ranchi: Ranchi University, 1965); L. P. Vidyarthi, *Cultural Configuration of Ranchi: Survey of an Emerging Industrial City of Tribal India* (Calcutta: J. N. Basu, 1969); F. Ivern, *Chotanagpur Survey* (New Delhi: Indian Social Institute, 1969).

tribal landlords collecting rent and paying revenue to their Mughal rulers.

In 1765 the region fell under the control of the East India Company, and by the end of the century it was incorporated into the British system of administration, with its courts, police, and revenue administration.

The region continued to remain among the least developed in India until the middle of the nineteenth century. In 1856 coal mining was developed in Dhanbad district, with coal-fields at Jharia, Bokaro, and Karanpura. The British discovered that the region was rich with minerals, and soon thereafter Chota Nagpur became a major producer of minerals—copper, bauxite, limestone, chromite, asbestos, graphite, and especially mica and coal. At Sindri near Dhanbad a state fertilizer factory was developed. And in 1906 a Parsi businessman, Jamshedji Tata, created the Tata Iron and Steel Company (TISCO) at Jamshedpur, which soon became the major producer of iron and steel in the subcontinent.

Alongside the extractive industries grew a manufacturing complex. At Hatia, just outside of Ranchi, the capital city of the region, an industrial complex was developed after independence with the creation of the public-sector Heavy Engineering Corporation (H.E.C.), assisted by the Czech government. Colleges multiplied and the University of Ranchi was opened, soon to become one of India's major educational centers. Government services also expanded: there were block development officers concerned with rural development, and a variety of extension officials from the ministries of agriculture, irrigation, forestry, and health.

Small towns grew into medium-size cities. By 1971, 19 percent of the population lived in urban areas, half of whom lived in four major urban agglomerations: Jamshedpur with 456,000, Dhanbad with 434,000, Ranchi with 255,000, and Bokaro with 107,000.

Today, Chota Nagpur is no longer a remote region. Busses, trains, and a daily air service link Ranchi and Jamshedpur to Calcutta and Patna. Its educational institutions, especially

147

Ranchi University, serve the entire state. The trade unions at Jamshedpur, the Lions Club in Ranchi, and Tata College in Chaibasa are all part of a network linking Chota Nagpur to the rest of India.

But in one critical respect regional development was unsuccessful: there were comparatively few benefits for the indigenous tribal population. Only a small number of tribals found employment in industry.[4] The improvement of agriculture was accompanied by what a government report referred to as the "usurpation" of land by outsiders.[5] Local services by government increased, but few tribals were em-

[4] Precise data on tribal employment are not available, but it is generally agreed that relatively few Munda, Ho, and Oraon tribespeople were employed by industry, while many Santals from nearby Santal Parganas did substantially better in industrial employment. In a study of the Heavy Engineering Corporation (L. P. Vidyarthi, *Industrialization in India: A Case Study of Tribal Bihar* [Ranchi: Department of Anthropology, Ranchi University, 1970]), it was found that in one plant only 335 workers out of 4,284 were tribal (p. 59). Vidyarthi reported that workers "even for unskilled jobs were recruited from outside." Migrants came from Bihar, Uttar Pradesh, and West Bengal. Vidyarthi reports that in 1961 there were 32,550 migrants in the Hatia region, and that the bulk of the tribals in the region—a locality that was predominantly tribal at one time—had moved elsewhere. Ironically, writes Vidyarthi, one reason for choosing the site "was the question of development of an underdeveloped tribal area and of providing opportunities for employment and for improving their standard of living" (p. 31).

For a contrasting account of the Santal experience with industrialization and urbanization, see Martin Orans, "A Tribal People in an Industrial Setting," in Milton Singer, ed., *Traditional India: Structure and Change* (Publication of the American Folklore Society, Bibliographical Series, Vol. x, Philadelphia, 1959); and Martin Orans, *The Santal: A Tribe in Search of a Great Tradition* (Detroit: Wayne University Press, 1965).

[5] "A high-level study team of the Union Home Ministry, which recently toured the tribal belt of Chota Nagpur and Santal Parganas in Bihar, has come to the conclusion that large-scale usurpation of the Adivasi (tribal) land and the nonavailability of any dependable means of livelihood have contributed to the growing unrest among the tribals in this region," reports the *Overseas Hindustan Times,* New Delhi, January 5, 1975 ("Unrest among Tribals," p. 10).

ployed by the expanding bureaucracy. The colleges and university grew, but few local tribal students attended.

It was migrants, not the local people, who primarily gained from the development of the Chota Nagpur region. Migrants from north Bihar and Bengal entered the colleges and university; migrants occupied most of the positions in the state and administrative services; migrants acquired most of the skilled positions created in the new mining, industrial, and commercial activities.

As the region itself prospered, a large number of tribals actually left. Starting in the middle of the nineteenth century, and accelerating later, thousands of tribals emigrated to the tea plantations of northern Bengal and Assam, where they found employment as tea pickers, and took jobs as far away as the Andaman Islands. With the emigration of tribals and the immigration of nontribals to Chota Nagpur, the indigenous population grew smaller. By 1971, Chota Nagpur—once, as far as we know, almost wholly tribal—was now only 32.2 percent tribal. (The figure was 33.9 percent in 1961.)

The indigenous tribal population had clearly failed to reap the benefits of regional development. Most remained outside the growing urban, industrial sector, and disproportionately outside the system of education. They were unable to compete with the migrants for jobs in either industry or government, for admission into colleges, and even for the use and control over their own land.

THE PROBLEM AND THE ARGUMENT

There are innumerable possible explanations as to why some social-cultural groups have been unsuccessful in the competition for education, employment, land, and income. Some will point to the way in which one people oppresses another: one group, with more wealth and political power than another uses its position to prevent others from sharing the wealth or power. Others will offer a "human capital" explanation, which emphasizes the lack of education and

149

skills by one group in relation to another—the results, perhaps, of unequal attention by government or some historic circumstances that gave one group a head start over the other. Still others prefer cultural and psychological explanations: it is not skills, but motivations, attitudes toward work and savings, a lack of innovativeness, the desire to achieve, the willingness to take risks, organizational abilities, or some other qualities deemed necessary for effective competition in today's universities and job market.

All of these are plausible explanations for why the tribals of Chota Nagpur were so much less able than the migrants to take advantage of the region's development. But why the tribals actually failed, if in fact we can ever really know, tells us less about tribal reactions to migrants than does an analysis of what explanations tribals themselves give for their failures. It is their perception of their relationship to outsiders that shapes their politics, provides them with an understanding of why they are in the position they are in, and how it might be remedied.

While the encounter between the tribals and nontribal migrants dates at least from the Mughal period, it has been primarily in the past century and a half, from the time the British took power, through several decades of independence, that these encounters have grown. The tribals have by no means been passive in their relationship to nontribals.[6] There have been millenarian and messianic movements, tribal secessionists groups, regionalists, and radicals. Some tribals have

[6] Christoph von Furer-Haimendorf, a British anthropologist specializing in India's tribes, however, noted that "anyone with first hand experience of conditions in areas where aboriginals are subject to exploitation by more advanced populations must be surprised not by the occurrence of uprisings, but rather by the infrequency of violent action on the part of aboriginals deprived of the ancestral lands and the freedom they enjoyed before their contact with populations superior in economic and political power." (Foreword to Suresh Singh, *The Dust-Storm and The Hanging Mist: Story of Birsa Munda and His Movement in Chotanagpur* [Calcutta: K. L. Mukhopadhyaya, 1966], pp. ix-x.)

been pro-British. Others have been pro-Hindu supporters of Jana Sangh, a right-wing party, or have supported the governing Congress party. Still others have supported wholly tribal parties, including the secessionist Jharkhand party and the more radical, youth-oriented Birsa Seva Dal. Each political movement, each political party, each tribal leader and political activist has sought to come to grips with the questions of who a tribal is, why the tribals are backward, and how they can move ahead more rapidly.

These are the themes we shall explore in this chapter. First we turn to a brief account, partly demographic, partly historical, partly ethnographic, of who the tribals are. This is followed by an examination of the relationship of the tribals to the land; the emergence of a small number of educated urbanized tribals with their own perspective of how tribals can relate to the nontribal world; and the schisms among the tribals, especially between the Christian converts and the nonconverted, and how the religious encounters of each, one with the Europeans, the other with their Hindu neighbors, shaped their conception of the problem. Finally, we shall suggest, by way of conclusion, how these different responses to the encounter between tribals and nontribals have led to radically different views of what kinds of politics the tribals ought to pursue to erase both their economic backwardness and their socially low status.

WHO ARE THE TRIBALS?

India's tribals are believed by ethnologists and classicists to be the descendants of the subcontinent's original population —the most authentic, if you will, of the sons of the soil. According to one widely regarded theory, the caste system was a device by which the Indo-Aryans, who migrated into northern India from their homeland somewhere in central Asia around 1500 BC, absorbed diverse indigenous tribes by converting them into castes and by borrowing many of their religious rituals and beliefs, incorporating these into Hinduism.[7]

Not all of the indigenous tribes were absorbed by the Indo-Aryans, by their descendants, or by the many subsequent invaders of the subcontinent. Some tribes moved into the hill regions and forest tracts of middle India, particularly around the Vindhya mountain range, away from the agriculturally more fertile lands of the river valleys that had been settled by the variety of invaders that came across the Hindu Kush mountains in the northwest into northern India.

Today there are several hundred tribes in India, totaling, in 1971, thirty-eight million, and concentrated in three major zones: the northeast, including Assam, Meghalaya, Arunachal Pradesh, Nagaland, and Mizoram; a zone in India's west, including parts of eastern Gujarat, western Madhya Pradesh, and southern Rajasthan; and a belt of middle India that includes southern Bihar, the hill areas of inland Orissa, southeastern Madhya Pradesh, and a portion of northern India. There is also a small tribal area in Himachal Pradesh in northern India, and another in and around the Nilgiri hills in south India.

Half the tribals belong to six large tribes—Gond, Bhil, Santal, Oraon, Mina, and Munda. About a tenth of India's tribals, 3.4 million, reside in Chota Nagpur, and another 1,154,000 in nearby Santal Parganas (1971 figures; see Table 4.1).

The largest tribes in Chota Nagpur are the Mundas, Oraons, and the Hos. The Oraon are the most numerous, numbering (in 1961) 735,000; the Mundas follow, with 628,000; and the Ho, to whom they are linguistically closely related, number 454,000. Three other tribes each numbered around 100,000—the Bhumij, the Kharia, and the Kharwar. The tribes are predominantly rural: in 1961 only 97,000 tribespeople, or 3.3 percent of the tribal population,

[7] Nirmal Kumar Bose, "The Hindu Method of Tribal Absorption," *Cultural Anthropology and Other Essays* (Calcutta: Indian Associated Publishing Co., 1953).

TABLE 4.1

Tribal and Nontribal Population,
Chota Nagpur (1971)

(THOUSANDS)

		Population	Tribal population	Nontribal population	Percent tribal
Palamau	Total	1,504	287	1,217	19.1
	Rural	1,433	283	1,150	19.7
	Urban	70	3	67	4.3
Hazaribagh	Total	3,020	331	2,689	9.0
	Rural	2,631	311	2,320	8.8
	Urban	388	20	368	5.1
Ranchi	Total	2,611	1,516	1,095	58.0
	Rural	2,254	1,451	803	64.4
	Urban	356	65	291	18.2
Dhanbad	Total	1,466	155	1,311	10.6
	Rural	828	127	701	15.3
	Urban	638	28	610	4.4
Singhbhum	Total	2,437	1,124	1,313	46.0
	Rural	1,798	1,050	748	58.6
	Urban	639	73	566	1.1
Chota Nagpur	Total	11,038	3,413	7,625	31.0
	Rural	8,944	3,222	5,722	36.0
	Urban	2,091	189	1,902	9.0

lived in towns; in 1971 it rose substantially to 189,000, or 5.5 percent of the population. By way of contrast, 25 percent of the nontribal population of Chota Nagpur resides in urban areas.

Most of the Oraons and Mundas live in Ranchi district, one of the five districts of the Chota Nagpur region. In 1971, 58 percent of Ranchi district (1.5 million out of 2.6 million)

153

was tribal. The city of Ranchi is the region's largest town, a fast-growing center that serves as the summer capital of the entire state. Hindustan Steel, India's nationalized steel corporation, has its headquarters there, and in the town are Ranchi University, several colleges, a number of church missions, a major hospital, and a well-known mental institution. Nearby, in the suburb of Hatia, is the factory complex of the Heavy Engineering Corporation.

South of Ranchi is Singbhum district, where the Hos live. Nearly half the population (46 percent) is tribal, 1.1 million out of 2.4 million. The district, with its primal forests and attractive hills, contains some of India's largest iron ore deposits. Within it is the major industrial steel city of Jamshedpur.

To the north of Ranchi is Dhanbad district, where the tribals constitute only 10.6 percent of the population (155,-000 out of 1.4 million), but the proportion that is urbanized (nearly a fifth) is larger than elsewhere in the region. Dhanbad contains some of India's largest coal deposits, and a considerable number of tribals work in its recently nationalized coal mines.

Bordering the five districts of Chota Nagpur, and often considered part of the region, is the district of Santal Parganas, with the large Santal tribe. There are 3.7 million Santals in India—they are India's largest single tribe—of whom about 1.1 million live in Santal Parganas; many of the Santals work in the steel mills at Jamshedpur, in the coal mines in Dhanbad, and outside the region.

Although indigenous to India, the Ho, Munda, and Oraon tribes, ironically, are not indigenous to Chota Nagpur. Of the three tribes, the Mundas were the earliest settlers in the region. What we know of their early history is largely derived from Vedic and Puranic texts written by invaders. They apparently retreated into the hill and forest tracts of Chota Nagpur from elsewhere in northern India. They were soon joined by the Ho, a sister tribe of the same linguistic family (generally referred to by linguists as the Austric family).

154

The Oraons came later. They are presumed to have migrated to the region from the south, for their language belongs to the Dravidian family, the indigenous language group of south India.[8]

The tribes of Chota Nagpur were much influenced by Hinduism. In the 1961 census nearly two-thirds of the tribals (64 percent) reported their religion as Hinduism,[9] though it is often a Hinduism far removed from that of their Bihari Hindu neighbors. Some observers question whether the Ho, Munda, Oraon, and other tribals in the region should be called tribal at all. They do not have the intense tribal spirit, tribal political organization, or distinctive cultural traits of the tribals of India's northeast. Some of the tribals of Chota Nagpur no longer speak their native language, but speak Hindi or Sadani, a dialect of Hindi widely used in southern Bihar (and reported as the mother tongue by 800,000 persons). They no longer engage in slash-and-burn agriculture and other practices of shifting cultivation; like their non-tribal Hindu neighbors, most of the tribals live as peasants, cultivating grain crops.

But everyone in Chota Nagpur can recognize a tribal. A distinctive racial type, known by physical anthropologists as belonging to the proto-Austroloid stock, they are somewhat darker than other Indians and have features that are sometimes Mongoloid in appearance. They live in their own

[8] The two classic accounts of the early history and ethnography of the Oraons and the Mundas are Sarat Chandra Roy, *The Mundas and Their Country* (Bombay: Asia Publishing House, 1970; original edition, 1912); and Sarat Chandra Roy, *The Oraons of Chotanagpur* (Calcutta: Brahmo Mission Press, 1915). A particularly good recent account of the Oraons is R. O. Dhan, *These Are My Tribesmen* (Ranchi: G.E.L. Church Press, 1967).

[9] According to the 1961 census, 14.3 percent of the tribals were Christian and 21.5 percent reported themselves as subscribing to a tribal religion. The 1971 census indicated a marked growth in the number of tribals who reported a tribal religion, from 626,000 in 1961 to 882,000 in 1971, an increase of 41.5 percent, as against an increase of only 5 percent of those tribals reporting their religion as Hindu.

155

villages, many of which are almost wholly homogeneous except for a handful of nontribal landowners, shopkeepers, or moneylenders. Like the nontribal peasantry, they are rice producers, but many continue to earn all or part of their income from forest products—by producing rope from bark, manufacturing wooden farm implements, selling wood for fuel, collecting various herbs and roots for medicinal purposes, producing a kind of plate from leaves, and other indigenous and ingenious ways of making use of forest produce.

While Hindu deities find a place in the religious pantheon of the tribals, the tribals continue to adhere to their own animistic creed known by a variety of names, but generically known as *Sarna*, or the religion of the sacred grove. Many villages do have a sacred grove, a forest of trees by the side of the village, in which religious ceremonies, weddings, and other tribal festivities take place.

But perhaps the most distinctive feature of tribal life is the very attitude toward life itself. In contrast with their Hindu neighbors, the tribals are a carefree people, hedonistic in their desire for simple pleasures. They enjoy their drink—a fermented and in some instances distilled drink from rice—which some take daily, often in noticeably large quantities, which incapacitates. Dancing is a regular part of their ordinary social life, and there is a freedom of social intercourse between tribal boys and girls that is viewed with some reprehension by the puritanical Hindus. Marriages are arranged, as with other Indians, by parents, but "abductions" are not infrequent. Although most tribals are too poor to eat fish, fowl, and meat (including beef), when they do it is without the sense of ritual contamination that so many Hindus experience when eating nonvegetarian food. All in all, the tribals have a distinctive style of life that at times appears more akin to practices familiar to the westerner than to the Hindu—one reason, perhaps, why British, German, and American missionaries found it so congenial to work among the tribals.

156

How the Tribals Lost Their Lands

"All our problems," summed up a tribal member of the Bihar Legislative Assembly and a lawyer by training, "come from colonization." But by colonization he didn't mean just British rule. "The British were here for a hundred and eighty years, before them Muslims for seven hundred years, and before them the Hindus for a thousand years. Before the Hindus, the tribals lived here alone. The lands, the best lands, were taken from the tribals by these invaders, taken by fraudulent means so that the tribals are now more or less slaves.

"When a tribal sees that he does not have the best lands," he continued, "he knows that someone exploited his father or his grandfather. He wants to take revenge. He commits a murder in public before witnesses, and then he tells the truth to the judge. I drank a lot, he says to the judge, and then went to the market where I saw this man who took my father's land, so I hit him with a lathi [stick] and killed him.

"The rise and fall of the *adivasis*"—he used the word Gandhi gave to the tribals, meaning original people—"depends on their land. If you take away their land they are like fish out of water. They do not want any other vocation in life. It used to be that half the land here was owned by the tribals as recently as the 1930s. Now, I think, it is only 25 percent. The tribals lost their lands to the new industries, especially to the Heavy Engineering Corporation. And then all the people who moved here took land from the tribals. Yes, the tribals were paid compensation, but what do they know about what to do with money? A Muslim or a Gujarati would know what to do with money, but tribals don't. So now the tribals have only the worst lands left, the waste lands that other people don't want."

The loss of land is a recurrent complaint of the tribals, echoed in all government reports. It purports to explain a great deal: the impoverishment of the tribes, the low regard

157

in which they are held by many Hindus, and the loss of self-esteem among the tribals. I took a closer look at the land problem, therefore, to see how and why it arose, how much of a problem it really was, and whether it explained as much as was supposed.

The "loss" of ancestral lands is generally assumed to have begun in the seventeenth century, that is, before the British settled in Chota Nagpur. The region was then governed by the maharaja of Chota Nagpur, a tribal who is believed to have descended from a *manki*, which means chief, or *raja*, as he was later called in Hindi terminology. According to legend, the first *manki*, was chosen in the sixth century by the chiefs of the Munda tribes to be their leader. Early in the seventeenth century, however, the maharaja, who then had a feudatory relationship with the Mughal emperor in Delhi, to whom he paid tribute, fell under Hindu influence. He formed an alliance with Rajput families in neighboring regions, and invited a number of Rajputs and Brahmans, mainly from Orissa, to settle in Chota Nagpur to serve in his wars against neighboring states. In return for services, the Brahmans and Rajputs were awarded grants of land or villages—not as cultivators but as rent collectors. Rent collecting worked like an elaborate marketing system. Each middle man took a share of the profits. The tribal peasant cultivated the soil and paid rent to the nontribal landlords, who paid a share to the maharaja of Chota Nagpur, who in turn paid a share to the Mughal ruler.

The East India Company initially superimposed its rule over the maharaja in much the same way as the Mughals. But in Chota Nagpur, as elsewhere, the British were concerned with establishing a legal and administrative structure that would assure them a stable system of revenue collection and provide a framework of order within which they could conduct their economic affairs. By the beginning of the nineteenth century a four-tiered system of administration had developed. At the top was the East India Company, followed by the maharaja of Chota Nagpur, then a number of local

158

rajas, mainly nontribal, who were subservient to the maharaja, and finally intermediary rent collectors appointed by the rajas, knows as *thikadars*. The *thikadars* actually collected rent directly from the peasants and were called *diku*, which means *foreigner* in the Munda language. There is also a word *dik* in Hindi, meaning a pain, to which some tribals attribute the word *diku*, capturing the double entendre of the term.[10]

How many nontribals actually lived in Chota Nagpur in the early nineteenth century is not known, and how much of the land they controlled is also uncertain. It seems evident, however, that even prior to the establishment of British rule, the tribal land system had been converted into a landlord-peasant system with a nontribal Hindu landlord class. The British passed the Chota Nagpur Tenancy Act in 1908 in an effort to arrest the alienation of tribal land. Its elaborate provisions specified the limited conditions under which tribals could sell land to nontribals or use land as collateral for loans.

While it is generally argued that the act slowed the pace of land alienation, reports by government and private scholars have pointed to continued violations of the law and the many loopholes that permitted the transfer of land from tribals to nontribals. A familiar story, one as common in Chota Nagpur as around the American Indian reservations of Oklahoma and New Mexico, is that nontribals provided tribals with liquor, persuaded them to sign documents showing that the land had been given as collateral for loans more than twelve years earlier and not repaid—which constituted grounds for the transfer of ownership under the act. But

[10] See S. C. Sinha, Jyoti Sen, and Sudhir Panchbhai, "The Concept of Diku among the Tribals of Chotanagpur," *Man in India*, 49:2 (April-June 1969), 121-138. The term *diku* is also used to characterize a tribal who has collaborated with outsiders to exploit tribals. And by extension, the word is also used to describe tribals who have taken on the undesirable qualities of nontribals, as in the following: "Tribals usually say what they mean. Now some tribals say things they do not believe. They are becoming dikuized."

precisely how much such illegal transferring took place is, of course, not known.

Tribal Emigration[11]

The growth of land alienation, the establishment of rent and moneylending that called for cash income, and the gradual increase of the tribal population as the death rate declined, led to the emergence by the second half of the nineteenth century of a pool of surplus agricultural laborers.

In the middle of the nineteenth century the British were looking for a labor force they could recruit to work on their plantations in Assam and Bengal as tea pickers. The tribals of Chota Nagpur were attractive recruits: they were "surplus," that is, they were in need of work; they were accustomed to hard labor; they were acclimated to the hill areas; and the distances, though substantial, could be traversed by railroad and steamer. British recruitment in the Chota Nagpur region began in the middle of the century, chiefly among the Santals and the Mundas. The Santals emigrated from Santal Parganas and Manbhum and the Mundas from Ranchi and Hazaribagh. By 1891 there were 190,000 tribals in the tea areas of Assam, and nearly 70,000 in Bengal. The emigration continued to rise steeply in the early decades of the twentieth century (see Table 4.2). Many went to the tea plantation areas of Assam and north Bengal, others settled as agricultural laborers in the Sundarban region, a delta

[11] Wolf Mersch, *Migration and Labour Recruitment for Coal Mines and Tea Plantations under Colonial Rule: The Case of Manbhum in Chota Nagpur, India 1881-1921* (manuscript, South Asia Institute, University of Heidelberg, May 1972); L. P. Vidyarthi, "The Ranchi Tribals in Andaman and Nicobar Islands," *Journal of Social Research*, 14:2 (1971), 50-59; Michael Van Den Bogaert, *The Influence of Caste, Education and Geographic Mobility on Labour Mobility at Jamshedpur, India* (Antwerp: Centre for Development Studies, Universitaire Faculteiten St. Ignatius, Universiteit Antwerpen, 1975); Hugh Tinker, *A New System of Slavery: The Export of Indian Labour Overseas 1830-1920* (London: Oxford University Press, 1974).

TABLE 4.2

Immigration and Emigration,
Chota Nagpur and Santal Parganas (1891-1961)[a]

	Immigration	Emigration
1891	96,000	333,000
1901	179,000	282,000[b]
1911	293,000	707,000
1921	307,000	947,000[c]
1931	307,000	NA
1941	NA	NA
1951	480,000	NA
1961	935,600	NA

[a] Based on place of birth data as reported in the decennial censuses.
[b] To Assam only. This can be compared with 190,000 in Assam in 1891.
[c] To Bengal and Assam only.

area in southern Bengal, and some found jobs as unskilled laborers in the industrial towns of Bengal.

Migration slowed after 1921, and declined sharply with the depression in the tea industry after 1931. In 1961, only 195,000 persons in Assam spoke a tribal language of Chota Nagpur, but this low number probably reflects linguistic assimilation rather than return migration. In 1961, there were 439,000 tea plantation workers in Assam. Inclusive of dependents, they numbered about a million or more. There are also several hundred thousand former tea plantation workers now engaged in cultivation, almost all tribals from Chota Nagpur or from the neighboring states of Orissa and Madhya Pradesh.

If we take 1921 as the peak year of emigration, when slightly under a million tribals were living in Bengal, Assam, and other parts of India, and when the tribal population of Chota Nagpur was approximately three million, we can estimate that nearly a third of the tribal population had emigrated. Or, to put the magnitudes another way, had there been no outmigration of tribals, the tribal population of Chota Nagpur and Santal Parganas in 1971, taking into account natural population increases, would have been about six million instead of four and a half.

Actually, it is likely that the long-term demographic effects have been even greater than the numbers indicate, since the migrants were young tribals of child-bearing age whose fertility would most probably have been higher than those who did not migrate. A striking feature of the migration streams from Chota Nagpur to both Bengal and Assam was the fairly even sex ratio, an indication that whole families migrated, and that the migrations were permanent rather than seasonal or short-term. There is, moreover, no evidence of any substantial return migration by either the original migrants or by second and succeeding generations.

Tribal Protest: Exit and Voice

This outpouring of tribals from Chota Nagpur in search of employment is generally pointed to as one indication of the severity of the land problem in Chota Nagpur. A second indicator is the growth of tribal protest. It has been suggested that outmigration is a political safety valve, that is, that a discontented people protest with their feet as well as with guns and bullets.[12] There is some plausibility to the argument in the case of Chota Nagpur. Throughout the nineteenth century, before large-scale outmigrations took place, there were frequent tribal agitations, many quite violent. There was the Kol insurrection in the beginning of the nineteenth century, when *diku thikadars* under attack were defended by the British administration and troops of the East India Company; there was the revolt of 1857, part of an all-India "mutiny" against the British, but which in Chota Nagpur was also directed at the landlords; there was an anti-*diku* agitation in

[12] Albert O. Hirschman, *Exit, Voice and Loyalty: Responses to Decline in Firms, Organizations, and State* (Cambridge: Harvard University Press, 1970).

162

the 1880s known as the Sardar movement, and perhaps the most famous and severe of all, the Birsa Munda uprising of 1899-1900.

The famous Birsa Munda rebellion of 1899[13] persuaded the British that the land problem of the tribals needed the attention of the government. At that time, a young man by the name of Birsa Munda, educated in a Christian missionary school, reportedly had visions of speaking with God. Deeply influenced by a Brahman pandit in a nearby village, then by a Vaishnava "saint," and then by his sojourn in a mission school in Chaibasa, Birsa became a critic of tribal customs and beliefs; he became a reformist preacher, calling upon the Mundas to "uproot" superstition, give up animal sacrifice, cease taking intoxicants, wear the sacred thread, but retain the tribal traditions of worshiping in the *sarna* or sacred grove of the village, not in the temples. A clash between Birsa and his supporters and the police at a time of growing agrarian unrest led to his arrest, trial, and imprisonment for two and a half years. Birsa subsequently organized a movement calling for open rebellion against the British and against nontribal landowners; bows, arrows, and swords were collected and recruits trained. On Christmas day in 1899 Birsa's forces attacked a mission house. In a battle between Birsa's forces and the police a number of policemen were killed, and the deputy commissioner sent government forces to break the rebellion. Hundreds were killed, the bows and

[13] For accounts of the Birsa movement see Suresh Singh, *The Dust-Storm and the Hanging Mist*; Surendra Prasad Sinha, *Life and Times of Birsa Bhagwan* (Ranchi: Bihar Tribal Research Institute, 1964); Stephen Fuchs, *Rebellious Prophets: A Study of Messianic Movements in Indian Religions* (Bombay: Asia Publishing House, 1965), Chapter 2, "Messianic Movements in Bihar," pp. 21-72; Sachchidananda, *Profiles of Tribal Culture in Bihar* (Calcutta: K. L. Mukhopadhyay, 1965). Earlier movements are described by John Douglas MacDougall, "Agrarian Reform vs. Religious Revitalization: The Sardar and Kherwar Movements among the Tribals of Bihar, India, 1858-1895" (Ph.D. dissertation, Harvard University, 1974).

arrows proving inadequate to meet the arms of the police. Birsa himself was captured, imprisoned in the Ranchi jail, and subsequently died there of cholera.

Birsa was a reformist and a revivalist. He believed that "the ideal order . . . would witness the liquidation of the racial enemies, the Dikus, European missionaries and officials and native Christians. The Mundas would recover their 'lost kingdom.' There will be enough to eat, no famine; the people will live together and in love."[14] The Birsa rebellion, like those that preceded it, was closely linked to alienation of land. "To them," wrote Suresh Singh in his account of the movement, "the land was not an arithmetic of a few acres, it was a part of their socio-cultural heritage: it contained the burial ground of their ancestors with whom they would be united after their death and the sacrificial grave where they propitiated their spirits. The emotional ties with their lands having gone, they were, to quote an anonymous Munda folk poet, 'adrift,' 'afloat like a tortoise.' "[15]

Birsa promised the Mundas as a solution to the agrarian problem the ejection of the foreigners and the establishment of "Birsaite Raj," with himself as the "New King." "He preached, healed, performed miracles and prophesied. The prophetic elements in his religion were obviously accentuated by the Christian influence. His fiery exhortations, warnings of the storm and the deluge, promise of advent and resurrection, his last outbursts in the jail were utterances saturated with earnestness, cast in the letters of fire."[16]

With his death, the Birsa movement dissipated, but Birsa himself became a folk hero. The movement was in any event never large, but the agrarian revolt was an important element in subsequent British efforts to halt, or at least slow, the loss of tribal land to nontribals.

After 1900, and until the early 1930s, political protest in Chota Nagpur subsided. One important exception, however,

[14] Suresh Singh, *Dust-Storm and Hanging Mist*, p. 193.
[15] *Ibid.*, p. 190.　　　　　　　　　　[16] *Ibid.*, p. 200.

was the Tana Bhagat movement among the Oraons from 1915 to the 1920s, another revivalist movement that launched a no-rent agitation against the *diku* landowners, and that associated itself with the Indian National Congress.[17] During this period, no comparable protest movement arose among the Mundas or among the Santals—the tribes, incidentally, with the largest outmigration. Moreover, while it is hard to measure the amount of participation in one movement as against another, the Tana Bhagat movement seems to have been less pervasive and certainly less violent than the political agitations of the mid and late nineteenth century.

Although it is by no means clear that emigration was a substitute for protest—the tribals did both—for several decades when emigration was at its highest, political protest did appear to diminish. And in the 1930s, when as a result of the world-wide depression and the decline in the tea market, emigration from Chota Nagpur to Assam and Bengal drastically declined, protest among the tribals again resumed, this time with the formation of the Jharkhand party.

Tribal leaders point out that in recent years industrialization has accelerated the loss of land by tribals. With the establishment of the industrial complex at Hatia large tracts of tribal land were acquired by the Heavy Engineering Corporation. Moreover, the towns of Ranchi, Jamshedpur, Singhbhum, and Dhanbad have all physically expanded into the surrounding countryside, on to land previously owned by tribals. There has been an extensive loss of land through sales by tribals to nontribals not only for business purposes, but for the erection of residential dwellings. By 1961 there were already more than a half million migrants in Dhanbad and Singhbhum districts alone (see Table 4.3). In the past

[17] For a short account of messianic and millenarian movements in the region, see Philip Ekka, "Revivalist Movements among the Tribals of Chota Nagpur," in K. Suresh Singh, ed., *Tribal Situations in India* (Simla: Indian Institute of Advanced Study, 1972), pp. 424-434.

TABLE 4.3

Migrants in Chota Nagpur and Santal Parganas (1961)

District	Population	Place of birth					Total migrants
		Bengal	Bihar	Orissa	East Pakistan	Other	
Dhanbad	1,158,000	68,000	139,000	2,900	10,500	66,000	286,400
Singhbhum	2,049,000	52,000	50,000	47,000	20,000	86,000	255,000
Ranchi	2,138,000	17,500	29,800	6,000	5,000	30,000	88,300
Santal Parganas	2,675,000	46,000	74,700	300	6,500	6,000	133,500
Hazaribagh	2,396,000	16,500	60,000	1,600	3,800	35,000	116,900
Palamau	1,187,000	1,000	42,000	—	500	12,000	55,500
Total	11,606,000	201,000	395,500	57,800	46,300	235,000	935,600

decade Jamshedpur has grown by 42 percent, Ranchi by 82 percent, and Dhanbad by 116 percent, and each has physically encroached upon the countryside.[18]

Wherever government has acquired land for industrial development, or individuals have acquired tribal land for residential construction, tribals have been compensated at market rates. But from the point of view of tribal leaders, no compensation, no matter how large, is adequate for the loss of land. "The tribals" explained one of the tribal representatives in the state assembly, "can only be agriculturists. They cannot work in industry. Agriculture is in their blood. They love to be surrounded by their animals and they are happy only when they are in the countryside. They are not very bright. They have limited intelligence so they cannot do well in school. There are a few exceptions but generally the tribals lack the natural aptitude for studies. If you want to improve their lot, then give them water, a tractor, good seeds. They must have their land. If they do not, then they will become extinct like the American Indians. That is why we are fighting against this colonization policy."

Notes from a Tour of Tribal Chota Nagpur

In an effort to gain a first-hand picture of the land situation in Chota Nagpur, I toured a number of tribal villages and talked to villagers about how much land they had, who else owned land, and what kind of jobs (with how much income) they held. I visited some of the Ho villages around the district town of Chaibasa in Singhbhum district, and some of the Munda and Oraon villages not too far from Ranchi town. In each of these tours I was accompanied by a tribal

[18] An account of this loss of land is provided by S. P. Sinha, *The Problem of Land Alienation of the Tribals in and around Ranchi (1955-1965)* (Ranchi: Bihar Tribal Welfare Research Institute, 1968, Studies in Tribal Bihar, No. 2); see also Sarat Chandra Roy, "The Administrative History and Land Tenures of the Ranchi District under British Rule," *Man in India*, 41:4 (October-December 1961), 276-323.

student from the Anthropology Department of Ranchi University who served as my guide, and, when need be, my interpreter, though most of the tribals could converse with me in my bazar Hindi. In this brief tour I chatted with dozens of villagers asking, in each instance, simple questions that would help me understand what the relationship was between tribals and *dikus* in a rural setting. The tribals were cordial and surprisingly unperturbed by a questioning foreigner.

I learned a great deal walking through the villages and attending markets, for one can readily see who is a tribal and who is not, who dresses well and lives in large houses, and who owns land and who does not.

The villages were small and, as is common in most of India, the houses were clustered together, surrounded by fields. In the Oraon villages paddy was cultivated. Holdings were small, sometimes only an acre or two, even less. No more than a few tribals I met owned four or five acres. Most of their land depended on annual rainfall, for there was little irrigation, although I saw a few newly dug wells.

Only a few of the tribals are able to grow more than a single crop. After the harvest in December many of the Oraons leave their villages to find seasonal work in the towns. Contract men (*sardars*) from Calcutta recruit some of the young Oraon boys and girls, pay their transportation, and provide them with accommodations in Calcutta. There they are paid four or five rupees a day as brick carriers or stone and brick breakers on construction projects. Some of the Oraons are gone almost all year, returning only for a few months during the harvest season to help their parents and brothers who continue to cultivate the family's small holdings. In several villages I was also told that one or two Oraons had left to join the army, and in two of the villages I encountered ex-soldiers.

The Oraon village leaders complained that the best lands in their villages were owned by *dikus*, and this appeared to be the case in the villages I visited. But the landholdings of

168

the *dikus* were not exorbitantly large. A few *dikus*—all of whom were Bihari Hindus—owned as much as fifty acres of land, but others had only ten or fifteen acres. Those I spoke to had been there for several generations. One Bihari explained that his family was given land by the raja of Chota Nagpur in return for serving as revenue agents. Another Bihari landlord explained that his great-grandfather had worked for the British administration in Chota Nagpur and had purchased land in this village near Ranchi, which he now owned.

The tribals invariably complained that they were exploited by the Bihari landlords. The Biharis, they said, paid only Rs. 1.75 for women and Rs. 2 for the men who worked as agricultural laborers, but they could earn more by taking a job in the town or by working in the brick factory outside of Ranchi. This disparity between the wages paid in the village and in the towns is sufficiently great that many commute daily into the nearby town for work—when they can find it. Some of the young Oraons, in spite of the high cost of living in the city or town have actually moved to Calcutta, Ranchi, Bokaro, or Jamshedpur. It is the older people and the very young who remain at home in the village, where they work locally at the lower wages. A few of the stay-at-homers work in the government community development program; others find employment in local road construction projects, but the wages for such jobs are not much higher than those paid by the Bihari landowners. In one village I visited, some thirty miles from Ranchi, the local Ranchi Rotary club had started a demonstration farm that employed tribal laborers. The wages, however, were only slightly more than what was paid by the Bihari landowner in the same village.

In a Ho village I visited near Chaibasa there were very few *dikus*. In these villages the local Ho leaders, or *mankis*, collected revenue from the villagers, kept a percentage as commission, paid another commission to the *tahsildar* (the land revenue officer), and passed on the remainder to the government as revenue. But even in these villages where the

169

land had not been alienated, Hos left after the harvest to find supplementary employment. Some work as day laborers in the town of Chaibasa, walking to town each day and then returning to their village at night. Many work in the steel mills at Bokaro and Jamshedpur, and some have found jobs in the coal mines near Chaibasa. Even then, most prefer to find quarters in a nearby Ho village with friends or relatives, and walk to town every day rather than live in the towns.

Contact between Hos and *dikus* occurs either in the towns in which they work, or at the local weekly market. The market is where the Ho villager sells his produce, and with the cash he earns buys the goods that he cannot produce. At the weekly market the Ho sell forest products such as rope, herbs and roots for medicinal purposes, leaves that are sewn together and used as plates for eating, wood for fuel, clay pots, wooden plows, and, of course, paddy. Some villagers produce a kind of yeast used for fermenting rice into *haria*, a local rice beer. The beer itself is readily available at the market. Other villagers produce vegetables for sale—chilies, eggplant, and potatoes, and some sell chickens and ducks.

Side by side in the market are the *dikus*. Some buy goods from the tribals, while others run their own shops. In the large market in the town of Chaibasa, most of the local merchants were Bihari Hindus. In the markets in the Oraon areas near Ranchi, however, there were many Muslim cloth merchants selling cloth.

Here again the tribal leaders complain that *dikus* cheat and exploit the tribals. Merchants in the weekly market sell their cloth at a higher price than in the larger towns, and they buy chickens from the tribals at five rupees each and sell them in Ranchi for twice the price. Whether the tribals would gain more by creating their own cooperatives to transport their produce to the larger towns, or whether the cost of cloth, cigarettes, and other consumer goods could be brought down through larger purchases by their own cooperatives is not clear. The disparity in prices is sufficiently great, however, for the tribals, especially educated tribal

170

leaders, to feel that they are being exploited by *diku* merchants.

To an outside observer there appears to be little difference between the level of living in the Ho villages on the one hand, where the land is exclusively Ho owned, and the Oraon and Munda villages on the other, where the *dikus* own most of the best lands. The only noticeable difference between the villages is that in some of the Ho villages the larger landowners and moneylenders are Hos rather than Bihari Hindus.

In recent years the land situation in Chota Nagpur has, by all accounts, grown worse. Although there has been some conversion of forest land to land for cultivation, it has not been sufficient to keep up with the rising population. The tribal rural population of the region has continued to increase in spite of the extensive outmigration. Between 1961 and 1971, the tribal population of Ranchi and Singhbhum districts increased by 15.5 percent, from 2,285,000 to 2,638,-000 (see Tables 4.4 and 4.5). Though there has been a substantial increase in the urban population of the tribals (an increase of 72.5 percent) and outmigration continues, the rural tribal population of these two districts rose from 2.2 to 2.5 million.

Increased rural density has been accompanied by the growth in the number of landless laborers and a decline in the number of owner-cultivators. In rural India as a whole, the proportion of workers that are owner-cultivators declined from 60.3 percent in 1961 to 50.9 percent in 1971, and the proportion of agricultural laborers increased proportionately from 18.9 to 30 percent. Bihar had one of the highest increases in the proportion of agricultural laborers of any state in India: from 24.4 to 40.9 percent between 1961 and 1971. Though data are unavailable by district, we have no reason to assume that the pattern has been any different in Chota Nagpur.

In other words, the increase in landlessness and the growth of small holdings appears to be a state and national

TABLE 4.4

Population Growth, Ranchi and Singhbhum
Districts (1961–1971)

(THOUSANDS)

	1961	1971	Percent increase
Rural population	3,545	4,052	14.3
Urban population	643	995	54.7
Total	4,188	4,947	18.1
Rural tribal	2,205	2,501	13.4
Urban tribal	80	138	72.5
Total	2,285	2,638	15.5
Rural nontribal	1,340	1,551	15.7
Urban nontribal	563	857	52.2
Total	1,903	2,408	26.3

TABLE 4.5

Population Growth, Chota Nagpur
(1961–1971)

(THOUSANDS)

	1961	1971	Percent increase
Rural population	7,741	8,944	15.5
Urban population	1,190	2,091	75.6
Total	8,931	11,035	23.5
Rural tribal	2,814	3,222	14.5
Urban tribal	97	189	95.9
Total	2,911	3,411	17.2
Rural nontribal	4,927	5,722	16.1
Urban nontribal	1,093	1,902	74.1
Total	6,020	7,624	27.3

172

phenomena, not limited to Bihar or to the tribals of Chota Nagpur. The tribal complaint, however, is not simply the loss of land, but the loss of land to nontribals. This is an important distinction, for there are some well-to-do tribals who have acquired land, some of whom are themselves substantial moneylenders. Traditional village headmen, or *mankis*, are often substantial owners of land and cattle, and in many of the Ho villages the largest landowners are Ho, not *dikus*. But there is virtually no antagonism to wealthy tribals. If anything, there is a tendency on the part of some tribals to be proud of those tribals who have become wealthy. Here we see a familiar feature of many multiethnic societies: the tendency on the part of members of an ethnic group to be antagonistic toward the wealthy of other communities, but not toward the wealthy of their own community.

Given a choice, people prefer to hate others because of their religion, or race, caste, or tribe, rather than because of their wealth. The wealthy in one's own community are a source of vicarious pride. The status (and accomplishment) of members of one's own community provides self-esteem to all members of the community. For this reason it is not easy to create class cleavages and class parties in a multiethnic society except where class and ethnic cleavages coincide. Class antagonisms then become veiled expressions of ethnic hostility. This is probably why ideological parties of the left based upon class appeal have not done very well in India, and why peasant revolts against landlords are more likely to occur when the peasants and landlords belong to different religions or castes, or one is tribal and the other is not.

Agricultural productivity throughout Chota Nagpur is low. There are a few areas with assured irrigation, and the new "miracle" strains of wheat cannot be used in dry zones. "Modern" agriculture is almost nowhere to be seen in Chota Nagpur except for a few government-run demonstration projects. The tribals, like most Indian peasants living in dry areas, have neither the resources nor the knowledge to move from traditional to modern agriculture.

173

At present the only opportunity tribals have for improving themselves is by leaving the village. As one anthropologist studying migratory patterns from an Oraon village has pointed out,[19] tribal peasants with small holdings and agricultural laborers simply cannot earn enough from the land to sustain themselves throughout the year. The unskilled jobs the villagers find in town, as "coolies" or unskilled laborers loading and unloading trucks, carrying bricks and dirt, and working as rickshaw pullers, provides them with more income than they can ever obtain in the village. Since many of the villagers migrate to towns for only a few months of the year, they do not see this as a permanent part of their lives, and do not seek—and in any event are not educated and trained to find—jobs as clerks or mechanics.

Those who travel long distances to the towns generally live in groups, and often return home to their village on the weekends. The main social activities of the tribals—dancing, drinking, religious festivals of one kind or another, marriage ceremonies—take place in the village rather than in the town, and as one observer put it, there is much more of a separation between work and pleasure for the migrants than for those who live at home. Still, the short-term visit to the town has its pleasures too, for tribals enjoy going to the cinema, and socializing and drinking occur in the evening.

What the migrants manage to save is used mainly for the purchase of household goods or clothing rather than for investment in agriculture. Some of the tribals return from Calcutta, Ranchi, or Jamshedpur after having been away for four to six months with 150 to 200 rupees in savings.

Each year a small number settle permanently in the towns, but most of the young people return home. The large towns of the region are mainly populated by nontribals. In 1971, only 5.5 percent of the tribals lived in urban settlement, and there was only a single "urban" settlement, the small town of

[19] Orvoell Roger Gallagher, "Migrant Labour from Tribal Chota Nagpur" (manuscript, Skidmore College, Saratoga Springs, N.Y., 197?).

Simdega in Ranchi district, where a bare majority—eight thousand out of fifteen thousand—were tribal.

In the past century there has been a small but constant exodus of tribals from their homeland, largely to points outside the region, and in recent years there has been a small but increasing flow to nearby towns and cities. Those who remain live on dwindling plots of land, some as owner-cultivators, but a growing number as agricultural laborers. And so for some tribals the dream persists that some day the non-tribals will be evicted and the land restored to the tribals, so that neither those who presently live on the land, nor their children, need move to the city or other regions in search of employment.

THE TRIBAL ENCOUNTER WITH THE CITIES

In contrast to the nineteenth-century rural tribal protests, which were directed against *diku* landowners, recent political activities have centered more around the concerns of the urban and educated tribal population. The numbers of such tribals are small: in 1961 there were only 43,000 tribals living in the urban areas of Ranchi district, and 37,000 in Singhbhum district, but the numbers have been growing. By 1971 there were 65,000 in Ranchi, and 73,000 in Singhbhum. In 1961 there were only 97,000 tribals living in the towns of Chota Nagpur; in 1971 there were 190,000. The number of educated tribals is very small—in 1961 only 9,532 tribals in the entire state of Bihar had matriculated (the rough equivalent of a high school education) or attended college, and of these only 231 had completed college. But between 1960 and 1965, secondary school enrollment of tribals in Bihar had increased by 130 percent, while 1,857 tribals were enrolled in colleges and universities.

In my several visits to Chota Nagpur, I talked to about thirty educated tribal leaders, plus a small group of tribal students at the university and tribal students in several of the colleges. I met most of them in the town of Ranchi, and

175

several in the smaller towns of Chaibasa and Kunti. They were a remarkably articulate group. Many were members of the Bihar state Legislative Assembly or political leaders accustomed to addressing crowds and speaking in legislative bodies. Others were Christian leaders, ministers in the German Lutheran Church or priests in the Catholic Church, soft spoken, but no less forceful in their views. Only one was a woman, an anthropologist who did her master's degree in London, and is the only tribal working for the state-sponsored Tribal Research Institute in Ranchi. Two other tribals I interviewed, both Christian ministers, had doctorates from abroad.

One of the educated tribals, a member of parliament, was an engineer who worked for H.E.C. before entering politics, the only tribal I met trained in something other than liberal arts, law, or theology—an exception to the general rule that tribals do not ordinarily study sciences or engineering. The oldest of the men was a Christian minister in his eighties, a vivacious man with a deep sense of history. However, most of the educated tribals were in their thirties and forties. They were each proud of their individual accomplishments, yet touched with a deep concern for what most of them felt was the failure of their people to keep pace with change.

By almost any standard these were successful individuals: they held responsible positions as teachers, ministers, politicians, and lawyers. They dressed well, and spoke English and Hindi. They earned typical middle-class incomes, lived in pleasant homes in Ranchi, with gardens in front and a servant or two to clean the house, help in the kitchen, and serve at the table. Their children were all in school, typically in private church-run schools, and the full-grown children were themselves members of the middle class. They had no special economic problems other than those shared by other members of the middle classes in India.

But for educated tribals being a tribal is in itself a problem. Not that they personally experience prejudice, but they cannot escape being identified with and identifying them-

176

selves with the community to which they were born—as an Oraon, Munda, or Ho—however much they might prefer to think of themselves as a Christian or Hindu, or even a lawyer, teacher, or minister. As one tribal politician, the leader of the militant Birsa Seva Dal put it: "When I was a student I was ashamed to be called an aboriginal. I always tried to hide what I was. I did not call myself anything. Can you grasp the feeling of a person who is ashamed to call himself a member of his community because there is something rotten in that community, and anyone who belongs to that community must feel shame? Only when the community gets rid of its bad traits, and people respect the community, can a person who belongs to that community not feel shame."

That sentiment was expressed by almost all the educated tribals I met. Although they were each in their own way successful, they knew that they belonged to a community that was looked down upon by others. Indeed, this sense of community failure was intensified by their own success. Some expressed the feeling that they were denied the respect they deserved because nontribals looked down upon tribals. It is not surprising, then, that educated tribals thought intently about such questions as: Why have the tribals remained "backward"? Why are they looked down upon by nontribals? Why have they not moved into skilled positions in industry, or into managerial posts? Why have they not successfully competed against the migrants who have moved into Chota Nagpur? What can be done to change the situation? My questions along these lines, therefore, opened a flood of ideas and emotions as each man sought to take the facts as he saw them and place them into his own explanation of social backwardness.

The most radical force among the tribals is a political organization known as the Birsa Seva Dal. The name is derived from Birsa Munda, the leader of the Munda messianic and millenarian anti-*diku* movement of the 1890s. The founder and leader of this political organization, Lalit Kuzur, is a man in his fifties, who has attracted many young people,

177

especially high school and college-educated youth, to his organization.

The organization was in the public eye in 1968 and 1969, when it launched violent attacks against landlords and led mass demonstrations in the streets of Ranchi for the creation of a tribal state. In recent years it has moderated its demand for a tribal state, and now advocates the creation of a state of Chota Nagpur, to include both tribals and nontribal "local" people. While not an explicitly urban movement— it has also been active in antilandlord movements—it particularly attracts young people in the urban areas.

When I met Kuzur in Ranchi he was surrounded by a half dozen young men of school or college age. Kuzur has a fairer complexion than most tribals, spoke English well and rapidly, as much to his youthful audience as to me.

I asked him what he thought was the main problem of the tribals.

"The adivasis," he said, "think of themselves as subhuman, a people without rights. We try to teach them that they are not inferior to others. They feel that way because there is reason to be ashamed of being called a tribal. After all, what does tribal actually mean? It means a primitive way of living. Everyone in the world once belonged to a tribe. A tribal doesn't believe in science. He has a blind faith in the deities. He doesn't reason, but has faith. He believes that because his father or some *pandit* [priest] said something that it is correct.

"We believe in detribalization. Some people want us to be proud of being tribal. They say we should carry on the old culture. We should make rice wine, we should get drunk, we should sleep on a mat on the floor. I am more interested in what we should change than what we should keep. We can keep our folk dances, but what else is there worth keeping? I admire Birsa Munda because he was a great social reformer who wanted to change his people. He told the Mundas that their beliefs were nonsense. He told them to give up drinking and to believe in one God.

"We can still be Oraons and Mundas and Hos, like the

178

Welsh and the Scots, but that doesn't mean we are tribal. As a schoolboy in Patna I thought 'adivasis' was as hateful a word as tribal. We can call ourselves Chota Nagpuris since this is the place we live. We belong to many different *races* —the Munda, the Oraon, the Ho, they are different races— but we all live in the same place. We have given the word Chota Nagpuri a new political meaning to cover all the tribes who live here. It expresses our desire to be detribalized."

Can a nontribal living in Chota Nagpur, I asked, be called a Chota Nagpuri? He answered indirectly.

"Look at the Board of Directors for H.E.C.," he said. "There is no one on it from Chota Nagpur. None of them have any love, any good feeling toward the people of Chota Nagpur. They come from other parts of India and they love their own people. The members of the Board of Directors chose the heads of each of the departments. Naturally those men hire their own people even when local people are qualified. All the officers bring their kith and kin from the other states because these officers have a duty toward their own people. It's only natural. Local people are not hired and all the good jobs go to outsiders. If we ran these institutions, like H.E.C., naturally we would hire our own people.

"The Government of Bihar says it has a program to provide technical training to the local people in each district so they can qualify for jobs in the new industries. But the head of the training institute in Ranchi is from Patna, not from Chota Nagpur. Only 25 percent of the boys are from here, and the rest are from other parts of the state. They say that competition for admission should be from all over the state, but that is foolish since every district has its own technical institution. It should only be open to boys from the district. That's the only way tribal boys from Chota Nagpur will have a chance. They are poor and have this inferiority complex, so they cannot compete with the boys outside."

But who is a local person, I asked?

"First of all the primitive people who have lived here for thousands of years, they are Chota Nagpuri. Then there are

many non-adivasis who have lived here for centuries—some
Rajput zamindars, some shopkeepers, quite a few Muslim
cultivators. I would never call a Bengali a Chota Nagpuri. We
call them domicile Chota Nagpuris. If you ask them who they
are, they say they are Bengalis not Chota Nagpuris, but if you
ask Muslims they will call themselves Chota Nagpuris. The
Rajput zamindars here call themselves Chota Nagpuris. The
Harijans are so backward politically that they call themselves
Harijans, but we would consider them Chota Nagpuris.

"The language spoken here is Sadani. It is a dialect of
Hindi spoken by all the communities—the Mundas, the
Oraons, the Rajputs, the Harijans, even the Muslims, though
some people speak Magadhi which is a little different from
Sadani. But the Bengalis don't learn Sadani or Hindi prop-
erly, they only speak Bengali.

"The Marwaris who own the businesses here, they consider
themselves outsiders, so we consider them outsiders. They
return to Marwar for their marriages. They say that 'we are
going to our *desh*—our country.' The same is true with the
north Biharis, they say they are going to their *desh* when they
go home but Chota Nagpuris say they are going to their *gaon*,
their village.

"The outsiders are turning Chota Nagpur into a colony.
The H.E.C. employs outsiders. The Bihar government offices
in Ranchi mainly employ outsiders. The Biharis who work
there even bring in their own peons from their own villages.
The private industries are all run by outsiders—there is
Bharat Ball Bearing, and Siddharta Industries, and Usha
Martin, all Marwari owned, and Birla has started some new
industries at Hatia. They all bring in more outsiders. Even
TISCO in Jamshedpur gives the best jobs to outsiders, though
they say they hire local people. It's like the time when the
Europeans went to the United States and colonized and ex-
ploited the Indians. The same thing is happening here."

One of the young men listening to Kuzur was Moses Guria,
the general secretary of the Birsa Seva Dal. He was in his
early thirties and is somewhat heavy-built for a tribal. Guria

180

met Kuzur at a rally attended mainly by young people in June 1967, and was much attracted to him. He joined Kuzur as one of the organizers of the Birsa Seva Dal. In mid-1968 they launched their movement against nontribal landlords, calling for the return of land to the adivasis. Both Kuzur and Guria were arrested and subsequently released.

Guria described himself as a socialist and sees socialism as the solution to the problems of the tribals. "We must do away with private business," he said, "for if we have private business here then the tribals will be left out. Only if government owns all businesses can we progress because if we controlled the administration we would control the employment exchanges and could be assured of jobs."

"But why can't tribals start their own businesses?" I asked.

"That is not possible. It is not one of our characteristics. The tribals who have started even small businesses have failed. There are very few shops that are owned and run by tribals."

"Why have they failed?" I asked.

"Because we do not cheat, we do not adulterate, we do not use the black market as the Punjabis and Marwaris and Gujaratis do. If you don't cheat in a capitalist society you do not succeed. In a socialist society there will be no cheating and no black market. And when cheating is gone, and capitalist production is gone, then the tribals will progress. The tribals can compete in honest sincere work, as technicians, administrators, cultivators, and doctors, but not as businessmen. If there is socialism, then the tribal people will work hard. Tribals cannot survive if capitalism continues."

I asked him how they would actually benefit if there were an autonomous state of Chota Nagpur.

"If we had power, then the tribals would be a majority in the administration. A tribal would be appointed vice chancellor of Ranchi University and the university would be run by tribals. We would take 90 percent of the jobs. If H.E.C. needed machinists, we would make sure that 90 percent of the jobs would be given to local people. The employment

181

exchange would only call Chota Nagpuris, local people, not Biharis. We would not allow national competition for these jobs—that's a loophole we would not allow. We would control licenses for businesses. We would give licenses to local people and only to outsiders if there were not enough who wanted licenses. We would give licenses to tribals who wanted to be entrepreneurs, but the main thing is that we would want to be sure that the tribals have employment."

Though the leaders of the Birsa Seva Dal are the most articulate on this question, many young tribals I met equated socialism with the public sector, and the public sector—in a government controlled by tribals—as the source of jobs.

I visited a number of employment exchanges in Ranchi and the personnel office at H.E.C. to inquire about the employment of tribals. Labor recruitment, I soon learned, is handled by several different agencies. The central government maintains an employment exchange in Ranchi that finds jobs for about three thousand persons a year. The Border Road Organization, under the Ministry of Transportation, hires another three to five thousand persons a year to work in Arunachal Pradesh in India's northeast as road construction laborers, and almost all of these are tribals who spend about six months at a stretch there. There is also a Tea District Labor Agency (TDLA) that recruits labor for the tea plantations in Assam, but the numbers recruited now are quite small.

Much political controversy has centered around the central government employment exchange. The public-sector industries in Ranchi, which include the Heavy Engineering Corporation and the headquarters of Hindustan Steel, legally must notify the exchange when there are job openings. They are only required, however, to hire through the exchange for jobs paying less than Rs. 500 per month that do not require special technical skills. The officers of the exchange privately admit that managers and engineers in the public sector do try to find jobs for their friends and relatives. One further complication is that friends and relatives of those who work in

182

the public sector come from other parts of India to register at the exchange in Ranchi, and then give a local address as their permanent residence. There is no way of knowing then whether a person who claims to be local is one in fact.

The employment exchange strongly presses public-sector firms to hire adivasis, but there are no "reserved" jobs for tribals in the public sector (as there are in state and central government employment), and in actual practice, very few tribals find jobs that require skills. One reason is that very few tribals have skills, or at least adequate skills to compete with outsiders. The officers of the exchange report that when there are openings for stenographers, or when the government health services need medical lab technicians, or H.E.C. needs machinists, there are few qualified tribals whose names they can submit.

There is no law requiring private firms to use the exchange. The law does require that they inform the exchange of an opening, but they need not hire from those registered at the exchange. The officers of the exchange estimate that no more than 5 or 10 percent of the people hired to fill openings in the private sector are recruited through the exchange in Ranchi.

The employment exchange keeps a list of individuals from scheduled tribes registered for employment, including a separate list by educational qualifications. In early 1970, there were 1,590 "educated" tribals on the register. Of these 945 were matriculates, who had roughly the equivalent of a high school education. Another 224 had some intermediate education equal to that of junior college, and the remainder, a little over 400, were college educated, mostly (273) arts graduates. In the first six months of 1970, the employment exchange found jobs for 59 educated tribals. No records are kept as to how many found jobs outside the exchange.

These figures reflect the substantial increase in the number of tribals who have attended secondary schools and colleges during the decade. In fact, each year the number of tribals registered at the exchange, educated or uneducated, has been

183

increasing, but the numbers placed continue to remain small. In 1967, for example, only 400 out of a total of 5,000 tribals, were placed in jobs.

The number of nontribals registered at the exchange has also sharply risen in recent years, and the number of placements for them is also low. Much—though by no means all—of the employment problems of the tribals, therefore, should be seen in the context of a labor supply that is growing more rapidly than employment opportunities.

Among the educated, both tribal and nontribal, it is unemployed matriculates who have been increasing at the most rapid rate, and who have the most difficulty finding employment. They are neither skilled nor educated enough to qualify for either the technical jobs or the more senior administrative posts that have opened in the new industries. Nor are they in the same situation as the wholly uneducated, who find employment as day laborers. An afternoon walk around the movie houses in Ranchi—and for that matter in most other Indian cities—reveals where most of the unemployed matriculates hang out. They constitute not just a reserve labor pool, but a reserve political pool as well.

SCHISMS IN THE TRIBES:
THE ENCOUNTER WITH CHRISTIANITY AND HINDUISM

In 1967 the following amendment to the constitution was introduced in the Indian parliament by the tribal member of parliament from Ranchi: "No person who has given up tribal faith or faiths and has embraced either Christianity or Islam should be deemed to be a member of a scheduled tribe."

The author of the amendment, Kartik Oraon, is an educated, articulate, well-dressed Congressman, who, before he entered parliament, was an engineer at H.E.C. He was elected in 1967, and was easily reelected in the Congress sweep of 1971. I met him on the eve of the election at the

Adivasi hostel, a youth hostel for tribal boys at Ranchi University. His nephew is director of the hostel, and Kartik Oraon was there to solicit support from the students. His amendment had first been introduced in 1967 but had not been acted upon. He introduced it again just before parliament's dissolution in 1971. It was, for most of the politically conscious tribals I talked with, the most controversial issue in the election.

I asked him why he had introduced a bill that would exclude all reservations—for admission into schools and colleges, and for jobs in the administrative services—for tribals who had become Christian.

"The Christian tribals" he said, "have taken all the reserved positions for themselves in the colleges and government service. The Christian missions have spent crores of rupees on the Christian tribals and built schools for them, so why should the government give them grants for their schools while the non-Christians get nothing? The government is actually supporting missionary work by giving their schools grants. In fact, why should anyone be allowed to propagate religion? When you propagate one religion that means you must attack other religions, and that leads to hatred of one group by another.

"The Christians dominate everything here. They have dominated the politics of the tribal people through the Jharkhand party. Jharkhand is a Christian party and their purpose is to keep the non-Christians down. When the government provides all these benefits, it's the Christians who get them. If the government reserved one hundred jobs, the Christians got them all. The constitution says that scheduled castes who are Muslims, or Buddhist, or Christians should not get any benefits from the government, so why should the Christian tribals?"

I suggested that perhaps an income criteria should replace caste and tribe as a basis for reservations. Those who come from poor and uneducated families should receive help, but those who come from the middle class, regardless of religion, should not. He strongly disapproved the suggestion, saying that it was particularly important to reserve seats in parliament and in the state assembly for members of scheduled tribes, since that was the only way they could be assured of representation. As for abolishing benefits based upon caste or tribe, he thought that might have been all right if it had been done when the constitution was written, but not now.

I asked him whether the non-Christian tribals were taking full advantage of the benefits given to them by the government. Wasn't it true, for example, that the drop-out rate of non-Christian tribals from school was very high?

"Yes, it is higher than for the Christians, but that's because the Christians spend more money on their schools and they are organized to motivate the boys to attend school. There has to be a plan to help uplift the tribals, but there isn't any."

"But isn't the result," I asked, "that there are many reserved positions for government jobs that are left vacant because there aren't enough qualified tribals? And if all the reservations aren't filled, what would be gained by excluding the Christian tribals?"

"If the Christians didn't get any benefits," he said, "the government would spend more on the schools, and then there would be more qualified tribals."

In 1961, 415,000 tribals, or 14.3 percent, were Christian. The largest number were Oraons (175,000), followed closely by the Mundas (165,000). A smaller number, 67,000, were Christian members of the Kharia tribe. Hardly any of the Hos—only 2,000—numbered among the Christians.

The largest concentration of Christians, 364,000, lived in Ranchi district, where they constituted 27.6 percent of the tribal population, and 17 percent of the population of the district. Another 27,000 Christian tribals lived in Singhbhum district. In other words, virtually all the Christian tribals resided in two districts, with 88 percent living in Ranchi district alone.

186

Jesuit missionaries began working in Chaibasa in 1869 under the leadership of a young Belgian Jesuit, and today Catholics form the largest Christian denomination in Chota Nagpur. The second largest denomination is the Gossner Evangelic Lutheran Church, named after the Rev. J. S. Gossner of Berlin, who in 1845 sent four Lutheran pastors to Chota Nagpur. The third mission, the Anglican Church, or as it is now called in India, the Church of India, has two dioceses each, with a large membership in Ranchi and Singhbhum districts.

The Christian tribals are more literate, more educated, and more urban than the non-Christian tribals. In 1961, only 3.5 percent of all the tribals in Chota Nagpur were living in urban areas; but the Christian tribals were considerably more urbanized (6.4 percent) than the non-Christians (2 percent). Both groups, however, were substantially less urbanized than the nontribals, 18.1 percent of whom lived in urban areas of Chota Nagpur.[20] Unfortunately, neither occupation nor literacy is broken down by religion in the census, but it is widely believed that Christian tribals are far more educated and have higher salaried jobs than non-Christians.

According to the data released for 1965-1966, there were 3,835 primary and middle schools in Ranchi district, with a quarter of a million students. Of the schools, 858 were run by the Christian churches, with an enrollment of 93,000 students. The proportion of children in church-run secondary schools is even higher, 15,000 out of 37,000. The Catholic Church runs two colleges affiliated to the university: Nirmala College for Women, and St. Xavier's, a prestigious, well-regarded college in Ranchi, as well as the Xavier Labour Relations Institute for Social Service at Ranchi and in Jamshedpur. In addition, the Catholic Church runs a number of

---

[20] In 1971, 24.9 percent of the nontribal population of Chota Nagpur lived in urban areas, as against 5.5 percent of the tribal population. Urbanization among the Christians rose sharply to 13.4 percent, while non-Christian tribals were 3.9 percent urbanized.

187

vocational schools that teach carpentry, commercial studies, weaving, and tailoring. Two other colleges are run by churches: St. Columbus is Anglican, and Gossner College is Lutheran.

The influence of the churches on education is greater than these numbers suggest. The churches created educational institutions in the nineteenth century at a time when there were few government schools. Most of the tribals were, as a result, educated in church schools. Moreover, the quality of the church-run schools has generally been higher than that of the government schools; the teachers are better trained, student discipline is greater, and the quality of instruction is generally regarded as superior.

The student body of the Christian-run schools is by no means exclusively tribal. Only 47 percent of the students at St. Xavier's College are Christians, and this reportedly is the highest percentage of Christians in any college in the state. No figures are available on the number of non-Christian tribals attending St. Xavier's or other Christian colleges, but the widespread impression is that the bulk of tribal students are Christian.

In the main, St. Xavier's provides occupational mobility for its tribal students. Most (67 percent) come from families in which the father is an owner-cultivator. Only 19 percent are from what could be described as "middle class" families, in which the father is a teacher, clerk, government official, or professional. A survey of tribal graduates reported that most (230 out of 307 students) had jobs as teachers, clerks, or accountants.

Until relatively recently, most tribal political leaders were Christian. The most influential of the non-Congress political parties in Chota Nagpur was the Jharkhand party. It was formed in the late 1930s by Christian tribals. At one time it had the support of a majority of the tribals. In India's first general elections of 1952, it swept most of the assembly and parliamentary constituencies, and remained a major force in

Chota Nagpur until 1963, when it temporarily merged with the Congress party.[21]

From the late 1930s till his death in the mid 1960s, the Jharkhand party was led by Jaipal Singh, an articulate, well-dressed Oxford-educated tribal who as a young man took part in the Olympics, worked as an officer of Burma Shell, then subsequently became a high official of one of the princely states. Though Jharkhand was not explicitly a Christian party, Jaipal Singh himself was a Christian, as were most of the activists in the party.[22] Working closely with him—some describe him as the chief organizer of the Jharkhand party—was Julius Tiga, an Oraon Christian and a graduate from the University of Cuttack in Orissa, who was general secretary of the party until 1955.

Jharkhand did not support the Indian National Congress. Like most of India's preindependence tribal parties, Jharkhand was outside the mainstream of India's nationalist politics. Indeed, during the Second World War, the Jharkhand party backed the British war effort, and Jaipal Singh himself helped to recruit tribals from Chota Nagpur to serve in the Indian army and to work for American and British military

[21] In the state assembly elections of 1952 Jharkhand won 32 seats, but declined to 30 in 1957, and 20 in 1962. Jharkhand did not take part in the 1967 elections. In the 1972 elections, the several splinter Jharkhand parties together won only seven seats. For a detailed analysis of voting patterns of tribals in Bihar and elsewhere in India, see Myron Weiner and John Osgood Field, "How Tribal Constituencies in India Vote," in Myron Weiner and John Osgood Field, ed., *Electoral Politics in the Indian States: Three Disadvantaged Sectors*, Vol. II (Delhi: Manohar Book Service, 1975).

[22] L. P. Vidyarthi, "Aspects of Tribal Leadership in Chota Nagpur" in L. P. Vidyarthi, ed., *Leadership in India* (Bombay: Asian Publishing House, 1967); B. N. Sahay, *Dynamics of Leadership* (New Delhi: Bookhive, 1969). For a sympathetic account of the Jharkhand movement, which sees the Birsa rebellion, with its opposition to alien rule (both Britishers and Hindu zamindars) as its historical precursor, see K. L. Sharma, "Jharkhand Movement in Bihar," *Economic and Political Weekly*, 11:1 (January 10, 1976), 37-43.

personnel stationed in southern Bihar. In this respect the tribals from Chota Nagpur were not very different from politically conscious tribes elsewhere in India. The tribes of India's northeast, for example, in the Naga hills and Manipur, supported the British struggle against the Japanese and played an active role in the famous battle of Kohima. And in the princely areas of Orissa, Madhya Bharat, and Gujarat, the tribals often remained loyal to the princes who, in turn, collaborated with the British.[23]

In the latter part of the nineteenth through the twentieth century, the European missionaries—British, German, Belgian, and American—supported the cause of the tribals, particularly with respect to land issues. Demands for the restoration of lands to the tribals, no-rent, and no-tax movements— movements directed more against the "alien" *dikus* and only indirectly against the government—were staunchly supported by the Jesuits, Lutherans, and Anglicans.

Since the *dikus* were Hindus, while the leadership of the agrarian movement and of the Jharkhand party were Christian, many Biharis looked upon these political movements— especially since they were not part of the nationalist struggle and often antagonistic to it—as antinational and anti-Hindu. Biharis spoke of the need to "integrate" the tribals into "national politics," a loosely used concept that meant—depending upon who used the term "integration"—pulling the tribals into Indian nationalist politics, "absorbing" the tribes into Hinduism, or reducing or eliminating Christian influence.

In the early fifties, efforts were made to restrict the flow of foreign missionaries into India. The Indianization of the churches in India was thereby accelerated and, to a lesser

[23] On the eve of Indian independence there were three major political tendencies among India's tribals: secessionist tendencies in the northeastern region; loyalist (to the princes) in Rajasthan, Madhya Pradesh, and Orissa; and separatists in southern Bihar and neighboring Orissa and Madhya Pradesh, who supported the Jharkhand demand for the creation of a tribal state within the Indian union of the tribals from these three states. See Weiner and Field, "How Tribal Constituencies in India Vote," pp. 81-85.

extent, in Chota Nagpur as well. Concomitantly, the Congress party of Bihar made every effort to recruit and nominate tribal candidates, a policy necessitated by the system of "reserved" parliamentary and state assembly constituencies. Irrespective of religious or caste affiliation, in certain constituencies only tribals could run. A major effort was made to woo the Jharkhand party into Congress, and funds were given to the Adimjati Sevak Mandal, a social reform organization working to improve the education of the tribals, but which many Christian tribals view as an organization concerned with the propagation of Hinduism.

The expansion of publicly financed schools throughout Chota Nagpur created, in effect, a school system competitive with that created by the missionaries. Though the government sought to "integrate" tribals by reducing Christian influence, there were limits to what the government could do, and some policies they pursued actually had the reverse effect. Since the government is prepared to support private schools of any religious sect and caste so long as they are open to all, the missionary schools were also entitled to public funds, and since the schools increasingly replaced foreign missionaries with indigenous instructors—the church missions in Chota Nagpur all support teacher-training institutions—the government was bound to continue to provide financial support. Moreover, while the government was committed to "integration"—whatever that might mean in practice—it was also committed to "development," and that led them to support many church-initiated development activities, including schools, health centers, hospitals, and a variety of agricultural development programs such as credit institutions and cooperatives.

So long as the educated tribal middle class—that is, the school teachers, professionals (mainly lawyers), and civil servants—were largely Christian, there was little conflict between Christian and non-Christian tribals. On the contrary, Christian tribals provided most of the political leadership for the tribals in their conflicts both with the local *dikus* and with

191

the state government. As the number of educated non-Christian tribals increased, however, a cleavage emerged between the Christian and non-Christian tribal middle class, especially as the latter produced its own political aspirants seeking tribal support.

Although there are exceptions on both sides, in the main the Congress party won the support of the non-Christian tribals, some of whom, like Kartik Oraon, explicitly identified with Hindu India. The Jharkhand party and the Birsa Seva Dal continue to be—though again there are exceptions—parties with a Christian leadership.

The growing ties between Hindu tribal politicians and Bihari Hindus accorded well with—some would say have largely been determined by—the political benefits each gain from an alliance. As the number of educated Hindu tribals has increased, Hindu tribal politicians have sought to wrest political influence from Christian tribals. An assertive Hindu identity helped distinguish the Hindu tribal politician from the Jharkhand and Birsa Seva Dal Christian leaders. At the same time, they were able to win electoral support as well as financial backing of Bihari Hindus in their constituencies. In turn, both Congress and Jana Sangh have wooed Hindu tribal politicians, particularly after the Congress party ceased to hold a majority of the seats in the Bihar legislative assembly, and the support of tribal legislators became important for creating coalition governments in the state. A majority of the tribal legislators are now tribal Hindus.

Kartik Oraon came to symbolize this new political force in Chota Nagpur, that is, those tribals who sought the support of Bihari Hindus and who spoke of "integrating" themselves into Bihar by asserting their Hindu identity. He explicitly calls himself a Hindu, wears a long strand of hair from the center of his head in the manner of orthodox Hindus, and is reportedly supported by Hindu politicians not only in Congress, but in Jana Sangh as well. He is a known critic of Muslims, and freely attacks Muslim politicians, a gesture intended to establish further his Hindu identity.

If Kartik Oraon symbolizes Hindu tribal identity, N. E. Horo, the other tribal MP, represents Christian tribal interests, and he has been a strong opponent of Kartik Oraon's efforts to delist the tribals. Unlike Oraon, Horo is in favor of creating a Jharkhand state. During an interview in Ranchi I asked Horo what his reaction was to Kartik Oraon's argument that the Christians were taking all the reserved positions, leaving little for the non-Christian tribals.

"The reason the Christians are getting a larger share of government appointments is that they are better educated than the non-Christians. But you must look at how many apply for jobs and how many get them. Government reserves 5 percent of the class I and II jobs (the highest ranking civil service positions), but only 1 percent are filled because so few apply. There may be twenty openings, but there are only, say, eight qualified adivasis. Of these six may be Christian and two are non-Christian. Kartik Oraon, however, doesn't speak of the twelve openings for which there are no qualified tribals. How would the delisting of Christian tribals give them more jobs when there are not enough qualified non-Christians?"

"Why was it that after more than twenty years and so much expansion of educational facilities, there were still so few qualified tribals," I asked.

"It's true that the tribals have not always taken advantage of many of the school facilities. Tribal parents don't encourage their boys to go to school. The Christian missions encourage the boys more and we need to have societies that will encourage the non-Christians. There was one MP who suggested that the government close mission schools and hospitals. The prime minister replied in Parliament by asking who would replace them? There is the Adimjati Seva Mandal, but their only work is to counter the missionaries. They have opened schools side by side with the mission schools but not in the remote villages where schools are needed.

"The tribals are now politically divided between the Christians and non-Christians. That is a fairly new development. I

193

think some of the businessmen in Chota Nagpur are encouraging and financing these groups so as to keep the tribals divided and prevent them from uniting to press for a Jharkhand state. They are afraid that a Jharkhand state would expel the Marwaris and make is difficult for outsiders to start businesses here. They were frightened by the Birsa Seva Dal when they spoke of Chota Nagpur for the adivasis."

I pointed out that Kuzur says he is in favor of Chota Nagpur for the Chota Nagpuris, not only for the adivasis.

"He says that now," replied Horo, "but last year their slogan was different."

How did he feel about the question? For whom would a Jharkhand state be? Who would be considered local?

"People who have lived here for a hundred years and who feel it is their home, I consider them local. The managers of all the firms here are outsiders and they employ outside people. If we have our own government then local people will have to be given preferences. When the central government opens a plant, they work with the state government and hire non-Chota Nagpuris from elsewhere in Bihar. Naturally, I think that central government concerns should recruit from all over India, but local people should be given their share of the jobs. I don't mind if outside businesses come here, but then the businessmen should not exploit us. I consider a *diku* someone who exploits local people."

Shortly after talking with Horo I visited the office of the Adimjati Seva Mandal in Ranchi to see its director, Mr. Narayanji, an elderly man from north Bihar, a Hindu and a Kyastha by caste, who had settled in Ranchi some thirty years ago as a Congress organizer to work among the adivasis.

"The Jharkhand party," he said, "was then an antinational party supported by the missionaries who told the tribals not to join the nationalists because they were Hindus. Personally I feel that the Christians are getting all the benefits of the reservations and if the Christians were delisted then the non-Christian tribals wouldn't have to compete against them.

"The tribals are a simple, honest people. They are best fit for work in agriculture. The difficulty here is that there is not enough irrigation. The tribals work hard. They built the tea plantations in Assam and many of the tribals have built the Andaman Islands. But the land here is not fertile and it needs water. It is difficult for the tribals to start their own businesses. They cannot compete with other businesses."

"Why not?" I asked.

"Because they have no self-control. They use the capital instead of the profit. If they have a cloth shop, then they give away cloth to other tribals when there is a wedding. They also drink a great deal. Their leaders are the worst sufferers since they drink so much."

We talked about the Jharkhand party and the Birsa Seva Dal. "They create friction between tribal and nontribal," he said. "All these frictions are due to the missionaries who encourage them. Wherever there is a missionary center there is conflict between the tribals and nontribals. . . . The Roman mission is the most powerful. Before the elections the bishop and the priests tell the people whom to vote for."

"The tribals are really Hindu," he said.

I asked him what *Sarna* was, the term generally used to refer to the tribal religion.

"That is all political. There is no separate tribal religion other than Hinduism. . . . The job of the Adimjati Seva Mandal is to combat the missionaries. We receive five lakhs rupees a year from the government. We run fifty-three schools, twenty hostels. . . . We can't work for political candidates openly but we do give our support to non-Christian tribals. In the last election I supported Kartik Oraon.

"The main problem is to end the barriers between tribals and nontribals. That is the most important thing we can do here."

Though the critics of the Christian tribal leadership look upon Christianity as a divisive force, separating, as Narayanji put it, tribals from nontribals, and as others put it, tribals from each other, all agreed that converted tribals are more successful than the nonconverts. A larger proportion of Christian tribals enter and remain in school than non-Christians, go on for advanced education, and enter the middle class as teachers, clerks, lawyers, and civil servants.

What factors separate the "successful" from the "unsuccessful" is even less well understood in India than in the United States, for it is not a subject that has received the attention of India's anthropologists studying tribal society. American social science literature has emphasized the importance of the student's family, and the social, cultural, and economic class from which the student comes, rather than the quality of the educational institution which he attends. But the limited Indian data we have points in the opposite direction, namely, that students who attend Christian schools appear to perform better than students in government schools, even the students of non-Christian as well as Christian background, and students of peasant as well as middle-class background. Obviously, some precise statistical studies are called for that would take a closer look at the performance of different social categories in each type of school system, and which would take into account the factors of self-selection at work. Nonetheless, in my interviews I was often struck by the very humble background of the middle-class tribal Christians I encountered, with village parents who appeared not to be the driving force in their educational success.

There is no doubt, too, that there is a substantial difference in the tone of the mission schools. The principals and teachers I met in the Christian schools, in contrast to those who worked for the government colleges and university, were greatly concerned with the motivation and conduct of their students. At the Christian schools, tribal students customarily introduced themselves and shook hands, a small gesture but obviously one intended to increase the self-confidence of tribal students in relating to strangers. Teachers also converse with students regularly, for I often saw students and teachers

196

walking together in the corridors. Emphasis is placed on discipline, orderliness, cleanliness, self-control. In these respects the contrast between the campuses of the Christian schools and colleges and those run by the government is quite noticeable. Mission-run schools have attractive gardens, students tend to appear neat, speak quietly, and rarely loiter; slogans on the walls are absent and strikes and demonstrations are rare. These aspects of the education system seem likely to affect student motivation and commitment to education, and their academic performance.

There is one other striking difference between mission-run and government-run schools: the number of tribal teachers employed by the mission schools. In the government schools, teachers and principals are almost exclusively Bihari; the missionary schools continue to have a small number of "foreign" (in origin, that is, but many of the Belgian, American, German, and British priests and ministers are now Indian citizens) teachers, and many have foreign principals, but several are now wholly run by tribals.

I met the tribal principal of one of the Christian colleges, the Reverend Nirmal Minz, principal of the Lutheran College in Ranchi. Dr. Minz is one of a small number of remarkable tribals of modest, even poor families, who have risen to positions of some eminence. Dr. Minz, a handsome man in his mid-forties, is an Oraon whose peasant father had no formal education, although he could read and write. Dr. Minz went to a Lutheran school run by the G.E.L. Church, then to St. Columbus College in Hazaribagh. He continued in Ranchi College and studied theology at a college in Serampore, West Bengal. In 1955 he was sent by the church for advanced study to St. Paul Seminary and to the University of Minnesota. He returned to India to teach at the Theological College of the G.E.L. Church in Ranchi. After several years he again returned to the United States, where he joined the Divinity School of the University of Chicago, and completed his doctorate there in 1967 with a thesis entitled "Mahatma Gandhi and Hindu-Christian Dialogue." Upon his return to Ranchi he was made principal of the Lutheran College. As the chairman of the Ranchi YMCA and a member of many local organizations, he is active in civic and tribal affairs. He is widely regarded by the Roman Catholics, by the leaders of political parties, and by his own church as one of the region's important tribal leaders. He is a soft-spoken man with an apparent capacity to relate well to other people and to communicate effectively with nontribals.

We began our interview by discussing the problems tribals have keeping their land. He described the many ways nontribals are able to acquire land from tribals, sometimes below the market price, and often in violation of the Chota Nagpur Tenancy Act, but he complained that none of the tribal leaders, "nor the churches," has educated tribals to prevent them from being cheated.

"The difficulty," he said, "is that none of the tribal leaders are willing to say how bad the tribals are. The truth of the matter is that the tribals have not been able to respond to outsiders positively. Their very outlook on life is shortsighted. Tribals don't think of the following day. What they have for the day is enough for them. They have no vision of the future. No tribal will plan for his land beyond this year. He doesn't plan for his children. Even the educated tribals who work for the government do not think about the long-term education of their children. Why, take this church. It is one of the most dynamic here, yet it does not plan for the next few years. I have a budget for this year, but I have no idea of what it will be next year.

"When you are psychologically unable to respond, then you say that your way of life is the best. Among the tribals there is a nostalgia for the past. The will to live better tomorrow is absent.

"You should watch people in a bus. Suppose a tribal boards a crowded bus and has to hang on the outside. He will not push in when space is available. He will just stay

198

in the same place even if a seat becomes available. But if a nontribal comes in, he will manage to find a seat. The tribals accept their position and only want to hold on to what they have."

"Are college educated tribals different?" I asked.

"Externally, they are. But once a tribal is appointed clerk, he will not try to improve himself to become the headclerk as a non-adivasi will. Some don't care for a promotion if it requires taking a departmental exam.

"There is a vast psychological barrier between the tribal and *dikus*, even among the educated. The barrier is so great that when outsiders come in, tribals feel that the progress is for them, not for us. There was a time when we used to walk, but now we just want to stand and watch."

"Would tribals have more confidence," I asked, "if they controlled those institutions like H.E.C., or had their own Jharkhand state?"

"I don't think so. Before a tribal can be a chairman of H.E.C., let him run a smaller industry. Before a tribal is made vice chancellor of Ranchi, let some tribals be college principals. If there were a Jharkhand state the leaders would bitterly fight one another. And if a tribal were made chairman of H.E.C., he would just be the tool of outsiders. Some tribals have become ministers in the government of Bihar, but what good have these ministers done for the tribals? The tribal politicians are exploiting their own people. They use their own people to get elected, then get money from the government, but they give nothing to the people in return. They are no better than *dikus*."

"Does the reservation of seats in colleges and jobs in the government improve the position of the tribals," I asked, "or does it make the barriers greater between tribals and nontribals?"

"You know, when I went to college there were no reservations so I had to compete. I was the best in my class so I felt equal to the nontribals. But now with reservations the boys can get into college and get government positions without competing. They do not change as I was forced to change. Personally, I'm in favor of economic criteria for reservations. I don't see why there should be reservations for me or for Kartik Oraon. Let our children compete against the nontribals. It's all right to give reservations to the poor, but not to the successful tribals. It would be a mistake to keep these reservations indefinitely."

"Some politicians I interviewed," I said to him, "felt that the adivasis could never be entrepreneurs and that the only solution was a socialist society in which they ran the institutions."

He laughed. "That might be a psychological solution, but in the real world, that is absurd. Whether this is a socialist or capitalist society, whether industries are privately or publicly run, you have to be an entrepreneur to run a business and factory. For these people socialism is their dream. You might say it is their eschatology."

TRIBAL RESPONSES: THE ARGUMENT RECAPITULATED

The incorporation of Chota Nagpur into the rest of India began in Mughal times, deepened still further with the establishment of British rule, and became complete from the end of the nineteenth century onward with the establishment of the coal, steel, and iron industries. Today, Chota Nagpur is the most industrialized and urbanized region of Bihar, and one of India's most important industrial regions.

But while the region is wholly incorporated into the rest of India, the tribals have not been incorporated into the process of urbanization or industrialization in Chota Nagpur. They have at best been passive participants in a process over which they have had virtually no influence. They have stayed aloof from the urbanization process and have not shared in the benefits of an expanding system of education and industry to the extent that other Indians have. Had they initiated or

200

at least been active participants in these processes of industrialization and urbanization, we would today be asking questions about the adaptation and absorption of migrants to Chota Nagpur rather than studying the responses of the indigenous tribal population.

Nor have they been able simply to "stand and watch," as Reverend Minz said, for the changes have transformed their lives. The agrarian changes that took place in the nineteenth century led hundreds of thousands of tribals to leave their lands, not to move to cities, but to find employment on tea plantations in Assam and Bengal. When these opportunities closed, tribals continued to migrate, some permanently but most seasonally, to the towns and cities of Bihar and West Bengal. These migrations have been of economic benefit not only to the migrants themselves, but to the families they have left behind—though their families and they, too, would have preferred to remain at home among their kinsmen.

The response to those changes has been as much political as economic. Throughout the nineteenth century there were periodic uprisings of the tribal peasants against the hated *dikus*. Since the 1930s tribal politics has shifted from millenarian, messianic movements based in the countryside, to party politics based on a more urbanized leadership. Tribal politics has changed from violent upheavals to electoral struggles, and from a politics that looked wholly inward and was exclusively tribal to a politics of coalitions with tribal leaders seeking political allies. But the fears and anxieties of tribals, especially of educated tribals, remains, and the anger and hostility of tribals to outsiders is great, deepened by the condescension with which many migrants, especially Bihari Hindus, continue to view the tribals.

Tribal politics in Chota Nagpur is focused exclusively on the issue of the relationship between tribals and nontribals. Even the question of the relationship between Christian and non-Christian tribals is linked to the question of how tribals should integrate themselves with Hindu India. The attitudes

201

of tribals on land policy, rural agricultural development, employment, and the role of the public and private sector are all shaped by this relationship between tribals and "aliens."

What have been the ideological forms of the tribal response? The political terrain is by now familiar.

Restoration

The early movements had a messianic component, an eschatology that assumed a cataclysmic decline followed by the restoration of the tribals to a golden age under the leadership of a savior: the Sardar movement of 1885 to expel the alien landlords and to restore Munda domination; the Birsa Munda movement of the late 1890s to drive out all foreigners —Hindus, Muslims, and British—to establish a Munda reign with Birsa as its ruler; and the 1915 Tana Bhagat movement, with its promise of a millennial era of Oraon rule, free from foreign settlers on their land.

Although messianic and millenarian movements do not exist among the tribals, the belief in a "restoration" is an important component of the outlook of many contemporary educated tribals as well as of tribal peasants. It takes the form of advocating the "restoration" of the land to the tribals and the establishment of a Jharkhand state that would restore the tribals to power and status. Even the cry for socialism has a restoration dimension, for in the tribal context socialism means that tribals, by controlling the means of production, could eject nontribals from control and could, moreover, assure tribals of employment. The tribals could thereby restore a world that they controlled and in which they did not have to compete with nontribals, nor suffer the humiliations of being subservient to outsiders.

Political Power

Some tribals hold to a theory of social change that is as old as nationalist politics: through the assumption of political power, it is believed, the ethos of the tribals can be changed.

202

This theory holds that the establishment of a state under the domination of tribals would not only increase the tribal share of employment by political means, but would also increase the self-confidence of the tribals and enable them ultimately to acquire the skills and ambition necessary to compete against others. This faith in the social transformation of individuals as a consequence of the acquisition of power is a faith on which the demand for a tribal state rests, and which links the outlook of political militants to religious millenarians.

Such a theory of social change, a theory that equates political power with self-pride, and pride with educational and economic performance, is one that is hardly likely to be tested in Chota Nagpur. The likelihood that India's central government would agree to create a separate Chota Nagpur state is small, and the prospect that even if there were such a state it would be politically dominated by the tribals (who form a minority) is even smaller. Conceivably, the struggle for political power itself could create pride and self-confidence among the tribals, which in turn would affect their performance; while such a transformation has not occurred even after a century of tribal rebellions, the search for self-pride through struggle is likely to continue.

Reservations

The British, and now Indian policy makers, have pursued a protectionist strategy for the tribals.[24] It began with the Chota Nagpur Tenancy Act, which sought to end the alienation of tribal land—a policy enshrined in the Indian constitu-

[24] The most comprehensive account of government policy towards tribals appears in the so-called Dhebar Commission Report of 1961: *Report of the Scheduled Areas and Scheduled Tribes Commission, 1960-61*, two volumes (Delhi: Government of India Press, 1962). A shorter version appeared in *A New Deal for Tribal India*, edited by Verrier Elwin (New Delhi: Ministry of Home Affairs, 1963). See also the annual *Report of the Commissioner for Scheduled Castes and Scheduled Tribes* (Delhi: Manager of Publications).

tion of 1950, which specifies that certain areas shall be reserved for tribals, and within these areas outsiders cannot purchase land.

The concept of reservations was soon extended to assure tribals of a fixed minimum proportion of educational and employment opportunities and positions in elected legislative bodies, in the state assemblies, and in parliament. Colleges have an admissions quota for tribals (with lower admissions requirements), and a percentage of jobs in the administrative services are reserved for tribals who meet the minimum educational requirements.

Many tribals argue that these reservations should be extended to include a larger share of the modern sector—that is, a proportion of jobs in the industrial sector under public control. Some are in favor of extending these guarantees to the private sector as well, or alternatively, expanding the public sector to incorporate what is now privately operated. Neither government nor industrial managers, however, is willing to extend the principle of reservations to the industrial sector. As the personnel officer of the Heavy Engineering Corporation put it, "Industry has its own culture—a culture in which competent men can compete. Some parties speak of taking over the H.E.C. and other industries here. But seizing industry is not like seizing politics. You need competent men to run industry."

By implication, the government assumes that reservations will not do irreparable damage to administration, but it could to industry. The one exception that both government and industrial managers are prepared to make is that local people can be given preferences in unskilled jobs where a level of competitive competence is not required beyond, say, a level of physical strength and stamina.

Among the tribals, as we have seen, there are disagreements over whether the reservations should continue to cover Christian tribals as well as non-Christians. The controversy only in part expresses the anxieties among non-Christian tribals that are not doing as well as Christian tribals;

more deeply it reflects the mood of some educated tribals that, like the Munda chiefs of old who adopted Hinduism to become the social equals of other rajas, their own "conversion" will win them the respect of Bihari Hindus.

Competition

Almost no tribal leaders have suggested that reservations and protections for tribals be removed, and that tribals compete in the open market place for education and employment. The few who hold this view support the establishment of improved educational facilities in tribal areas and scholarships for tribal students, but argue that the standards of performance in colleges and universities and the criteria for employment and promotion for tribals be no different than for nontribals.

Most tribals (and nontribals) believe that in the absence of protective land laws and reservations the plight of the tribals would be even worse, for tribals are believed to be too "weak" and "ignorant" to protect themselves against clever nontribals, and too unskilled, unambitious, and unaggressive to effectively compete against nontribals for college admissions and jobs. Some view such reservations and protective laws as temporary measures, like tariffs that protect infant industries, until such time as tribals can "catch up," but others believe that the characteristics of tribals are so fundamental and so enduring that they must be protected indefinitely.

The competitive alternative is also rejected on the grounds that there is not, in any event, a competitive merit-criteria marketplace. Many tribals argued that even if they were able to compete, Bihari and other *diku* managers of industries and officials of government public service commissions are likely to prefer nontribals unless the reservation system requires that they act otherwise. As one Oraon Catholic priest put it: "You can do away with reservations only if there is fair play." Sometimes tribals are not hired out of simple prejudice, but often it is because employers give preferences to

205

their own "people" in employment. Then too young tribals often do not feel self-assured in interviews, and thus appear to be less competent than nontribals.

Ultimately, though, as a few perceptive tribal leaders saw it, the issue for the tribals remains their capacity to change in such a way that they can eventually compete on equal terms with the nontribals who have settled in their midst and who continue to arrive. With assured quotas, tribals (or at least a proportion of them) have jobs, but not status, for outsiders assume that they hold their positions by virtue of reservations, not performance. Moreover, reservations mean that tribals compete against each other, an arrangement that generates, as we have seen, political schisms among the tribals as those who lose out in the competition try to redefine the category of who should be entitled to reservations. Finally, even with reservations tribals must compete with others in an open market—for the paradox of reservations is that the best graduates are assured employment in reserved positions, while the second best must be thrown into the open market.

Partnership

In recent years another alternative has been posed by some tribal leaders—that both tribals and nontribals join together for the improvement of Chota Nagpur. Those who advocate this position speak of ending the division between Christian and Hindu tribals and between tribals and nontribals by creating a new attachment to the region, to, as one tribal expressed it, "our soil." "Tribal or nontribal," he went on to say, "our fate is the same." Among those who share this outlook, the creation of the Chota Nagpur Development Council was greeted as the institutional framework within which this partnership could be nurtured. They see the council as the instrument for making demands upon the state and central government for additional resources for the development of the region, particularly for the construction of roads, the improvement of irrigation, the expansion of

206

education, and other programs that would particularly benefit the rural population.

This notion of partnership leaves unresolved, for the tribals at least, who among the nontribals is a "local" person—those who have been born in Chota Nagpur, residents for at least thirty years, or less?

Among many Bihari Hindus and other nontribal residents in Chota Nagpur there is a sense that the system of reservations stands as a barrier to a workable partnership. As one professor at the University of Ranchi explained: "Now a third of the new lecturers appointed to the colleges must be tribals. We have had some instances where a first-class nontribal was rejected for a position while a tribal with barely a second class was appointed. As long as few tribals apply for positions there will, of course, be little resentment, but once the tribals begin to fill up the 33 percent reservations then the resentment will grow. Many students," he continued, "don't like to oppose the demands of the tribals because that would make them right-wing, but they are privately critical. There is much resentment over reservations. First it was for fifteen years, then another ten years. How much longer should it go on?"

For many nontribals, then, partnership implies the end of special rights for tribals, a position that few tribals are yet willing to accept. For tribal leaders, partnership implies a joint effort on the part of those who live in Chota Nagpur to develop the region in such a way as to improve the education, the employment, and the social position of the tribals.

Trends

What lies ahead? Dwindling holdings and more landlessness in the countryside? More low-income, unskilled, and uneducated tribals moving to the cities? More educated tribals in search of urban employment? Resentment among nontribals against the reservation of jobs for tribals? All of these.

The opportunities for migration to the tea plantations of Assam and Bengal have come to an end, but the opportuni-

207

ties—and certainly the need—to work in the towns and cities of eastern India grow. For a substantial and increasing part of the rural tribal population, therefore, the necessity for urban migration is irreversibly under way. Within a single decade, from 1961 to 1971, the population of the tribals in urban Chota Nagpur nearly doubled.

While the number of tribals enrolled in primary school actually exceeds that of nontribals, the drop-out rate is substantially greater. Only 24,105 tribals were enrolled in secondary schools in the mid-sixties, and a mere 3,491 were enrolled in colleges and universities, but these figures represent major increases in less than a decade.[25] With the expansion of education there is now emerging a tribal middle class of secondary school and college-educated graduates seeking nonagricultural employment.

Neither the urbanized tribal middle classes nor the non-tribal urban migrants and their descendants will be content with what lies ahead. As the new tribal middle class increasingly penetrates the modern sectors—that is, the universities, administration, and industrial employment—many will experience the humiliations that have thus far characterized encounters between tribals and nontribals. Moreover, tribal youth with secondary school education, perceiving themselves as too educated to work in the fields, aspire to move into higher status and income positions that are not available. As this lower middle class grows, the combination of status

[25] For a review of educational trends among tribals in India as a whole, see J. P. Naik, *Education of the Scheduled Tribes* (*1965-66*) (New Delhi: Indian Council of Social Science Research, 1971). According to Naik's calculations, the spread of higher education among scheduled tribes in India is only one-seventh that in other communities, while in Bihar it is nearly a third (p. 29).

See also A. B. Bose, "Problems of Educational Development of Scheduled Tribes," *Man in India*, 50:1 (January-March 1970), 26-50; Nirmal Kumar Bose, *The Scheduled Caste and Tribes and their Present Condition*, University of Calcutta: Bijay Chandra Mazumdar Memorial Lectures, 1969 (Calcutta: Sakti Press, 1969); Jyoti Sen, "Problems in Tribal Transformation," *Man in India*, 46:4 (October-December 1966), 319-330.

humiliation and limited employment opportunities will constitute a formidable politicizing force.

Nor will the position of the nontribal middle class remain
unchanged. Their numbers too will increase and, barring a
more rapid increase in the number of jobs than the region
has experienced in recent years, so will the number of educated or semieducated unemployed. Many nontribals who, it
must be recalled, now constitute a majority of Chota Nagpur
no longer willingly accept the notion that a percentage of
jobs should be reserved for tribals. Nontribal resentment
against reservations, especially in the midst of increasing unemployment among educated tribals, is a sure formula for
bitterness among tribals. The dream of a "partnership,"
when economic opportunities for everyone remain so limited, seems as ill-fated as the dream of "restoring" the land.

In the context of scarcity, each group blames another for
its plight. For the lack of opportunities and for their exclu-
sion from Hindu society, non-Christian tribals blame Christian tribals. For trying to exclude them from what little patronage is available, the Christian tribals cast stones at the
tribal Hindus. Some of the tribal anger will be turned, as it
has in the past, toward the *dikus*, who are viewed by tribals
as responsible for their low status and their low mobility.
And in turn many nontribals in Chota Nagpur see reservations for tribals as restrictive of their own opportunities for
advancement.

Though the tribals of Chota Nagpur will continue to remain predominantly a rural people concerned with land issues and rural development, the new urban tribal classes
seem likely to play an ever more important role in defining
the political issues for the tribals and in working out a relationship with the nontribal settlers who are destined to remain in their midst.

BIBLIOGRAPHY:
CHOTA NAGPUR, BIHAR

Government Publications

Bihar District Gazetteers: Dhanbad District (Patna, 1964), *Hazaribagh District* (Patna, 1957), *Palamau District* (Patna, 1967), *Ranchi District* (Patna, 1970), *Singhbhum District* (Patna, 1958).

Bihar, Government of, *Handbook on Tribal Statistics of Bihar* (Part 1). Ranchi, 1969.

Chota Nagpur Tenancy Act, 1908, as modified up to 25th January 1950. Patna: Superintendent, Government Printing, 1950.

Report of the Advisory Committee on the Revision of the Lists of Scheduled Castes and Scheduled Tribes. Government of India Department of Social Security, Delhi: Government of India Press, 1965.

Report of the Commissioner for Scheduled Castes and Scheduled Tribes. Delhi: Manager of Publications. Annual.

Report of the Scheduled Areas and Scheduled Tribes Commission (The "Dhebar" Commission), 1960-61 (two volumes). Delhi: Government of India Press, 1962.

Social Mobility Movements Among Scheduled Castes and Scheduled Tribes of India, Office of the Registrar General. Delhi: Manager of Publications, 1970.

Census of India

1951, Volume V (Bihar), Part II-A.
1961, Volume V (Bihar), Parts I-A, II-D.
1971, Series 1—*India, Final Population*, Paper 1 of 1972.

Books and Articles

Ahmad, Enayat. *Bihar: A Physical, Economic and Regional Geography*. Ranchi: Ranchi University, 1965.

210

Bogaert, Michael Van Den. *The Influence of Caste, Education and Geographic Mobility on Labour Mobility at Jamshedpur, India.* Antwerp: Centre for Development Studies, Universitaire Faculteiten St. Ignatius, Universiteit Antwerpen, 1975.

Bose, A. B. "Problems of Educational Development of Scheduled Tribes," *Man in India*, 50:1 (January-March 1970), 26-50.

Bose, Nirmal Kumar. "The Hindu Method of Tribal Absorption," *Cultural Anthropology and Other Essays.* Calcutta: Indian Associated Publishing Co., 1953.

————. "Some Observations of Industrialization and Its Effects on Tribal Life," *Man in India*, 42:1 (January-March 1962), 5-9.

————. "National Integration and the Scheduled Castes and Scheduled Tribes," *Man in India*, 48:4 (October-December 1968), 289-296.

————. *The Scheduled Castes and Tribes and Their Present Condition.* University of Calcutta: Bijay Chandra Nazumdar Memorial Lectures, 1969. Calcutta: Sakti Press, 1969.

Burman, Dr. R. K. "Population and Social Process among the Tribes of India," *Plural Societies*, 6:4 (Winter 1975), 17-23.

Chatterjee, B. B.; Singh, P. N.; and Rao, G. R. *Riots in Rourkela: A Psychological Study.* Gandhian Institute of Studies. New Delhi: Popular Book Services, 1967.

Chaudhary, Vijay Chandra Prasad. *The Creation of Modern Bihar.* Patna: Krishna Chandra Chaudhary Yatin Press, 1964.

Dhan, R. O. *A Study of the Problem of Unemployment among the Trained Tribal Technicians in Ranchi.* Ranchi: Tribal Welfare Institute, 1965.

————. *Problem of Land Alienation in the District of Ranchi.* Ranchi: Tribal Welfare Institute, 1966.

————. *These Are My Tribesmen.* Ranchi: G.E.L. Church Press, 1967.

Ekka, Philip. "Revivalist Movements among the Tribals of Chota Nagpur," in K. Suresh Singh, ed., *Tribal Situations in India.* Simla: Indian Institute of Advanced Study, 1972, pp. 424-434.

Elwin, Verrier. *A New Deal for Tribal India.* New Delhi: Ministry of Home Affairs, 1963.

Fazal, A. *Principle and Practice of Land Tenure.* Ranchi: New Publishing Agency, 1969.

Fuchs, Stephen. *Rebellious Prophets: A Study of Messianic Movements in Indian Religions.* Bombay: Asia Publishing House, 1965. Chapter 2, "Messianic Movements in Bihar," pp. 21-72.

Gallagher, Orvoell Roger. "Migrant Labour from Tribal Chota Nagpur." Manuscript, Skidmore College, Saratoga Springs, N.Y., 197?.

Gupta, Satya Prakash. *Steps to Check the Tendency of Purchase and Resale of Tribal Land by the Clever Tribals.* Welfare Department, Government of Bihar, 1969.

Hoffman, J. "Principles of Succession and Inheritance among the Mundas," *The Journal of the Bihar and Orissa Research Society,* September 1915. (Reprinted in *Man in India,* 41 [October-December 1961], 324-338.)

Ivern, F. *Chotanagpur Survey.* New Delhi: Indian Social Institute, 1969.

Kunstadter, Peter. "Conflicts in the Development of Tribal Leadership in the Modern World," in L. P. Vidyarthi, ed., *Leadership in India.* Bombay: Asia Publishing House, 1967.

MacDougall, John Douglas. "Agrarian Reform vs. Religious Revitalization: The Sardar and Kherwar Movement among the Tribals of Bihar, India, 1858-1895." Ph.D. dissertation, Harvard University, 1974.

Mersch, Wolf. *Migration and Labour Recruitment for Coal Mines and Tea Plantations under Colonial Rule: The Case of Manbhum in Chota Nagpur, India 1881-1921.* Manuscript, South Asia Institute, University of Heidelberg, May 1972.

Misra, B. R. *Report on the Socio-Economic Survey of Jamshedpur City.* Patna: Bihar Legislative Council, 1959.

Naik, J. P. *Education of the Scheduled Tribes (1965-66)*. New Delhi: Indian Council of Social Science Research, 1971.

Orans, Martin. "A Tribal People in an Industrial Setting," in Milton Singer, ed., *Traditional India: Structure and Change*. Publication of the American Folklore Society, Bibliographical Series, Vol. x. Philadelphia, 1959.

————. *The Santal: A Tribe in Search of a Great Tradition*. Detroit: Wayne State University Press, 1965.

Panchbhai, S.C. "Group-Image, Identification and Preference in a Multiple Group Membership Situation and Their Significance in Intergroup Relations," *Bulletin of the Anthropological Survey of India*, 12:3-4 (1963), 171-184.

————. "The Levels of Regional and National Identification and Intergroup Relations Among Harijans and Adivasis," *Journal of Indian Anthropology Society*, 2 (1967), 75-83.

Prasad, Narmadeshwar. *Land and People of Tribal Bihar*. Ranchi: Bihar Tribal Research Institute, 1961.

Prasad, Narmadeshwar, and Sahay, Arun. *Impact of Industrialisation on Bihar Tribes*. Ranchi: Bihar Tribal Research Institute, 1961.

Report to the Bengalee Association, Bihar, 10th Conference. Dr. Bimanbehari Majumdar, President. Patna: 1968.

Roy, Sarat Chandra. *The Oraons of Chota Nagpur*. Calcutta: The Brahmo Mission Press, 1915.

————. "The Administrative History and Land Tenures of the Ranchi District under British Rule," *Man in India*, 41:4 (October-December 1961), 276-323.

————. *The Mundas and Their Country*. Bombay: Asia Publishing House, 1970 (reprinted from 1912 edition).

Sachchidananda. *Profiles of Tribal Culture in Bihar*. Calcutta: K. L. Mukhopadhyay, 1965.

Sahay, B. N. *Dynamics of Leadership*. New Delhi: Bookhive, 1969.

Sarkar, Sourindranath. *Psycho-Dynamics of Tribal Behavior.* Calcutta: Bookland Private Ltd., 1965.

Sen, Jyoti, "Christian Missions and their Programs of Training Workers," *Man in India,* 46:2 (April-June 1966), 114-120.

———. "Problems in Tribal Transformation," *Man in India,* 46: 4 (October-December 1966), 319-330.

Sharma, K. L. "Jharkhand Movement in Bihar," *Economic and Political Weekly,* 11:1 (January 10, 1976), 37-43.

Silent Revolution: A Report of the Second All-Chotanagpur Seminar. Samtoli, December 1969. Ranchi: Vikas Maitri, 1970.

Singh, Amar Kumar. *Alienation and Social Change in India.* Paper presented at a Transnational Symposium on Social-Psychological Dimensions of Social Change, American Psychological Association Convention, Washington, D.C., September 3-7, 1971.

Singh, K. Suresh, ed. *Tribal Situation in India.* Simla: Indian Institute of Advanced Study, 1972.

———. *The Dust-Storm and the Hanging Mist: Story of Birsa Munda and His Movement in Chotanagpur.* Calcutta: K. L. Mukhopadhyaya, 1966.

Sinha, R. K. *The Bihar Scheduled Areas Regulation, 1969.* Patna: Eastern Book Agency, 1971.

Sinha, S. C.; Sen, Jyoti; and Panchbhai, Sudhir. "The Concept of Diku among the Tribals of Chotanagpur," *Man in India,* 49:2 (April-June 1969), 121-138.

Sinha, Surendra Prasad. *Life and Times of Birsa Bhagwan.* Ranchi: Bihar Tribal Research Institute, 1964.

———. "Portrait of a Munda Leader: Birsa Bhagwan (1895-1900)," in L. P. Vidyarthi, ed., *Leadership in India.* Bombay: Asia Publishing House, 1967.

———. *The Problem of Land Alienation of the Tribals in and around Ranchi (1955-1965).* Studies in Tribal Bihar, No. 2. Ranchi: Bihar Tribal Research Institute, 1968.

Tinker, Hugh. *A New System of Slavery: The Export of In-*

dian Labour Overseas 1830-1920. London: Oxford University Press, 1974.

Vidyarthi, L. P. "Aspects of Tribal Leadership in Chota Nagpur" in L. P. Vidyarthi, ed., *Leadership in India*. Bombay: Asia Publishing House, 1967.

————. *Cultural Configuration of Ranchi: Survey of an Emerging Industrial City of Tribal India*. Calcutta: J. N. Basu, 1969.

————. *Industrialization in India: A Case Study of Tribal Bihar*. Ranchi: Department of Anthropology, Ranchi University, 1970.

————. "The Ranchi Tribals in Andaman and Nicobar Islands," *Journal of Social Research*, 14:2 (1971), 50-59.

————. "University Youths in Chotanagpur: A Study in Campus Life," *Journal of Social Research*, 15:2 (September 1972), 1-23.

Weiner, Myron, and Field, John Osgood. "How Tribal Constituencies in India Vote," in Myron Weiner and John Osgood Field, ed., *Electoral Politics in the Indian States: Three Disadvantaged Sectors*, Vol. II. Delhi: Manohar Book Service, 1975.

Andhra Pradesh, Administrative Divisions

216

FIVE

MIDDLE-CLASS PROTECTIONISM: *MULKIS* AGAINST MIGRANTS IN HYDERABAD

INTRODUCTION[1]

THE curious feature of the antimigrant movement in Hyderabad is that it is directed against people from the same state,
who speak the same language, who belong to the same religion, and who intermarry. Yet in 1969 a major political
movement developed in the city of Hyderabad that quickly
spread to towns throughout the western districts of Andhra
Pradesh in the region known as Telangana, a movement demanding that jobs for the people of Telangana (called *mulkis*)
be "safeguarded" (to use the term then widely employed)

[1] Data for this study rest on four sources: 1. published literature
by or on the Telangana movement, including Telangana Praja Samiti, Congress, and other political party literature, official statements,
and reports by central and state governments, and abundant newspaper coverage; 2. thirty-eight interviews with participants in the
movement and their opponents, including members of parliament and
the state Legislative Assembly, officials of the Andhra and Telangana
Non-Gazetted Officers Associations, Congress, and T.P.S., politicians,
student leaders, lawyers, academics at Osmania University and several colleges in Hyderabad, Muslim leaders, and journalists; 3. the
Andhra census of 1961 and 1971 and earlier reports of the Hyderabad State census; and 4. a survey of 148 students at five colleges in
Hyderabad. I am particularly grateful to three local scholars: Waheeduddin Khan, the coauthor of the best book on Hyderabad, who took
me on an invaluable and memorable tour of the city; K. V. Narayana
Rao, author of two excellent books on the politics of Andhra; and
P. Satyanarayana who, as a friend and knowledgeable guide, introduced me to the key persons in the complex Andhra political scene.
All three, along with Carolyn M. Elliot of Wellesley College, were
kind enough to read and comment on an earlier draft of this chapter. I also wish to take this opportunity to express my appreciation
to the helpful staff of the census office in Hyderabad.

against the "Andhras," that is, people in the eastern part of the state.

It was the students who launched the movement. It escalated in the now-classic fashion of student agitations. In early January 1969, two groups of students at Osmania University took out separate demonstrations: one calling for "safeguards," while the more militant group called for separating the Telangana region from the rest of the state. A clash occurred, accompanied by a *lathi* (baton) charge by the police. At the end of January, students throughout Hyderabad rallied in protest at Nizam College. The police entered the college grounds (reportedly without the permission of the principal), and the demonstrations became violent. Counter demonstrations were organized by students in the eastern part of the state to protest the anti-Andhra student agitations in Hyderabad.

Like an epidemic, the agitations spread throughout the state. Looting and arson broke out in the town of Warangal, a government officer was burnt to death in Nalgonda, and in various parts of Telangana migrants from the Andhra region began to flee in terror back to Andhra. As refugees moved into the train station in the coastal town of Vijayawada, people in Andhra became inflamed. At the border villages of Andhra and Telangana violence broke out. The government sent in troops to restore order, thousands were arrested, and the university was closed.

The violence subsided, but the movement continued to grow. Lower-level civil servants in the state government—the nongazetted officers (or N.G.O.s)—joined in the demand for safeguards against the Andhras. So did the Teachers Union. In March 1969, a Separate Telangana Convention was held in Hyderabad, chaired by a professor at Osmania University. It formed an organization to be known as the Telangana Praja Samiti (T.P.S.), committed to the formation of a separate state and the reservation of jobs for domiciles in a new Telangana government. Branches of the new organiza-

218

tion were quickly formed throughout Telangana. The T.P.S. entered candidates in two by-elections to the state assembly, and won. But its first popular test took place in the parliamentary elections of 1971, when Mrs. Gandhi, then the leader of a left-leaning reorganized Congress party, sought a national mandate for a campaign to abolish poverty. Mrs. Gandhi's Congress won the largest parliamentary majority in its history, but it suffered a defeat in the Telangana region of Andhra, where Congress lost ten of the fourteen parliamentary seats to the Telangana Praja Samiti.[2]

How did it all begin? Why should a movement, initiated by students and supported by teachers and state government clerks, sweep over an entire region? Why should there be such bitter hostility to migrants from another region of the same state, who belonged to the same culture, who spoke the same language, and whose numbers, as we shall see, were quite small?

One explanation was offered by the dominant political elite of Andhra, who saw the movement as motivated by dissident political leaders from Telangana unable to get what they regarded as an adequate share of the spoils of office. Guided by this theory—which reflected their own view of politics as a struggle for control over the patronage dispensed by the state—many Andhra leaders concluded that the movement could be ended by the incorporation of some of the dissident elites into the state political system. Hence, efforts were subsequently made to bring more Telangana leaders into the state cabinet, to appoint a Telangana man to the post of Congress president, and eventually to make

[2] Among the best brief accounts of the rise of the Telangana Praja Samiti are the following articles: D. B. Forrester, "Subregionalism in India: The Case of Telangana," *Pacific Affairs*, 43:1 (1970), 9; K. V. Narayana Rao, "Separate Telangana State? Background to the Current Agitation," *Journal of the Society for the Study of State Governments* (July-September 1969), 139; and Hugh Gray, "The Demand for a Separate Telangana State in India," *Asian Survey*, 11:5 (May 1971), 463-474.

219

someone from Telangana chief minister of the state. But the efforts to incorporate dissidents did not succeed in undermining the substantial social base of the Telangana Praja Samiti.

The theory that the movement merely represented an intra-elite struggle, with dissident politicians seeking popular support by bringing together a variety of grievances against the Andhras, does not bear up under scrutiny. Though this became a factor later, it was clearly not the case in the movement's early phase, since the 1969 agitations were politically leaderless. Not a single political party in the state endorsed the agitation. It was condemned by the governing Congress party. The communists, ordinarily sympathetic to student movements, denounced the agitation—for the communists were among the earliest and strongest advocates of a single Andhra identity and of a united Andhra state. Other opposition parties, including Jana Sangh, opposed the movement.

Moreover, in this initial phase none of the dissidents within the Congress party took part in the movement. It was not until it became clear that the Telangana Praja Samiti was a popular movement with a social base, not only in Hyderabad but in towns and rural areas throughout Telangana, that dissident politicians joined the movement; indeed, many of the student leaders were resentful of the johnnies-come-lately who were displacing them as spokesmen for the movement.

At the heart of the controversy was the question of whether the people of Andhra were a single people who shared Telugu as a common language, or whether they were two peoples—the Telanganas in the west, the Andhras in the east—and if they were two peoples, what distinguished them? On this issue the people of Telangana were themselves initially divided, but as the months went on more and more people argued that Telangana had an identity of its own quite apart from Andhra, and in time the movement itself began to define a new cultural identity.

To understand how the movement began and how it grew, we need an explanation of a dynamic character—one that

220

will explain why the movement started among students and civil servants, spread throughout the country, emphasized jobs first, then focused on defining a group identity and a distinctive culture. Finally, we shall take a look at how and why the political movement—but not the issues that it raised —came to an end in late 1973.

HISTORICAL ROOTS

The movement was rooted in history. Andhra is a composite state made up of three regions: Telangana, a region with nine districts, 44,000 square miles, and a 1971 population of 15.8 million, that had previously been part of the princely state of Hyderabad; coastal Andhra, with seven districts; and the Rayalaseema region in southern Andhra, with four districts, 62,000 square miles, and 27.7 million people, that had previously been a part of Madras state.[3]

A political movement for uniting the Telugu-speaking peoples of south India into a single state originated in Madras state in the 1920s. But not until after independence in 1953, after several years of militant agitation in the Telugu districts of Madras, were the Rayalaseema and coastal Andhra regions separated from Madras to create an Andhra state. There was less enthusiasm for a union of all Telugu-speaking peoples (a "Visalandhra" or greater Andhra) in the Telangana region.[4] Telangana was less developed economi-

[3] For this study the 1961 census data are taken from *Census of India, 1961*, Vol. II, *Andhra Pradesh*, Part I-A (i) *General Report*, New Delhi: Government of India; 1971 data are from *Census of India, 1971*, Series 2—*Andhra Pradesh*, Part II-A, *General Population Tables* (Hyderabad: Director of Census Operations, Andhra Pradesh, 1972).

[4] The pros and cons of transferring Telangana to a Visalandhra are described in the *Report of the States' Reorganisation Commission* (Delhi: Manager of Publications, Government of India, 1956). This government commission, appointed to review proposals for the reorganization of states along linguistic lines, recommended that Telangana be kept as a separate state, but the recommendation was not accepted by the central government.

221

cally, compared with coastal Andhra, and its population was considerably less educated. Many Telangana leaders feared that if a single state were formed they would be dominated by the people of the more developed coastal Andhra region. But the ties of language and of a common Telugu culture were strong, and both the Congress party and the communists in Telangana endorsed the idea of a Visalandhra. To allay the anxieties concerning the status of a backward Telangana in a Visalandhra, an agreement was reached between Congress representatives from Andhra and from the Telangana region. The document, known as the Gentlemen's Agreement, provided for a variety of safeguards for Telangana.[5] These included the formation of an autonomous Regional Council for Telangana with responsibility for the development of the region, restrictions on the admission of students to colleges and technical institutions in Telangana to students from the region, recruitment to government services in proportion to population, control over the sale of agricultural land in Telangana by the Regional Council (this provision was subsequently dropped), proportional representation in the state cabinet, and the establishment of domicile rules to ensure that local people would have proportionate recruitment in government service.

The domicile, or *mulki* rules, as they were called—that is, the notion of safeguarding employment and educational opportunities for local people—has a long history. The term itself comes from the Urdu *mulk*, meaning country, and *mulki* was a native or subject of the Nizam or Muslim ruler of Hyderabad. Those who were not *mulkis* were *ghair* (non) *mulkis*. Throughout the nineteenth and early twentieth cen-

---

[5] For an account of the events leading up to the formation of Andhra and the merger of Telangana, see K. V. Narayana Rao, *The Emergence of Andhra Pradesh* (Bombay: Popular Prakashan, 1973). For an account of the working of the regional committees and of the various safeguards, see K. V. Narayana Rao, *Telangana—A Study in the Regional Committees in India* (Calcutta: Minerva Associates, 1972).

turies the Nizam of Hyderabad recruited officials for his government from among the Muslims of northern India and even from western Asia. The local Muslims of Hyderabad, and eventually the Hindus as well, became increasingly resentful, especially as their educational level increased, and the demand arose for restricting employment in government service to local people. The Hyderabad Civil Service Rules were amended to provide that only *mulkis*, or domiciled individuals, could be employed; *mulki* was defined as a subject of Hyderabad state by birth, by residence if the person resided in the state for at least fifteen years, and by marriage if she is the wife of a *mulki*. The rules were quite elaborate, also specifying the status of children of civil servants, the status of divorced persons, and so on. In effect, the civil service rules were an instrument for defining citizenship in a state that had no sovereign status.

These guidelines for defining *mulki* were implicitly incorporated into the Gentlemen's Agreement, for if the rights of Telanganas were to be safeguarded then there had to be a precise definition of who was a native of Telangana.

HYDERABAD CITY: PERIPHERY CONTROLLING THE CENTER

The city of Hyderabad was made the capital of the new composite state. One of India's more attractive cities, Hyderabad shares with Delhi the distinction of being one of the few large cities in India that predates British rule and, like Delhi, was a center for the Mughal rulers. Hyderabad was founded in 1591 by the Muslim king of Golconda. It was initially the capital of the Mughal viceroyalty of the Deccan, but subsequently became an independent state when the Mughal empire in Delhi disintegrated. The city has attractive public gardens, many public buildings constructed by the Nizam, several large palace complexes and mansions built by members of the governing Muslim aristocracy, numerous mosques —including one of the largest in India—and the Charminar, a handsome sixteenth-century archway with four tall mina-

223

rets in the heart of the Muslim quarter, which has become the city's symbol.

After independence and the merger of Hyderabad state into India, the leadership of the Hyderabad State Congress, the ruling party, demanded that non-*mulkis* be sent back to their respective states to enable *mulkis* to take positions in the government.[6] In the early fifties there were demonstrations in Hyderabad city and in several districts towns with slogans "non-*mulkis* go back," "*Idli-Sambar* (Tamils and coastal Andhras) go back," and "Hyderabad for Hyderabadis."

The city grew slowly between 1951 and 1961,[7] largely because of an outmigration of Muslims to other parts of India, Pakistan, and western Asia. The 1971 census, however, reported a substantial increase in population, from 1,118,000 to 1,607,000, an increase of 489,000 persons, or 44 percent. The growth is partly related to the establishment of central government public sector factories in and around the city: Hindustan Machine Tools, Hindustan Aeronautics, Bharat Heavy Electricals, and the Electronic Corporation of India. The city also attracted private investors: Union Carbide, Usha Refrigeration Works, United Breweries, Shaw Wallace Distilleries, and Warner Hindustan.

When Hyderabad became the capital of an enlarged Andhra state, government officials were transferred to the city.

[6] For an early account of the rise of the *mulki* movement in Hyderabad, see Syed Abid Hasan, *Whither Hyderabad?* (Madras: B.N.K. Press, 1938). See also Rao, *The Emergence of Andhra Pradesh*, chapter XI; and Karen Leonard, "The Mulki-Non-Mulki Conflict in Hyderabad" (manuscript, November 1974).

[7] The city of Hyderabad grew substantially between 1931 and 1951, slowed thereafter, and resumed growth after 1961. Here are the population and decadal growth figures for the Hyderabad Municipal Corporation:

1901	448,000		1941	720,000	61%
1911	502,000	12%	1951	1,026,000	43%
1921	405,000	−19%	1961	1,118,000	9%
1931	427,000	10%	1971	1,607,000	44%

The state government constructed housing for the relocated government officials, and provided government loans to make it possible for the Andhras to acquire ownership. In time, "Andhra colonies," as they were called, sprung up in the city. Many businessmen from the Andhra region also moved into the city. Some started vineyards on the outskirts of the city (an attractive enterprise, since agricultural income is not subject to income tax), and some opened small firms and shops. The children of the new settlers entered the schools and colleges of Hyderabad and sought entrance into Osmania University. As the civil service expanded in size, following a trend in all the states, more and more Andhras found jobs in the government and moved to the city.

By 1961, a substantial proportion of the city were already migrants. In 1961, the census revealed that 284,000 persons were born outside the city: 29,000 came from rural areas of the district, 174,000 from other districts of Andhra, and 80,000 from outside the state, particularly from Mysore (21,000), Maharashtra (18,000), and Madras (14,000). In all, a fourth of the city's people were migrants.[8] (For figures on migration to and from Telangana and the Andhra region, see Table 5.1.)

Of the migrants, 119,000 were workers, the remainder their dependents or unemployed. Fewer than half (54,000) were illiterate, 22,000 were literate without an educational level, 15,000 had completed primary school, 20,000 had completed secondary school, and 8,000 had university degrees or equivalent. The educated classes, that is, those with high

[8] According to the 1961 census, the largest number of migrants to Telangana districts from outside the region are to Hyderabad (65,000); Khammam (79,000)—a border district; Nizamabad (20,000)—which attracts migrants to irrigated lands near the Nizam-sagar dam; and Nalgonda (42,000) which has the Nagarjunsagar dam (see Table 5.1). In all there were a quarter of a million migrants in Telangana from non-Telangana districts of the state. The Andhra districts with the largest number of emigrants to Telangana are Krishna (75,000) and Guntur (68,000), which together account for well over half the migration.

225

TABLE 5.1

Intraregional Migration in Telangana (1961)

District	Emigrants to Andhra region	Immigrants from Andhra region	Net balance	Migration rate per 1000 population
Mahbubnagar	18,166	15,932	− 2,184	− 1.37
Hyderabad	9,953	65,298	+55,345	+26.82
Medak	712	2,922	+ 2,210	+ 1.80
Nizamabad	1,677	19,910	+18,122	+17.84
Adilabad	473	5,144	+ 4,671	+ 4.63
Karimnagar	6,372	5,141	− 1,231	− 0.76
Warangal	6,988	17,854	+10,866	+ 7.03
Khammam	27,521	78,786	+51,265	+48.47
Nalgonda	31,954	41,600	+ 9,646	+ 6.12
Total	99,666	253,487	-153,821	+12.11

SOURCE: Computed from *Census of India, 1961*, Vol. II, *Andhra Pradesh*, Part I-A (i), *General Report.*

school and college degrees, constituted 24 percent of the migrant labor force, well above the educational level of the local population.

No census figures are available as to how many migrants into Hyderabad *city* came from districts outside of Telangana, but the census does report migration into the entire *district* of Hyderabad; 65,000 came from non-Telangana districts and 190,000 from other parts of Telangana. If nearly all of the non-Telangana migrants had moved to the city (which seems probable), then about a fourth of the city migrants came from the Andhra and Rayalaseema regions. The 1971 census reports that total migration to the *district* of Hyderabad had risen to 324,000 (as compared with 225,000 in 1961), of whom 104,000 came from non-Telangana districts and 220,000 from other districts of Telangana. Four districts of the Andhra delta—East Godavari, West Godavari,

226

Krishna, and Guntur—sent 70,500 migrants to Hyderabad district, as compared with only 39,300 in the 1961 census (see Table 5.2). Though we do not have educational statistics for these groups, there is evidence that coastal Andhra migrants were among the more educated migrants to the district.

TABLE 5.2

Migrants from Coastal Andhra to
Hyderabad District (1961, 1971)

	1961	1971	% increase
Srikakulam	1,500	1,800	20
Vishakhapatnam	3,200	4,600	44
East Godavari	8,400	16,000	90
West Godavari	7,700	12,500	62
Krishna	12,500	23,000	84
Guntur	10,700	19,000	78
Ongole*		4,000	
Nellore	4,600	6,000	30
	48,600	86,900	79

* A new district carved out of Guntur, Nellore, and Kurnool districts. The name of the district was subsequently changed to Prakasam.

SOURCE: *Census of India, 1961*, Vol. II, *Andhra Pradesh*, Part I-A 9 (i), *General Report*; and the *Census of India, 1971, Andhra Pradesh*, unpublished data made available by the Hyderabad office of the Andhra Pradesh census.

According to a study by Shah Manzoor Alam and Waheeduddin Khan[9] based on a field survey of migrants in Hyderabad, unskilled migrants are largely from other parts of Telangana, while Andhra migrants hold clerical and other middle-class positions. They estimate that 30 to 35 percent of the migrants are in government service, and that migrants

[9] Shah Manzoor Alam and Waheeduddin Khan, *Metropolitan Hyderabad and Its Region* (Bombay: Asia Publishing House, 1972).

from Andhra and from other states tend to hold the higher-income positions. Migrants from other states often hold executive positions in the central government undertakings located in Hyderabad city.

But as important as numbers was the question of political control. When Telangana was merged with Andhra, power shifted to political leaders from the Andhra region. The chief minister of the state was from the Andhra region, and so was the leader of the ruling Congress party. The most powerful portfolios in the cabinet were held by Andhras. Though according to the Gentlemen's Agreement one-third of all new positions in the state bureaucracy were to be allocated to the Telanganas, Andhra politicians reportedly used their position to provide proportionately more jobs for Andhras, largely through the method of accepting bogus domicile certificates. Telangana civil servants also became resentful of the government practice of allocating government-built residences to Andhra employees, while local Telangana civil servants continued to live in old and inferior housing. The Andhra colonies in Hyderabad soon became the symbol of the government's discriminatory policies toward the local population.

As one Hyderabad scholar, Waheeduddin Khan, put it, it was a case of the "periphery taking control of the center." The people of the periphery—the Andhras—used their control of the center—Hyderabad—to benefit themselves and the people of the Andhra region. Telangana politicians felt that more money and attention was given by the state government to the Andhra region than to the backward Telangana region. Large numbers of statistical tables and technical papers were prepared by each side to prove their case— the Telanganas claiming discrimination, the Andhras arguing that funds had been expended and appointments made on an equitable basis. But more important from the Telangana point of view was the visual impression of Andhra becoming prosperous, while Telangana remained stagnant. The coastal Andhra region has always been a more prosperous

228

agricultural region than the other areas that made up Andhra Pradesh, even before a united Andhra was created. But the advent of the green revolution in agriculture in the Andhra districts, particularly in the areas along the Godavari and Krishna rivers, widened the gap between the Andhra region and Telangana. In Krishna, Guntur, and East and West Godavari districts, paddy and tobacco production increased, new agro-industries to process sugar, rice, and tobacco were constructed, and there was a spurt in the construction of hotels and restaurants in the towns. With a rise in income more consumer goods flowed into the Andhra districts. Visitors could readily see more trucks and cars on the road, construction in the towns, and a more prosperous-looking population. Some Andhra peasants sold their land at high prices and purchased lands at lower prices in the newly irrigated districts of Telangana, especially in Nizamabad district. Andhra businessmen started a wine industry outside Hyderabad. Andhras built homes in Hyderabad and opened their own businesses and shops. Local Andhra leaders were frequently seen in government offices in Hyderabad arranging credit, pressing the government for fertilizers, seeds, and other agricultural assistance, trying to arrange for the admission of their sons to the local colleges, or finding a job for their sons in government service. In contrast, the people living in the dry areas of Telangana remained largely unaffected. Telangana peasants were hardly touched by the green revolution, since few had the irrigated lands that are a precondition for the use of the new hybrid varieties and fertilizers. Industries grew in Hyderabad, but public-sector firms recruited staff from all over India, while businesses started by Andhras tended to hire staff from the Andhra region, not *mulkis* from Hyderabad. Meanwhile, more young people in Hyderabad went to secondary schools and colleges, and there were far more graduates each year than the number of jobs that became available.

One statistic dramatically illustrates how unemployment grew, even though the city experienced considerable economic growth. In 1970, 66,000 persons registered for jobs at the employment exchange in Hyderabad, of whom only 3,000 were provided jobs.

The number of unemployed seeking clerical positions rose sharply from 10,400 in 1968 to 21,700 in 1970. Hyderabad had developed a class of middle-class youth, mainly high school graduates, who were unable to find employment in the city.[10]

"How would the people of Telangana gain if a separate state were formed?"[11] I asked a number of people in Hyderabad, including the principal of a prominent law college who was a staunch advocate of a separate Telangana state. With great clarity he stated a view that I heard frequently.

"First of all," he explained, "in a separate state there would be more employment opportunities since the Andhras would leave the state government. Some would leave because the state secretariat itself would be bifurcated and many officials would move with the new Andhra government. Perhaps the Andhras working in Telangana districts as school teachers and in the district-level administration wouldn't be able to move so readily since there might not be new jobs for them in an Andhra state. But there would be social pressures on the Andhras to leave. A new Andhra government would also have to create many supernumerary posts to accommodate the Andhras in Telangana who want to return to their own state."

"How many jobs do you think would be created in the state government?" I asked.

[10] Elsewhere in the state there was also a severe unemployment problem, but not as great as in Hyderabad. In the coastal town of Vijayawada, the registered unemployed rose from 14,000 to 18,000. The port town of Visakhapatnam has experienced a considerable growth in unemployment, from 11,000 to 22,000; but Visak, with its expanding port facilities and shopping industry is a boom town, its population having grown from 108,000 in 1951 to 211,000 in 1961, and 355,000 in 1971 (a 68 percent increase between 1961 and 1971).

[11] The case for a separate Telangana is presented in A. R. Thota, ed., *The Telangana Movement* (Hyderabad: Telangana University and College Teachers' Convention, 1969).

"I think that about 50,000 Andhras would go back, providing that many new jobs for people in Telangana.

"Secondly," he continued, "if the Andhras left, there would be more housing available in Hyderabad. Many of the Andhras working for the state government live in accommodations built by the Housing Board of the Andhra government, and if they left the Telanganas would take over their housing.

"Thirdly, as a separate state, Telangana would no longer be a neglected region. With our own political leadership we would utilize our own tax resources for development, and we would obtain assistance from the central government. Look at how well Haryana has done since it became a separate state! It has improved economically because it is a small state.[12]

"Finally, the movement of the wealthy Andhras into Hyderabad has increased inflation in the city since they buy so much consumer goods."

"But doesn't that help local merchants?" I asked. "No," he replied, "because the Andhras only patronize the Andhra-owned businesses. Besides, even if some Telangana businessmen gain, for people like me on fixed salaries we lose when there is a rise in prices."

We shall return to some of these points later. Now we shall only note how many of the grievances, such as employment, housing and prices, relate specifically to Hyderabad city and how the ejection of "outsiders" is seen as a way of relieving each of these problems.

The Social Base of the Telangana Praja Samiti

Earlier we described the explanation offered by Andhra politicians to account for the rise of the Telangana Praja Samiti —one that emphasized the role of dissident politicians. An alternative explanation, much more compatible with the

---

[12] Actually, Haryana was a high-growth region of the Punjab even before it became a separate state.

231

hypotheses offered here, has been put forward by Carolyn Elliot in her study of factional politics in Andhra.[13] She argues that the movement was sustained not by dissident politicians, but by dissident social classes who were no longer able to obtain benefits within the existing system of patronage. She identifies three such social classes: university students, seeking urban employment at a time when government was no longer hiring and Andhras held most of the posts in Hyderabad and in the Telangana region; peasants of Nizamabad and Nalgonda districts, who had sold their land to richer Andhra migrants and who were now resentful of their richer neighbors; and, finally, middle-level government employees, especially nongazetted officers resentful of government employees from Andhra who had obtained promotions.

This analysis fits well with our proposition concerning the ways in which local social classes feel blocked by migrants. All three groups perceived migrants from Andhra as obstacles—to employment, promotion, and enhanced income. The three groups were also linked to one another. Many lower civil servants are related to small landholding peasants, and the students at the colleges are often the children of civil servants or of landholding families. A substantial proportion of the N.G.O.s and many of the students are themselves migrants to Hyderabad from portions of rural Telangana. In a survey of several colleges in Hyderabad (see appendix, Hyderabad Student Survey) we discovered that more than half of the students had fathers working for the civil service. This is hardly surprising when one considers the enormous role played by government as an employer. In the state of Andhra, there are 663,000 persons working for the local, state, or central governments. If we add dependents, and note that in a society with an extended kin system the burden of unemployment falls not upon the state but upon employed relations, then we can grasp the extraordinary

[13] Carolyn M. Elliot, "The Limits of Patronage Politics" (manuscript, 1975).

232

role that government employment plays for the educated population of Hyderabad and other urban centers in the state.[14]

Many of the early student organizers of the Telangana movement were themselves of peasant background and were recent migrants to the city. Jaleel Pasha, one of the prominent organizers of the student movement in Hyderabad, comes from a rural area of Telangana. His father, an absentee landowner presently living in Hyderabad, reportedly owns a hundred acres of agricultural land. Pasha is the oldest of three sons. The family hopes to see his two younger brothers become an engineer and a doctor, but he envisages a political career for himself.[15] As president of the Hyderabad High School Student Union he was instrumental in bringing high school students into the movement for a separate Telangana. Like most of the students I interviewed, he emphasized the importance of government jobs as the main reason for advocating the creation of a separate state. As he sees it, a separate Telangana would vigorously "enforce the rules requiring *mulki* certificates for employment."

[14] There is no precise way of calculating what proportion of the educated classes are employed by government. Hyderabad city has nearly half a million (496,000) workers, of whom 103,000 are in industry, 23,000 in construction, 106,000 in trade and commerce, and 175,000 in what the census calls "other services," which includes most government employment. In the urban areas of the entire state (that is, settlements with more than 5,000 persons) a total of 1,945,000 are in these categories. Since government workers reside primarily in the urban areas, we can assume that from a third to a fourth of all of those employed in what can be loosely called the "modern" sector work for government. Actually, the ratio is considerably higher if we consider only those jobs that require some level of education. My own guess is that approximately half the jobs for secondary school and college graduates are in government and in public-sector firms. (Data computed from *Census of India 1971*, Andhra Pradesh, Part II-A, *General Population Tables.*)

[15] Pasha explained that he had chosen to enter a Muslim college when he completed high school "so that I could be elected president of the student union. I wanted to win support for a political career."

233

One of the leaders of the student movement at Osmania University, Shreedar Reddy, comes from a peasant family living sixty miles from Hyderabad. His father died when he was three, but his mother and other members of the family managing their hundred acres of land earned enough to send him to college. He was the first member of his family to be educated.[16] "My family has always been well-to-do," he said, "but they never thought of education." He emphasized that it was the students who started the movement for a separate Telangana, and only later were they joined by N.G.O.s, "who followed our call." Reddy sports a Castro-like beard, which he says he will not cut until a Telangana state is created. He emphasized the importance of "sincerity" in political leaders —a quality he felt none of the older politicians in Telangana had; like Pasha, he looks forward to a political career.

A third student leader I interviewed was a migrant from coastal Andhra but, surprisingly, he was a spokesman for a separate state. "I decided to support the movement," he explained, "when it became clear that all the students in my high school were in favor of a separate Telangana. I realized that I could no longer be a student leader [he is president of the student union at his high school] unless I supported the movement." Evidently, sentiment for a separate state was so intense among both high school and college students that only those who supported the movement had any chance of achieving positions of leadership.

It was always the job issue that was raised by the students. In early 1973, in the midst of the agitation for a separate state, I interviewed a group of students at a Muslim college in Hyderabad who were taking part in a hunger fast. A large tent had been erected on the college grounds (with the support of the college officials) with three or four students in the tent at any one time taking part in a twenty-four hour relay fast. "Why," I asked the fasting students, "do you want

16 Observers of the January 1969 agitation noted that many of the prominent student leaders came from rural peasant backgrounds and that they were often the first in their families to attend college.

a separate state?" "For jobs," was the immediate reply of one of the students. "We will get jobs because the Andhras will leave their government posts when a Telangana state is formed." "How many will leave?" I asked. "Fifty thousand will leave, so there will be that many new jobs," was the reply. "And what kind of jobs do you personally want?" I asked. "I want to be a clerk in the government," said one. "I would like to be a clerk in a bank," said another. "I want to be an upper divisional clerk [a more senior clerical position] in the government," replied the third.

It is evident that the Telanganas see opportunities for employment and promotions as finite. Since migrants from Andhra hold positions in government coveted by the Telangana middle class, it is they who must be ejected if jobs and promotions within the services are to become available to young men from Telangana.

The perception of employment as a zero-sum system is, under present circumstances in Hyderabad, probably accurate. The number of people entering the labor market each year in the city is substantially larger than the number of new jobs being created, especially for educated young people seeking middle-class positions. Unfortunately, the solution advocated by the T.P.S. is not likely to make much of a difference to job seekers. In a smaller state, the number of people employed by the state government would necessarily be reduced, so that the number of jobs acquired by the Telanganas—even if 50,000 Andhras left—would probably be small. Moreover, there would only be a one-time increase in employment that would benefit those currently seeking jobs, but each year thereafter there would be no greater increase in the number of positions for local people than probably would have been available in a larger state.

The demand for local employment at the cost of migrants is thus a response to a stagnant labor market which, in turn, is related to the slow pace of economic growth in Hyderabad and, indeed, elsewhere in much of urban India. State-wide development expenditures between 1965 and 1972 in Andhra

235

actually declined by 50 percent, though the state budget has remained constant at about Rs. 3 billion. Development expenditures declined for two reasons: an increase in nondevelopment expenditures by the state government, mainly in wages and benefits to state employees; and second, increased costs in the form of debt repayment to the central government for money borrowed for the construction of the Nagarjunasagar multipurpose dam in eastern Andhra. Nor have revenues increased, since the state government has been unwilling to increase either land or income taxes on farmers who have profited from irrigation expenditures and from the introduction of new agricultural technologies.

Thus, in the context of declining employment opportunities in proportion to growing demand, and with little investment that might accelerate economic growth, the demand for the expulsion of migrants and the employment of local people, even if its benefits are limited to a small proportion of those currently seeking employment, is politically attractive. For young people presently completing high school and college, the demand seems eminently rational.

CREATING A TELANGANA IDENTITY

If one is to displace a section of the labor force, it is psychologically necessary to persuade oneself that those who are being displaced are "outsiders," not entitled to the positions they hold. Supporters of the movement for a separate Telangana thus sought to define themselves as culturally distinct from the Andhras.[17] The task of identifying a distinctive Telangana identity is made difficult by two factors. The first is that the majority of people living in the Telangana region are Telugu-speaking Hindus who share a common language and religion with the people of coastal Andhra and Rayala-

[17] The Telangana Graduates Association (of Osmania University) passed a resolution that said that "what the people want is a state of their own which will establish their identity with a firm emotional and psychological base."

236

seema and who, as we have noted earlier, tend to wear the same dress (with minor exceptions, as we shall see), eat similar food (again with some exceptions), and racially belong to the same stock. Second, the Telangana region also contains a substantial proportion of Telugu and Urdu-speaking Muslims (constituting 10.8 percent of Telangana),[18] and a considerable number of people whose native language is Marathi and Kannada. How does one define a Telangana identity that encompasses such diversity? How do political leaders single out elements in the culture of Telangana that distinguish *mulkis* from the non-*mulkis* or Andhras, and that simultaneously link the diverse people of Telangana while distinguishing between Telangana and Andhra Telugu Hindus?

The search for such a distinctive cultural identity formed a significant feature of the Telangana movement. The heart of that search, hardly a claim to generate pride, but which served to justify the movement, was the assertion that the people of Telangana are "backward" in relation to people elsewhere in the state. The Telangana region was part of a princely state (in general the areas governed by the princes remained less developed than the areas governed directly by the British), with fewer educational facilities than the rest of India.[19] Illiteracy was high and few attended colleges and

[18] The 1971 Muslim population of Telangana was 1.7 million (out of 15.8 million), or 10.8 percent. In the remainder of Andhra there were 1.8 million Muslims out of a population of 27.7 million, or 6.5 percent. In the state as a whole, Muslims form 8 percent of the population. In the city of Hyderabad 38 percent of the population is Muslim. Between 1961 and 1971 the Muslim population in Andhra Pradesh increased more rapidly (29.5 percent) than that of the state as a whole (20 percent).

[19] Telangana is still educationally more backward. In Telangana districts the literacy rate ranges from a low of 14 percent in Adilabad district to a high (excluding Hyderabad) of only 18.5 percent in Khammam district. In contrast, literacy in the more developed coastal districts is between 30 and 35 percent. For the state as a whole, 24.6 percent of the population is literate. Data from *Census of India 1971*, Andhra Pradesh, Part II-A, *General Population Tables*.

237

universities. The civil service was less developed than in neighboring Madras, and less attention was given by the government to the development of agriculture. "The Andhras lived under the British," explained a Telangana Hindu, "while we lived under feudal rule. We were not exposed to modern competitive life as they were, so we remained a complacent, closed, contented society." An orthodox Muslim explained, "We were no match for the Uttar Pradesh Muslims and now we are no match for the Andhras. We are educationally backward and even our agricultural productivity is lower. We cannot do as well in education or on the land as the Andhras."[20]

It is this sense of being unable to compete that provides the principal justification for the system of safeguards. A young (age 30) Hyderabad lawyer who was an active participant in the Telangana movement noted that of the eight hundred lawyers practicing in the Hyderabad High Court, only a fourth were from Telangana. "Their lawyers," he noted, "have all had experience practicing in the Madras High Court while most of us are less experienced and younger." This young man from a peasant family in Nizamabad district was the first member of his family to be educated. "If the people here," he added, "must compete on merit alone, they do not stand a chance of winning even local posts. If there is an opening for an engineer and there is open competition from all over the country, then the Kerala man will get it. He probably has more degrees and may have worked in the U.S. or England. Our engineer will only have a local diploma. So what is his chance? If jobs are open to all and merit is the criteria, then the engineers from outside will get the jobs here. The people from Bombay, Madras, and Calcutta are better qualified.

[20] A professor at the university, caricaturing the different groups in Hyderabad and their capacity to work, said that "what the Malayalee [from Kerala] could do in a half hour, the Tamil Brahman would take one hour, the Tamil non-Brahman one-and-a-half hours, the Andhra Telugu two hours, and the Telangana two-and-a-half hours."

"The same holds for teachers," he continued. "We did not have qualified teachers or nurses. The nurses came from Kerala and the teachers from Andhra. If you threw all these posts open, outsiders would take them all. When our people become better educated, where will there be jobs for them?

"People here don't take to the principle of competition. The constitution says you will not discriminate because of religion, caste, place of birth—that means free competition. But because there are differences in culture, education, and so on, this principle cannot be followed. There must be equality in the social sense, equality in education, before there can be free competition."

It was evident that he, like many supporters of the Telangana movement, believed that the responsibility of the state was not to guarantee free competition to individuals, but rather to protect individuals *against* competition.

A persistent argument of Telangana supporters is that in a state with "advanced" and "backward" regions it was inevitable that the advanced regions would dominate, for the advanced people would move to the poorer areas and take the better jobs. "The issue," explained one member of the state Legislative Assembly, "is not whether the states in India are big or small, but whether one people shall be overlords of another. When you combine advanced and backward areas as you have in Andhra, that will happen. This is the main reason we want a separate state."

It was not simply that the Andhras had taken jobs and occupied land, but, from the viewpoint of the Telanganas, they had taken control of the political system. The civil servants in the state government, the judges in the high court, the chief political figures in the state government, and the leaders of the ruling party were from the more advanced regions. Once Telanganas came to feel that they were dominated by outsiders, no proposal for greater regional autonomy, or for more effective regional councils, or even for a system of reserving positions for local people by decentralizing government appointments could cool the sentiment

239

of the separatists. "Once we were governed by the Nizam," said one Telangana leader, "who was protected by the British raj, and after Andhra was formed we became dominated by the Andhras, who are now protected by the central government."

But for most Telanganas the notion of "backwardness" was hardly sufficient to define a distinctive identity; for that, one must identify some *cultural* characteristics that they all share. These elements have been found in Islamic culture, the culture of the political class that dominated Hyderabad state prior to independence. Speech, dress,[21] cuisine, and manners have in subtle but countless ways been influenced by Muslim culture. Urdu words have been incorporated into the Telugu widely spoken in Telangana. Muslim dishes are eaten. Tea is preferred (while Andhras, along with Tamils, Malayalees, and other south Indians are coffee drinkers). Educated Telanganas describe themselves as more gentle in their speech and manners, more cordial to guests, more leisurely, and less aggressive than the people of Andhra. A middle-aged Muslim, a prominent figure in the alumni association of Osmania University, explained: "I give a *salaam* [a gesture of greeting with the hand touching the forehead], but the Andhra man will never raise his hand. Young people should always salute older people. A government officer should return a salute to a servant. We are polite in dealing with subordinates. We speak to a rickshawalla or to an N.G.O. politely, but the Andhras don't behave this way. Feudalism gave us some traditions that we try to maintain."

A Telangana Hindu, an activist in the Telangana movement, expressed similar thoughts. "Feudal culture had its finer elements like social courtesies and human relationships.

[21] A few upper-class Telangana Hindus emulate the aristocratic Muslim style of dress by wearing a *sherwani*, an elegant long jacket with high collar, rather than the *dhoti* commonly worn by Andhras and most Telanganas. A more distinguishing feature of the Andhras, however, is the scarf they often wear around their neck (called a *paipancha*), which is almost never worn by Telanganas.

We can always feel the vulgarity of the Andhras. The Andhras suffered from living under the Tamils. They felt persecuted by the Tamils and they learned the art of doing to others what the Tamils had done to them. That is why they are aggressive and coarse."[22]

An orthodox Muslim leader, the principal of a Muslim college in Hyderabad, gave his feelings about a Telangana identity. "The differences between Andhras and Telanganas is over language. The Andhras say that the Telanganas don't speak Telugu well. They condemn Telangana culture because they say that it has been influenced by Muslim culture. The people from Uttar Pradesh used to look down on the Hyderabad Muslims for speaking an inferior Urdu, and now the Andhra people look down upon the people of Telangana for speaking bad Telugu!"

A Telangana Hindu saw the Urdu influence in his Telugu as a source of his sense of Indianness. "We studied Urdu, not English the way the Andhras in Madras did. It gave us some identification with the north. So we don't have that southern complex that the Tamils and the Andhras have. When they started an anti-Hindi agitation we laughed at that. You see, we never had the linguistic feelings that the Andhras had because they emphasized language in order to separate themselves from the Tamils. The notion of language as the basis of hostility was their invention, not ours.

[22] The Andhras, of course, use different words to describe the same traits. Andhras speak of "initiative" rather than "aggressiveness" to describe themselves; and while the Andhras agree that the Telanganas are educationally backward, they describe them as culturally backward as well. An Andhra trade unionist in Hyderabad, a leader of the Andhra N.G.O.s, said that "the Andhras are culturally more advanced than the Telanganas. Our doctors, lawyers, and civil servants are not only better educated, but they have more initiative. The Telanganas are accustomed to a feudal administration while we know the advanced British administration. We also speak Telugu better than they do because we conform more to the written Telugu. The Telanganas have produced no eminent scientists, educators, or technocrats as the Andhras have. In that way you can say they are culturally backward."

"We are also closer to the north on matters of religion. For example, our main religious festivals are Holi and Dessera [festivals of northern India], while the Andhras celebrate Pongal [a Tamil festival]."

Muslim supporters of Telangana were not only proud that the Muslim influence was seen by Hindus as a key ingredient of a Telangana identity, but they also saw the political advantages of a smaller state in which Muslims would constitute a larger minority. In Andhra Pradesh, Muslims (in 1971) are 8 percent of the population, but as we noted earlier, they are 10.8 percent of Telangana. Many Muslims incorrectly believe that the proportion is substantially higher.[23] Evidently the high proportion of Muslims in the city of Hyderabad (26 percent) gives many Muslims an exaggerated view of the demographic position of Muslims in Telangana. Muslim supporters also believe that the Urdu language would be given greater prominence in a smaller state, and that in a separate Telangana Muslims would have a greater chance of asserting their own identity. "We Muslims," explained the official of the Osmania Graduate Association, "are emotionally and sentimentally attached to Telangana."

Another theme that appeared in discussions of a Telangana identity was the notion of its cosmopolitanism as distinct from the parochialism of an Andhra identity. The same Muslim noted that the city of Hyderabad consists of many linguistic communities—"Tamil Brahmans who came here fifty years ago from Madras to escape the anti-Brahman movement, the Maharashtrians, the Kannarese, and so many others. These people all call themselves Hyderabadis because they feel they belong here."

This sentiment was enthusiastically echoed by members of linguistic minorities in Hyderabad, several of whom were prominent at rallies supporting a separate Telangana. Indeed,

[23] When I asked the orthodox principal of the Muslim college in Hyderabad how Muslims would benefit by a Telangana state, he bluntly—but inaccurately—said, "Now we Muslims are 7 percent in Andhra. In Telangana we will be 18 percent."

Telangana leaders were particularly eager to have members of linguistic minorities participate in the movement, since their involvement demonstrated that they were not anti-Indian and that nativist sentiments were directed against the dominating Andhras, not against all outsiders residing in the region. Telangana supporters spoke more broadly of the advantages of smaller states as a way of breaking up linguistic provincialism. The Telangana movement, as they saw it, was in the forefront of the movement to break up the large states like Uttar Pradesh, Bihar, Madhya Pradesh, and Maharashtra.[24]

Many Telangana supporters spoke with enthusiasm of the cultural diversity and cosmopolitanism that marked the culture of preindependence princely Hyderabad. Critics of the Telangana movement, especially members of the left parties, described this sentiment as a romantic myth. But whatever the reality, it is important to note that supporters of an independent Telangana, eager to find a distinctive cultural identity, have chosen to identify themselves with much of the style of the Muslim aristocracy of older Hyderabad, its language, cuisine, manners, even dress, and some (imagined or real) notions of its cosmopolitan outlook—the social class, ironically, which the Telangana middle class fought to dispossess during the struggle for independence.

[24] Indeed, it was precisely this fear that the Telangana movement might trigger similar movements elsewhere in India that led politicians from the larger states to express their opposition. Dilip Mukherjee, writing in the *Times of India* ("The Crisis in Andhra: Serious Challenge to New Delhi," November 25, 1972), noted that "the reason why the Centre is adverse to Andhra's division is the repercussions it might have on other states, particularly Uttar Pradesh, Bihar, and Madhya Pradesh. In May this year, an action committee came into being in Lucknow, spearheaded by Congress MLAs of western Uttar Pradesh to agitate for division of this sprawling state of ninety million people into three units—Braj Pradesh, Avadh, and Purvi Pradesh. In Bihar, the tribal people of Chotanagpur division have long been arguing that their future will remain insecure until they become masters of their own house. The Vidarbha area of Maharashtra nurses a similar feeling."

Explaining the Movement

We began this study by posing the question of how a nativist movement could arise against a people with whom the natives shared so much in common, with whom they had so much social contact and, indeed, with whom they even inter-married? Neither a cultural difference model nor a communications interaction model provides satisfactory explanations. Nor does an intraelite conflict model fit a movement that initially attracted none of the political party elites in the region.

Three factors seem to be crucial for explaining the Telangana movement.

The first is the disparity, not only in the levels of economic development but, more critically, in the levels of skills (including education) between the Telangana region and coastal Andhra. Historical circumstances, primarily related to the fact that one region was ruled by a native prince and the other by the British, seem to account for many of these differences.

Second, the emergence of new economic opportunities in the Telangana region, particularly in the capital city of Hyderabad, and in several rural districts with new irrigation facilities, led to substantial migration into the region. Between 1931 and 1971 there was a net in-migration to Telangana (with a substantial increase after 1961), while there was a net out-migration from the Andhra region (Table 5.3). Contrary to most conventional wisdom about migration flows, the movement was from the more to the less prosperous region of the state. The resulting influx was unwelcomed by the Telanganas, who saw themselves losing in the competition for jobs in government services, in private firms, and even in the competitive struggle for land.

Third, and most critically, education in the entire state, but especially in Telangana, expanded more rapidly than employment opportunities. The number of students in secondary schools in Telangana leaped fivefold from 82,000 in

244

TABLE 5.3

Net Decadal Migration by Regions
of Andhras Pradesh (1931-1971)

	Telangana region		Andhra region	
Decade	Total Migrants	Net migration per 1000 population	Total migrants	Net migration per 1000 population
1931–1941	+214,029	+22.9	−208,140	−11.6
1941–1951	+282,274	+25.9	−272,925	−13.5
1951–1961	+105,365	+ 8.3	−107,128	− 4.6
1961–1971	+585,262	+40.0	−632,587	−22.8

SOURCE: Computed from *Census of India, 1971, Andhra Pradesh,* Part II-A, *General Population Tables,* pp. 90-94.

1956 to 440,000 in 1966, compared to little more than doubling in the Andhra region from 299,000 to 620,000. During this same decade, college enrollment tripled in Telangana from 12,300 to 37,700, while increasing by 50 percent in Andhra from 39,400 to 59,100.

The employment situation substantially deteriorated after 1965. In that year some 41,000 persons found jobs through the state employment exchanges (251,000 were registered), but by 1970 the number employed dropped to 26,000, even as the number seeking jobs increased to 312,000. The decline in the Andhra Pradesh economy, as we noted earlier, was related to the sharp drop in state government plan expenditures; with a decline in developmental investments after 1965-1966, economic stagnation set in.[25]

[25] For a review of the economic development of Andhra Pradesh from 1951 to 1971, see the excellent introductory essay in the *Fifth Plan, Andhra Pradesh: Review of Development,* Technical Papers, published by the Planning and Cooperation Department of the Government of Andhra Pradesh, Hyderabad, n.d. (1972?). Its author is B.P.R. Vithal, then secretary of the Planning and Cooperation Department.

The decline in employment after 1965 was particularly acute in the public sector. In 1966, for example, the state government had 15,700 new jobs; in 1967 it dropped to 10,200, and in 1968 to 8,800. When the student movement commenced in early 1969, it was at a time when the number of new jobs available had reached a low point, and a time when the number of secondary school and college graduates was increasing.

Many young Telanganas, lower-level civil servants—and in time much of the Telangana electorate—attributed growing unemployment to what they believed was the neglect of their region by the government, and by the domination of political elites from coastal Andhra. There was, as they saw it, an uneven distribution of political power among the elites within the state to the detriment of the Telanganas. Some Telanganas did hold positions of authority within the state government, but they were seen as ineffectual "stooges," or —to use the more colorful Urdu word to describe Telugu ministers who supported Brahmananda Reddy, the Andhra chief minister—*chamcha*, or spoon. By virtue of their political positions in the state government, it was argued, Andhras were in a better position to exercise *pairavi*, another Urdu word that conveys the steps one takes to further one's case before the government. In a political system that rests so heavily on patronage and influence, and where access to government resources and jobs are widely perceived as the key to both educational and economic advancement, the disparity in political power between the two regions was popularly seen as disadvantageous to the people of Telangana and as responsible for the growing unemployment.

Had the economic disparity between the people of the two regions and the worsening job situation for the Telangana middle class not been reinforced by a disparity in political power between the two regions, perhaps the separatist movement might not have persisted. But when the "periphery took control of the center," again to quote Waheeduddin Khan,

246

the political leadership in Telangana fought back, and since they had no prospect of asserting their control over the entire state (Telangana constitutes only 36 percent of the total population of the state), separation appeared to be the most feasible means of reestablishing political control over their own region.

It was these elements rather than cultural differences that shaped the Telangana movement. It was political circumstances engendered by a constricting employment situation for the Telangana middle class—and the psychological need to find a difference between Telangana and the rest of the state—that necessitated the search for a distinctive cultural identity. The Islamic component of Telangana culture was elevated, for it was the one element that could simultaneously bring diverse Telanganas together and distinguish them from the Andhras. But we should also note that each community within Telangana chose to emphasize different features of a Telangana identity, and each had different motives for supporting the movement. The Telangana Hindus wished to free themselves from political and economic competition from the Andhras; the Muslims hoped to improve their balance of power and status in a smaller state; and the non-Telugu sought to identify themselves with a local sons-of-the-soil movement and thereby demonstrate that they too had been domiciled.

It is premature to say that there is now a distinctive Telangana identity. To an outsider the identity appears to be quite shallow and, in any event, to be so closely linked to a political movement that its future rests more on political circumstances than on any underlying forces of cultural change. This is by no means to suggest that it has no future, for we have seen elsewhere in the world that political experiences can shape a community's cultural identity; moreover, as the sense of group identity based upon self-defined cultural differences grows, in time these cultural differences may themselves become the source of irritations and social cleavages.

247

THE END OF THE TELANGANA MOVEMENT?

The demand for separation on the part of the Telanganas— and then later the demand for the bifurcation of the state by the Andhras—was closely linked to a set of legal and constitutional issues. In each stage of the agitation, decisions by the state and central governments, and more often by the courts, proved to be decisive in either accelerating or calming the claims of the respective groups. Of critical importance was the Public Employment (Requirement as to Residence) Act of 1957, which was passed by parliament to permit the Andhra government to impose domicile rules on employment within regions of the state. This law, which perpetuated the *mulki* rules formulated by the Nizam, and which provided the social contract that made the unification of Andhra possible, was undermined by a decision of the Andhra High Court in January 1969, when the court ruled that the State Electricity Board did not come under the purview of the act—a decision that precipitated the student agitations for the implementation of the *mulki* rules. A few months later India's Supreme Court declared unconstitutional that portion of the act (Section 3) providing residence qualifications for people seeking jobs in the Telangana region, on the grounds that no discrimination could be made between people *within* a state as to their residence, though such a restriction could be made for the state as a whole: "Requirement as to residence within the State in Article 16 (3) can only mean a requirement as to residence anywhere within the State and not in a particular region of the State."[26] The court decision was interpreted to mean that a state could impose a residence requirement for government employment, but it could not discriminate among individuals who lived in different portions of the same state.

Many Telangana political leaders concluded that if there were a separate state of Telangana, it would then be constitutional to limit employment to those who were domiciled

[26] K. V. Narayana Rao, *Telangana: A Study in the Regional Committees in India* (Calcutta: Minerva Associates, 1972), p. 281.

in the region. In an effort to undermine the growing sentiment for secession, the state government first pressed New Delhi to amend the constitution, and, failing that, it then proceeded to decentralize appointments to the administrative services so as to permit "local" people to have preferences in employment. At the same time, an intensive legal battle began to determine whether the *mulki* rules were revived or not by the Supreme Court's decision if the court rejected Section 3. In October 1972, the Supreme Court ruled that the *mulki* rules were "laws in force" immediately before the commencement of the constitution under Article 35B. According to this constitutional provision, any law in force immediately before the commencement of the constitution in the territory of India shall "subject to such permissible adaptations and modifications under the Constitution continue in force until altered, repealed or amended by Parliament."

With the restoration of the *mulki* rules, the strict legal position was that every person holding a government position in the Telangana region, including Hyderabad city, both state and central government personnel, had to be *mulkis*. While the Public Employment Act (Section 3)provided that in the composite government employment should be in the ratio of two to one as between Andhra and Telangana employees (that is, roughly corresponding to the population ratio of the two regions), and that only the nongazetted employees (that is, the lower ranks of the civil services) were covered, the *mulki* rules affected all ranks of government employees and provided for no ratios.

The Andhra political leadership argued that if the *mulki* rules were enforced and the Andhras denied employment in the state services in the capital city, then there was no longer any reason to keep the state intact, and two separate states should be created. Separatist leaders in Telangana agreed. The Telangana Praja Samiti called for the bifurcation of Andhra, saying that the implementation of the *mulki* rules and the continuation of an integrated state "are two incompatible propositions." An Andhra member of the state as-

249

sembly said that "this is really a question of the honour and dignity of the Andhra people, enabling them to live in their capital as equal citizens, educate their children and compete for jobs with a sense of pride and equality."[27] The *Hindu*, a prominent Madras daily, editorially urged the government to amend the *mulki* rules so that there would not be "total" recruitment of *mulkis* for all government posts in all levels of administration, and to limit whatever new rules are formulated for ten years. "It would be against the spirit of the Constitution to deny the right of equal opportunity for any citizen in any part of the country. The sooner Telangana outgrows the need for such invidious protection the better."[28]

"Merit, not *mulki*!" declared the leader of one of the Andhra student organizations, but a prominent Telangana student leader replied, "*mulki* rules are like medicine to ailing Telangana and they should be there till Telangana is developed fully. The medicine cannot be withdrawn if a patient continues to be sick."[29]

Telangana leaders insisted that some form of protection or bifurcation was necessary. One prominent Telangana leader, a former member of parliament, had this to say: "If we have a separate state, then most of them will leave and there will be more jobs for our people. Since they control the government, their people are always getting the jobs and the industries ministry makes sure that even private businessmen hire their people. Yes, it is true that they are also better qualified for many of the jobs than we are. Maybe they are better qualified but why is merit so important? We can have some inefficiency. That will be necessary if our people are to get jobs. Are we not entitled to jobs just because we are not as qualified? [When would the reservations end?] I don't think they will ever end. We came from a feudal background and we have less education than they do. Their people are more aggressive than we are. It is in their character. Our boys

[27] *Hindu*, November 3, 1972.
[28] "*Mulki* and Non-*Mulki*," *Hindu*, October 19, 1972.
[29] *Hindu*, November 15, 1972.

250

are not as ambitious as theirs. So how can we ever catch up? If one tree is four feet high and another is six feet high, will the four-foot tree ever catch up? By the time the four foot tree is six feet the other tree may be nine or ten feet high, maybe even more. If our people are not protected from them, we will not have jobs and they will come here and dominate us."[30]

On only one point did the opposing groups agree. Article 35B of the constitution, which kept the controversial *mulki* rules alive, also provided a remedy—an act of parliament. In late November 1972, Prime Minister Gandhi proposed a five-point formula for resolving the *mulki* dispute. "At the time of the formation of the State of Andhra Pradesh in 1956," she explained, "it was realized that the people of Telangana would need some safeguards in the matter of public employment and an agreed formula was evolved by the representatives of the Andhra and Telangana regions. As a matter of national policy, residential qualifications for public employment was removed in other areas, yet Parliament enacted the Public Employment (Requirement as to Residence) Act in 1957, in order to provide for posts in the subordinate services in the Telangana area being filled subject to the requirement of residence in that area. This law was envisaged as a temporary measure and was to expire in March 1974; however, it was struck down by the Supreme Court early in 1969. Since then, the question of devising suitable measures to secure representation of the people of the Telangana region in the public services of the State has been engaging the attention of the Central and State Governments. The recent judgment of the Supreme Court has brought about a new situation requiring the adoption of further measures to give effect to the objectives envisaged earlier."

She then announced a five-point formula to resolve the crisis: 1. residential qualifications would apply only for recruitment of nongazetted posts and posts of *tahsildar* and

[30] Interview with the author, February 1973, Hyderabad.

251

civil assistant surgeons in the Telangana region (that is, most of the senior administrative posts would be excluded from the rules); 2. these safeguards would remain operative in the Telangana region up to 1980, and Hyderabad till 1977; 3. promotion within the government would be regionalized up to the first or second gazetted level, but would not apply to the services that act as direct feeders to the all-India services (where, presumably, merit and seniority would continue to apply); 4. educational facilities would not be affected; facilities would be expanded and additional facilities would not be subject to any restrictions on the basis of residence; 5. there would be a "composite" police force in the capital city.

Mrs. Gandhi's proposal did not initially end the demand, either in Telangana or Andhra, for separation; Andhras remained concerned that too much had been conceded to Telangana, while Telangana leaders feared that the protections were not sufficient. In Delhi, many national leaders, while supporting the prime minister's move, expressed fears at its implications for a common citizenship. The New Delhi newspaper, the *Statesman*, editorially supported Mrs. Gandhi's proposal as necessary for maintaining a united Andhra, but asserted: "While the concept of preferential treatment is admittedly repugnant to the spirit and letter of the Constitution, this is a relic of the past which cannot be abrogated overnight without serious dislocation."[31]

Even Mrs. Gandhi expressed an ambivalence. Speaking to the Lok Sabha (December 21, 1972), she said, "Rightly there is a strong feeling in the country that any residential qualification for public employment goes against the very concept of common citizenship which is enshrined in our Constitution. But at the same time, the framers of the Constitution did realise that the safeguards available to people who suffer from special hardships could not be abrogated straightaway."

Mrs. Gandhi also implied that "protections" were a legacy

[31] "Counsel of Despair," *Statesman*, December 27, 1972.

of the past, to be replaced in due course by a "common" citizenship. But is this the direction in which Indian law is proceeding? Subsequent developments in Andhra suggested otherwise.

In December 1972, Mrs. Gandhi's five-point formula was incorporated into the *Mulki* Rules Act passed by parliament. But in the Andhra region there was considerable opposition to the act from junior engineers, civil assistant surgeons, and nongazetted officers, all directly affected, and from Andhra lawyers, students, and politicians who felt that they would remain "second-class" citizens in the capital city. In early 1973, as the agitation continued, the central government announced the imposition of president's rule upon the state.

A month later, in a bizarre ruling, the Andhra High Court announced on a technicality that the *mulki* rules applied only to a person born outside of Telangana and residing there for fifteen years, but did not include the native-born, a decision that invalidated the key provisions of the new *Mulki* Rules Act. Still, a new formula was sought, this time after extensive discussions between leaders of the two regions and the minister of state for home affairs. By mutual agreement, India's constitution was amended[32] so as to enable the president of India to issue orders permitting the Andhra government to regionalize appointments and promotions in the state services, and to take residence into account for the purpose of admission to educational institutions under the control of the state government. Moreover, under this constitutional amendment, the president could "specify any part or parts of the State which shall be regarded as the local area" for these purposes.

Even as the central government took action on the constitutional front, it also acted politically. The central government removed the dominant Andhra leadership from control over the state government, and placed Congressmen from Telangana in politically stronger positions. The cooptation of Telangana politicians, along with promises to enforce the

[32] The Constitution (Thirty-Second Amendment) Act, 1973.

safeguards, did much to undermine the Telangana Praja Samiti's demand for a separate state.[33]

The constitutional amendment was soon followed by a series of presidential orders. The first defined local candidates and local areas for purposes of admission into educational institutions. Andhra was divided into three regions: Telangana, seven coastal districts, and the remaining southern districts. Of seats in all government colleges and universities, 85 percent were reserved for candidates from the region in which the educational institution was located.[34] In another presidential order the state was divided into seven zones, each with two or three districts, "for the purposes of recruitment, appointment, discharge, seniority, promotion, and transfer . . . in respect of that category of posts" in the state administrative services.[35] Under this order, a fixed percentage of posts was allocated to each zone—for example, 80 percent of lower-division clerks, 70 percent of other nongazetted categories, 60 percent of *tahsildars* and junior engineers, and so on. In addition, each of the seven zones was allocated a prescribed share of the 60 percent of the posts of civil assistant surgeons reserved for local candidates.

Both orders were specific as to what constitutes domicility: residence in the area for not less than four years and, when an educational qualification has been prescribed, four years in an academic institution within the local area. Under this definition, then, students would be admitted into the university in the area in which they attended four years of secondary school, except for a few selected statewide institutions (such as the Agricultural University) where recruitment would be based on a quota system for each region.

[33] For a detailed account of how the central government attempted to resolve the conflict between Telangana and Andhra, see Hugh Gray, "The Failure of the Demand for a Separate Andhra State," *Asian Survey*, 14:4 (April 1974), 338-349.

[34] Andhra Pradesh Educational Institutions (Regulation of Admissions) Order, 1974.

[35] Andhra Pradesh Public Employment (Organization of Local Cadres and Regulation of Direct Recruitment) Order, 1975.

No expiration date was placed upon any of these presidential orders. The constitutional amendment and the subsequent presidential orders not only legitimized the principle of domicile restrictions on employment and education, but extended the principle so that it would be applicable in accordance with whatever seemed to the government to be an appropriate way for defining "locality," either by region or district.

With the new ordinances and constitutional amendment, and through the political intervention by the central government, the state of Andhra was kept intact and the demand by the Telangana Praja Samiti for a separate Telangana state was brought to an end. But the distinction between *mulki* and non-*mulki*, between sons of the Telangana soil and outsiders was not ended; on the contrary, the political movement succeeded in modifying the law and the constitution so that the principle of preferences for local people was extended to the entire state. While in other states the demand of the sons of the soil for preferences meant the natives of the *state*, the Telangana movement succeeded in extending the principle of preferences to the sons of the regional soil *within* the states.

Appendix: Hyderabad Student Survey

As we have seen, the students in Hyderabad played an important role in the movement against the Andhra migrants and for the creation of a separate Telangana state. This is a report on a survey of the attitudes of 148 students at five colleges in Hyderabad; two Muslim colleges (the Urdu Arts College and the Anwar-ul-Uloom College), a liberal arts and commerce college (AV College), a science college (New Science College), and one evening science college (Agarwal Evening). The students in the survey had diverse backgrounds: 60 percent were Hindu and 40 percent were Muslim; 77 percent came from the Telangana region, and 23 percent came from outside; nearly half (46.5%) came from the lowest income groups (their fathers earned less than Rs.

255

200 per month), while a fifth (20%) had fathers with income above Rs. 500. More than two-thirds (69%) reported that their fathers were in white-collar and professional occupations, while the remainder had fathers who were peasants (21%), or workers (10%). The largest number of the students surveyed were in the arts (39%), followed by science (35%), and law and commerce (26%).

A striking feature of their background—in itself an interesting finding—is that 76 of the 148 students surveyed, or 51 percent of the students, reported that their fathers worked for the government. Twenty-eight students (19%) reported that their fathers worked for the central government, another 19 percent had fathers who held gazetted positions in the state civil service, and 13 percent had fathers who held nongazetted positions in the state government.

The survey was administered in one or two classes in each of the colleges by a member of the faculty. The questionnaire was in English, since English is the medium of instruction in the colleges, but the instructor explained the questions in Telugu or Urdu as seemed appropriate. Some of the questions were open-ended, but these did not have a high response rate. Only questions with a high response are reported here.

The survey was intended as a pilot study, but circumstances prevented a follow-up survey from being conducted. Among the limitations to the survey are the following: 1. we do not know how representative these students are of the larger student population in Hyderabad; 2. since the number surveyed is small, few cross-tabulations are statistically reliable, and the use of controls is difficult or impossible; 3. in the absence of surveys of the adult population in Hyderabad, we are unable to compare the response of these students to the larger population; 4. finally, there were omissions and poorly worded questions characteristic of a preliminary survey.

Major Findings

1. Nearly 60 percent of the students from Telangana favored the formation of a separate Telangana state. Muslim

256

students were evenly divided, but Hindu students were over-whelmingly in favor.

2. Of the Telangana-born students, 58 percent were in favor of discouraging people from other states and other parts of Andhra from coming to Telangana, as contrasted with 26 percent who came from outside the region. Neither religion nor father's income is significantly associated with this view. Law and commerce students were most in favor of discouraging migrants, science and arts students less so.

3. Nearly half of the Telangana-born students (49.6%) were in favor of restricting the purchase of land in Telangana to domiciles; among the non-Telangana students, only 23.5 percent were in favor.

4. A surprising finding is that the non-Telangana students who have migrated to Hyderabad report that they are indifferent as to whether they live in a neighborhood with people from their own community (59%), while less than a fifth (17.6%) say they would like to live in their own community. Among native-born Telanganas, however, more have firmer feelings on the matter (only 40% are indifferent), with 37 percent preferring to live in mixed areas, and 23 percent (slightly higher than the migrants) preferring to live in their own community. Students whose fathers are in the lowest income group (below Rs. 200) are more likely to prefer to live in their own community than others (30%). On this question there does not appear to be any significant difference between Muslims and Hindus, though the non-Telangana Hindus are more in favor of mixed neighborhoods or are indifferent. The arts students are the most indifferent, the law and commerce students are the most for mixing, and the science students are the most in favor of living within their own community.

5. Two questions were asked concerning the attitudes of students toward violence and toward dictatorship. Fifty-three percent of the students agreed that "these days to counter the violence of certain groups we must be prepared to use violence." The survey showed that students whose fathers were professionals or peasants were most in favor of violence, and

257

the richer students more than the poorer students, but there was no significant difference between migrants and non-migrants, or between Hindus and Muslims, although (with a small N) the Hindus from outside of Telangana appeared to be more in favor of violence than others.

Of all the attitudinal questions, the one receiving the greatest approval was the statement, "At least over the short run, what India needs is a dictatorship." Sixty-three percent of the students agreed, and among the non-Telangana students, 76 percent agreed. There were no significant differences between Hindus and Muslims, but the Brahmans and Sunni Muslims gave the highest agreement (79 and 71%). Students with well-to-do fathers (earning above Rs. 500) were the most in favor (81.5%), as were the science students (75.5%), while the arts students were the most opposed to dictatorship.

6. The survey of party preferences showed that the students could be simultaneously in favor of both the Congress party (71%), which governed the country and the state, and the Telangana Praja Samiti (58%), its opponent on the issue of forming a separate state. Clearly the students saw the T.S.P. as a one-issue party, while their basic sympathies on other issues were with Congress. The Muslims expressed greater support for Congress than did the Hindus, and correspondingly less support for the T.S.P.

NOTE: The field survey was administered by Dr. P. Satyanarayana, a lecturer in public administration at AV College in Hyderabad. The statistical analysis of the data was prepared by Jesse L. White, Jr. at M.I.T. The survey was conducted in 1971.

BIBLIOGRAPHY

Public Documents (Chronological)

Constitutional Rules of H.E.H. the Nizam's Government. Hyderabad, 1925

Government of Hyderabad, Hyderabad Civil Service Regulations, 1st November 1949, Chapter III, General Rules for Regulating Allowances (Mulki Rules).

Report of the States Reorganisation Commission. Delhi: Manager of Publications, Government of India, 1956.

Gentlemen's Agreement arrived at on 20th February 1956 between Andhra and Hyderabad Leaders for the formation of Andhra Pradesh.

Public Employment (Requirement as to Residence) Act, 1957. Passed by the Houses of Parliament.

The Andhra Pradesh Regional Committee Order, 1958.

The Andhra Pradesh Public Employment (Requirement as to Residence) Rule, 1959.

The Public Employment (Requirement as to Residence) Amendment Act, 1964.

Committee of Jurists, Report on Telangana Safeguards (Public Employment). New Delhi: Ministry of Home Affairs, Government of India, 1969.

All Party Agreement of 19th January 1969 on Telangana Safeguards.

Judgment of the Supreme Court of India, Writ Petition No. 65 of 1969, A.V.S. Narasimha Rao versus the State of Andhra Pradesh, 28th March 1969.

Prime Minister's Eight Point Plan statement in Parliament on April 11, 1969.

Report of the Committee on Telangana Surpluses. Delhi: Ministry of Home Affairs, Government of India, 1969.

First Report of the Ad-Hoc Committee on Services on Telangana Services Problems, Andhra Pradesh Regional Committee. Hyderabad, 1969.

259

Judgment of the High Court of Judicature Andhra Pradesh. Hyderabad, 9 December 1970.

Second Report of the Sub-Committee on Services on Integration of Services and Other Matters, Andhra Pradesh Regional Committee. Hyderabad: Andhra Pradesh Legislature, 29 June 1971.

Third Report of the Sub-Committee on Services on Mulki Rules, Andhra Pradesh Regional Committee. Hyderabad: Andhra Pradesh Legislature, 1972.

Andhra Pradesh Regional Committee, Fifth Report of the Sub-Committee on Services on Service Matters. Hyderabad: Andhra Pradesh Legislature, 1972.

Prime Minister's Five Point Formula Statement in Parliament on 27th November 1972.

The Constitution (Thirty-Second Amendment) Act, 1973, received the assent of the President on 3rd May 1974. Published in Andhra Pradesh Gazette, 27 June 1974, Part III-B, pp. 505-511.

Andhra Pradesh Educational Institutions (Regulation of Admissions) Order, 1974, Order issued by the President of India with respect to the State of Andhra Pradesh, 3 July 1974.

The Andhra Pradesh Administrative Tribunal Order, Order issued by the President of India, 19 May 1975.

Other Government Reports

Census of India

1961. Vol. II, Andhra Pradesh, Part I-A (i), *General Report*. New Delhi: Government of India.

1961, Vol. II, Andhra Pradesh, Part IX, *State Atlas, Andhra Pradesh*.

1971, Series 2, Andhra Pradesh, Part IIA, *General Population Tables*. Hyderabad: Director of Census Operations, Andhra Pradesh, 1972.

Fifth Plan, Andhra Pradesh: Review of Development, Technical Papers. Planning and Cooperation Department, Government of Andhra Pradesh, n.d. (1972?).

Statistical Abstract of Andhra Pradesh 1960. Bureau of Economics and Statistics. Hyderabad: Government of Andhra Pradesh, 1962.

Statistics on Employment and Unemployment. Director of Employment and Training, Andhra Pradesh. Hyderabad, 1970.

Books and Articles

Alam, Shah Manzoor, and Khan, Waheeduddin. *Metropolitan Hyderabad and its Regions*. Bombay: Asia Publishing House, 1972.

Bernstorff, Dagmar. "Eclipse of 'Reddy-Raj'? The Attempted Restructuring of Congress Party Leadership in Andhra Pradesh," *Asian Survey*, 13:10 (October 1972), 959-979.

Colossal Loss to Telangana (Sequel to Agitation). Department of Information and Public Relations. Hyderabad: Government of Andhra Pradesh, 1969.

Elliot, Carolyn M. "Decline of a Patrimonial Regime: The Telangana Rebellion in India, 1946-51," *Journal of Asian Studies*, 34:1 (November 1974), 27-47.

————. "The Limits of Patronage Politics." Manuscript, 1975.

————. "The Problem of Autonomy: The Osmania University Case," in Susanne H. Rudolph and Lloyd I. Rudolph, *Education and Politics in India*. Cambridge: Harvard University Press, 1972.

Forrester, D. B. "Subregionalism in India: The Case of Telangana," *Pacific Affairs*, 43:1 (Spring 1970), 5-21.

Gour, Raj Bahadur. *Mulki Tangles in Andhra Pradesh: The Communist Approach*. New Delhi: Communist Party of India, 1972.

Gray, Hugh. "The Demand for a Separate Telangana State in India," *Asian Survey*, 11:5 (May 1971), 463-474.

————. "The Failure of the Demand for a Separate Andhra State," *Asian Survey*, 14:4 (April 1974), 338-349.

————. "The Landed Gentry of Telangana, Andhra Pradesh," in E. Leach and S. N. Mukherjee, *Elites in South Asia*. Cambridge: Cambridge University Press, 1970.

261

Hasan, Syed Abid. *Whither Hyderabad?* Madras: B.N.K. Press, 1938.

Implementation of Prime Minister's Plan for Telangana. Information and Public Relations Department. Hyderabad: Government of Andhra Pradesh, 1969.

Khan, Rasheedu-din. "Muslim Leadership and Electoral Politics in Hyderabad," *Economic and Political Weekly,* 6:15 (April 17, 1971), 783-793.

Leonard, Karen. "The Mulki-Non-Mulki Conflict in Hyderabad State." Manuscript, November 1975.

Memoranda to the Central Advisory Committee on a Few of the Grievances of Telangana Gazetted Officers. Hyderabad: Hyderabad Services Association, 1969.

Memoranda Submitted to the Prime Minister on Behalf of the Telangana Service Associations Rejecting Five Point Formula and Reiterating the Request for Implementation of the Judgment of the Supreme Court on Mulki Rules. Hyderabad, December 8, 1972.

The Mulki Rules: Their Genesis and After. Hyderabad: Andhra Pradesh Legislature Congress Party, n.d. (1972?)

Narain, Vatsela. *Demographic Study of Andhra Pradesh: A Census Analysis.* Demographic Training and Research Center. Bombay: Chembur, 1971.

National Council of Applied Economic Research. *Techno-Economic Survey of Andhra Pradesh.* Hyderabad, n.d.

New Deal for Telangana. Hyderabad: Department of Information, Public Relations, and Tourism, 1970.

Rao, A. Vasudeva. *Telangana—An Economic Problem.* Department of Information and Public Relations. Hyderabad: Government of Andhra Pradesh, 1969.

Rao, C. H. Hanumantha. "Budgetary Surplus of Telangana." *Economic and Political Weekly,* 4:42 (October 18, 1969), 1665-1676.

Rao, C. H. Venkateswara. *Reception Address.* Telangana Convention, March 8-9, 1969.

Rao, J. B. Narsing. *Separate Telangana—A Suicidal Slogan.* Department of Information and Public Relations. Hyderabad: Government of Andhra Pradesh, n.d.

Rao, K. V. Narayana. *The Emergence of Andhra Pradesh.* Bombay: Popular Prakashan, 1973.

————. *Telangana—A Study in the Regional Committees in India.* Calcutta: Minerva Associates, 1972.

————. "Separate Telangana State? Background to the Current Agitation," *Journal of the Society for the Study of State Governments* (New Delhi, July-September 1969), 129-143.

Reddy, G. Ram. "Uni-Party Dominance in Centre-State Relations: Andhra Pradesh Experience," in B. L. Maheshwari, ed., *Centre-State Relations in the Seventies,* 1973.

Reddy, K. Subhas Chandra. *Telangana: A Study in Regionalism: An Opinion Survey of the Political Elite.* Hyderabad: Osmania University Department of Political Science, n.d.

Reddy, M. Narayan. *Facts about Mulki Rules.* Hyderabad, n.d. (1972?)

Select Documents on Telangana. Andhra Pradesh Legislature. Hyderabad, 1972.

Sen, Mohit. "Twists in Telangana," *Economic and Political Weekly,* 6:15 (April 10, 1971), 774-775.

"Separatism and Strife in Andhra," *New York Times,* July 15, 1969.

Seshadri, K. "Administrative Problems in Andhra Pradesh Panchayati Raj," *Journal of Administration,* 9 (January 1970).

————. "The Telangana Agitation and Politics of Andhra Pradesh," *Indian Journal of Political Science,* 31:1 (January-March, 1970), 60-81.

Shakha, Janasambandha. *Facts about Telangana.* Hyderabad: Government of Andhra Pradesh, n.d.

————. *Telangana and Employment.* Hyderabad: Government of Andhra Pradesh, 1969.

Social Area Analysis of Metropolitan Hyderabad. Hyderabad Metropolitan Research Project, Technical Bulletin 3. Mimeographed, Osmania University, May 1966.

"Telangana in Turmoil," *Mainstream* (8 February 1969, 15 February 1969).

Telangana Praja Samiti. *Police Atrocities in Telangana.* Hyderabad, 1969.

Telangana Safeguards. Issued by Andhra Employees Coordination Committee. Hyderabad, n.d.

Thota, A. R., ed. *The Telangana Movement.* Hyderabad: Telangana University and College Teachers' Convention, 1969.

United We Stand. Hyderabad: Andhra Pradesh Congress Committee, 1969.

Violation of Telangana Services Safeguard. A Report. New Delhi: Telangana Non-Gazetted Officers Union, 1968.

Voice of Telangana Employees. Hyderabad: Telangana Non-Gazetted Officers Union, n.d.

SIX

MIGRATION AND
THE RISE OF NATIVISM

OVERVIEW

THUS far, we have examined three nativist movements. In Assam we looked at the struggle by the indigenous Assamese to gain control over their own administration and educational system, and to assert the special claims of Assamese in relation to the Bengalis and other migrant communities. Fearful of being overwhelmed in both the cultural and economic spheres, the Assamese turned to politics to establish their dominant position. In Chota Nagpur, a native tribal population—a poor, illiterate, and predominantly rural people—have been overwhelmed by waves of migrants who have settled in their region over the past century. The migrants dominate the steel and mining industry, industrial establishments, and the region's schools and colleges, so that the indigenous tribesmen are today a minority, living in a region whose administrators, teachers, factory owners, lawyers, and merchants come from outside. Unable to cope with these changes, many tribesmen have turned to messianic cults, separatist movements, and radical politics. In contrast with the Assamese, who as a majority within their own state can exercise political power, the tribals, as a minority, remain a politically powerless people. Finally, we have looked at the conflicts that have arisen in the Telangana region of Andhra over the migration of people from the more prosperous eastern agricultural delta districts. Both anxious and jealous over the entrance of migrants into the state administrative services, their purchase of housing in the capital city of Hyderabad, their acquisition of land in the countryside, and their predominant power in the state government, the educated middle classes of Telangana turned against the Andhras, sought

265

greater power in the state government, and demanded preferential rules for employment. The result was not only a triumph for the Telanganas, but the extension of preferential policies in employment to all "local" people throughout the state.

To these three examples, let us briefly add two other instances of significant antimigrant nativist political movements.

In Bombay, a city known for the wide variety of its linguistic, religious, and cultural communities, a political party called the Shiv Sena[1] has demanded that jobs in the city not be given to migrants from other Indian states. The Shiv Sena has been particularly hostile to the Tamil migrant population for occupying the middle-class jobs sought by the local Marathi-speaking population. Within two years of its founding in 1966, the Shiv Sena became the largest single opposition party in the Bombay municipal elections, supported by a majority of the Marathi-speaking people in the city. And though the Shiv Sena did not gain power in the state government, the governing Congress party adopted many of its demands: by putting pressure on private employees to recruit Marathi-speaking people rather than migrants, by giving preferences to local people for employment in the state government, and by tacitly supporting moves to place Marathi signs on both public and private places so as to convert Bombay from a cosmopolitan multiethnic center to a Marathi city.

In the south Indian city of Bangalore in the state of Mysore, a political party emerged in the late sixties known as the Kannada Chaluvaligars (the Kannada word for "agita-

[1] For accounts of the Shiv Sena, see Ram Joshi, "The Shiv Sena: A Movement in Search of Legitimacy," *Asian Survey*, 10:11 (November 1970); Mary Fainsod Katzenstein, "Origins of Nativism: The Emergence of Shiv Sena in Bombay," *Asian Survey*, 13:4 (April 1973); and Mary Fainsod Katzenstein, "Politics of Population Movements: The Case of Bombay," *Economic and Political Weekly*, 10:51 (December 20, 1975).

tors"), calling for restrictions against Tamil, Malayali, and Telugu migrants to the city, and demanding that employment preferences be given to the local Kannada-speaking population. The party won several seats in elections to the municipal corporation in a city widely regarded throughout India as a model of linguistic harmony. But like the Shiv Sena, its political support was largely confined to a single city with a large migrant population; it did not spread its influence either to the countryside or to the more ethnically homogeneous urban centers.

In each of these instances, antimigrant sentiment took a highly organized political form; in four of the five cases (Assam is the only exception) opposition parties ran on nativist platforms calling for employment preferences for sons of the soil. In several of these states, there has been substantial violence against the migrant communities. In both Assam and Andhra, the military had to be called upon to restore order as a result of clashes between the local population and migrant minorities. And in Bombay there have been attacks against businessmen who failed to hire local people or post Marathi signs.

In other states, nativism has taken a less organized and generally a less virulent form, but it has been present.[2] Meghalaya has adopted a residential permit bill that requires that persons from outside the state have to obtain a permit from governmental authorities even to stay in the state for more than four months. In Kerala, an agitation at a factory demanding that jobs be provided for local people resulted in police firing to disperse the crowd when it set fire to the factory. In West Bengal, the state assembly passed a law stipulating that anyone living in the state for ten years should be treated as a "son of the soil," entitled to preferential treatment in employment. In Tamil Nadu, where people speak of *mannin mainder* (Tamil for "sons of the soil"), the state

[2] These examples of nativism are cited in several articles in the November 3, 1974 issue (95:36) of the *Illustrated Weekly of India*.

government retaliated against Maharashtra's anti-Tamil policy by sending employers a replica of the Maharashtra government's order on job reservations, though this proved to be largely a political gesture in a state where skilled local labor and the local middle class compete effectively against migrants.

In this chapter, we shall look at the growth of opposition to intercultural migrations in India, consider why opposition has become highly organized in some but not in all high-migrant areas, why nativist sentiment is stronger among some classes and ethnic groups than among others, and why opposition emerged in the late 1960s and 1970s, though intercultural migrations have taken place for a long time.

"Nativism" is a term widely used in the United States to indicate intense opposition to minorities because of their foreign origin.[3] At different times in American history nativists have had varying antagonists—Roman Catholic Irish, the new migrants from southern and eastern Europe, and the "hyphenated" Germans and Japanese. At times nativists were concerned with the volume and character of migration, as these affected the rate at which newcomers culturally and politically assimilated into American life. At other times nativists expressed avowed racist views, dwelling on the special racial qualities of Anglo-Saxons on the one hand, or of Orientals, southern Europeans, Jews, or Slavs on the other. Nativism in America also took a variety of organizational forms—the Know Nothing Party before the Civil War, the American Protective Association at the end of the nineteenth century, and the Ku Klux Klan in more recent times. But whoever the antagonists, and whatever the tone, or the or-

---

[3] Among the standard accounts of nativism in America are John Higham, *Strangers in the Land: Patterns of American Nativism, 1860-1925* (New Brunswick: Rutgers University Press, 1955); Marcus Hansen, *The Immigrant in American History* (Cambridge: Harvard University Press, 1940); and Barbara Miller Solomon, *Ancestors and Immigrants: A Changing New England* (Cambridge: Harvard University Press, 1956).

ganizational form, nativism always has been linked to various concepts of American national identity.

Antimigrant movements in India can also be seen as nativist phenomena; that is, they represent the response of emerging "nationalities" (a term that requires special explanation in this context) to internal minorities with foreign connections. In the Indian context, the emerging "nationalities" are regionally, linguistically, and tribally defined; and the "foreign" minorities or migrants are defined as people who speak the language and share the cultural beliefs and identities of those who live in other regions of India. It should be apparent, of course, that in one fundamental respect the Indian case differs from the American: the nativist reaction in India is not to foreign migrants from another country, but to so-called "foreigners" from other cultures within the same political system. In this respect, however, the Indian experience is more typical of what is found in many other developing countries where plural conceptions of nationality (or what may be more precisely called "regional cultural identities") are often emerging within a single political framework.

The nativist phenomenon in such societies is particularly complex, since various conceptions of nationality or of regional cultural identity are in the process of being formulated, and nativism is often a way of defining what one is and what one is not. It is, so to speak, a way of defining the boundaries of one's own culture in relation to others. It is in this context that we can ask what the conditions are under which nativist movements arise, and why some migrant groups are defined as alien while others are not.

THEORIES OF NATIVISM

Since social scientists concerned with understanding and explaining the nativist phenomenon first looked at the United States, it is only appropriate that we first turn to theories derived from the American experience. At the risk of oversimplification, we can classify the various theories under five

269

general groups: 1. economic competitive models that explain the rise of nativist movements in terms of employment fears, especially on the part of the working class; 2. status mobility models that emphasize the threats posed by migrants to the social status of the upper and middle classes, especially to New England Anglo-Saxons; 3. political interest models that stress the fears of certain social classes to the political threat of migrants to their interests, as was the case in the reactions of the antebellum South to the demand by migrants for homestead legislation, and early twentieth-century urban elites to the growing political power of the "new" migrants in urban areas; 4. psychological models that emphasize the relationship between frustration and aggression and the importance of displacement, particularly as exemplified by the hostility often expressed by one minority group against another; and 5. demographic models that suggest that the rate and volume of migrants into a given social space may pass some "optimum" threshold of tolerance by the native population.

The most common-sense explanation is one that points to cultural differences as a determinant of native-migrant conflicts. It is useful, therefore, to consider first to what extent cultural differences explain the rise of nativism.

The cultural-difference explanation holds that People A (the local people) and People B (the migrants) subscribe to antagonistic cultural norms: People B eat beef or pork, while People A consider such food practices counter to their religious sensibilities; People A respect cleanliness (or orderliness, or punctuality), in contrast with the slovenliness (or disorderliness, or indifference to time) of People B; People A admire the arts, while People B prefer business activities to aestheic pursuits; People A are warmhearted and generous, while People B are clannish and aloof to strangers; People A believe in one God, People B are polytheistic; People A worship their God directly without intermediaries, while People B have elaborate rituals and a hierarchical priesthood; People

270

A are attached to the land, while People B prefer urban life; People A prefer leisure to work, while People B are thrifty, hard working, enterprising; and so on.

The Indian experience suggests that a cultural explanation of conflict is inadequate in three respects: first, there are numerous instances in India of people with widely differing cultures living side by side without conflict. Indeed, in India's agglutinative society it would be difficult to find a rural district or an urban settlement in which there were not people speaking different languages, subscribing to different religions, differing in cultural beliefs and social practices. All of India's large cities are multilingual and multicultural, and have large migrant populations. But while Bombay, Hyderabad, Gauhati, Bangalore, and Ranchi have nativist movements, Delhi and Calcutta do not. Moreover, two communities with cultural differences may clash in one locale, but not in another. There is, for example, nativist sentiment in Bihar and Orissa against Bengali administrators, teachers, office clerks, and lawyers, but no significant nativist sentiment in Calcutta against Oriya and Bihari workers.

Second, there are innumerable instances of conflicts between our hypothetical People A (the locals) and People B (the migrants) when the cultural differences between these two groups are not as great as between People A and People C (another migrant community). Wherever there is a clash between the local population and a culturally different migrant community, one can often point to another migrant community with whom the local people do not clash, but with whom their cultural differences are at least as great. The nativist movement in Bombay opposes Tamil migrants but pays little attention to the more numerous Telugu-speaking migrants, though both are equally alien people from the south. The local population of the city of Hyderabad is hostile to migrants from the eastern part of the state with whom they share a common language, culture, and religion, but there is little resentment against Marathi, Kan-

271

nada, and Tamil-speaking migrants from other states, with whom the cultural differences are far more substantial.

Finally, the cultural-difference theory does not explain why nativist movements have arisen in the past few years, although in most regions there have been no major increases in interregional migration, and cultural differences are no greater now (and in some instances are reduced by an increase in bilingualism) than a few years ago. Why did nativist movements emerge in the 1960s and 1970s in the towns all along the Brahmaputra valley of Assam, and in the cities of Bombay, Hyderabad, Bangalore, and Ranchi? Why are there fluctuations in nativist movements in India over time? For example, in its various guises nativism was a political force in Chota Nagpur at the end of the nineteenth century, declined for several decades, and became important again in the late thirties. In Hyderabad, nativism was important in the 1920s for several years but then remained dormant until the 1960s. And Bangalore had no history of nativism until the Chaluvaligar party emerged in the late sixties.

In short, there are many instances in which migrants and natives with substantial cultural differences do not conflict, instances in which cultural differences appear to be slight but conflicts are intense, and instances when cultural groups are currently in bitter conflict though at other times their relationship was either cordial or indifferent.

But if cultural differences are not causes of nativist hostility to migrants, they surely accompany such conflicts. It is a distinguishing feature of nativism that its adherents emphasize differences, no matter how slight, between the culture of the native and the culture of the migrant, for nativism defines who is local in cultural, not territorial, terms. Local people, the natives, or what Indians call the "sons of the soil," are defined by the tribe to which they belong, their mother tongue, or the ethnic community with which they identify, rather than the locale of their birth. The Marathi-speaking person, for example, who migrated to Bombay from a town in Mysore state may be considered local by the na-

272

tivist, but not the Bombay-born Tamil whose parents or even grandparents came to the city decades ago.

Nativism magnifies cultural differences precisely because it is a way of defining cultural identity. In Hyderabad, as we have noted, supporters of the nativist Telangana Praja Samiti, seeking to restrict the employment of "outsiders" in the Telangana region and in the capital city of Hyderabad, have attempted to define a Telangana cultural identity that would distinguish them from the Telugu-speaking people in the rest of the state. They emphasize small differences in food habits (Telangana people drink tea, while the people in the eastern districts drink coffee!), language (there are more Urdu words used in the Telugu spoken in the Telangana region), and clothing (the men in the east wear a characteristic scarf not worn by men from Telangana). Much is made of small nuances in manners, gestures, attitudes, and accents, most of which reflect the historic domination of the Telangana region by the Muslims. Yet little more than twenty years ago, when there was a movement for uniting the Telugu-speaking people into a single state, the political movements in Telangana sought to minimize the importance of Islamic culture and to emphasize the similarities of all Telugu-speaking people. Here again we see how political movements attempt to define cultural identities.[4]

In short, nativist movements convert cultural differences into cultural conflicts. Cultural conflicts should be viewed as the effects, not the determinants, of nativism. What, then, are the determinants? Are there any factors that must be present when there are nativist political movements and which, conversely, can never be present in the absence of nativist movements?

---

[4] For an excellent discussion of how the political process determines which ethnic ties become politically salient, see Paul R. Brass, *Language, Religion and Politics in North India* (Cambridge: Cambridge University Press, 1974). Brass quite properly rejects the notion that ethnicity is a "given" to which the political system responds. His theoretical perspective is close to the viewpoint expressed here.

CONDITIONS FOR NATIVIST MOVEMENTS IN INDIA

This chapter attempts to specify a set of conditions for nativist movements in India. First, we shall ask what conditions are present in each of the regions and cities in India that have nativist movements, which are not present in locales without nativist movements; and second, we will ask what changes have taken place in each of the regions preceding the emergence of nativist movements that may explain why at a given time these movements emerged. Since in several areas there have been nativist cycles over a period of decades, whatever variables account for the rise of nativist movements must also help explain their decline.

We shall draw our analysis from the five cities or regions where in recent years there have been major nativist movements: Bombay city, the Brahmaputra valley of Assam, the Chota Nagpur region of southern Bihar, the city of Bangalore, and the Telangana region of Andhra.

In four of these areas there are explicitly nativist political parties: the Shiv Sena in Bombay, the Jharkhand party and the Birsa Seva Dal in Bihar, the Kannada Chaluvaligars in Bangalore, and the Telangana Praja Samiti in Telangana. In Assam, nativism informs the sentiment of the governing Congress party, but there is also a loosely structured nativist movement known as the Lachit Sena. The focus of this analysis will not be on the parties themselves, but on the social context within which these movements emerged.

As we have noted earlier, in three of these areas nativism is not a new phenomenon. In the former princely state of Hyderabad, in which the Telangana region is located, the movement against non-*mulkis* developed shortly after World War I, when the local educated population expressed its opposition to the government policy of recruiting Muslims from northern India into the state administrative services. Similarly, the anti-Bengali movement in Assam began in the mid-nineteenth century, when the Assamese protested the domination of their educational system and administrative services

274

by Bengali Hindus who had migrated from Bengal. At that time Assam, along with Orissa and Bihar, was part of the presidency of Bengal, with its capital in Calcutta. And in Chota Nagpur the hostility of tribals to nontribal Bihari settlers was a central theme of the major political movements and upheavals in the region in the middle of the nineteenth century, culminating in the great Birsa rebellion in the 1890s, calling for the "restoration" of tribal lands.

What are the conditions shared by these diverse contemporary and historical situations? *The first condition is that each area with a nativist population has migrants from outside the cultural region.* The number of migrants and their descendants can even be greater than the local population. The extreme case is the Chota Nagpur region, where the indigenous tribal population now constitutes a minority of 33 percent. Only in two districts of Chota Nagpur, Ranchi and Singhbhum, are the tribals a majority, with 2.3 million out of a total population of 4.2 million, or 54 percent.

In the six districts that make up the Brahmaputra valley of Assam (population in 1961, 9.1 million), 73.3 percent report themselves as Assamese speakers, 7.4 percent speak indigenous languages other than Assamese, and 19.3 percent speak migrant languages. But in the urban areas of the valley, 350,000 people are Bengali out of an urban population of 913,000 (38 percent), as against 304,000 Assamese (33 percent). (Another 13 percent are Hindi-speaking migrants, and the remainder a mixture of migrants and some local tribals.)

In Bombay, the Marathi-speaking population in 1961 also constituted a minority, 42.8 percent of the population. Similarly, in Bangalore the local Kannada-speaking population in 1951 had dropped to 23.8 percent, for the first time falling below that of the Tamil-speaking population.

Of the five cases, the Telangana region has the smallest migrant population. According to the 1961 census, migrants constitute one-fourth of the population of the city of Hyderabad—a smaller proportion than that of many Indian cities.

And for the Telangana region as a whole, in-migration from other states and from other parts of Andhra is considerably smaller. But since 1961, only a few years after Hyderabad was made the capital of the new state of Andhra, there has been a substantial influx of migrants from the eastern districts of Andhra to take jobs in the administrative services and to open small businesses.[5] There are now many "Andhra" (as the migrants from the eastern districts are called) housing colonies in or close to the city.

In each of these five cases, the migrant population and its descendants belonging to "alien" ethnic communities constitute anywhere from a fourth to two-thirds of the population, perhaps somewhat less in the Hyderabad case, though the recent figures are not yet available.

A second condition is that there must be some perceived cultural differences, no matter how small, between the migrants and the local community. These differences can take any one of many forms: language, religion, preferences in food and dress, and belief systems. But above all, the native community must have some awareness of a cultural identity by which they distinguish themselves from the migrants. The litmus test for such a separate cultural identity is the use of a distinguishing name.

---

[5] More than half (52.7%) of the growth of Hyderabad between 1961 and 1971 was due to migration, the remainder from natural population growth. It should be noted that of India's twenty largest cities, in five more than half of the growth was due to migration: in addition to Hyderabad, Madras (65%), Bangalore (52.6%), Jaipur (53.7%), and Surat (56.6%). Other high-migration cities included Greater Bombay (47.4%), Poona (46.4%), Indore (48.5%), Madurai (48.3%) and Jabalpur (48.9%). In Ranchi, the other city with a nativist movement dealt with in this study, 75.7 percent of the growth was due to migration. In most Indian cities, however, growth is more by natural population increase than through in-migration.

In contrast, a larger proportion of the urban growth of African cities is more the result of migration than natural population increase. For data, by region and by country, see Kingsley Davis, *World Urbanization, 1950-70,* Vol. 1 (Berkeley and Los Angeles: University of California Press, 1971), especially Table D, pp. 141-160.

In three of the five cases, the names are linguistic. In Assam, the distinction is between the Assamese (those who speak Assamese as their mother tongue), and the non-Assamese Bengalis, Marwaris, Nepalis, Biharis, and so on. In Bombay, it is the Maharashtrians (Marathi-speakers) as distinct from the Tamils, Telugus, Gujaratis, Sindhis, and Hindi speakers. In Bangalore, it is the Kannadas (sometimes called Kannadigas or Mysoreans), as distinct from the Tamils, Telugus, and Malayalis.

In Chota Nagpur, the tribal people group themselves together as *adivasis*, a term used by Gandhi to mean the "original" people; outsiders are called *dikus*, a word with pejorative overtones.

In Telangana, the term *mulki* is used to refer to people originating from the region, irrespective of language and religion. The term was initially used before Andhra was created to refer to anyone born in Hyderabad state; it implied that one was a citizen of the state, or more properly, a subject, for the state was, until 1948, governed by a monarch. When the Telangana region was merged with other Telugu-speaking districts of south India to form Andhra, the term was used more narrowly to mean the people who lived in the Telangana region (one of several regions that formed the old state of Hyderabad). The term, originally intended to specify who was qualified for employment in the state administrative services, is even now used in that sense. Someone who is not qualified, an outsider, is a non-*mulki*.

Although all nativist movements are by definition antimigrant, not all antimigrant movements should be called nativist. A community or government may want to slow or halt the rate of in-migration for a variety of reasons: overcrowding of schools, inadequate urban services, such as sewerage facilities, water, electric supply, and mass transportation; concerns over the environment, general anxieties concerning overcrowding, and so on. A community may also be hostile to the class composition of migrations: well-to-do communities often want to keep out the poor.

277

The characteristic feature of nativism is its ethnic selectivity. It accepts or rejects migrants (and their descendants) because of the ethnic community to which they belong and with which they identify or can be identified. Without such perceived cultural differences there cannot be a nativist political movement.

A third condition of nativism is that in areas with a nativist movement, the local population is likely to be immobile relative to other groups in the population. Out-migration from Assam, Maharashtra, and Andhra is below the national average, Mysore is at the mean, and Bihar is above average. But statewide census figures are an unsatisfactory measure of mobility on the part of the native population; for one thing, it is more relevant for our purposes to know whether there is out-migration from the region, district, or city in which the nativist movement thrives; for another, it is more relevant to know whether the native ethnic group is mobile or not, not simply how much out-migration there is from a locality. State-wide out-migration figures, therefore, are only a crude index (see Table 2.3 Migrant's State of Birth); regional out-migration figures are better, but still not adequate; a linguistic dispersal table indicating what proportion of the people speaking a given language lives outside of the region in which the language is spoken provides us still a third crude measure (see Table 2.6 Linguistic Dispersal).

By any available measures, the Assamese are among the least mobile linguistic group in India. Only 1 percent of those born in Assam live outside the state—and some of these migrants are not ethnically Assamese. Only 19,000 Assamese, or 0.3 percent of the total Assamese speakers in India, can be found outside Assam, according to the 1961 census. Even within Assam there is relatively little movement of Assamese from one district to another, or from rural to urban areas within the state. Only 3.5 percent of the population of Assam live outside the district of birth, and this figure includes both the non-Assamese and Assamese-speaking people born in the state. Assam has one of the highest in-migration rates of any

278

state in India, but the Assamese themselves remain a predominantly nonmobile people in a status-based society.

The linguistic dispersal index is unsatisfactory for measuring out-migration among the Marathi and Telugu-speaking people, since state boundaries have been drawn in such a way that substantial numbers of speakers of both languages are found in districts bordering the state. Both states, however, are among the lowest (along with Assam) in the proportion of population living outside the state: 2.2 percent for Maharashtra and 2.7 percent for Andhra. The census also reports low out-migration from the Telangana districts, including Hyderabad, into other districts of Andhra.

Out-migration from Bihar is of less importance for this analysis than out-migration from Chota Nagpur, which has a long history of tribal out-migration to the tea plantations in Assam and northern Bengal. The 1891 census reported that as many as 421,000 persons born in Chota Nagpur had emigrated. The number rose to 707,000 by 1911, and 947,000 (to Bengal and Assam alone) by 1921. Out-migration figures are not available thereafter, but we have some evidence to suggest that out-migration dropped sharply in the 1930s, when the tea industry was no longer expanding. There may have been a small increase in the 1940s, when some tribals found employment in Assam, since the British and American armies were engaged in constructing roads, airports, and other military installations. In the 1950s and 1960s, migration out of the area appears to have declined. The period between 1900 and 1931 is thus the major period of out-migration; tribal emigration evidently provided an alternative to political unrest, for there was a marked decline in tribal political protest between 1900, the year of the death of Birsa Munda, the leader of the most famous tribal rebellion in the region, and the 1930s, when the nativist Jharkhand party was formed.

While the evidence for this condition still remains incomplete, there is data to support the inverse condition; that is, *states or regions with a high in-migration and a high rate of*

279

out-migration tend not to have nativist movements. Neither the Punjab nor West Bengal has nativist movements, though they have the largest migrant populations of any states in India, 14.2 and 15.7 percent, respectively. The Bengalis and Punjabis are also among the most mobile people in India; 15.5 percent of all Punjabis live outside the Punjab and Haryana (in 1961), and 12.9 percent of all Bengali speakers live outside West Bengal.

The quantity of out-migration is a surrogate for another variable: the ability of a people to compete in the labor market. A competitive employment situation locally may be tolerable if there are employment opportunities outside the region. This leads us to the fourth condition: the rate and pattern of unemployment.

There is no town, city, or region in India that does not have a high and growing unemployment rate. It is officially estimated that in the early 1970s there were 7.5 million unemployed in India, apart from disguised rural unemployment and seasonal unemployment, but all unemployment figures either for the country as a whole, by region, or by city, are likely to be imprecise, since not all job seekers register at the employment exchanges. The employment exchanges do, however, report an alarming increase in the number of people seeking employment. In 1961, there were 1.8 million registered, and in 1970 the number was up to 4 million. The sharpest increase occurred after 1966, reflecting the slowdown in industrial growth and, for much of Indian industry, an actual decline in employment. In Bombay, for example, the number of workers employed in factories rose from 505,000 in 1961 to 572,000 in 1966, and then declined thereafter to 551,000 by 1969.

Raj Krishna, in his presidential address to the Indian Society of Agricultural Economics in December 1972, estimated that if one includes among the unemployed those who are severely underemployed and available for additional work, nearly 21,500,000 workers are unemployed (of whom

280

19.3 million live in rural areas and 2.2 million in urban areas), or approximately 9 percent of the labor force.[6] The growth of unemployment in India is associated with the following factors:

1. There has been an accelerated increase in the size of the labor force in the mid-sixties as a result of the declining death rate of the previous decades. Infant mortality has substantially declined, and survival rates for all age groups have improved so that the "drop out" rate from the labor force through mortality has declined, while the entry rate has increased. The growth in the labor force between 1951 and 1961 was greater than in the *total* previous fifty years:

Labor Force 1901-1961 (thousands)[7]

1901	110,712
1910	121,301
1921	117,764
1931	122,168
1951	139,890
1961	189,190

It is estimated that additions to the labor force now total 4.8 million annually, increasing each year, so that by 2007 the annual increase will exceed 7.5 million; changes in the birth rate will have no impact on the annual inflows into the labor force until the 1990s.[8]

[6] Raj Krishna, "Unemployment in India," reprinted in *Teaching Forum*, No. 38 (March 1974), Agricultural Development Council, New York.

[7] J. N. Sinha, *Census of India, 1961*, Vol. 1, Monograph No. 11, *The Indian Working Force: Its Growth and Changing Composition*, p. 23. The 1971 census estimates the labor force at 227 million, but comparisons with 1961 labor-force figures are difficult because of changes in the criteria for measuring participation in the labor force.

[8] John C. Cool, "The Dynamics of Indian Population Growth," paper presented at the Wingspread Conference on the Social and Cultural Responses to Population Change in India, November 1974.

2. Increases in employment have not kept pace with the expansion of the labor force. Between 1961 and 1969, factory employment rose from 3.9 million to 4.77 million, an annual increase of 2.5 percent, about equal to population growth. But employment in mining has grown at only 1 percent per annum since 1956, and India's plantation sector, which employs about a million and a quarter workers, has actually been declining. According to the National Commission on Labour, employment in the private sector actually decreased by 1.9 percent in 1966-1967, and by 2.4 percent in 1967-1968, reflecting the impact of the economic recession that emerged in 1966-1967.

The number of employees in the entire organized sector in 1968 was 16.3 million, about the same as the previous year, for while employment in the private sector declined there was a slight increase in public-sector employment from 9.63 million in 1967 to 9.8 million in 1968. It should be noted, incidentally, that state governments, with 3.8 million employees, are the largest employers, followed by the central government (2.72 million), local bodies (1.8 million), and quasi-government establishments (1.48 million).[9]

Why the demand for labor has not kept pace with the growth in the supply of labor is a complex matter that need not concern us here, except to report that the rate of investment, according to Raj Krishna, has been declining or stagnating since its peak of 13.4 percent in 1965; for the four years from 1968 to 1972, reports Krishna, it was less than 10 percent.[10] "In a poor developing economy," he notes, "investment growth and employment growth are highly complementary."

3. A rapid expansion of the educational system since independence, particularly at the matriculation and college

[9] *Report, 1968-69*, Vol. II, Employment and Training, Ministry of Labour, Employment and Rehabilitation, Government of India, New Delhi, 1969, p. 8.

[10] Raj Krishna, "Unemployment in India."

levels, has substantially increased the number of young educated people seeking employment, especially in urban areas.

Since independence there has been a tendency for the higher levels of education to expand more rapidly than the lower levels. The proportion of children attending middle school increased from 12.7 percent in 1951 to 31.7 percent in 1965-1966, while there was a more than threefold growth in secondary school enrollment (from 5.3 to 16.8 percent) and an even greater growth in undergraduate enrollment, from 1.89 to 6.38 percent.[11] The proportion of expenditure going to higher education grew substantially, from about 23 percent in 1950-1951 to 29 percent in 1965-1966.[12]

Paradoxically, an important incentive for the expansion of college enrollment has been the growing unemployment of secondary school graduates. As unemployment increases, parents send their children to college with the hope that additional education will increase their chances of securing employment.

Defining the educated unemployed as those who have completed at least eleven years of schooling and who are totally without employment but seeking work, Blaug, Layard, and Woodhall estimated that there were at least a half-million educated unemployed in India in 1967, and if all educated people registered with employment exchanges are counted (including those who work part-time), as many as 900,000 were unemployed.[13]

The expansion of higher education has tended to transfer[14]

---

[11] Mark Blaug, Richard Layard, and Maureen Woodhall, *The Causes of Graduate Unemployment in India* (London: Penguin Press, 1969), p. 44. This study provides an excellent account of the uncontrolled expansion of secondary and higher education in postindependence India.

[12] *Ibid.*, p. 47.   [13] *Ibid.*, p. 1.

[14] The word "transfer" may be misleading, for we are not suggesting that the growth in education is increasing unemployment, but simply that the unemployed are more educated, more urban, and more middle-class than if there had been a smaller expansion of

unemployment from rural to urban areas, from the unskilled to the skilled labor markets, and from the laboring classes to the middle classes. As unemployment increases, the rate of unemployment among the educated appears to increase more rapidly than among the uneducated. India's growing unemployment in the late sixties and early seventies has been accompanied by a sharp increase in the numbers of educated registered at the employment exchanges.

But unemployment rates, even if they were accurately measured by registrations at employment exchanges, are an unsatisfactory index of competitiveness between migrants and the local population. There are many jobs that local people do not want even though unemployment is high. Educated Bengalis do not seek work in the jute and textile mills near Calcutta, where the labor force is largely from Orissa and Bihar. In Assam, neither the urban educated nor the uneducated peasantry sought employment in the tea industry when it was expanding, preferring instead to see tribals take the jobs as tea pickers. In Bombay, Marathi-speaking workers seek employment in factories, but generally do not compete against unskilled Rajasthanis for jobs on construction projects, or against Telugu migrants for jobs as dockworkers.

A high degree of occupational specialization by ethnic groups among the working classes in India tends to reduce, though not wholly eliminate, competition within the labor force among ethnic groups, even when unemployment levels are high.

However, for middle and lower-class positions—defined broadly as nonmanual occupations irrespective of salary levels—there is a decline in ethnic specialization. Within every large ethnic group in India, there are now substantial

---

secondary school and higher education. As Blaug *et al.* note, "The rate of unemployment among the uneducated turns out to be a much better predictor of educated unemployment than the proportion of educated people in the state labour force. . . . Over a third of the variance in matriculate unemployment is associated with the unemployment rate of those below matriculation" (pp. 93-94).

numbers of people seeking middle-class jobs as office clerks, typists, teachers, office messengers, clerks in retail shops, and so on. Probably no social class has grown in size more than India's middle classes; in every state the most rapidly expanding occupational category has been employment in government services, including employment in the educational system. And the entrance requirement for middle-class employment is a matriculation certificate or college degree.

A locale in which there is a high level of unemployment among the indigenous middle class (middle-class in education and aspirations, but often not yet in employment and income) *and a substantial proportion of middle-class jobs are held by culturally alien migrants, is a likely candidate for a nativist political movement.* In Gauhati, Hyderabad, Bombay, Ranchi, and Bangalore, most of the lower middle-class positions are held by migrants and their descendants, while in each of these cities—as in other cities of India—the number of educated registered at the employment exchanges has sharply increased. Other cities also have high levels of educated unemployment—cities such as Calcutta, Kanpur, Lucknow, Allahabad, Trivandrum, and Madras—but in these cities the middle-class jobs are already held primarily by the native population.

A fifth condition is that *areas with nativist movements have experienced a rapid growth of educational opportunities for the lower middle classes.* In four of the five regions with nativist movements, the local populations were historically late-comers to education. While the Bengalis and Tamils were among the first communities to be exposed to the British-created system of education, and hence were among the first to produce a substantial middle class, the Assamese, the Marathis, the *mulkis* of Telangana, and the Munda, Santhal, Ho, and Oraon tribesmen of Chota Nagpur are among the most recent groups to become educated.

In Assam prior to 1947, the middle class was almost entirely Bengali Hindu; teachers in the schools and colleges, a

285

substantial portion of the state administrative services, and most of the professionals were Bengali Hindus. After 1947, the newly independent government made use of a considerable portion of the state's resources to expand educational facilities, especially for the local Assamese. The number of students in Assam increased from 934,000 in 1950 to 3,154,-000 in 1965. There was a proportionately even larger educational explosion in the secondary schools and colleges. The number of students attending colleges and universities in Assam almost doubled every five years:

1950	8,601
1955	14,595
1960	28,226
1965	45,387

Thus there developed in Assam an educated class that aspired to become middle-class before it achieved any of the occupations and material standards of middle-class life. For this aspiring Assamese middle class, the Bengali Hindu middle class stood as an obstacle to advancement.

A similar situation obtained in Bombay. Though the Marathi-speaking population was by no means as educationally late as the Assamese, they tended to lag behind the Parsis, the Gujaratis, and the Sindhis in Bombay. The proportion of Marathi speakers in semiskilled and middle-class positions in Bombay was substantially below the proportion of Marathi speakers in Bombay. A study conducted by D. T. Lakdawala of Bombay University in the early 1950s reported that 4.9 percent of the Marathis earned more than Rs. 500 monthly, compared with 17.3 percent of the Gujaratis, and 10.1 percent of the south Indians.[15]

[15] D. T. Lakdawala, *Work, Wages and Well-Being in an Indian Metropolis* (Bombay: Bombay University Press, 1963), p. 281, cited by Mary Fainsod Katzenstein, "Political Nativism: Shiv Sena in Bombay," Ph.D. dissertation, M.I.T., 1974.

According to estimates made by Mary Katzenstein, there has been a sizable increase in the number of matriculates throughout western Maharashtra. In a study of the social composition of the nativist Shiv Sena party in Bombay, Katzenstein reports that almost all of the party workers surveyed belong to the lower middle classes. "The list of specific jobs," she writes, "reads like a directory of lower-middle class occupations—including on the one hand neither professionals (teachers, doctors, or lawyers), big businessmen, nor simple, unskilled laborers or menial workers on the other hand. Rather, the job descriptions—accounts clerk, bookshop owner, salesman in bookshop, clerk in bank, towing operator, assistant supervisor in auto works, inspector in municipal corporation—suggest that Shiv Sena organization leaders are predominantly of middle and lower-middle class backgrounds."[16] Katzenstein goes on to report[17] that the elected Shiv Sena members of the Municipal Corporation are less well educated (26 percent have college degrees, compared with 53 percent of the two Congress parties and the Praja Socialist party municipal councilors), and more often in the lower middle class (42 percent are clerks or skilled and supervisory factory personnel, as compared with 25 percent for the other three parties in the corporation). The Shiv Sena is the party of a new, expanding, lower middle class of Marathi speakers in competition with the non-Marathi middle classes.

Few communities in India are as educationally backward as the tribal population. In Bihar only about a third as many tribal students as nontribals attend secondary schools or colleges. In 1961 as few as 9,532 tribals in the entire state of Bihar (whose 4.2 million tribals live primarily in Chota Nagpur) had completed high school.

As we noted in our study of Chota Nagpur, there has been a marked increase in tribal education within the past decade.

[16] Katzenstein, "Political Nativism," chapter 6, p. 18.
[17] *Ibid.*, chapter 7, pp. 7-8.

While the increases have taken place at all levels of education, they are the greatest for the secondary schools and colleges. These increases are reflected not only in enrollment figures (there were 24,105 tribals enrolled in secondary schools in 1965 compared with 10,500 in 1960), but also in the growth of educated unemployment. In 1970 there were 1,590 "educated" tribals registered for employment at the exchanges, of whom 945 were matriculates, 224 had some college education, and about 400 were college graduates. Though education among tribals still remains substantially below that of other communities in Bihar, for the first time there is now emerging among the tribals a young, educated, largely urban group seeking middle-class employment.

While the Jharkhand party remains the major nativist political movement among the tribals, the more militant Birsa Seva Dal has won support among young tribals in the major towns. The organization achieved public recognition in 1968 and in 1969, when it launched violent attacks against nontribal landlords and led demonstrations in the streets of Ranchi demanding the creation of a tribal state. Although the size of the Birsa Seva Dal is not known—in any event it does not appear to be a well-organized membership organization, and with the arrest of some of its leaders in the last few years it has become dormant—it is generally agreed that its supporters have mainly been young matriculates. There are jobs reserved for tribals in the state and central administrative services, but no such reservations exist in the public-sector enterprises that have sprung up in and around Chota Nagpur. Moreover, the largest expansion of the state and central administrative services took place in the 1950s and early sixties, when there were few educated tribals, while there has been comparatively little job expansion since 1965, when the number of tribal graduates was rapidly increasing.

Telangana, our fourth case, is educationally the most backward region in the state of Andhra. In 1960-1961, only 40.6 percent of the 6-11 age group in Telangana (even though it includes the city of Hyderabad) attended school,

288

as compared with 61 percent in coastal Andhra (north) and 85.5 percent of coastal Andhra (south).[18]

Even when Telangana formed part of Hyderabad state, it was educationally the least developed region. For Hyderabad state as a whole, literacy in 1949 was only 9.2 percent, but for each of the Telangana districts (excluding Hyderabad city), it was typically only 6 or 7 percent.[19] When the Telangana region was joined with the Telugu-speaking areas of neighboring Madras to form a united Andhra, there was considerable anxiety within Telangana that their small, but also growing, educated middle class would lose out in the competition for employment in the state administrative services and in the state educational system. The "Gentlemen's Agreement" reached between the political leaders of the Telangana region and those of the rest of the new state of Andhra provided that "future recruitment to services will be on the basis of population from both regions," and that "some kind of domicile rules; e.g., residence for 12 years should be provided in order to assure the prescribed proportion to recruitment of Services for Telangana area."[20]

Even in 1956, when the new state was formed, the Telangana middle class feared that they might lose out in competition for employment unless some legal safeguards were created. Since Telangana, including Hyderabad city, has a small industrial base and a small private sector compared with Bombay, the concerns were mainly over employment in government, or "services," to use the Indian term. In 1966, there were 663,000 persons employed in the public sector of Andhra: 137,000 worked for the central government, 231,000 for the state government, 101,000 for quasi-government establishments, and 194,000 for local bodies.

A decade after the state was formed, the Telangana political leadership complained that the Gentlemen's Agreement had been violated, and that non-*mulkis* were taking

[18] K. V. Narayana Rao, *Telangana: A Study in the Regional Committees of India* (Calcutta: Minerva Associates, 1972), p. 232.

[19] *Ibid.*, p. 70.   [20] *Ibid.*, pp. 82-83.

positions in the state services that should rightfully go to the *mulkis*. There were protests from the Non-Gazetted Officers' Central Union, the trade union of lower middle-class government employees, that the Public Employment (Requirement as to Residence) Act of 1957, which specified the rules for employment of *mulkis* and non-*mulkis*, had been violated. This was accompanied by similar protests from the major student organizations in Hyderabad, particularly the Osmania University Students Union. "The growing acute unemployment, particularly since 1966 owing to the slackening of the tempo of development, agitated the minds of the students and the lapses, though minor, in the implementation of the Public Employment Act, 1957, only enraged them," wrote one local observer.[21]

In one important respect, the Kannada-speaking people of Bangalore—our fifth example—are not educationally backward compared with the migrant communities that have settled in the city. Mysore state has for some time been well advanced in engineering colleges, technical institutions, and polytechnics. The major private firms in Bangalore (such as Kirloskar Electric Motors, the Indian Tobacco Company, Mysore Electrical, and International Instruments) and the public-sector firms (Indian Telephone Industries, Hindustan Machine Tools, Hindustan Aeronautics, and Bharat Electronics) all have a substantial number of Kannada engineers and managers. Moreover, many educated Kannadigas have successfully competed for high-level appointments in public and private firms outside of Mysore state. Although out-migration from Mysore is not high (it is only 3.4 percent), Mysore does have a larger and more mobile managerial and technical class than many states.

Nonetheless, Mysore's educational development still remains below that of her neighboring states of Tamil Nadu and Kerala, two states from which migrants come. Of the Mysore population, 31 percent is literate, as against 39 percent for Tamil Nadu and 60 percent for Kerala. Literacy in

[21] *Ibid.*, p. 336.

290

Bangalore is 59 percent, as against 62 percent for Madras city, 63 percent for Madurai, and 65 percent for Coimbatore—the largest cities in Tamil Nadu—and literacy rates near 70 percent for Kerala cities.[22]

Mysore experienced a rapid growth of its educational system between 1957 and 1968, as figures of school enrollment reveal (Table 6.1).

TABLE 6.1

Educational Enrollment in Mysore

Enrollment	1956-67	1967-68	% increase
Primary school students	1,727,000	3,662,000	112
Secondary school students	178,000	510,000	185
College students	30,000	86,000	183
Technical institutions, polytechnics	9,000	32,000	240
Literacy: 19.3% (1951), 25.3% (1961), 31.5% (1971)			

Support for the Kannada Chaluvaligars, Mysore's nativist party, comes neither from the most educated sectors of Kannada society, nor from the working class, both of whom have found a place in the industrial and managerial sectors,[23] but from the secondary school graduates. The leader of the Chaluvaligars is a young man, born in 1942 in a village twenty

[22] Literacy figures are from the 1971 provisional census.

[23] While a substantial part of the industrial labor force in Mysore is Kannada, employment in Mysore's plantations and in construction is largely non-Kannada; here, again, is an example of ethnic specialization, for neither construction nor plantation employment is sought by the Kannada working class. In the large-scale construction projects, Tamils are generally employed for "earth work" and Telugus for "stone work." Plantation workers generally come from Kerala, and forest operations—that is, cutting, loading, and trucking—are also mainly carried out by Kerala laborers.

miles from the city of Mysore, whose father was an agricul-
turalist and small shopkeeper. He went to school in his village, then attended secondary school in Mysore, where he
matriculated. He started but never completed college in Bangalore. He created a weekly Kannada newspaper, ran for
the Bangalore corporation and, in 1967, successfully won a
seat in the state assembly. He formed his own party, which
won 6 of the 62 seats in the Bangalore municipal elections in
1971. His active party workers are sociologically similar to
those of the Shiv Sena and the Telangana Praja Samiti; they
are young, often below voting age, matriculates, and have
jobs in shops, restaurants, cinema halls, or are unemployed.
Their dress is distinctively lower middle-class: bushshirts,
trousers, and chaples (sandals). The Chaluvaligar election
symbol is the bicycle, which effectively identifies the social
class and the age group that gives it support, as well as the
way the lower middle class moves about.

Unemployment has become increasingly acute among secondary school graduates. The live registers of the Directorate
of Employment showed that while 175,000 registered themselves for jobs in the state in 1967, the figure rose to 304,000
by mid-1972. The Kannada Chaluvaligars singled out the
five major Government of India firms in Bangalore—who
together employ about 60,000 people—for failing to hire
Mysoreans. The state government claimed that more than
75 percent of the middle income staff positions were held by
Mysoreans, but the Chaluvaligars argued that the government had not properly defined a "Mysorean," for they included anyone who registered for a job in the state, including
resident Tamilians and Keralites. "Grievances against the
Central undertakings are mounting, as hundreds of 'luckless'
Mysorean candidates throng ministerial chambers for help
and intervention. Probably 50% of callers on ministers in a
day are candidates who are unsuccessful in getting jobs."[24]
In arguing for a system of preferences in employment for

[24] *Times of India*, October 7, 1972.

292

"sons of the soil," the chief minister of the state declared,[25] "Can you name any state which does not prefer its own people?"

SOCIAL MOBILITY VERSUS SPATIAL MOBILITY

The cities and regions with nativist movements analyzed here share the following characteristics:

1. the locale contains a substantial number of middle-class migrants belonging to culturally distinguishable ethnic groups originating from another section of the country;

2. there is a native middle class, expanding under the impetus of a growth in secondary and higher education;

3. there is a highly competitive labor market in which the native middle class seeks employment in private and public-sector firms and in government, where middle-class positions are already held by migrants or their descendants;

4. there are limited opportunities for the native middle class to find employment outside their own locale.

These conditions suggest a single proposition: *nativism tends to be associated with a blockage to social mobility for the native population by a culturally distinguishable migrant population.*

This proposition explains why, in India at least, nativism is largely a middle-class sentiment, not a movement among the industrial labor force or the peasantry, even though there are culturally distinguishable migrants in the industrial labor force in many cities and in some rural areas. At present there continues to be a high level of ethnic specialization within the industrial labor force, but should India's native urban working classes seek employment in industries and in job categories currently held by alien migrants, we can anticipate that nativism will also become a working-class phenomenon. This proposition thus explains why nativism tends to emerge even when there is no noticeable change in the rate of mi-

[25] *Ibid.*

293

gration; of greater importance are social changes within the native community that change job aspirations.

Were the labor market in Indian cities expanding more rapidly, then there might be a niche both for the migrants and for the growing native middle classes, but under conditions of slow economic growth the labor market is correctly perceived by job seekers as a zero-sum situation in which employment for the local population depends upon restricting employment for the migrants. Nativism in India is fundamentally a protectionist movement whose tariff walls are domicile regulations for employment and whose middle-class population is like an infant industry seeking protection against competitive foreign imports.

Nativism in India is a movement toward ethnic equality. Nativists believe that by pursuing a policy of favoring the native inhabitants over migrants they can equalize their income, their occupation, and their class position in relation to the migrants. If this analysis is correct, then the question of how close the migrant population is to the language and culture of the native population—and by inference, how much it assimilates—is less important in shaping the attitudes of native populations toward culturally alien migrants than the question of how effective the local population is in competing against migrants for the jobs they both want in a labor market of few opportunities and a plentiful labor supply.

Nativism in India is a political response to conflicting forms of mobility: the spatial mobility of migrants and the aspiring social mobility of a social class within the native population.

NATIVISM AS A VARIETY OF ETHNIC POLITICS

How does nativism differ from other political expressions of ethnicity, and particularly from other kinds of regional movements?[26] Is there a theoretical difference between nativist

[26] I am grateful to Professor Paul Brass of the University of Washington, Seattle, for probing me on this issue.

political movements and other ethnic movements in India—
such as the Akali Dal, a political movement in the Punjab;
the Dravida Munnetra Kazhagam (D.M.K.), the regional
party that once governed the southern state of Tamil Nadu;
or the various political movements that agitated for linguistic
states in the mid 1950s and early 1960s, such as the Andhra
Mahasabha and the Samyukta Maharashtra Samiti? In what
sense can we call the Jharkhand party nativist but not the
Akali Dal, or the Telangana Praja Samiti but not the Andhra
Mahasabha? Why the Shiv Sena but not the Samyukta Maharashtra Samiti? Is nativism not simply a logical extension of
regionalism in India, a short leap from demanding a separate
state for one's people to demanding that alien migrants from
other states be excluded and even expelled?

To answer these questions let us first consider what differences there are between nativist and regional movements,
then turn more generally to consider how nativism might be
viewed as one of several alternative types of political expressions of ethnicity.

What are generally referred to as "regional" movements in
India are political movements by ethnic groups to create or
govern states organized around an explicit ethnic identity:
hence, the Akali Dal (and what was more broadly known
as the Punjabi Suba movement) demanded the creation of a
Punjabi-speaking state; in Assam's hill areas various tribal
parties agitated for the creation of the tribal state of Meghalaya; and the Samyukta Maharashtra Samiti called for the
creation of a Marathi-speaking state. After these and other
ethnically (mainly linguistically) defined states were created,
regional sentiments persisted and deepened. In each state the
governing party expressed (some would say used or even
exploited) regional sentiments in clashes with the central
government or with neighboring states. Moreover, regional,
but particularly linguistic, sentiment affected state government policies concerning the choice of language in education
and administration, and the adoption of a variety of cultural
policies.

295

The development of either a regional or national identity—both expressions of a sense of ethnicity when "ethnic" becomes synonymous with "region" or "nation"—is a precondition to the development of nativism, but nativism is not its inevitable consequence. Nativism is that form of ethnic identity that seeks to *exclude* those who are not members of the local or indigenous ethnic group from residing and/or working in a territory because they are not native to the country or region: nativism is antimigrant. To the extent that the D.M.K., the Akali Dal, the Andhra Mahasabha, and the Samyukta Maharashtra Samiti were not antimigrant, they should not be classified as nativist. In contrast, the Jharkhand party and the Telangana Praja Samiti are regional parties that are *also* antimigrant; that is, they are nativist.

Nativism is thus one form of ethnic politics. Subnational ethnic movements seeking to create a state, either within or apart from the country, are still another form. When the ethnic group identifies itself with a given territory within the country, we generally speak of *regionalism*; when it seeks statehood outside, we describe the movement as *secessionist*. If the ethnic group believes that people of the same ethnic and linguistic heritage should belong to one state or nation and makes claims upon the territory of a neighboring state because it contains the same ethnic group, we speak of the movement or demand as *irredentist*. Then there are ethnic groups that make specific interest claims and engage in coalition politics to achieve their objectives, a pattern common in the interest group politics of the American political system. All of these forms—nativism, regionalism, secessionism, irredentism, and interest articulation—should be understood as varieties of demand making on the part of ethnic movements, as varied as the forms of demand making among class-based political movements. All these forms of ethnic group politics can be found in India.

To the extent that an ethnic group is characterized by a high degree of solidarity, demand making on the part of one class within the ethnic group may become adopted by the

296

ethnic group as a whole. Thus, while nativism may first develop within one class—in the Indian case, within sections
of the middle class—nativism may become widely accepted
by most politically participant members of the ethnic group.
The electoral results demonstrate that in several regions described here nativist parties won support that extended well
beyond the social class that initiated the movement.

Moreover, each of these nativist movements tends to have
multiplier effects. When nativism develops in one region, it
is not long before other regions soon develop nativist movements as well, although the same proximate causes may not
be present. The hostility to migrants in one region creates a
counter hostility in another. Thus, anti-Tamil movements in
Maharashtra give rise to anti-Marathi sentiments in Tamil
Nadu, and anti-Bengali sentiments in Bihar and Orissa stimulate anti-Bihari, anti-Oriya sentiments in Bengal. A new set
of determinants begins to operate quite apart from those thus
far propounded. The *diffusion* process has a dynamic of its
own, independent of origins. It is thus only in the early stages
of the development of this form of ethnicity that its determinants can be understood. The same elements of cohesion and
diffusion may similarly affect our understanding of the determinants of other types of ethnic politics.

Finally, we need to consider whether nativism need be the
only political response to blockages to social mobility. Can
there be a secessionist response or even a revolutionary, class-
oriented response? Anyone who has witnessed the political
responses of the middle classes in neighboring Sri Lanka or
Pakistan to blockages to their quest for power, status, and
wealth must recognize that there can be a variety of alternative responses, depending upon whose gains are blocked, who
is doing the blocking, and the political context within which
the response takes place. Indeed, when one considers the
alternatives, nativism may well be among the least destructive
choices, both for the political system and for individuals
within it—for in one sense nativism contains within it the
seeds of its own destruction. As nativism within a multi-

297

ethnic society spreads from one region to another, as each region creates barriers to migrants from other regions, each ethnic group must ask whether it gains when all regions behave in the same way. Like economic protectionism, when practiced by a few there are gains, but when practiced by all many of the gains are cancelled out. As the principle of reciprocity serves to diffuse nativism, so too does it suggest the means by which nativist restrictions can be brought to an end.

SEVEN

WHO IS LOCAL?
TERRITORIAL VERSUS ETHNIC IDENTITIES

THE demand by nativist political parties and movements that employment preferences be given to "local" people has raised the issue, who is local? Indian laws, administrative rules, and college and university entrance requirements define "local" in a territorial sense to refer to an individual born or for a specified period of time residing in a state, portion of a state, district, or city, but this legal conception is at variance with the popular understanding of who a "local" person is.

Indians do not ordinarily identify themselves by the place from which they come, but by the ethnic group to which they belong. When an Indian says he is a Maharashtrian, he does not mean that he comes from the state of Maharashtra, but that he belongs to that group of people who speak Marathi as their mother tongue. Similarly, when an Indian identifies himself as a Bengali, it does not mean that he necessarily comes from West Bengal, but that Bengali is his mother tongue. Self-identity terms in India are, with rare exception, not territorial but ethnic, that is, religious, linguistic, tribal, or caste.

This chapter first analyzes the words Indians use to describe themselves and to identify others in an effort to understand the criteria Indians employ for choosing an identity. It is followed by an analysis of a survey of members of the Indian parliament representing constituencies with large numbers of "nonlocal" constituents in an effort to see how they define who is local, how this relates to their own religious, linguistic, and cultural identity, and how these definitions affect their attitudes toward the claims that various groups make within their constituencies. The effort here,

299

therefore, is to relate conceptual notions of identity with concrete political attitudes and to link the structure of thought to political conduct.

TERRITORIAL IDENTITIES

We start first with the question of how the presence or absence of a terminology for territorial identities influences the nature of political discourse in a political system.

Indians living in a state where the majority language differs from their own mother tongue identify themselves by the linguistic community to which they belong. Thus, a Tamil speaker in Maharashtra is a Tamil or Tamilian, a Malayali speaker is a Malayalam, a Telugu speaker is a Telugu; none is ever called Maharashtrian. Collectively, Marathi speakers may call them south Indians or Madrasis, but the terms are ethnic rather than geographic. A Tamilian can only become a Maharashtrian if he adopts Marathi as his mother tongue and assumes the dress, customs, and identity of Marathi speakers, that is, if he culturally assimilates. An individual cannot be both Tamil and Maharashtrian, for these are mutually exclusive ethnic terms. *Jus soli*, the concept of citizenship by place of birth and, by extension, identity by place of birth, is not an accepted concept.

Similarly, Bengalis living in the state of Assam are Bengali so long as Bengali is their mother tongue. To be Assamese one must belong to the culture of Assam, an *Ahomiya*, to use the term employed by the Assamese to refer to themselves.

Since the Indian states were reorganized in the mid-1950s they are, in the main, linguistic units. Each state has an "official" language and, by implication, an "official" or at least "dominant" (numerically, if not politically) ethnic community. Ethnic minorities in each state can, therefore, only identify themselves in ethnic, not territorial, terms. Thus, the Bengali from Assam cannot call himself Assamese (as a resident of New York, irrespective of his ethnic identity, can call himself a New Yorker), nor can the Tamilian in Bombay call himself a Maharashtrian. In each state the migrants or descendants of migrants from other states remain, in identity, territorially stateless.

There are, however, several striking exceptions. In multi-ethnic Bombay city, non-Marathi residents often call themselves Bombaywallas to signify they belong to and identify with a culturally and linguistically heterogenous city. A Bombaywalla thus asserts his independence from any exclusive ethnic identity: he may be Tamil, Gujarati, or Parsi; he may come from "mixed" parentage; or, whatever his origin, he may have attended an English-speaking school and identify himself as an Indian with no particular regional roots.

Similarly, residents of Delhi often call themselves Delhiwallas. Here again, long-term residents, wherever their place of birth or ethnic background, often consider themselves "natives" of the capital city, emphasizing their "cosmopolitanism" or Indianness rather than any particular ethnic or regional identity.

The third example is from Hyderabad, a city that was once the capital of a composite state in which Telugu, Marathi, Kannada, and Urdu speakers resided; here many call themselves Hyderabadis to emphasize their liberation from an exclusive linguistic or religious identity.

But these cities are exceptions:[1] in none of the states are there comparable terms for territorial identities. Even indigenous minorities sense that they reside in but cannot identify with the state. What, for example, does one call a Khasi tribesman in Assam, a Munda tribesman in Bihar, a Pahari-speaking hillsman of Uttar Pradesh, or a Konkoni speaker in Mysore? Why not, these native minorities often argue, cor-

---

[1] Sometimes the term Calcatian is used to refer to someone from Calcutta, but the term is generally used by residents of the city to refer to a Bengali who is urbane, that is, not of recent rural origin. See D. N. Basu, "The Language and Dialects of Calcutta during the Last One Hundred Years," in Surajit Sinha, *Cultural Profile of Calcutta* (Calcutta: Indian Anthropological Society, 1972), p. 22.

rect their anomalous position by making their ethnic identity coterminous with statehood? Thus, the Khasis (and others) have fought for (and won) a separate state in the northeast carved out of Assam, while the Mundas (and others) in Bihar have called for the creation of a tribal state in southern Bihar. Not to have a state is to remain a permanent minority; to be a cultural minority within a state is also to be—in identity—stateless.

Why no territorial concepts for identity? The reason is that since the formation of linguistic states, in each state the dominant ethnic group defines the state in ethnic terms. The dominant communities argue that their states should not be viewed as culturally composite entities: Assam, they assert, is the homeland of the Assamese, not simply a state in which Assamese-speakers reside along with Bengalis, Khasis, and others; similarly, Tamil Nadu, Maharashtra, Kannada, Kerala are the "homeland" of a particular people, while others who live there are, in effect, guests who cannot share the same "joys and sorrows" (as Marathi nativists say) of those who "belong" to the state, nor therefore are they entitled to all the rights and benefits. For the dominant communities the possession of political power ultimately defines their identity, and their political identity defines their rights and benefits.

It is in this political context that we can understand why words do not ordinarily exist for those who reside within a political-territorial unit apart from the words used to describe the ethnic group that is dominant within the unit. Those who do use territorial terms for identity not only signify a detachment from an exclusively ethnic identity, but they are also asserting a particular conception of their cities as multiethnic units, a position at variance with the viewpoint of those who support nativist political movements. Those who call themselves Bombaywallas, Delhiwallas, and Hyderabadis are not simply asserting their identity; they are taking a political position. *Terms for identity need to be understood not only in a cultural and psychological sense, but as political concepts.*

302

The Assamese, or *Ahomiya*, as they call themselves, have a rich vocabulary to distinguish between what is local and what is alien. The closest word to native is *thalua*, an indigenous person, or more specifically a person belonging to a particular village or locality. The word is related to the Sanskrit *sthala*, meaning locality, and Assamese *thai*, meaning place. (A more literary term, having the same meaning, is *khilanjia*.) When the Assamese speak of hiring local people, they generally mean *Ahomiya*, or people who are culturally and linguistically Assamese, but in a particular context they may also mean a *thalua*, or local man, from the village or district. *Thalua* thus can include both *Ahomiya* and the tribal population indigenous to Assam, but it never includes Bengalis or other migrant communities, no matter how many generations they have settled in Assam. *Thalua* is thus more than a territorial concept; it means one whose cultural roots are in the soil.

The opposite of a *thalua*, or local person, is a *pamua*, a nonlocal. The term is used to refer to people originating from outside the state, or those who are from elsewhere in Assam but are not of that locality. A *pamua* lives in the locality and possesses a *pam* or plot of land, but he is an outsider by origin. Even more removed from the community is a *bideshi*, someone who has come to the locality to make a living, but who owns no land and who also remains an alien no matter how long he resides in the community. He is an *Ona-Ahomiya*, a non-Assamese; thus, Marwari and Punjabi businessmen, Bengali teachers, and Bihari construction workers residing in Assam are *bideshi*.

Since the earliest and most influential migrants to settle in Assam in the nineteenth century were Bengalis, the Assamese tended to call all foreigners Bengalis. Even the European tea planters, army men, and civil administrators were called *Boga Bengali* or white Bengalis. Soon the Assamese began to distinguish among various categories of aliens. Bengali Muslims who came as peasants from Mymensingh district of East Bengal in search of land were called *Mymensinghias*.

The British imported tribals from Bihar and Orissa to work in the tea plantations; they called them *coolies*—a term they brought from China—to refer to tea plantation laborers, a word, with all its overtones, soon taken on by the Assamese. The Hindi-speaking people who came from Bihar and Uttar Pradesh into the northern districts of Assam to ply rickshaws and do construction work were called *deshwali*, meaning a country man (from the word *desh*, or country), suggesting a crude and coarse peasant. The term *deshwali* is now widely used for nearly all Hindi speakers, wherever they come from.

The Assamese recognize that migrants can assimilate. Since many of the tea plantation laborers (*coolies*, often called *cha-bonua* or tea laborers) have learned to speak Assamese, and their children have become linguistically assimilated, they are sometimes called *Na-Ahomiya*, or new Assamese. But to be a *Na-Ahomiya* it is not sufficient to speak Assamese: one must culturally identify with the Assamese, for it is a term that bespeaks cultural assimilation. Thus, the prominent Agarwala family of Tezpur, one of whose members represents his constituency in parliament, are *Na-Ahomiya* even though they are Marwaris; some Bengali Muslims are also *Na-Ahomiya*, but almost never Bengali Hindus.

The Assamese lack a single word to refer to the indigenous tribal population of Assam. They are called by their specific tribal names: Mikir, Khasi, Garo, Mizo, Bodo, or sometimes *thalua*, a local person. No single term links them with the *Ahomiya*, the people who claim Assam as their homeland, for the tribals are never called either *Ahomiya* or Assamese. Excluded from the conception of Assam, most of the tribes pressed for separate states of their own. Today, with the exception of the Bodo, the major tribes in the northeast now have their own states—Meghalaya, Mizoram, Arunachal Pradesh, and Nagaland.

304

Like Assam, the state of West Bengal also has a large number of migrants from other regions, with a rich vocabulary to match. Bengalis are particularly fond of puns, for by slightly varying the pronunciation of the word in another language to suit their own, a new meaning is conveyed. Thus, *Ahomiya* (the *h* pronounced as a gutteral *ch* by the Assamese) is pronounced by Bengalis (who lack the guttural *ch*) as *Asami*, in Bengali, a culprit or thief. Similarly, Bengalis call anyone from south India a *Madrasi*, a word frequently converted by Bengali school boys, taunting their south Indian classmates, into the cry of *madrasisala*, the unpleasant relative, the brother-in-law.

Marwaris, perhaps the least liked of all migrant communities in Bengal, are called *Maura* (by those from East Bengal) or *Mero* (by those from West Bengal), puns again—a Bengali word meaning lamb or sheep, thought of by Bengalis not as gentle, obedient, lovable animals, but as dumb, inferior creatures.

Food, of much ritual importance in Indian culture, provides a particularly rich source for invective. Bengalis call Bihari laborers in Calcutta *chhattu* or *chhattu khor*, an eater of chhattu, corn flour turned into a paste, a coarse dish commonly eaten by Bihari laborers. Another way Bengalis may express their disdain for the peasant Bihari is to ask him, where is your *khaini?*—a tobacco prepared with lime, chewed by Biharis, a practice viewed as disgusting by *pan* (betel)-chewing Bengalis.

Bengalis do not limit their use of derogatory terms to non-Bengalis, for they also have a rich vocabulary for each other. West Bengalis call East Bengalis *Bangal*, a somewhat offensive term if the voice is raised on the second syllable. (When the Assamese launched a nativist attack against East Bengalis in 1962 they raised the slogan, *Bangal kheda, kheda* being a term used to refer to the rounding up of elephants; hence the slogan can loosely be translated, "Oust the Bengalis.") Bengali Hindus and Bengali Muslims can be particularly

305

offensive to each other; Bengali Hindus may call Bengali Muslims *kata bora*, or one who has been circumcised, a phrase so crude that educated Bengalis report that it is only used by lower-class Bengali Hindus.

In cultures so rich with verbal distinctions for ethnic groups is it not possible to create words suggesting territorial identities, thereby reducing the sense of alienation felt by both indigenous minorities and migrants from other states? A few Indians have suggested that each state have a term to denote residence in the state as distinct from ethnic identity —Mysorean as distinct from Kannada, Maharashtrian as distinct from Marathi, Assamese as distinct from Ahomiya, and Orissan as distinct from Oriya, but each of these words has in turn acquired ethnic meanings, again illustrating the conceptual difficulties of distinguishing between territorial and ethnic concepts of identity in the Indian political context.

At the national level, of course, multiethnic societies do have a territorial-political term for identity that is distinct from ethnicity: thus, the Walloons and Flemish are Belgians, the Serbs, Croatians, and Slovenes are Yugoslavs, the Afrikaans and Bantus are South Africans, the Maharashtrians, Bengalis, and Assamese are Indians. It is at the level of the locality where the problem arises, that is, where the ethnic group expresses an exclusive claim on a piece of territory within the country, a region, or province thought of as the homeland of a specific ethnic group. By recognizing the special claims of ethnic groups to territories within the political system, India's national political leadership had hoped thereby to acquire the loyalties of its diverse peoples—and indeed has done so—but it was at a price paid by minorities residing in each of the states. When linguistic states were being formed, the central government was concerned with finding ways and means of protecting linguistic minorities, including migrants, and to assure such minorities the same rights and benefits as local people. But once linguistic states became established, the mood has been one of ethnic exclu-

306

siveness and a desire to impose restrictions on migrant minorities.

For many years the city of Bombay offered itself as an alternative to ethnic exclusiveness. With a population drawn from all over India, and many of its residents calling themselves Bombaywallas, some Indians suggested that Bombay be declared an independent city-state, a multiethnic city whose residents would take pride in their cosmopolitanism. The emergence of several cities like Bombay and the development of a sense of territorial identity for those who lived in them, it was argued, could prove to be as important to India's national development as the growth of wholly provincial cities would prove important in the strengthening of India's many regional cultures.

Had Bombay been placed directly under the central government (like Delhi), such a model might have emerged. But once Bombay was made the premier city within the state of Maharashtra, Marathi speakers sought to turn Bombay into a Marathi city. Other ethnic communities could remain in the city and even retain their own distinctive cultural identities, but it should be understood, argued the Marathi nativists, that the city belonged to Maharashtra, that native Marathi speakers had special rights within it, and that all who resided in the city had to speak Marathi at least as a second language. Thus, the Marathi nativists explicitly reject the territorial concept of the Bombaywalla in favor of more exclusive ethnic identities. Gujaratis, Tamils, and other alien communities are welcome to retain their own exclusive identities and maintain their own cultural traditions, but to call them Bombaywallas implies that they have the same rights within the city as the local Marathis.

The question of defining who is local remains fundamentally a political issue. Let us turn, then, to examine the viewpoint of a select group of political leaders in India who are potential pace setters for political ideas. We shall report on the attitudes of a group of members of the Indian parliament who represent multiethnic, multilingual constituencies and whose notions, therefore, of who is local is a central element in their own political outlook and conduct.

MIGRANT CONSTITUENCIES

The focus here is on legislators from a small group of constituencies in India. Most members of the Indian parliament represent constituencies that are highly diversified in their class and caste structure, and some MPs have constituents who speak a variety of languages and adhere to a variety of religions and cultures. But one feature that almost all constituencies share is that they consist primarily of people born in the constituency. As we have noted earlier, most Indians are born, go to school, marry, work, and die within a relatively small area, and often in a single village or town. Though women marry outside their village, few move long distances. Among the men, only 9.8 percent live outside the district in which they were born, and a good proportion of these in villages and towns in nearby districts of the same state. The voting population, therefore, is highly stable. Voter turnover is mainly the result of young people coming of age and the death of some voters. Most MPs need not be concerned that many of their voters will leave the constituency or that new voters will migrate from elsewhere.

Even in those urban constituencies that have substantial numbers of migrants from surrounding rural areas, new voters are ordinarily people of the same language, race, and culture as those of the constituency to which they have moved. In the Hindi-speaking towns and cities of northern India, for example, most of the migrants come from nearby Hindi-speaking localities.

But there are about 47 parliamentary constituencies in India, out of 520 seats in the Indian parliament (less than 10 percent), that constitute an exception. In each of these constituencies there is a modest number of migrants from other states—5 percent or more of the male population. In

308

each of these, at least 20 percent of the population speaks a language that is not local to the state or region of the state in which the constituency is located. In several instances the indigenous population is actually less than a majority of the constituency. These constituencies, then, all have a substantial ethnically distinguishable population of migrants or descendants of migrants, speaking a nonlocal language, or belonging to a nonlocal culture. Many of these are urban constituencies: five are in Bombay, four in Calcutta, two in Madras, one in Bangalore, and two in Hyderabad. Nine of the constituencies are in Chota Nagpur, and six are in the Brahmaputra and Surma valley districts of Assam. In addition, there are four constituencies in Madhya Pradesh, three in Maharashtra (including the urbanized districts of Nagpur and Thana), three in Mysore, two in Uttar Pradesh, two in northern Bengal, and one each in Rajasthan, Tamil Nadu, Orissa, and Tripura.

THE SURVEY

For this study, sixteen of the MPs from these constituencies, about a third, were interviewed.[2] Three were from Bombay, two from Hyderabad, four from Chota Nagpur, six from Assam, and one from Bangalore. The Bombay, Hyderabad, and Bangalore constituencies are urban, while the Chota Nagpur and Assam constituencies are mainly rural.

Each MP was asked to describe the ethnic composition of his constituency: which groups lived there, what occupations they were engaged in, where in the constituency they lived, what kinds of demands they made, and how the various groups got on with one another. The MP was then asked a series of questions intended to elicit his attitudes toward outsiders. Should local people be given preferences over outsiders in employment in the state government and for jobs as teachers in colleges, universities, technical and medical

[2] The numbers are too small to warrant a detailed statistical analysis with cross-tabulations.

309

schools? They were also asked whether they thought local people should have preferences in gaining admission to engineering and medical colleges, and obtaining financial support from the government for their businesses. Should outsiders be allowed to purchase land in the locality, or to start their own businesses? Should they be permitted to send their children to schools in their own languages when the schools were financed by the government?

I was particularly concerned with trying to find out what the MP meant by a "local" person. Was "local" defined in ethnic or territorial terms? By length of residence? Or by place of education? And did the MP feel that local people had more (or the same) claims on the resources and authority of the government than migrants or the descendants of migrants? In short, for whom did the MP speak? Did he see himself representing the claims of "local" people (as he defined them), or representing the claims of both groups of voters?

Of the sixteen MPs interviewed, a dozen belonged to the ethnic community indigenous to the locale. These included MPs from Hyderabad (1), Bangalore (1), Assam (4), and Bombay (2), who belonged to the dominant linguistic community in the state. Three of the MPs from Chota Nagpur were tribals whose communities were indigenous to the region, though they were not the majority ethnic group in the state. A Bengali represented Cachar district in Assam, but the predominantly Bengali district was historically once part of neighboring Bengal.

Only four of the MPs were themselves ethnic outsiders in their own constituencies. One MP representing a district in Assam was a Marwari (originally from Rajasthan) whose family settled in Assam in the early part of the nineteenth century. He and his family are widely thought of as domesticated Assamese. One of the MPs from Chota Nagpur was a Bengali, and his family also settled in the region several generations ago. A Gujarati representing one of the seats in Bombay moved to the city fifty years ago as a young man to attend college. Finally, one of the MPs from Hyderabad was born in the city of a Kannada-speaking family that moved to Bangalore when he was a child. He returned to Hyderabad as a young man to attend college, and he too has lived in the city continuously for fifty years. In other words, none of the MPs was a recent immigrant; indeed, only one MP was born outside of the region in which his constituency is located.

Eleven of the sixteen MPs were members of the ruling party and five belonged to the opposition. Two MPs from Hyderabad were members of the Telangana Praja Samiti, two from Chota Nagpur were members of the Jharkhand party, and the fifth belonged to the Congress (O), a dissident Congress group that had been expelled from the ruling Congress party in 1969.

WHO IS "LOCAL"?

The MPs had divergent views as to who constituted a local person. For some, local meant someone from the *region* in which their constituency was located. The MPs from Hyderabad, for example, distinguished between *mulkis* from the Telangana region and non-*mulkis* from outside the region, whether from other parts of Andhra or from other states of India. For other MPs, local meant someone who belonged to the *ethnic* group indigenous to the state or to the region of the state in which the constituency was located. The tribal MPs from the Chota Nagpur region of Bihar, for example, distinguished between *adivasis*, or tribal people, and *dikus*, the pejorative for nontribals.

We can distinguish, therefore, between those MPs who have a territorial and those who have an ethnic conception of who is a local person. MPs, like other Indians, sometimes use the English phrase "sons of the soil" to refer to local people, but the phrase is neither as rich nor as complex as the many terms used by local people in their own language to refer to themselves or to outsiders. In some instances, the indigenous term is explicitly ethnic, while in other instances

311

the term may be explicitly territorial. *Diku* and *adivasi*, for example, are ethnic concepts, while *mulki* and non-*mulki* are territorial.

The English phrase "sons of the soil" ambiguously incorporates both concepts. It may refer to those who are born, raised, or permanently settled in a given territory, or it may refer to those who belong to, identify with, and are accepted as part of a given cultural group without regard to their place of birth. This ambiguity is a major source of tension between those who belong to the dominant culture of a state or locality within the state, and those who were born within the area but are considered by members of the dominant culture as outsiders because their parents or ancestors migrated and they belong to a culture that has its roots elsewhere.

The territorial-regional definition of local was expressed by an MP from Hyderabad who enumerated the problems created in Hyderabad by migrants from the coastal areas of Andhra. "They have created a housing problem for us. The government built housing for the Andhras because they felt that outsiders needed housing while the local people could always live with their relatives. That has created much resentment. The migrant children have also overcrowded the schools and created difficulties for the local students seeking admission into colleges and the university. And a disproportionate number of Andhra people have been given jobs by the state government, and many have been given promotions faster than the people from Telangana."

I asked him whether he was regarded as a non-*mulki* since he spoke Kannada, not the regional language (Telugu), and spent his early years in Bangalore. "No, everyone here considers me a *mulki*. I was an active participant in the independence struggle in Hyderabad and I was elected to the state assembly in the first election in 1952, and then to parliament in 1957. To become a *mulki* is more than just a matter of how long someone lives here, but whether he supports local causes. Some of the migrants from Andhra came here in 1957, but they are not one of us because they

312

don't give us support. For example, they didn't support us when we protested that the tax money raised in Telangana was spent elsewhere in the state. Telangana is a backward region. Its people come from all over, speaking many languages, not only Telugu. The region is less developed and the people are less educated than in other parts of the state. So we need to be developed and we need to be given preferences in education and in jobs. If people who live here do not support us then they are not *mulkis*." Like the other members of parliament from Telangana, he was in favor of carving a separate Telangana state out of Andhra.[3]

Among the MPs from Bombay city, one of the three had a strong sense of territorial identification, while the other two tended to think of only those who spoke Marathi as local. One of these two, however, a Harijan born in Maharashtra, but outside of Bombay, welcomed the cosmopolitan character of the city though he adhered to an ethnic conception of local. The one MP with a territorial conception was himself a Gujarati who had settled in the city as a young man to attend Elphinstone College. He spoke of the other Gujaratis in his constituency as local, not only because many had lived there for several generations, but also because they had their roots in Bombay. "The Gujaratis in Bombay spend their money in Bombay for building schools and hospitals, and financing charities. If there is a public fund to be raised, then Gujaratis here contribute generously." He pointed out that in his constituency, a quarter of the population is Gujarati in origin—engaged mainly in business, trade, and commerce. Another 15 percent of the constituency comes from Uttar Pradesh, and they work in the city as milk vendors and producers and sellers of sweets made from milk. Some also work in the factories. The constituency also has some south Indians, a few Bengalis, some Parsis, and a variety of other ethnic groups. Only 40 percent of the population is native

[3] If a Telangana state were formed, he explained, "the people from Andhra might remain, but the influx of Andhra people into government employment would stop."

Marathi-speaking.[4] Each ethnic group lives in its own neighborhood and each has schools in its own language. The migrants from Uttar Pradesh and Bihar send their children to Hindi-medium schools, the Parsis and Gujaratis send their children to Gujarati schools, while the Marathi children go to Marathi schools. In his view, all of these are local people. "Anyone who goes to school here, anyone who passes the examination for a secondary school certificate in Maharashtra should be considered a Maharashtrian," he said.

A very different conception of local was expressed by an MP from Chota Nagpur, a member of the Ho tribe. His constituency has many Gujarati, Bengali, and Punjabi businessmen, and he noted that most of the people who worked in government offices, including the local police and revenue officers, were from north Bihar. He spoke of both the businessmen and government officials as outsiders. "The tribals are fed up by the outsiders who exploit them. All the government jobs are held by Biharis so the government doesn't build us enough schools and we do not have proper roads. There is only a dirt road going to the district town and it is washed away during the rainy weather. Posts in government are supposedly reserved for tribals with an education, but in the personnel interviews for government jobs, the Biharis turn the tribals down as unqualified. The tribals can't start their own businesses either, since they have no money and the government won't give them loans. The capitalists are all outsiders, while the tribals are the workers."

Like other tribal leaders, he spoke of outsiders as *dikus*. "Who are the *dikus*?" I asked. "They are the upper caste Hindus. The Biharis are all *dikus*. So are the Bengalis.[5] They

[4] This constituency has never elected a native-speaking Maharashtrian to parliament.

[5] Not all tribals use the term *diku* in this restrictive sense. Another MP, himself a tribal, said that not all nontribals were *dikus*, only those "who exploit the tribals." Some tribal leaders have sought the support of nontribal local residents in the region for the creation of a Chota Nagpur state arguing, as this MP put it, that "even the non-adivasis in this area are being neglected by the government."

314

are the people who exploit us and who reject us for jobs. They are people without sympathy for the tribals, people who do not like us. The tribals live in the rural areas, while the Biharis, Marwaris, Bengalis, and other outsiders live in the towns. But with the growth of population in the rural areas and the spread of education, the younger tribals are looking for jobs in the towns. They aren't finding any, or sometimes they get only the most menial jobs in mining at low wages.

"We are colonies of the Biharis. The Biharis don't allow us to use our mother tongue in the schools.[6] They don't give us jobs. So we want a state of our own. In a tribal state the government would give financial support to tribals to build up small scale industries and give contracts to tribals for timber instead of helping the north Biharis. If the Chota Nagpur region were a separate state, then we would have our own public service commission and the officers of the government would be tribals. All the taxes would be spent in Chota Nagpur instead of being collected here and spent in north Bihar. Now that we are well educated we can govern ourselves."[7]

The other tribal MPs representing constituencies in Chota Nagpur shared this notion of tribals as locals while all others were outsiders, though not all agreed that there ought to be a separate tribal state.

EMPLOYMENT FOR LOCALS AND NONLOCALS

Whatever criteria an MP used for who was local, whether ethnic or territorial, all the MPs agreed that preferences

But thus far, the demand for a separate state has mainly received support from tribals.

[6] Hindi is used as the medium of instruction in the primary schools in the tribal areas, not the various tribal languages: Munda, Oraon, and Ho.

[7] He referred to the recently created state of Meghalaya, a predominantly tribal area carved out of the state of Assam, as an example of tribals capable of governing themselves.

315

should be given to local people in employment. Without exception, all the MPs asserted that whenever new jobs for the unskilled were available in their constituencies, preferences should be given to local people. Three of the MPs said they felt that in unskilled jobs *only* local people should be hired, but the other MPs agreed with the statement in the survey that "local people should be given preference, but if no qualified local people can be found then people from other states should be employed."

Where the MPs diverged, of course, was on the question of who qualified as a local person. In this particular context most of the MPs meant the indigenous population: the MPs from Chota Nagpur meant the tribals, the MPs from Bombay meant Marathi speakers, and the MPs from Assam meant the Assamese. The one exception was the Bengali MP representing a constituency in Chota Nagpur. By "local," he said, "I don't mean just the *adivasis* (tribals), but all local people including the Muslims, the local Biharis who have settled here, the Bengalis, and so on. By local I mean the people from Chota Nagpur."[8]

There was also nearly universal agreement among the MPs that in hiring for skilled positions, local people should also be given preferences before migrants were employed. Two of the MPs wanted to impose a minimum quota on employers for hiring local people,[9] but other MPs simply asserted that

[8] The MP estimated that only 50 percent of the population of his constituency is tribal. The constituency includes the town of Ranchi. He estimated that about 10 percent of the voters are Bengalis, mainly in the professions and central government services; 10 percent are Bihari Muslims, mainly cultivators; a substantial proportion consists of Biharis in land, in state government service, and in industry; and there is a scattering of Oriya factory workers and Punjabi businessmen. Ranchi is the site for the Heavy Engineering Corporation, Hindustan Steel, and Ranchi University, all of which attract personnel from outside Chota Nagpur.

[9] An MP from Bombay said that even in skilled positions, 80 percent of the jobs should be reserved for local people, by which she meant Marathi speakers.

316

qualified locals should be hired before others. Only one MP —the Gujarati representing a Bombay constituency—endorsed the statement that "the most qualified persons should be employed no matter which part of India they come from." Another MP from Bombay, an educated member of a scheduled caste who had converted to Buddhism—said that he would give preferences to local people, but "I would rather hire a competent Keralite than an incompetent Maharashtrian."[10] Other MPs, however, made no such qualification.

Most of the MPs, for example, argued that in the hiring of teachers for colleges, universities, technical and medical schools, local people should be hired first, and only if a qualified person could not be found locally should someone from another state be employed. Only one of the MPs, the Gujarati from Bombay, agreed with the statement that the colleges and universities "should hire qualified teachers from all over India."

The MPs were just as locally minded when it came to the appointment of civil servants. Almost all agreed with the statement that "local people should be given preference, but if no qualified local people can be found then qualified people from other states should be employed as top officials." Two of the MPs adamantly expressed the view that *all* the top officials of the state should come from within the state. The two MPs from Hyderabad went further, arguing that the top officials within the Telangana region of the state should be recruited only from within Telangana; similarly, the tribal MPs from Chota Nagpur argued that officials in the area should be recruited primarily from among the tribals. In both instances, the MPs favored converting their regions into

[10] This MP reported that his main electoral support came from the non-Maharashtrians who constituted a majority of his constituency—Telugu construction workers, Tamil clerks and owners of restaurants, Gujarati shopkeepers, and Uttar Pradesh mill workers. In the election he was opposed by a candidate of the Shiv Sena, who not only wanted to give employment preferences to local people, but who "wants to force the migrants to leave Bombay."

separate states in which government officers would be recruited from within the region. Only the Gujarati from Bombay agreed with the statement in our survey that "it doesn't make any difference where the top officials of the state come from so long as they do their work well and speak the regional language."

INVESTMENT IN BUSINESS AND LAND

When it came to the question of whether migrants should be allowed to open businesses in their constituencies, the MPs were in the main much more open. About a third of the MPs agreed that "in order to develop the economy of the state, the government should encourage investors from all over India to start new enterprises in the states." Most of the remaining MPs agreed that "the state government should give special assistance to local businessmen, but businessmen from other states should be welcome too." Only an MP from Hyderabad asserted that "businessmen from other states [and other parts of his own state, he added] should be kept out or local people will lose control of their own economy." He went on to say that "when it comes to investment I would keep out all the Andhras [people from other parts of the state, outside of Telangana]. We should encourage local people in Telangana to start small industries, and if there aren't enough local businessmen, then let the government start more industries here." This was, however, an extreme view, for the other MPs generally welcomed outside investors, though they emphasized the importance of outside businessmen hiring local people.[11]

But while the MPs were cosmopolitan when it came to investment in industry, they were highly protective when it came to investment in land. Nearly half of the MPs representing rural constituencies agreed with the statement that "people who come from outside the state shouldn't be al-

[11] "There is a tendency," said an MP from Bombay, reporting a widely shared sentiment, "for employers to hire their own people."

lowed to buy land in the state." The other half agreed that "in general anyone in India ought to be allowed to buy land any place in the country." Almost all of the MPs from tribal constituencies of Chota Nagpur felt that outsiders (in this case, nontribals) should not be allowed to buy land; a similar viewpoint was expressed by one of the two Telangana MPs, who expressed his concern over the purchase of land in Telangana by migrants from the eastern districts of Andhra.[12] One of the MPs from an urban constituency in Bombay said that the land belonged to Maharashtrians; they could sell the land, but then that entitled them to jobs locally. "After all," she said, "the Tamil and Gujarati migrants can find jobs elsewhere but the Marathi boys cannot."

EDUCATION FOR LOCALS AND NONLOCALS

The MPs were enthusiastic supporters of efforts to increase educational opportunities for young people in their constituencies, especially in engineering and medical schools. They were in favor of providing preferences for local students, agreeing with the statement that there "should be admission to qualified local students first, and only if there is sufficient place should students from other states be admitted." Several MPs took a somewhat more liberal view by agreeing that "there should also be some reserved places for students from other states." Only a single MP, again the Gujarati from Bombay, said that "the engineering and medical colleges in the state should be open to all qualified Indians no matter what part of the country they come from." Another Bombay MP presented the more widespread view when she said that "without these preferences the boys from backward areas would not get a chance to be admitted to the medical and engineering colleges. In fact, some states would probably not

[12] He complained that people from coastal Andhra were buying land in Hyderabad, thereby pushing up the price of urban land. He also reported that the richer Andhra farmers were purchasing newly irrigated lands in Telangana at low prices.

319

have any medical students at all. There are disparities all over India in all fields. We must not extend these disparities to our children; that's why the local children from the backward communities should be given preferences in admissions."

ASSIMILATION AND INTEGRATION

An interesting finding in this survey is that the MPs were not in favor of culturally assimilating migrants from other states. None of the MPs believed that migrants should surrender their cultural identity. When they were asked about the language of instruction in government-supported schools, for example, every MP in our survey agreed with the statement that the "regional language of the migrant should be used as the medium of instruction if requested by the parents," and not one accepted the statement that "the official language of the state should be the medium of instruction in all schools even for migrant children from other states."[13] However, most of the MPs quickly qualified their statement by saying that the regional language should be compulsory as a second language for all migrant children.

Nor was there any overwhelming sentiment in favor of integrated housing. A few of the MPs agreed that "migrants from other states should be encouraged by government to live in neighborhoods with local people so that they can learn the regional language and culture." But most of the MPs felt that the migrants "should be completely free to live wherever they want to."[14] One MP, a woman from Bombay, said that "where people lived shouldn't be a concern of the

[13] On this issue the MPs took a more liberal view than many state politicians and officials, who would prefer to see all the secondary schools conducted in the regional language. It is interesting to note that several of the MPs, when asked, reported that they sent their own children to English-medium schools.

[14] The Gujarati MP from Bombay, a strong advocate of equal opportunities for locals and migrants in jobs and education, said that "normally each group lives separately in its own locality. I like to stay in a place where my wife can speak Gujarati to the neighbors."

320

government." This sentiment was widely shared, for even those who felt that it was desirable for migrants to live among local people were unable to suggest any steps government might take to bring about greater integration in housing. On the question of housing there was an uncharacteristic laissez-faire attitude among MPs.

The integration of migrants into the local culture was not the issue among Indian MPs from mixed constituencies that it is in American and British constituencies. The MPs did not press for the linguistic assimilation of migrants, for the incorporation of migrants into schools with local children, or for integration in housing. It seemed perfectly natural to the MPs that people of each culture should prefer to live in their own neighborhoods and send their children to their own schools in their own languages.

When the question of schools and higher education arose, it was not over the issue of "integration," but rather over the question of who should be hired to teach and, at the higher levels, who should be admitted.

Some MPs did talk about the importance of migrants acquiring knowledge of the regional language, and many spoke of the need for migrants to identify with local causes and support the claims of the state (or region) against other areas of the country, even those from which the migrants came. But it was quite evident that most of the MPs would simply prefer that migrants from other states and other cultural regions of their state not come into their constituency to compete for jobs, college admissions, and land.

WHY THE DIFFERENCES?

What accounts for whether an MP thinks in territorial or ethnic terms, and whether "local" people, however defined, are entitled to rights and benefits that outsiders are not entitled to? The handful of cases we have hardly permits us to do more than touch upon these issues, but even with these small numbers we can suggest several hypotheses. The first

321

is that an MP who is himself the member of an ethnic minority that originates outside the constituency and the region is more likely to see himself as the representative of all ethnic groups within his constituency, and more likely to think of "local" as anyone who has resided in the constituency for an extended period of time. The Bengali representing a constituency in Chota Nagpur, the Gujarati from Bombay, the Kannada from Hyderabad, the Marwari representing a constituency in Assam are all examples of MPs whose conception of local is multiethnic. Not all ethnically mixed urban constituencies produce such MPs, however, for most of the urban MPs belong to the indigenous ethnic group, identify with them, and define local in ethnic terms. But then we also find some urban MPs belonging to the indigenous ethnic group who have a territorial conception of what is local: a Kannada-speaking MP representing Bangalore, for example, who spoke with pride of the multilingual features of "cosmopolitan" Bangalore, and the Marathi-speaking Harijan MP from Bombay who said, "I have an affinity to migrants since I, too, belong to a minority community."

MPs from rural constituencies are more likely to see themselves as spokesmen for the indigenous ethnic community, but even some of these MPs are concerned lest they alienate their constituency. The MPs from Assam believe that the Assamese alone among the major linguistic communities are indigenous, but they expressed a tolerance for their Bengali Muslim agricultural constituents, even as they expressed their hostility toward the less numerous urban-dwelling Bengali Hindus and Marwaris. Similarly, one tribal MP from Chota Nagpur had created an alliance of Bihari Hindus and non-Christian tribals in opposition to Bihari Muslims and Christian tribals.[15] The strategic need to build electoral coalitions of

[15] This MP, who considered himself a Hindu tribal, was in favor of removing job and educational reservations for Christian tribals on the grounds that Christian tribals were educationally more advanced than non-Christian tribals. His views won him considerable support from the Bihari Hindu community that constitutes a substantial part of his constituency.

diverse ethnic communities often forced MPs not to rely exclusively upon their own ethnic group.

Anxiety over employment led almost all the MPs to advocate restrictive policies toward one or another group. They differed only on who should receive preferences in employment, not on whether such preferences should be given. The Christian tribals were in favor of preferences for all tribesmen. The non-Christian tribal MP wanted preferences only for the non-Christian tribals. The Hyderabad MPs wanted preferences for *mulkis*, the Assamese MPs for the Assamese. Many echoed the opinions of a Bombay MP who said that "Maharashtrian boys [by which she meant Marathi speakers] should get preferences even though the other boys are born here too. If three boys equally qualified come for a job, all born in Maharashtra, then the Marathi boy should be given preference over the Tamil and Gujarati for they could find a job elsewhere and the Marathi boy could not." The case for a system of preferences was forcefully expressed by an MP from Assam who said, "Ideally, the best man should get the job, but in our state of development if we left it to merit alone the backward areas and the backward communities would always remain backward. So in this transitional period our state must be helped as must other backward areas and backward peoples. We cannot leave the economy to free competition and that includes the question of hiring people. One day we can leave employment and admissions to college entirely to merit, but until we can reduce poverty and provide a minimum living for everyone, special measures will have to be taken by the government."

The sense that job opportunities are limited, that in a wholly open competitive job market those with more education and skills would get the jobs, that "outsiders" (whether they be ethnic outsiders, people from elsewhere in the state, or people from other parts of India) would take jobs was clearly an obsession with virtually all the MPs. None questioned the right of the government to make distinctions as to who would get preferences in employment, public or private,

323

skilled or unskilled. Where people lived, what languages they spoke, what languages were used as the medium of instruction in primary schools—these were not the issues that divided people; the issue of employment was.

Employment is primarily an urban, not a rural, issue. When the MPs from predominantly rural constituencies expressed their concern over employment, they were identifying an issue for their urban constituents, and for wealthier rural peasants who had aspirations that their sons could obtain urban employment. The rural MPs tended to share an ethnic conception of who was local, and to share attitudes on preferences in education and employment, but the urban constituencies seem capable of producing MPs who are more broadly cosmopolitan as well as MPs who are militantly nativist.

The divergences reported by this survey, even among MPs from the same cities, simply reflect the conflicts that exist within India's urban centers. Urban voters, like MPs, are themselves often uncertain as to whether they should adopt territorial or ethnic identities, as our linguistic analysis has shown. Some will call themselves Bombaywallas, others will call themselves Marathis or Maharashtrians; some will call themselves Hyderabadis, and others will call themselves Telugus or Andhras. The choices are as old as mankind: who am I, who are they? Are we alike because we live in the same place, or different because we belong to different tribes or speak different languages? Do I have more rights than you because I belong here and you do not? These issues will shape political life and public policies in India for many years, and they will not easily be resolved in a society where migration patterns are changing and where the political system itself is in flux—for the choices that individuals make will be shaped not simply by the social changes that they experience, but by the political struggles among contenders for public office and by the public policies adopted by governments. Group identities are molded in the political and public policy arenas.

324

EIGHT

CITIZENSHIP AND INTERNAL MIGRATION LAWS

CITIZENSHIP AND NATIONAL IDENTITY

IN multiethnic societies, "citizenship" and "national identity" are different and, at times, conflicting conceptions. Citizenship implies a relationship between the individual and the state in which certain rights and duties are specified under law. Citizenship implies universality of rights and duties, that is, a notion of equality under law. To the Greeks a slave was not a citizen of the *polis*, for he did not share the rights of free men. To Aristotle citizenship meant the right to share in the administration of justice and in office, that is, legislation and adjudication, a definition appropriate for a democracy but not to other regimes in which political participation is restricted and where few people are permitted to hold office. The modern usage, however, is to use "citizen" to mean one who owes allegiance to a government and is entitled to its protection, without necessarily implying any rights of participation; thus, one can be a "citizen" of an authoritarian state.

"Nationality," though more complex in its usage, is sometimes used interchangeably with citizenship, implying protection by the state but without Aristotle's notion of political rights. In either case, "national," like "citizen," denotes a relationship to the state.

In contrast, however, "national identity" denotes a relationship to society rather than to the state, and implies a subjective rather than legal relationship. A national identity may be learned at home or in school, transmitted from one generation to another, or it may be the outgrowth of a po-

325

litical process as a given tribe, caste, linguistic group, or culture choses to assert its own identity or declare a national identity. Identities are thus learned or chosen by individuals or social collectivities, while citizenship is conferred by the state.

Citizenship and national identity are by no means coterminous. A Frenchman is born French, both by cultural identity and citizenship. But a Tamil child born in the tea plantations of Sri Lanka is not necessarily a citizen of Sri Lanka, whatever identification either he or his parents choose, for in Sri Lanka place of birth is not the sole criterion for citizenship.

How states have defined citizenship is by no means uniform. The widespread convention is that citizenship is acquired by birth in a given territorial state, descent from a citizen parent, marriage, or naturalization, but there are numerous historical and contemporary exceptions. In 1492 the Spanish monarchy expelled the Sephardic Jews as noncitizens, and not until the middle of the nineteenth century were the Jews of England given full citizenship rights. The Edict of Nantes (1598) extended rights to the Huguenots in France, while its revocation nearly a century later (1685) denied French Protestants the rights and protections extended to Catholic citizens.

Among developing countries, the governments of Burma, Sri Lanka, and Uganda denied automatic citizenship to Indians born in their countries, while many African countries have expelled as noncitizens members of tribes whose original homeland is a neighboring country, again without regard to the individual's place of birth. Neither *jus soli* (citizenship by birth, irrespective of parental citizenship) nor *jus sanguinis* (the citizenship of one's parents, irrespective of place of birth) is the only principle for relating birth to citizenship; in some political systems, citizenship is determined by one's membership in a specified race, linguistic community, tribe, or culture.

326

Nor is the "classical" conception of citizenship, which assumes that rights and obligations are conferred upon individuals rather than collectivities, and that these rights and obligations are universally shared under a system of law, uniformly followed by all governments. Indeed, conceptions of citizenship within the multiethnic societies of many African and Asian states often take into account the special claims of ethnic collectivities, so that governments fashion laws that allocate rights and benefits to some ethnic groups but not to others.

Even states whose constitution and national political leadership assert the classical conception of a universal, uniform citizenship may find it necessary to modify this conception as a consequence of the emergence of subnational identities as a political force. The Indian experience described here provides us with just such an example. A government, deeply shaped by British conceptions of citizenship, has gradually changed that conception under the political pressures of linguistic, caste, and tribal groups seeking special protections and rights under law. The policies adopted by India's state governments with respect to employment and education have in effect created separate classes of citizenship, as local ethnic groups assert the special rights of "sons of the soil" to jobs and education, in spite of provisions of the Indian constitution that explicitly prohibit job discrimination and proclaim equal opportunity for all citizens of India. The political process by which the conception of a common citizenship has been modified by internal migration policies in India is the theme of this chapter.

CITIZENSHIP AND FREEDOM OF INTERNAL MOVEMENT

Within democratic societies, the right to move freely within the boundaries of the country is widely regarded as a claim of citizenship. This right is implied in Article IV, Section 2 of the American constitution, which says that "the citizens of each state shall be entitled to all privileges and immunities of citizens in the several states." The post-Civil War amendment, Article XIV, even more forcefully asserts that "no State shall make or enforce any law which shall abridge the privileges or immunities of citizens of the United States." Several court cases have interpreted these articles to mean that whatever rights or restrictions imposed by a state upon its citizens shall be applicable, neither more nor less, upon the citizens of other states residing within its jurisdiction.

The right to move as a right of citizenship is similarly asserted in the French Rights of Man (which guarantees "le droit de libre séjour et libre circulation") and in the French constitution of 1791 ("liberté d'aller, de rester, de partir"). The Australians, torn, as were Americans, between the upholders of states' rights and the upholders of federal rights, followed the Fourteenth Amendment of the American constitution by declaring in their constitution that "a subject of the Queen resident in any State shall not be subject in any other State to any disability or discrimination which would not be equally applicable to him if he were a subject of the Queen resident in such other State."

In India, the first legal assertion of this right is Section 87 of the Government of India Act of 1833 (subsequently incorporated into the Government of India Act of 1935, and, with slight variations, into the Constitution of India, 1950). "No native of British India nor any subject of His Majesty resident therein shall by reason only of his religion, *place of birth*, descent, colour or any of them be disabled from holding any office under the Crown in India" (italics mine). Though the "place of birth" provision presumably intended to eliminate the distinction between those born in India and those British subjects born outside of India, the provision was interpreted to provide equal rights to all Indians irrespective of the province of birth. British and Indian constitution and law makers repeatedly rejected proposals for creating provincial citizenship side by side with Indian

328

citizenship. In contrast with the American constitution, the Indian constitution does not provide for dual citizenship.

The right to migrate within India is explicitly asserted by the Indian constitution (1950), which specifies that all citizens "shall have the right to move freely throughout the territory of India," and "to reside and settle in any part of the territory of India" (Article 19).

The right to move within national boundaries is inherent in the doctrine "equality under the law"; citizens of a country shall not suffer any disabilities under the law by virtue of place of birth. Moreover, were local and provincial units of governments within a federal system permitted to bar individuals from entering their territory or permitted to impose legal disabilities on newcomers that were not imposed on long-term residents, then the sovereignty of central authority would be severely limited. Thus, both citizenship and sovereignty imply that local bodies shall not restrict internal migration.

But the right to move within a nation's boundaries is not an unqualified, fundamental right; it is weighed against other rights and it is subject to some of the same political forces that seek to impose limitations on any rights. In this Chapter, we analyze the kinds of conflicting values and interests at work in India that limit—some would say erode—this dimension of both individual rights and of national authority, for an analysis of the concept of citizenship, the linchpin of any system of jurisprudence, necessitates a consideration of the conflicting values and political interests upon which legal concepts rest.

ETHNIC GROUPS AS LEGAL ENTITIES

One striking feature of the Indian legal system is its recognition of ethnicity, that is, of caste, religious, tribal, and linguistic communities as legal entities entitled to certain rights as well as protections against disabilities. There are two pro-

329

visions of the constitution dealing with ethnicity that are particularly relevant for an analysis of the freedom to migrate within the country.

The first is a constitutional provision that guarantees individuals the right to retain their cultural identity irrespective of where they reside. "Any section of the citizens," declares Article 29, "residing in the territory of India or any part thereof having a distinct language, script or culture of its own shall have the right to conserve the same." Article 30 goes on to say that "all minorities, whether based on religion or language, shall have the right to establish and administer educational institutions of their choice" and "the State shall not, in granting aid to educational institutions, discriminate against any educational institution on the ground that it is under the management of a minority, whether based on religion or language."

This provision is strengthened still further by Article 350A, which provides that "it shall be the endeavor of every State and every local authority within the State to provide adequate facilities for instruction in the mother tongue at the primary stage of education to children belonging to linguistic minority groups; and the President may issue such directions to any State as he considers necessary or proper for securing the provision of such facilities." To ensure the protection of linguistic minorities, Article 350B creates a special officer to be appointed by and responsible to the president of India.

These provisions thus make it possible for individuals to retain their cultural-linguistic heritage even when they migrate to another state. State governments are required to provide primary and secondary schools in the mother tongue of migrants when the migrants speak one of the official languages listed in the constitution, and when they are sufficiently numerous within a given school locality. When migrants are numerous within a state or even a district, state governments are under obligation to provide translations of state laws and ordinances into the language of the migrants.[1] In short, cultural diversity rather than a melting-pot strategy is constitutionally prescribed not only for India as a whole, but for each state.

The second constitutional provision relevant to migrants limits the right to move into specified areas of the country. The fifth and sixth schedules of the constitution provide for the special administration of India's tribal areas, and empower the governor and the state in which these areas are located to prohibit or restrict the transfer of land from tribals to nontribals and to restrict or regulate moneylenders. Article 19 of the constitution (which provides for freedom of movement, the right to reside and settle in any part of India, and the right to acquire property) explicitly permits states to make laws imposing "reasonable restrictions on the exercise of any of (these) rights . . . either in the interests of the general public or for the protection of the interests of any Scheduled Tribe," an exception freely used with respect to the scheduled areas.[2]

The constitution also provides that the president of India prepare a list of "scheduled" castes and tribes suffering from economic and social disabilities, that are entitled to special representation in the state assemblies and in the national parliament, and special benefits both in education and in government employment. However, a tribe or caste may be deemed "scheduled" only "in relation to that State or Union

[1] Article 347 of the constitution provides that if the President "is satisfied that a substantial proportion of the population of a State desire that the use of any language spoken by them to be recognised by that State, [he may] direct that such languages shall also be officially recognized throughout that State or any part thereof for such purposes as he may specify." Note that the central government (in the person of the President) rather than the state government has the right to give official recognition to minority languages.

[2] In addition to the scheduled areas, the constitution also permits the government of Kashmir to restrict the sale of land in the state to non-Kashmiris.

territory, as the case may be" (Articles 341, 342). Thus, a member of a tribe or caste is only entitled to the special representations, benefits, and protections granted by law in the state in which his tribe or caste is listed as scheduled, and loses these once he leaves the state.

In contrast, then, with the language provisions of the constitution, which facilitate migrations across state boundaries, the special protection clauses of the constitution are spatially restrictive. Let us now consider how these two sets of constitutional provisions have been modified under the exigencies of conflicting values and interests.

CLASHING CLAIMS: CITIES AND STATES AS HOMOGENEOUS OR HETEROGENEOUS CULTURES

Almost every urban center in India has schools for linguistic minorities. Multilingual Bombay, for example, supports a large network of public and private schools in Gujarati, Hindi, English, and Sindhi as the medium of instruction, as well as in Marathi, the official language of the state. Migrant minorities in many other cities have also created their own private schools, financially supported by the government, which provide instruction in the mother tongue or in English.

Nonetheless, state and local government have tended to drag their feet in response to demands for separate schools and classes for linguistic minorities of migrant origin. The annual report of the Commissioner of Linguistic Minorities— the central government officer empowered to investigate claims by linguistic minorities that their rights are not protected by state governments—is full of accounts of unresolved demands and unanswered letters from the commissioner to state governments.

One reason that state and local educational authorities are often unresponsive is convenience and cost: materials for teaching in another language need to be brought in from a neighboring state, special materials need to be prepared that are compatible with existing school materials, and special

332

examinations have to be written and evaluated. Another reason is that the state or locality must recruit teachers who speak the migrant languages, often from neighboring states, when in a situation of job scarcity there is great reluctance to give jobs in the state services to "outsiders."

Privately, and now increasingly publicly, there is growing opposition to the constitutional requirement that migrant minorities be permitted to maintain an educational system in which their own language is used as the medium of instruction. There is strong sentiment that the children of migrants learn the language of the region to which they have moved, and that learning it as a second language in the schools is a poor substitute for using the regional language as the medium of all classroom instruction.

State governments are under no constitutional obligation to provide colleges for linguistic minorities, either "indigenous" minorities or migrant minorities. Since many state colleges have switched from English to the regional language as the medium of instruction and examination, students belonging to linguistic minorities must either develop a competence in the regional language equal to the local students against whom they must compete for college admission, or seek admission in the college of the states from which they or their parents originally come.

State governments have also resisted enforcing the provisions that laws and ordinances must be issued in the languages of migrant minorities, partly because it means that the state government and local authorities must recruit migrant minorities in the state services, when they are under political pressure to expand employment for the native population, and partly because it implies that states are or should be officially multilingual when in every state there is strong political sentiment that asserts that one language should have exclusive official status.

Again, it is important to emphasize that many state governments do satisfy these requirements of the constitution; the point is that in most states there is considerable resent-

333

ment against the demands, both by the migrants themselves and by the central government, to provide migrants from other linguistic regions facilities to maintain their linguistic identity. In state after state, government leaders have urged migrants to learn the regional language and to accept the notion that the state is, or ought to be, linguistically homogeneous. The provisions of the constitution are by no means dead, but clearly they have little political support from the dominant ethnic groups in the states.

What is at stake in this controversy is whether India is to be a multilingual, multicultural country in which each state is linguistically and culturally homogeneous, or whether the states themselves are to be heterogeneous. Since 1956, when the states were reorganized along linguistic lines, there has been sentiment in each state for creating greater cultural-linguistic homogeneity. Many regional universities have replaced English with the regional language; the regional language is used increasingly, and in some instances nearly exclusively, for government communications; regional histories are being written, regional heroes proclaimed, and regional holidays declared.

The indigenous regional minorities—as distinct from migrant minorities—are ill at ease with these developments and have, as a consequence, been provoked to seek their own statehood. Here we see a familiar phenomena at work: cultural nationalism on the part of the dominant ethnic group tends to provoke anxiety, separatism, and often secessionism among minorities.

India's tribal minorities have been most affected. These thirty-five million people, scattered in a half-dozen or so states, have not, until recently, had states of their own, but the more strident the claims of linguistic minorities, the more fearful some tribals have become that they will be culturally submerged. Cultural regionalism has thus stimulated tribal secessionist movements, particularly in India's northeast, where there are many districts that are almost exclusively tribal. In recent years most of the tribal areas of the north-

334

east have won their claim for separate states. There have also been political movements for separate statehood, not only among tribals in other regions of India, but among other cultural minorities, reflecting the growing sentiment in India for culturally more homogeneous political units.

But at the same time that there are political pressures for culturally homogeneous units, there are demographic pressures for culturally heterogeneous units. As we have noted earlier, the movement of people from one cultural-linguistic region to another has tended to increase the heterogeneity of many Indian cities and states.

In spite of the constitutional provisions, and in spite of demographic changes that tend to accentuate cultural and linguistic heterogeneity, there are strong political tendencies at work to discourage migrants from maintaining their own cultural-linguistic traditions. These political forces, as we shall soon demonstrate, are directed less at facilitating linguistic assimilation than at discouraging migration.

THE ORIGIN AND DEVELOPMENT
OF PROTECTED LABOR MARKETS

The concept of "reservations," that is, the provision of special benefits and safeguards under law for portions of the Indian population, has a long and controversial history in India. Initially used by the British in the Morley-Minto reforms of 1909 to meet the claims of the Muslim community for special political reservations, the system was extended in 1919, under the Montagu-Chelmsford reforms, to other minorities. By the time India became an independent state, an elaborate system of reservations had been created for Muslims, Anglo-Indians, tribals, scheduled castes, Sikhs, Christians, and so on. Some minorities had reserved seats in state assemblies, while others had reserved positions in employment (the Anglo-Indians, for example, were given preferences in employment in the railroads). The constitutional provisions for scheduled castes and scheduled tribes, and a

335

number of related provisions for "backward" communities, was thus a continuation of this policy toward minorities.

Reservation was a policy intended to assure that a given ethnic group—initially a minority—would receive a share of preferred goods in proportion to its population; the policy assumed that in the absence of such a governmental intervention, minority groups would not get their proportionate share, and by implication, those who belong to the majority ethnic group would get a disproportionately larger share. Since the preferred values are power, status, and wealth, reservations were soon extended from the areas of political representation to preferential arrangements in education and employment, and protection with respect to land ownership and land use.

The Indian National Congress was initially hostile to the system of reservations, particularly for the Muslim community, whose political leadership argued that in its absence the dominant Hindu community would control such a disproportionate amount of power that Muslims would be denied any benefits within the political system. Gandhi and many of his supporters were also initially opposed to reservations for scheduled castes, or Harijans, on the grounds that the British were seeking thereby to create a separatist mentality among the Harijans, creating the possibility of a dangerous alliance between the Harijans, Muslims, and other minorities against the nationalist movement.

But in due course, the nationalist leadership accepted the principle that some communities were entitled to special benefits under the law because of their low status and occupations.

In time, however, the notion of reservations was extended to benefit not minorities, but majorities who sought to protect themselves against the competition of economically and educationally more successful minority communities. The process by which a legal principle originally intended to benefit minorities was extended to benefit majorities is revealed by an examination of the controversy between Bihari

336

natives and Bengali migrants in the north Indian state of Bihar in the 1930s, a controversy that set an important precedent for subsequent protectionist policies.

The Bengali-Bihari Controversy

In 1938, the chief secretary to the Government of Bihar, W. B. Brett, wrote a memo to the departments of the state government entitled "Percentage of members of different communities in Government Services." The Brett Circular, as it came to be called, noted that a high percentage of positions in the provincial government were held by Bengalis, many of whom were migrants from the neighboring state. "It is not the intention of Government that the appointment of Bengalis or of any other class should be stopped nor the efficiency of the service should be lowered in order to secure representation of particular communities. They do, however, desire that in making appointments, the percentage of posts which the particular community holds in the service to which appointments are being made and the percentage which that community bears to the total population should be taken into consideration. Subject to the consideration stated above, the communal distribution of new appointments should aim at bringing each of the principal communities to its proper share and in redressing present excesses and deficiencies."[3]

After the circular was denounced by the Bengali community, and supported by the Biharis, the Working Committee of the Congress party asked Rajendra Prasad, then a leader of the Bihari Congress (subsequently president of the Congress party and, after independence, president of India) and himself a Bihari, to examine the controversy. Prasad concluded that Bengalis who permanently resided in Bihar should be treated as Bengali-speaking Biharis, but that "Bengalis who have not made Bihar their home but have come

---

[3] Quoted in *Bengali-Bihar Question: Report of Babu Rajendra Prasad together with the Resolution of the Working Committee*, issued by the All India Congress Committee (Allahabad: Kitabistan, 1939), pp. 18-19.

for service or profession or business" should be excluded from appointments.[4] Prasad argued that it is "just and proper that the residents of a province should get preference in their own province in the matter of public services and educational facilities."[5]

He noted that the state government of Bihar had written to the various provincial governments to find out whether recruitment to government services was restricted to "natives of, or persons domiciled in the province and as to what the rules relating to domicile are."[6] The government of Assam replied that a man was considered a domicile in the province if he owned a "homestead" (house and land), had lived in the "homestead" for ten years, "and intends to live in the homestead until he dies."[7] There were, Prasad reported, similar domicile requirements for government employment in Bengal, the Central Provinces, Madras, the North West Frontier Province, Orissa, Sindh, and Uttar Pradesh. Only the Punjab reported that there were no domicile rules for employment in the state services.

Prasad observed that as communities and groups that were once backward in education became educationally more advanced, they demanded that their own provinces ensure them a larger share of jobs in public services. "It is neither possible nor wise," concluded Prasad, "to ignore these demands, and it must be recognized that in regard to services and like matters the people of a province have a certain claim which cannot be overlooked."[8] Prasad then analyzed the employment situation in the Bihar civil service and reported that Bengalis held a large proportion of appointments in most departments, the judiciary, and police; Bengalis, he wrote, can have no just grievance if the government attempts to redress the deficiency in the number of Biharis. "Bengalis in Bihar," he concluded, not distinguishing between the na-

[4] *Ibid.*, p. 10.   [5] *Ibid.*, p. 14.   [6] *Ibid.*

[7] *Ibid.*, p. 15. This latter proviso, the intention of living in one's home until death, surely must be the most unusual legal definition of domicile ever formulated.

[8] *Ibid.*, p. 21.

tive-born, the long-term residents, and recent migrants, "speak a different language and insist on having Bengali schools. They should have due and fair share—no more and no less—in services also."[9]

Prasad suggested that a system of employment preferences need not contradict the notion of national citizenship. "The desire of Provincials to seek employment in their own locality is natural and not reprehensible, and rules providing for such employment to them are not inconsistent with the high ideals of the Congress, particularly *when they exist in all Provinces*"[10] (italics mine).

Without so specifying, Prasad was calling for a concept of provincial citizenship side by side with Indian citizenship.

LEGAL TRENDS: EQUALITY OF OPPORTUNITY VERSUS PROTECTION

What are the present legal trends with respect to the protection of local majorities? Let us consider what has happened in employment, then turn to education.

Article 16 of the constitution asserts that "there shall be equality of opportunity for all citizens in matters relating to employment or appointment to any office under the State. No citizen shall, on ground only of religion, race, caste, sex, descent, place of birth, residence or any of them, be ineligible for or discriminated against in respect of any employment or office under the State." However, Article 16, Section 3, makes the following qualification:

"Nothing in this article shall prevent Parliament from making any law prescribing, in regard to a class or classes of employment or appointment to an office (under the Government of, or any local or other authority within, a State or Union territory), any requirement as to residence within that State or Union territory prior to such employment or appointment."

In 1968, the Ministry of Labour, Employment and Re-

[9] *Ibid.*, p. 30.   [10] *Ibid.*

habilitation of the central government declared that all public-sector enterprises in the country had been asked to fill vacancies carrying a monthly salary of less than Rs. 500 through the local employment exchanges. Recruitment to higher posts, the ministry added, would continue to take place on an all-India basis, that is, no preferences would be given to local people. The ministry also asked the all-India Organizations of Employers to ask their members to follow the same procedures. A similar request went to state labor ministers asking them to persuade private employers in their states to do the same.

The government's decision was commended by the National Integration Council, a high-level advisory body of chief ministers, opposition party leaders, and central government officials, with the following statement: "The National Integration Council recommended the removal of discontent in the States arising from the inadequate share of the local people in employment opportunities in the public and private sectors, by giving a major share of the employment to qualified local persons from among the people of the State, bearing in mind at the same time the vital importance of common citizenship to national unity" (March 20, 1969). Again, the concluding phrase indicated an awareness of the way in which the new policy had qualified the notion of "common citizenship."

It was pointed out that, while the government required public sector firms to *hire* through the local employment exchanges where salaries were less than Rs. 500, private firms were only required to *notify* the exchanges of vacancies, and remained free to recruit outside the exchanges. But the labor minister of Kerala said that if statutory insistence was not possible, then his government would consider the use of "indirect pressure." Business leaders said that they would provide jobs for local people, but that they opposed compulsory recruitment through employment exchanges. "Introduction of compulsory recruitment," explained the president of the Bharat Chamber of Commerce, "through the ex-

340

changes at this stage would interfere with the proper selection of personnel and operational efficiency."[11]

Under the rules of the employment exchanges, only residents of a district can register at local exchanges. An exception is made for graduates and other technically trained people who can apply to exchanges wherever they are located *within the same state*. To the extent, then, that recruitment did take place through exchanges, and registration rules were effectively enforced, there would be limited migration of graduates outside the state, and no migration of others even across district lines, except when the manpower needs of a district exchange exceeded the available supply.

At a meeting of the employment officers in charge of employment exchanges in Mysore, it was agreed that only individuals who had studied at educational institutions within the state should be permitted to register at the employment exchanges. "The parents of the applicants should be residents of the state and their mother-tongue should be Kannada," while all other applicants would have to produce certificates to show that they had been living in Mysore for at least five years.[12]

The registration rules are in any event difficult to enforce, since migrants living with friends and relatives can register by reporting a local residence. Where domicile certificates are required, as in Telangana, it is often possible to persuade or bribe local officials to provide certificates. A bitter complaint in Telangana after the unified state of Andhra was created was that thousands of people from the eastern districts of Andhra, armed with "bogus" domicile certificates, were able to obtain appointments as nongazetted officers and teachers throughout the Telangana region. Easy to evade, the domicile rules, like prohibition, tended to generate widespread cynicism.

Several state governments now have official policies that

[11] *Financial Express*, September 21, 1972.
[12] "Mysore Steps To Give Jobs to 'Sons of Soil,'" *Hindustan Times*, February 10, 1973.

all, or a fixed proportion, of available jobs, both in the public and private sectors, for state government and local bodies, should be reserved for "sons of the soil." In August 1974, for example, the cabinet of the Tamil Nadu government announced that 80 percent of all jobs, public or private, should be reserved for local people; the state government said that they would also seek the cooperation of the central government to implement the policy in the central government projects in the state. The chief minister explained that "local" meant anyone who had lived in the state for at least fifteen years, following the same definition employed by the government of Maharashtra.[13]

The increasingly widespread domicile requirements for employment have left the linguistic minorities in each state uneasy. Fluency in the regional language is a prerequisite for employment in the administrative services in most states. Since employment exchanges and public service commissions tend to view "local" as someone whose mother tongue is the regional language, the descendants of migrants often find that their employment opportunities are shrinking rapidly. One recalls the statement made by Rajendra Prasad advocating employment preferences for Biharis even if it meant limiting the job opportunities for the local Bengali-speaking minorities. "They should have due and fair share—no more and no less—in services also."[14]

Trends in education are somewhat similar to those of employment, with one striking exception. While agencies of the central government—the Ministry of Labour, the National Labour Commission, and the National Integration Council —have generally supported the claims of state governments and state political parties that employment preferences be given to local people (always with the qualification that skilled people be recruited on an all-India basis), in the

[13] *The Overseas Hindustan Times,* August 8, 1974, "Concern over job policy."
[14] *Bengali-Bihari Question,* p. 30.

342

field of education the central government has opposed domicile requirements for admissions.[15]

The National Integration Council, the Ministry of Education, and the prime minister have all called upon state governments to remove the domicile restrictions on admissions to academic institutions that have by now become widespread. In 1968, the National Integration Council surveyed the states to find out the extent of such domicile restrictions. The council found that many states had domicile restrictions for admission into arts, science, and commerce colleges run directly by the government, but imposed no domicile restrictions on private colleges even when they received government funds. Several states—including Maharashtra, Gujarat, and Madhya Pradesh—restricted admission to engineering colleges and polytechnics to students who had passed qualifying examinations only from institutions in the state. Many states, including Maharashtra, Assam, Bihar, Orissa, Andhra, Tamil Nadu, Mysore, and Kerala have explicit domicile restrictions for admission to medical and/or engineering colleges.

Interstate mobility among students has, in any event, been reduced by the adoption of the regional languages as the language of instruction and examinations in many state colleges and universities. The several national universities and institutes of technology under the jurisdiction of the central government are significant exceptions, for these are open to students from all over the country on a competitive basis. The national universities and technical institutes are widely regarded as among India's premier educational institutions.

The shift to regional languages in the states, combined with a widespread sentiment at the state universities that em-

[15] The reverse position could be argued: that domicile requirements in education provide opportunities for less developed communities to "catch up" without limiting the freedoms provided by a common citizenship, while domicile requirements for employment are restrictive.

343

ployment preferences should be given to local people, have combined to reduce substantially the mobility of faculties.[16] In Orissa, Assam, and Bihar, for example, efforts have been made to appoint local people in preference to Bengalis, who in the past formed a "disproportionate" share of the faculty; similarly, south Indian universities have sought to reduce the number of Tamils on their faculties.

In mid-1968, the National Integration Council passed a resolution calling for the elimination of domicile restrictions on admissions to colleges and universities. The prime minister wrote to each of the state chief ministers urging them to accept the recommendations of the council. Few of the chief ministers replied, but most of those that did expressed their reluctance to eliminate domicile rules, either because they felt that their students could not educationally "catch up" if they had to freely compete with students who applied from elsewhere in the country, or because they wanted "reciprocity" for their students. "As very few students of Jammu and Kashmir," wrote the chief minister of that state, "are considered for admission to technical institutions in other states, the State Government is unable to take further steps unless reciprocal arrangement is made."[17]

CONCLUSION: COMMON OR DUAL CITIZENSHIP?

Let us recapitulate the argument thus far. Constitutionally, citizenship is unitary in India. Individuals reside in, but they are not citizens of, states: they are only citizens of India. According to the constitution, all citizens are free to migrate to any state and within any state and to receive the same rights, protections, and benefits as those born in the state and locality to which they move. The only constitutional exception is that selected minorities are entitled to special benefits.

[16] See V. V. John, "Universities Swim with the Tide," *Times of India*, May 9, 1969.

[17] Report of the National Integration Council, New Delhi, March 20, 1969.

The policies of states governments, with the support or at least the acquiescence of the central government, have eroded this conception of a single citizenship. Two factors—the high level of unemployment and the ethnic basis of India's states—have generated political pressures for creating domicile requirements for both education and employment. In most states, "domicile" legally means birth within the state or residence in the state for at least fifteen years, but politically it is often applied to the dominant ethnic group within the state.

Though domicile laws and rules predate independence in some states, they have by now been extended to most of the states and, in the case of Andhra, even to regions within the state. Indeed, given the requirement that workers can only register for employment at exchanges within their own district, "domicile" has in some instances come to mean residence in the district, not the state.

Domicile rules thus create protected labor markets and protected educational markets. The object of such rules is to protect ethnic communities that are economically weak and educationally backward, irrespective of whether they are a minority or majority community. The supporters of domicile rules argue that a market in which all Indians could, without restrictions, compete with one another wherever there are educational facilities and employment opportunities would leave some ethnic groups indefinitely behind. Would the tribal population, for example, with so little experience with education, urban life, industrialization, and a competitive environment, ever catch up with their more sophisticated Hindu neighbors? And if the state is willing to provide special protection for backward minorities, such as tribals and scheduled castes, then why not provide protection for all groups that are backward? And, to complete the argument, when migrants from other regions are more educated, more skilled, more enterprising, should not the state take steps to protect the local population? In short, the claims of ethnic equality are asserted to justify public policies by central, state, and

345

local authorities to keep out migrants of another ethnic group who, by virtue of their education or culture, can more effectively compete for jobs than the local population.

What has weakened the claims of those who assert "merit first, local afterwards," is the counter assertion that neither public nor private employers in India actually hire on the basis of merit, but tend to recruit from among their own kinsmen, caste, and linguistic community. Since merit doesn't count anyway, argue nativists, why shouldn't local people be recruited rather than outsiders?

Moreover, few Indians have any expectation that the country as a whole, or their region in particular, is likely to experience rapid economic growth and an expansion of employment opportunities. Advocates of domicile rules are persuaded that the labor market will not substantially expand in the foreseeable future, that the demand for employment will grow more rapidly than supply, that the allocation of a large number of jobs will not be on merit, but on ascriptive ties and political clout, and that, hence, one should use political means to gain control over the labor market.

In a no-growth or limited growth economy, the nativist argument is politically unassailable, for under such conditions the success of one individual and one ethnic group is at the expense of another. The argument that restriction on interstate migration would itself affect growth has, moreover, not been persuasive, for it is not easy to demonstrate any relationship between which ethnic group is employed in the public sector, the state administrative services, and the state educational system, and the state's rate of economic growth. The impact on growth could be substantial if private investment were reduced because entrepreneurs from other states were reluctant to invest in a region whose government restricted their freedom to recruit anywhere in the country they chose. But the decision of entrepreneurs to invest in a particular location is influenced by a wide range of factors, and freedom to "import" labor is only one of many con-

346

siderations. Moreover, the domicile restrictions currently imposed on employment in India have not, thus far at least, limited the recruitment of engineers, managers, and other highly skilled or senior personnel.

The erosion of the concept of a common single citizenship and its replacement by dual citizenship (not constitutionally, but by legal accretion and administrative practices), based on residential qualifications, work permits, linguistic tests for employment, and domicile certificates, is ultimately likely to have more political and psychological than economic effect. India's dilemma, put starkly, is that a body of law providing rights and benefits to some that are denied to others appears politically necessary to meet the demands for greater equality among ethnic groups; but the creation of such discriminatory rights and benefits erodes some of the advantages of common citizenship and threatens to weaken, thereby, the cement of loyalty on which all political systems ultimately rest.

India is by no means a unique case. On the contrary, the notion of a single citizenship resting upon universally applied legal rights and obligations does not sit well in multiethnic societies where ethnic groups are in a political position to demand special rights. The ancient cry of justice, in its modern guise of equity, provides the legitimation of special rights. How otherwise, it is asserted, are the weak ever to catch up? But the claim is not for individuals, but rather for ethnic collectivities. The state is not simply asked to provide assistance to enable the poor and uneducated to catch up, but to establish legal walls to ensure that each ethnic group will get its share, "no more and no less." India is not the only country to follow this route, nor is it clear yet how far and how permanently this path will be followed even by India. In India, as elsewhere, these protectionist policies conflict with two values: merit and common citizenship. But while many Indians recognize the conflict, there have been few political pressures for policies based upon criteria of merit or for reasserting the rights of citizenship as specified by Article 19 of the constitution.

To the extent that the policies described here continue to be pursued, and are implemented, there are likely to be far-reaching consequences for the pace and distribution of development, the patterns of social and spatial mobility, the relationship between governmental units and, above all, for the kinds of identities and loyalties that Indians choose.

NINE

CONCLUSION:
TRENDS AND CONSEQUENCES

BOTH migrants and natives have their intellectual partisans. There are some who see the migrant as both pioneer and victim. The migrant, according to this perspective, has left his native place because of lack of employment, low wages, shortages of land, political or religious persecution, or threats to his safety—and in search, therefore, of religious or political freedom, personal safety, and new economic opportunities for himself and his children. But all too often, according to this perspective, the government of the area to which he has moved denies him equal oportunities in employment, tears down the squatter settlement he has constructed, and attempts to force him to give up his language and cultural identity.

In contrast, other scholars are concerned that the local people may be "disrupted" by the "encroachment of outsiders" on their "ancestral lands," who "exploit the local population," impose "too rapid a process of social change," and thereby force local people to "unexpected and violent reactions."[1]

The holders of these divergent perspectives are likely to share a critical view of government, but for opposing reasons. The anthropologist—who is more likely to hold the latter position—will be critical of government for failing to protect the native from rapacious migrant creditors, rack-renting migrant landlords, and forest poachers, while the sociologist

---

[1] These quotations are from Christoph von Furer-Haimendorf, a distinguished British anthropologist who has written extensively on the tribes of India. These quotes are from his introduction to Suresh Singh, *The Dust-Storm and the Hanging Mist: A Study of Birsa Munda and His Movement in Chotanagpur* (Calcutta: K. L. Mukhopadhyay, 1966).

—who is most likely among the academic partisans to hold the former position—will criticize government for ejecting the migrant from his squatter settlement, harassing migrants for lacking proper papers, and for imposing a policy of forced assimilation. For the anthropologist, government has failed to be the protector of the weak; for the sociologist, the government has failed because it has become oppressive.

These different perspectives are related to different values. One emphasizes the importance of preserving community and its cultural traditions in the face of social change; the other admires the successes of individuals who have overcome adversity. The partisans, therefore, each have their own heroes. For the partisan of the natives, the hero is the man who remains within his community to become a leader, defending the culture and values of the community against both intruders and government. The native who becomes educated, moves into a modern profession or business, and migrates away from the community is not admired, but one who stays and plays a role in improving the well-being and preserving the culture of the community is. For the partisan of the migrant, the hero is one who by his initiative, wits, and hard work, achieves wealth or fame, moves out of his ghetto environment, and provides his children with new opportunities.

Since the partisan of the migrant is primarily concerned with how the migrant has benefited from the opportunity to move, he is likely to pay little attention to the effects of migration upon the local population; and since the partisan of the native is concerned with the steps government can take to protect the natives against the disruptive effects of migrants, he is likely to pay little attention to the impact of such policies upon the migrant. It is to these consequences of migration and of migration policies that we now turn.

Costs and Benefits, Winners and Losers

It is a commonplace observation that migrants benefit from having migrated. People do not migrate unless there is a perceived disparity between the place in which they live and the place to which they move. Most migrations in India —the major exceptions are international refugee migrations from Uganda, Sri Lanka, Burma, Pakistan, and Bangladesh —have been by free choice. People who migrate generally do so because they believe employment and income opportunities are better; if they are not, they are likely to return home. But while the migrant may gain, it does not follow that local people necessarily benefit from an influx of migrants. While some gain, others may lose. Let us consider some of the effects of migration upon the local population.

1. A considerable amount of migration in India is of individuals who are willing and able to engage in occupations that local people choose not to enter. In many parts of the country workers on construction sites, dams, irrigation schemes, roads, and railroads are migrants doing work that local people do not want. In these instances migrants contribute to the development of a region's infrastructure, and thereby make it possible for local people to expand their own economic activities. Even if migrants continue to man the railroads, the hydroelectric and irrigation dams, the postal and telegraph services, and road maintenance, the local population has gained.

2. The migrant entrepreneur—the Marwari and Punjabi in Assam, the Gujarati in Maharashtra, the Tamil in Bangalore—makes a contribution to the local community even if a large part of the labor force he employs are migrants. The local community gains if the manufacturer is required to pay local taxes. Other local producers gain if the manufacturer purchases products and raw materials produced or sold by local people. Migrant workers employed in the factory buy consumer goods and food supplies, thereby providing income for local producers and traders. Finally, the goods produced by the migrant manufacturer and his migrant workers may be sold in the local market in prices and quantity that are advantageous to local consumers.

To what extent local people gain, however, depends upon

351

how many are engaged in these activities. If the manufacturer is a migrant, the labor force consists of migrants, and the shopkeepers and tradesmen purchasing agricultural produce from local people are also migrants, then the economic benefits to local people are likely to be very small. In some instances there may exist a dual economy in which the modern sector is in the hands of outsiders, while the traditional, marginal agrarian sector remains predominantly local. Such dualism characterizes the economies of Chota Nagpur and, to a less marked degree, Assam. The problems of changing the opportunity structure for the local population embedded in a dual system is somewhat different from the problem of local people in a more open, competitive urban labor market in which some, even if not all, elements of the modern sector involve the participation of the local population.

3. When migrants and local people compete for the same jobs, then gains for migrants do mean losses for natives. As we have seen, at present it is primarily in the middle-class occupations that such competition exists. Lower-income working classes do not compete to such an extent because of the high degree of ethnic segmentation by occupation in India. If that comes to an end, then nativism will spread among the working class in India, as it did historically in the United States.

4. Some existing local occupations may lose through migration. Marginal local producers and merchants may be eliminated by more efficient migrant entrepreneurs and traders. Some traditional occupations—the handloom weavers, or the village smith, for example—may be put out of business by more modern migrant-run industries (though the losses may take place no matter who develops the modern industries and where they are located). Some local peasants may sell their land to migrants because the price is high, only to discover that they cannot find alternative employment. The new owner, with more capital and skills, and with his land

352

newly irrigated, earns a high income, while the former land-owner becomes a low-paid landless laborer.

5. Even when the real income of local people has in-creased as a consequence of the economic activities of mi-grants, local people may become resentful at their subordinate economic role. If the more prosperous farmers, owners of factories, administrative personnel and floor managers of factories, and the owners and staff of shops are all migrants, local people may suffer a lowering of status that is not com-pensated by a rise in income. If the smaller producer or tradesman has gained an expanding market for his goods, he may be economically subordinate to alien manufacturers and wholesalers. If local peasants are able to buy goods that they could not previously afford, they may be resentful that migrant factory laborers are able to buy even more goods. If a manufacturer employs migrants for half of his labor force but still recruits half locally, the local population may turn against him, believing that if the manufacturer were a local person he would have hired his entire labor force locally.

6. Migrants may create social and economic costs for the local community. A large migrant influx imposes new de-mands upon the local water and sanitation systems and upon health and education services. There may be shortages of drinking water, the sanitation system may be overloaded, and schools and hospitals may become overcrowded as a result of a population influx. As far as local people are concerned, a large migrant population may be responsible for increasing environmental pollution and a diminution of their health and educational well-being.

7. Migrants may be psychologically threatening, since their very success implies a defect in character on the part of local people. Are outsiders more successful because they work harder, have more skills, are more education-minded, more punctual and efficient in their work, better attuned to the market requirements of the outside world? A major issue

353

for many local communities has been the question of whether they should modify their own behavior in order to compete with the migrants. Shiv Sena leaders have urged Marathi young men to go to secretarial schools to learn typing and stenography so that they can compete with Tamils, and to improve their English so that they can enter the middle-class labor force. In Chota Nagpur some tribal leaders have urged their young men to go to secondary schools and colleges, and to seek training in technical and vocational schools to prepare themselves for positions in government or industry. And in Nizamabad district in Telangana, many peasants have learned the skills of wet-rice cultivation from migrants from the delta districts.

But should local people try to compete? Can the small local merchant or manufacturer successfully compete with a migrant who has banking and trade connections outside the local community and has greater knowledge of the larger market? Can the local middle class compete with migrants who are willing to work harder in the office during the day and go to school in the evening to improve their typing, stenographic, and accounting skills? Can the local farmer compete with the migrant who has brought in new seeds, is more experienced in the use of irrigation, and is experimenting with new crops, insecticides, and fertilizers?

The compulsion for change created by migrants may not be welcomed by local people. While the local person does not wish to become subordinate either in income or status to the migrant, the changes he needs to make in himself to compete successfully may be ones he prefers not to make. For one thing, his cultural heritage may be one that devalues competition. The very notion of changing oneself to compete may be anathema. For another, the specific qualities of the migrant that he perceives as the reasons for his success may be viewed by the local person as qualities he would prefer not to emulate—such as working hard or long hours, following more punctual work habits, taking fewer holidays, or adopting what is seen as a more aggressive personal style.

354

8. Local people may perceive migrants as a political threat, particularly if the migrants are numerous, wealthy, or politically cohesive. Influence on the political system by persons perceived as outsiders is ordinarily viewed by local people as particularly threatening to their *cultural* system in a society in which the cultural system is so interlocked with the political order. In Chota Nagpur, for example, the domination of the tribals by nontribals has resulted in the creation of an educational system in which the local tribal languages are subordinated to Hindi. Similarly, in Assam, the subordinate role played by the Assamese in their own political system in the nineteenth century, when Assam was part of Bengal, meant that the Assamese language remained secondary to Bengali as the language of administration and education, a pattern that was only effectively reversed when Assam became an autonomous state.

The linguistic and cultural norms of the migrant may be both hated and emulated, simultaneously. The dominance of migrants in the world of business and administration may lead local youth to emulate their dress, their style of living, even their language; but as they do so they may simultaneously fear that the migrant has forced them to lose their own cultural identity.

From the viewpoint of the local person, migration is—to use the language of economists—an externality, that is, an event that confers costs or benefits on persons who were not consenting parties to the decision that created the event. If there is a net loss for the local person, if he *believes* he has lost more than he has gained through the presence of migrants, he will take political action to stop migration rather than choose to emigrate himself. The Assamese middle class, having won power in their own state, do not feel the need to emigrate; the middle class of Telangana, like the aspiring middle class of many regions into which more enterprising and more educated migrants have moved, do not feel that they can compete effectively outside their home territory; and a similar attitude exists among the new tribal middle class of Chota Nagpur, an attitude reinforced by the system of reservations, which entitles them to special educational and employment benefits in their own state, but not in other states. Nativists link ethnicity with territory. Committed as they are to the land in which the natives reside, they are opposed to emigration. Hence, the nativists of Chota Nagpur would prefer a society in which the local tribal population would never need to emigrate. The emigration of one's own people represents a failure to preserve community. *Nativists are thus not only opposed to migrants from outside, but they oppose the spatial mobility of their own people.*

As we have seen, within the nativist movements themselves there can be conflicts between those who advocate a return to traditional agriculture, those who advocate a protectionist strategy to ensure local people a larger share of the preferred jobs in the modern sector, and those who are willing to compete in the open marketplace for education and employment. The larger the benefits accruing from migration for the local population, the more likely it is that local people will not press hard for restrictions on migration and will make some competitive response; the smaller the gains and, conversely, the greater the losses, the more likely it is that the local population will seek restrictions on the free entry of migrants, demand protectionism in the labor market, and press for reservations on the land.

THE EFFECTS OF NATIVIST POLITICS AND POLICIES

While it may be too soon to assess the impact that recent restrictive policies and political agitations have had, some preliminary consequences can be observed, if not measured.

The efforts of state governments to give residents preference in government employment seem to have been the most successful of these policies. Indeed, there are many accusations that state governments have in practice limited these preferences to those who speak the regional language as their mother tongue and have avoided giving appointments to descendants of migrants. In Assam and Bihar, for example, there have been sharp decreases in the proportion of Bengalis employed in the state governments, though the state governments have argued that this is primarily a consequence of the growing educational accomplishments of the local Bihari and Assamese-speaking people.

No statistics are available on the migration of students across state boundaries, but in any event it would be difficult to ascertain whether any change in mobility was a result of the restrictions imposed by colleges and universities or by the shift to regional languages. Moreover, the growth of nationally run educational institutions may have compensated for some of the reduction in mobility to state-run institutions.

The impact of restrictions on employment in the private sector is equally difficult to ascertain. Many Indian businesses are under the same pressures as foreign firms all over the world to employ local people, and they know that restrictions can be imposed upon them if they do not take into account local political sentiment. There are a number of reasons, however, why in practice entrepreneurs often find it difficult to change their recruitment patterns. For one thing, in the employment of technical and professional personnel, employers prefer to recruit more widely than from the local community. Consideration may be given to the friends and relations of those who are already employed within the firm, as well as to the skills of the candidates. Even in the employment of unskilled and semiskilled workers, as we have noted, there are often well-established labor migration streams that managers are reluctant to disrupt. Similarly, as we have also observed earlier, there are well-organized work gangs that are regularly employed by contractors for the construction of buildings, roads, hydroelectric projects and irrigation schemes. Finally, in the employment of office personnel, such as typists, stenographers, accountants, and clerks, many employers prefer people from Kerala and Tamil Nadu, since it has often been their experience that they are reliable and efficient office workers.

Nevertheless, business firms in Bombay, Hyderabad, Gauhati, Bangalore, and other cities with large migrant populations are making an effort to hire local personnel, especially for clerical positions and for front-office jobs where employees deal with the public. While statistically the effects may still be small, business managers often see such shifts in recruitment as essential to maintaining good relations with the local community.

The 1971 census does not reveal any noticeable change in the pattern and rate of migration to areas in which there have been antimigrant agitations or protectionist policies. Assam, though one of the most disturbed areas for migrants, actually showed an increase of interstate migration from 490,000 in 1961 to 551,000 in 1971. Similarly, there was an increase in interstate migration to urban Maharashtra, from 2,099,000 in 1961 to 2,665,000 in 1971. According to calculations made by G. K. Mehrotra,[2] the number of interstate migrants to India's urban areas increased from 8.6 million in 1961 to 10.9 million in 1971.

Since migration figures for individual cities have not yet been published, it is not possible to assess the effect of nativist activities on such cities as Bombay and Hyderabad. However, greater Bombay, the site of Shiv Sena agitations, had an accelerated growth from 1961 to 1971, 42.9 percent, as against 38.7 percent in the preceding decade. Similarly, Hyderabad showed a phenomenal increase in population from 1.1 million in 1961 to 1.8 million in 1971, a 63 percent increase, much of which was due to migration from the delta districts.

Looking ahead, there is reason to expect substantial urban increases which, as we noted in Chapter Two, are likely to

[2] G. K. Mehrotra, *Birth Place Migration in India,* Census of India, 1971, Special Monograph No. 1, Office of the Registrar General, New Delhi, 1974, section II, Table 9, pp. 20-21.

change the composition of India's cities. In 1961, 45 million Indians, or about 10 percent of the population, lived in towns and cities with a population of 50,000 or over. A decade later 70 million persons lived in urban centers of this size, an increase of 56 percent as against an overall population increase of 24 percent for the country as a whole during the decade.

India's urban population in 1971 was 109 million, a growth rate of 38 percent from 1961 to 1971. If India's urban population continues to increase at the same rate, then by 1981 urban areas will have 150 million people; by 1991, 207 million; and by 2001, a population of 286 million, when the country's population is likely to pass the billion mark.[3]

Fifty of India's cities have populations exceeding a quarter of a million. Any city in 1971 with a population of 100,000 and a growth rate of 38 percent per decade will exceed a quarter of a million by the end of the century. In 1971, 92 cities had populations exceeding 100,000 and less than 250,-000. In other words, by the end of the century India is likely to have 142 cities with a quarter of a million people. Another 65 cities will have populations exceeding a half-million, and 25 cities will have populations in excess of a million.[4] In 1971, only 8 cities exceeded a million.

[3] The estimates of urban growth by Jaipal Ambannavar in *Second India Studies: Population* (Delhi: Macmillan, 1975), p. 74, are slightly higher: 151.5 million in 1981, 210.5 million in 1991, and 291 million in 2001, with similar estimates of population growth. Ambannavar expects that by 2001 29 percent of the Indian population (as against 20 percent in 1971) will be living in urban areas, and by 2011 the urban population will be 35 percent, or 406 million, in a country of 1,159 million.

[4] These estimates are arrived at by assuming that any city with a current population of at least 400,000 (in 1971), growing at 38 percent a year, will have a million by 2001. Actually a few cities in this size range are growing more slowly, while several below 400,000 are growing more rapidly. Were Indian cities increasing at the same pace as the country as a whole, that is, without any migration, then every city with a population of 500,000 or more in 1971 (17 cities) would have a million by the end of the century. Many of the cities in the 300,000 to 400,000 population range are

To continue urban growth at this pace, at least a third of the population increase in the urban areas must be the result of migration.[5] This is by no means high, either by comparison with India's recent past, or by international comparisons with other developing countries.

As India's population growth rate declines, the role played by migration in urban growth will increase. For this reason, the urbanization rate will rise as population growth slows down. Generally speaking, the slower a country's population growth rate, the more important migration is in accounting for urban growth.

Thus far, we have assumed no significant change in the rate of rural-to-urban migration. Actually, the migration rate in India is low compared to many other developing countries. Should India's industrialization rate substantially increase, then many of India's cities will attract larger numbers of migrants than at present.

While there is no way of estimating what proportion of India's future urban migrants will be moving from other cultural-linguistic regions, historical and contemporary trends suggest that interstate mobility is growing (see Chapter Two). Already, as we have seen, there are many cities whose

---

currently growing at 50 percent per decade or faster (7 such cities), and if they continue at this rate they too will pass the million mark by the end of the century.

In 1961, seven cities had populations exceeding one million: Calcutta, Bombay, Delhi, Madras, Hyderabad, Bangalore, and Ahmadabad. In 1971, Kanpur was added to the list. In 1981, the cities of Nagpur and Lucknow, and possibly Poona, are likely to pass the one million mark. In 1991, if they continue to grow at the present rate, the cities of Agra, Jaipur, Indore, and Jabalpur will contain at least a million. In 2001, the cities of Banaras, Madurai, and possibly Allahabad will have a million. There are several cities in the 400,000 to 500,000 range whose current rates will lead them to have a million by the end of the century: Patna, Surat, Baroda, Jamshedpur, Cochin, Dhanbad, and Ludhiana.

[5] According to calculations I have done for 121 cities where data were available, in 94 cities one-third or more of the growth in the 1961-1971 decade was the result of migration.

linguistic heterogeneity has been increasing, while the tribal-nontribal mix of many cities in Bihar, Madhya Pradesh, and Gujarat seems likely to increase as tribals become more urbanized. As these trends continue, then, quite a few of India's largest cities (for these tend to attract migrants from the longest distances) will be multiethnic cities surrounded by a more linguistically homogeneous countryside. To some extent, as we have seen, that has already happened to Bombay, Bangalore, Ranchi, and Gauhati, and cities such as Delhi, Ahmadabad, and Calcutta, though still predominantly populated by people who speak the regional language, have large and growing migrant populations speaking the languages of other regions.

The absence of a decline in the interstate migration to urban Assam and to Bombay suggest that antimigrant campaigns and antimigration legislation have had little if any effect on population flows. The anti-Bengali riots in Assam in the early sixties were reportedly accompanied by a substantial exodus of Bengali Hindus, but, according to newspaper accounts, most of the Bengalis returned when the violence subsided. The anxieties over returning were apparently weighed against the absence of alternative jobs in Bengal. Similarly, there is no evidence thus far that the Tamil influx into Bombay has subsided, in spite of the bitter and sometimes violent attacks against Tamils by Shiv Sena supporters, and government directives to private employers to give preferences to Marathis for clerical and administrative positions. It is possible that nativism has succeeded in slowing the pace of interstate migrations over what would have taken place in its absence, but the present trend toward the growth of more heterogeneous urban centers does not appear to have abated.

This is not a demographic formula for intergroup harmony in India's urban areas. Nor is it a pointer toward good relations between ethnically heterogeneous cities and the homogeneous countrysides that surround them. Experiences in India and elsewhere do not give grounds for optimism. Nor does it seem likely that these demographic tendencies can be

361

reversed or even significantly slowed. India's ambitious, enterprising, upwardly mobile young people with higher education and skills are likely to move long distances, some across cultural-linguistic boundaries, in search of jobs and higher wages. It is hard to see how any public policy directed at influencing the selectivity of migration is likely to overcome two significant counter tendencies: the differential levels of education and skills among individuals belonging to different states and ethnic groups; and the differential rates of economic growth (and hence employment opportunities) between states and regions of the country. So long as these two trends diverge—and it is hard to see how they could not in a country as large as India and as ethnically diverse—and so long as the skilled, the educated, the enterprising, and the unemployed are in one locality and the opportunities are in another, people will migrate. Laws and regulations that are intended to prevent people from entering an area for employment when it is in their economic interests to do so, and when there is a demand for their labor, are likely to be evaded. Enforcement officers can be bribed, identification papers forged, and exceptions sought. In a country in which employment opportunities continue to grow more slowly than the size of the labor force, relatively small differences in employment opportunities and in wages between states and regions seem likely to lead migrants to seek ways to overcome both nativist hostility and protectionist policies.

But the failure of policies is rarely a reason for governments to change them. As we have seen, state governments have been responsive to the demands of their middle classes, who have become mobilized to seek protective legislation against outside competition. When these policies have not worked, or have been evaded, demands for more stringent policies and for more effective enforcement have grown.

More important, perhaps, than the effects of this legislation upon future patterns of migration may be its effects upon the position of those who have already migrated. Many nativists assert that inasmuch as a particular culture and language is associated with the land and the indigenous people who dwell there, outsiders should be required to adapt themselves to the customs of the land, and those who do not identify with the land and its culture should not be allowed to dwell within it. Almost every culture has an expression like that voiced by one Tibetan: "He who drinks the waters of the land must abide by its customs."

It follows, according to many nativists, that only those who speak the local language, adapt to local customs, identify with the land and its people, and treat local people and their culture with proper respect ought to remain. Thus, migrant manufacturers and shopkeepers who do not employ local people have by their acts betrayed the local community and demonstrated that they do not properly identify with the land and its people. From the point of view, therefore, of the local person who is hostile to migrants, the terms "domicile" and "sons of the soil" had best be left vague precisely because they assume a certain emotional identification with local people and certain standards of behavior which only local people can adequately define. The nativist political movement may be as concerned with encouraging the identification of migrants to the local community as with pressuring employers and government to give preferences to local people in employment.

Nativists advocate some ill-defined form of migrant "integration" with the dominant linguistic culture of the state, not necessarily "assimilation." Nativists recognize that migrants may retain their mother tongue in the home, and continue to observe their own distinctive habits and customs with respect to food, dress, and religious rituals. What is sought by the nativist is a change in the public behavior of the migrant: migrants are asked to speak the regional language, to take part in public festivities observed by the regional culture, and to support the political claims of the state upon the center and upon other states.

The demands of the nativists have created considerable anxiety among migrants and ethnic minorities of migrant

363

descent. Tamils in Bombay and Bangalore, Bengalis in Assam, Biharis in Chota Nagpur, coastal Andhras in Hyderabad, fear that their position and that of their children will be limited by sons-of-the-soil movements and policies. They fear that what is at stake is not merely future migration, but their own position within the community—their opportunities for sharing power, for educating their children, and for achieving jobs and promotions. From their point of view, reservation is simply a policy of discrimination. This concern that they, not potential migrants, are the real targets of protectionist policies has often been confirmed by nativists themselves. Indian law does not permit a distinction between those who belong to the regional culture and those who are born locally but who identify with another culture, but it is a distinction very much in the minds of nativists pressing for reservations for sons of the soil. The distinction—and the clear intent of such policies—was alluded to in a report of a committee appointed by the Assam state Legislative Assembly to inquire into the employment of Assamese: "In the absence of any clear-cut definition of the term 'local people,' the Committee has had to base its analysis as place of birth in Assam being the yardstick of local people. This yardstick is palpably inadequate and misleading and a clear understanding should be there in government and all others concerned in the matter as to what is meant by the term 'local people.' "[6] But the committee judiciously refrained from providing a "clear-cut definition."

Many migrants also fear violence. In Assam, Bombay, Chota Nagpur, and Telangana there have been frequent agitations against migrants. There are many forms of what the British call "Pak Bashing." Marwari shops have been burned in Gauhati, Bengalis have been beaten in Lakhimpur, Tamil signs have been torn off shops and Tamil cars have been overturned in Bombay, and Andhra-owned shops and houses have been attacked in Hyderabad. Those who use violence

[6] *Report of the Employment Review Committee, Third Report,* Assembly Secretariat, Assam, December 1973, p. 357.

364

have many objectives—to force migrant businessmen to employ local people, to humble "arrogant" migrants, to encourage migrants to leave, and to discourage others from coming. Moreover, the violence of young militants is used by the established political leadership of the community as an argument for passing protective laws and ordinances, and to pressure businessmen into giving preferences to local people on the grounds that such measures are necessary if further violence is to be avoided.

Only a small number of migrants—the most educated—have had to change their linguistic behavior as a consequence of nativism. The low-income, less well-educated migrants tend already to be conversant in the regional languages. In Assam, for example, the tribal tea plantation laborers and the Bengali Muslim peasants appear to be more willing to speak Assamese, and even to adapt to Assamese customs than the educated middle-class Bengali Hindus. Similarly, bilingual Telugus in Bombay, mostly members of the working class, speak Marathi as their second tongue, while the Tamil middle class is largely bilingual in English.

It is now widely argued that everyone, including migrants, must speak the regional language. The children of migrants must therefore learn a variety of languages: their mother tongue, which they use at home and which many use in the primary grades; the regional language, which is compulsory in secondary schools; Hindi as the official language of India and as an essential "link" language; and for those who come from families who want their children to enter the professions, English. At each stage of the educational process, educated parents must make decisions for their children based on language considerations: should they send their children to schools in which the language of instruction is the regional language, their own mother tongue, or English? Should they plan to send their children for higher education to the regional college, to the college in the state of their origin, where they could study in their own mother tongue, or should they prepare their children for entrance into one of the national universities or institutes of technology where English is the medium?

Some migrant businessmen take nativist sentiments into account not only in their employment, but in their investment policies. Fearful less of the policies of reservations than of violence, some migrant businessmen and merchants have geographically dispersed their investments. While hard data on this subject are impossible to find, a number of businessmen report that they are cautious about expanding their investments in areas where provinicial feelings are strong. Marwari businessmen in Gauhati whose shops and offices were set on fire in the 1960s have invested some of their capital in the Hindi-speaking region. There are reports that some Gujarati businessmen in Bombay, while not withdrawing from the city, have invested new capital in Ahmadabad and Baroda, two cities that have expanded since the state of Bombay was reorganized along linguistic lines. New Delhi, it should be noted, has profited from its reputation as a city that is hospitable to entrepreneurs from all over India—a reputation that once contributed to the growth of Calcutta and Bombay.

It is premature to conclude that nativist movements discourage investment by migrant entrepreneurs, but some state governments have been concerned about the possible flight of capital should nativism become too aggressive. In this respect state governments have been more far-sighted in encouraging investors from all over the country than some of the nativists, who would prefer to see an expansion of the public sector—though there is no evidence (and some to the contrary) that public-sector firms are more solicitous about employing local people than private firms.

THE FUTURE OF PROTECTIONIST POLICIES

Protectionist regulations are now so widespread in India that even if the nativist parties were to disappear from the political scene they would have had an enduring impact on the educational system and on the employment market. The political leaders of virtually every state see as one of their primary responsibilities "protecting" their own people against outsiders by imposing domicile restrictions in education and in state employment, and by pressing private firms to give preferences to local people. A state government whose leadership belongs to the same ethnic group as the majority of the population, and which relies upon the support of that majority, is likely to be responsive to "local" (widely understood as the ethnic majority) claims for preferences against migrants.

The pressure for such protective policies seems hardly likely to decrease, given the expected increases in India's labor force for the rest of this century. According to Ambannavar,[7] India's labor force will grow from 227 million in 1971 to 251.8 million in 1976, 280.6 million in 1981, and 347 million by 1991. These estimates, it should be noted, are based largely on an analysis of the age structure of a population that has already been born. Assuming that the labor force includes those who are fifteen years of age, all who enter the labor force until the early 1990s have already been born. By the year 2000, Ambannavar further estimates, the labor force will be about 420 million.

In annual terms, this means that 4.8 million young people entered the labor force each year in the early 1970s, 5.7 million will enter annually from 1976 to 1981, 6.3 million in the first half of the eighties, 6.9 million from 1986 through 1991, and 7.5 million annually by the end of the century.

Between 1971 and 1991, the rural labor force will grow from 191 to 278 million (45.5 percent in two decades), while the urban labor force will leap from 36.2 to 69.2 million, a staggering 91 percent increase.[8] By the year 2000, the rural labor force should increase to 322 million (a 68.5 percent increase over 1971), and the urban labor force to 97.4 million (an increase of 169 percent). Barring a far more rapid increase in nonagricultural employment than has taken

[7] Ambannavar, *Second India Studies*, p. 85.
[8] *Ibid.*, p. 87, table 3.9.

367

place so far, it seems likely that there will be an accelerated increase in India's urban unemployment, with the burden increasing on each year's entry of young people into the labor force. It is no wonder, then, that the political struggle for control over the urban labor market has already loomed so large in the politics of urban India, and why it seems likely to become even more important in the future.

There are, however, two elements that may restrain state governments from acceding to all of the restrictive demands advocated by nativists.

One is that some state government leaders recognize that what their state does, others may do as well. For those states with emigrating populations, restrictions on migrants from other states may lead neighboring states to impose restrictions on their migrants as well. Thus, should West Bengal restrict the employment of Oriya and Bihari workers, the states of Orissa and Bihar might further restrict the employment of Bengalis. Should Kerala restrict Tamils, Tamil Nadu could restrict Malayalis. When there were agitations in Bombay against the showing of Tamil films, there were threats in Tamil Nadu that Hindi films might be restricted—thereby creating a severe blow to Bombay's large Hindi film industry. If the Assamese have been harsher in their treatment of migrants and linguistic minorities than have many other states, surely it is because they need not fear that other states will mistreat Assamese, since Assamese emigrants are so few in number. It is the fear of reciprocity rather than some overriding concern for national integrity or individual rights that often discourages state governments from pursuing protectionist policies.

The second restraint is the central government. The central government has substantial powers to limit state government efforts to restrict migration. Though state governments can regulate their own public employment, they cannot regulate the employment of central government personnel within the state, including employment in public-sector industries under central government control. Nor can state governments impose domicile requirements on employment in the private sector, though they can often put considerable pressure on businessmen to hire the local ethnic majority. It would take an act of the central parliament to require private firms to hire through local exchanges, a policy the central government would hesitate to impose, since it would be opposed by their own public-sector managers who, like private businessmen, want to hire their work force—especially their skilled labor and managerial staff—nationally. Finally, it should be noted that state governments can regulate admissions into state-supported educational institutions, but they cannot affect the centrally run educational institutions within their own state. The national universities, the Indian institutes of technology, and the many centrally run teaching and research institutes all recruit faculty and students in a national competition.

The interests of the central and state governments diverge. While state governments seek to protect their own people, the central government seeks to make national institutions accessible to all. The central government, the larger all-India private firms, the public sector under central control, the nationally run educational institutions, the scientific laboratories and research centers, and, though they are not numerous in India, the multinational corporations, are all stimulants to migration, including migration across state boundaries; in contrast, state governments, state-run public sector industries, businesses run by local entrepreneurs, and state-run educational institutions are likely to side with nativist demands for protectionist policies. The success of nativist policies is thus likely to be in inverse proportion to the strength of central authority in India.

Are there alternatives to protectionist policies for governments committed to increasing the employment opportunities of the local population? The system of reservations assures the local population that a fixed proportion of admissions into educational institutions, jobs, and promotions will be available to them without having to compete with those out-

369

side their own community or ethnic group. An alternative set of policies would be directed at enhancing the capacity of the local population to compete against outsiders. The government could, for example, finance the job training programs for firms prepared to hire local people without requisite skills. Government could also provide short-term wage subsidies to provide incentives to employers to hire local people in selected job categories. The government could establish educational programs to train local people for jobs that will be created as a consequence of anticipated public or private investment. Counseling services and training programs within secondary schools and colleges could assist in guiding students into the existing local labor market. Finally, antidiscrimination legislation with enforcement procedures could be passed to cope with complaints that employers are discriminating against the local population.

These alternatives are not as attractive politically as the policy of reservations. State and local political leaders nearly universally believe that government should assure a distribution of educational and employment benefits between ethnic groups, and should protect ethnic groups against the inequalities that result from competition. At the state and local level few subscribe to the notion that government's role is to enhance the opportunities by individuals to compete for education, jobs, promotions, and higher salaries. It would require the intervention of a central government firmly committed to the free movement of individuals within an open labor market to reverse the protectionist policies that have already been adopted.

Many of the policies pursued by the state and central governments in India to cope with the problem of uneven development have been understandable political responses to severe social tensions. One can hardly fault a government for trying to find policies that will prevent a state from being divided by regional claims, or for pacifying local people anxious over the successes of migrants, or for coopting the platforms of parties winning elections on nativist platforms.

370

In a society where development is both uneven and slow, where economic differences overlap with ethnic and regional differences, and where social groups are politically mobilized by political parties, government has little choice but to give high priority to programs and policies to reduce social tensions and minimize the political losses for government. However, policies that successfully diffuse social tensions and antigovernment activities also incur costs. The political costs of protectionist policies are actually small, for in most instances it matters little that a small number of linguistic minorities, potential migrants, and employers are critical. The real losses are the costs in opportunity, those unseen would-have-beens that might have taken place if governments and citizens had been creative and imaginative enough to forgo short-term benefits for long-term gains. What India loses are the advantages of a common market in a continental economy where investments, goods, and people can freely move from one region to another in response to local opportunities. The challenge of a political leadership is to find a way of assisting those who are falling behind in the development process, without adopting policies that constrict the innovative, ambitious, creative elements of a society whose talents are essential if the entire country is to move forward. One of the major questions for the Indian government is whether it uses its authority to build an internal common market, with spatial mobility as one of its features, or lends its support to those groups that want government to pursue internal protectionist policies. India seems likely to develop with either set of policies; the question is, what kind of India will it be?

371

INDEX

Adimjati Seva Mandal, 191, 193, 194
Adivasis, definition, 157, 312. See also Chota Nagpuri tribals; scheduled tribes
Ahmadabad, 19, 36, 55; development, 22, 366
Ahom: administration under British rule, 91-92; employment of Muslims, 102n; rule in Assam, 80, 80-84
Ahomiya, 300, 303-304; see also Assamese (people)
Akali Dal, 295, 296
Alam, Shah Manzoor, 227
All Assam Students Union, 117-20
American constitution, 327-29; Fourteenth Amendment, 328
American missionaries, see missionaries
Andaman Islands, 149, 195
Andhra High Court, 248, 253
Andhra Mahasabha, 295, 296
Andhra Pradesh, 12, 29, 37, 217, 219, 229, 238, 304; creation, 221-22, 251; development, 229, 235-36, 244, 245; education, 244-45; ethnic tension in, 77, 248, 253; imposition of President's rule, 253-55; linguistic composition, 56, 58; literacy rate, 237n, 289; migrant communities, 67-71, 242; outmigration, 61, 224, 278. See also Andhras; Congress

party; Hyderabad; Jana Sangh; mulkis; Telangana; Telangana Praja Samiti
Andhra Pradesh government, 225; employment, 227-28, 232-33, 265; Legislative Assembly, 239; preferential policies, 248-49, 251-52, 266; use of military, 267. See also employment exchanges; Indian Constitution, 1950; mulki rules; Public Employment Act of 1957
Andhras, 218, 238, 241, 248; as migrants, 224, 226-31, 276; as political elite, 219, 239, 246, 265-66; conflict with mulkis, 249-50, 253; cultural identity, 220, 236-38, 241; language, 220, 241
Arunachal Pradesh, 30, 83, 87; tribals in, 152, 182
Assam, 12, 29, 37, 39, 64, 65; development, 125-30, 134-36, 352; disturbances of 1960, 117-24; education, 108, 125-28, 285-86; employment, 90-91, 126-30; language policy, 107-108, 111-12, 117-24, 355; linguistic composition of, 22, 79-80, 275; members of parliament from, 310; migrant communities in, 14, 24, 52, 65-69, 79-105, 128, 134, 152, 303-304; migration and ethnic tension, 77-136; migration policy,

373

Assam (*cont.*)
116, 361; migration rates, 81-82, 278-79; opportunity in, 80-81, 100-101, 104-105, 109, 130, 134-35; political movements, 118-19, 129-30, 134-36, 274-75; preferential employment, 129-30, 135, 265; state organization, 84-87, 122. *See also* hill tribes, plains tribes
Assamese (language), 117-124
Assamese (people), 22, 47, 132, 136-38; and Bengali migrants, 92-95, 106-124, 131, 136-38, 265; and language policy, 107, 111-12, 117-24; as migrants, 66-67, 130, 133; assimilation of immigration, 112-13, 121-23, 133, 304; cultural identity, 107-117, 132, 277, 299, 300-301, 303-304; Hindus, 83-86, 110-111; middle-class, 94-95, 107, 111-13, 128, 133, 285-86, 355; relations with Marwaris, 128-29, 131, 134-35; relations with tribals, 120-23. *See also* hill tribes; plains tribes
Assam Land and Revenue Regulations, 109
Assam Plantation Labour Rules of 1956, 91
Assam Sahitya Sabha, 119
Assam state government, 85-86, 91-93, 125; and political movements, 129-30, 274; employment, 128; preferential policies, 118-20, 126-27, 131-32, 136, 286, 364; use of military, 119. *See also* Congress party

Bangalore, 36, 285, 309, 358; development, 22, 24; linguistic composition, 22, 54-55, 58, 65, 361; migrant communities, 60,

68, 267, 275; political movements, 271, 272, 358. *See also* Kannada Chaluvaligars
Bangladesh (formerly East Pakistan), 23, 75-77; emigration, 21, 32, 35, 66, 83, 351
Baroda, 366
Bengali (language): and language riots, 117-24; in education, 107, 108, 111; speakers, 51n, 52, 56, 60, 79, 113, 117n
Bengali (people): cultural identity, 305-306; in Assam, 9, 92-95, 106-24, 131, 136-38, 265, 303-304; in civil service, 48-49, 337-39; language riots, 117-24
Bengali Hindus: and language policy, 117-24; in Assam, 85-86, 93, 94, 101, 108, 115, 134, 138; middle-class, 115-17, 285-86; relations with Assamese, 106-108, 110-17, 131, 361; relations with Bengali Muslims, 108-109, 305-306
Bengali Muslims: and migration policy, 109, 110n; dominance, 104-117, 304; impact on land use, 98-101, 108; in Assam, 80, 85-87, 95-102, 134, 138; relations with Assamese Hindus, 100, 110-11, 122-23, 131; relations with Bengali Hindus, 108-109, 305-306. *See also* Mymensinghias
Bentinck, Lord William, 88
Bhashani, Maulana, 110
Bhil, 27, 51n, 152
Bhojpuri, 29
Bhumij, 152
Bihar, 12, 22, 29, 30, 37, 64; emigration, 104, 137, 149, 278; government, 179-80, 337-39; literacy rate, 287; migrants in,

47, 66, 71, 77, 152, 361; political movements, 243; preferential recruitment, 337-39. *See also* Bihar Legislative Assembly; Chota Nagpur
Bihari, 51n, 73-74; and tribal politics, 190-92, 205, 207; as migrants, 83, 86, 197; Hindus, 169
Bihar Legislative Assembly, 176, 192
Bihu festivals, 90, 116
Birsa Munda, leader, 163-64, 178, 279; movement, 163-64, 202, 275
Birsa Seva Dal, 151, 177-78, 181-82, 288; as Christian party, 192, 194, 195
Bodo, 86, 87, 120-21, 304
Bodo Sahitya Sabha, 120
Bogue, Donald, 77
Bombay, 9, 12, 36, 267, 286; cultural identity, 227, 301, 307, 313-14; development, 22, 24, 366; government, 266, 309; indigenous population, 22, 266, 358; linguistic composition, 22, 53-54, 64, 275, 361; migrants in, 66, 67, 72, 266; political movements, 266, 271. *See also* Maharashtrians; Shiv Sena
Bombaywallas, 301, 302, 307
Brahmaputra valley, 66, 80, 83, 87; and language policy, 117-24; distribution of ethnic communities, 136-38, 275; migrants in, 86, 87, 98-99, 102
Brett Circular, 337
Britain, 72, 74
British colonies, 73-74
British missionaries; *see* missionaries
British rule: and labor recruitment, 48, 61; and preferential

policies, 92-93, 107-109, 131, 159, 163-64, 203-204, 335-36; in Assam, 80, 84-86, 108-109, 110; in Chota Nagpur, 147-49, 150, 158, 162-63. *See also* preferential admissions; preferential recruitment; tea plantations
Burma, 73, 75, 90, 351; and Assam, 80, 83, 84

Cachar, 83, 85, 86, 117-24
Calcutta, 36, 301n, 309; development, 22, 24, 366; linguistic composition, 55-56; migrants in, 65, 67, 69, 168
census, 1891, 102, 103, 279
census, 1921, 90
census, 1931, 97, 98n
census, 1951, 96-100, 101n
census, 1961: in Assam, 79n, 90, 101, 103n, 116n, 117n, 122, 133, 278; in Brahmaputra valley, 137-38; in Chota Nagpur, 155; in Hyderabad, 225, 227, 275
census, 1971, 31, 34, 35-37, 59-61, 63, 81n, 224, 244-45, 291n, 358-59
central government: and preferential policies, 339-44, 368-71; and recognition of ethnic groups, 20-21, 306-307; in Assam, 81, 86-87, 119, 127, 133; in Telangana, 228, 231, 248-50, 253-55. *See also* employment exchanges; Indian constitution; preferential admissions; preferential recruitment; reserved constituencies
Chinese, 9, 75, 88-89
Chota Nagpur, 151-52, 180-82, 189-90, 200-201, 275; and preferential policies, 149, 288,

Chota Nagpur (*cont.*)
355; colonization, 157, 167, 180; cultural identity, 314-16; education, 147, 183-88, 191, 193, 196-97, 208-209, 265; emigration, 160-65, 279; employment, 148n, 179-80, 183-88, 208-209, 265; ethnic conflict, 162-73, 288; development, 145-54, 157, 165-67, 171, 181-83, 191, 200-201, 206, 352; land loss, 148, 157-67, 198, 202; land system, 146-47, 158-59, 169-73; members of parliament, 314-317; political parties, 150-51, 162-65, 175-84, 188-92, 275; separatism, 178, 181-82, 194, 202-203, 265, 334-35; socialism in, 181-82, 200, 202. *See also* Birsa Munda; Birsa Seva Dal; Chota Nagpuri tribals; Congress party; employment exchanges; Jharkhand party; Kuzur, Lalit; Tana Bhagat

Chota Nagpur government, 183, 190-92; preferential policies, 185-86, 191, 193, 199, 203-207, 288; services, 147-49, 179, 288

Chota Nagpur Tenancy Act, 159, 198, 203-204

Chota Nagpuri tribals, 151-56; and development, 148-51, 200-209; and preferential policies, 183, 185-86, 193, 199-200, 203-205, 316-17; as cultivators, 155-56, 159-67, 173; as migrants, 87, 104, 134, 148n, 149, 160-65, 174-75, 186-87, 201-208; conflict among tribals, 185-200, 205-206; cultural identity, 177-79, 277, 314-16; educated, 175-84, 287; employ-

ment, 148-49, 167, 171-74, 179, 181-84, 195; ethnic conflict, 150-51, 162-73, 201; middle-class, 176-77, 191-92, 196, 355-56; politics, 188-89, 201-209, 265; population, 149, 153-54, 160-62, 171, 275; relations with nontribals, 149-51, 155-59, 181, 190-92, 201-202, 265, 315. *See also* Christian tribals; *dikus*; employment exchanges, non-Christian tribals; scheduled tribes

Christian tribals, 187n, 188-89, 204; education, 184-88, 193, 196; relations with Hindus, 190-92, 195, 206-20

citizenship, 300, 327-29; definition, 325-36; dual, 329, 344-48; impact on migration, 327-29; varying conceptions of, 326-27

Congress party, 29, 189, 336; in Assam, 86, 110-11; in Bihar, 191; in Bombay, 266; in Chota Nagpur, 151, 188-89, 192; in Telangana, 219, 220, 224, 258

contract labor, 77, 89-90, 168

Darjeeling, 65

Das, H. P., 106

Delhi, 36, 37, 301; development, 24, 366; linguistic composition of, 19, 22, 55; migrants in, 67, 68

Delhiwallas, 301, 302

Dhanbad district, 147, 154, 165-67

dikus: and anti-*diku* movements, 162-65, 177, 190, 191, 201; definition, 159, 312, 314; in

Chota Nagpur, 159, 168-74, 190, 194, 277

D.M.K., *see* Dravida Munnetra Kazhagam

domicile requirements: for admissions, 343-44; for employment, 338, 341-42. *See also mulki* rules; preferential admissions; preferential recruitment

Dravida Munnetra Kazhagam (D.M.K.), 295, 296

East Africa, 73

East Bengal, 37, 96-102, 109. *See also* Bengali Hindus, Bengali Muslims

East Godavari, 226-27, 229

East India Company, 92, 95, 147, 158, 162

East Pakistan, 55, 60-61, 86, 114. *See also* Bangladesh

educational opportunities: and unemployment, 283-85; growth, 282-83. *See also* by name of individual states and cities; preferential admissions

education policies: and language policies, 320-21, 332-33; and state colleges, 333; as viewed by MPs, 319-20. *See also* preferential admissions; preferential policies

Elliot, Carolyn, 232

employment exchanges: and unemployment, 280, 285, 288; in Chota Nagpur, 181-84; in Hyderabad, 230, 245; in Mysore, 341; legal provisions for, 340-42, 369

English (language), 27, 115, 117, 123, 365-66

ethnic conflict, 3, 7, 75-78, 364-66; in Andhra Pradesh, 77, 249-50, 253; in Assam, 77-136, 361; in Bombay, 361; in Chota Nagpur, 162-73; in Telangana, 218, 220, 239, 248, 253; use of military, 81, 162, 163, 267; use of police, 163, 267. *See also* by individual state or city

ethnic demography, 3-4

ethnic group politics, 294-98

ethnic infrastructure, 10

Fancy Bazar, 103, 129

French Rights of Man, 328

Gandhi, Indira, 12, 119, 219, 251-53

Gandhi, Mahatma, 157, 336

Garos, 30, 86, 304

Gauhati, 9, 119, 271, 361; middle-class, 285, 358

Gauhati University, 117-19

Gentlemen's Agreement, 222-23, 228, 289-90

Goalpara, 96

Gond, 152

Gondi, 27, 51n

government, *see* central government

Government of India Act of 1833, 328

Gujarat, 19, 62, 65-67, 69; tribal population, 152, 361

Gujarati (language), 19

Gujarati (people), 67, 73-74

Guntur, 226-27, 229

Guria, Moses, 180-82

Harijans, *see* scheduled castes

Haryana, 30, 37

Hatia region, 147, 154

Heavy Engineering Corporation (H.E.C.), 147, 154, 157; tribal employment, 148, 179, 182

377

hill tribes, 80, 83-84, 86; reorganization, 86-87, 122-23, 304. *See also* Garo; Khasi; Mikir; Mizo; Naga
Himachal Pradesh, 39, 152
Hindi (language), 21, 28, 79, 155; as dominant, 19, 27n, 51n, 67, 365, 366; -speaking population, 52-56, 58, 60, 67-68, 73-74, 113
Hindu, The, 250
Hinduism, 155-59, 190, 192; and Indo-Aryans, 151-52; rule, 146, 157
Ho, 173, 186; in Chota Nagpur, 146, 148n, 152, 154-55; relations with *dikus*, 170-71
Horo, N. E., 193
Hyderabad, 223-25, 309; civil service, 227-28, 276; cultural identity, 236-247, 301, 311-13; employment, 229-30, 233n, 235-36, 358; ethnic conflict, 218-19, 234, 239, 253; development, 24, 229, 235; linguistic composition, 56, 58, 68, 242-43; migrants, 60, 225-28, 275-76, 285; political movements, 230-36, 271-73; student survey, 255-58. *See also mulkis*; Telangana; Telangana Praja Samiti
Hyderabad Civil Service Rules, 223
Hyderabad High Court, 238
Hyderabadis, 301-302. *See also mulkis*

Ibo, 75
Illustrated Weekly, 13
Indian Army, 81, 163
Indian Constitution of 1950, 25; and citizenship, 328-29; and discrimination, 327-28;

and linguistic minorities, 118, 330; and migration policy, 116, 329; and preferential policies, 185, 203-204, 239 249-55, 344; and scheduled tribes, 184-85; Article 16 (equal opportunity), 339; Article 19 (freedom of movement), 331; Article 29 (protection of cultural identity), 330; Article 30 (right to education), 330; Article 350A (language policy) 330
Indo-Aryan, 80, 151-52

Jalpaiguri, 65
Jamshedpur, 165-67
Jana Sangh, 151, 192, 220
Jharkhand party: and separatism, 193-94, 199, 202-203; as Christian party, 185, 191-95; as nativist movement, 151, 165, 274, 279, 288
Jorhat, 127

Kachari, 86, 87
Kannada (people), 52-60, 72, 237, 275; and preferential policies, 266-67, 292-93; literacy rate, 290-92
Kannada Chaluvaligars, 266-67, 272, 274; social base, 291-93
Karnataka, *see* Mysore
Katzenstein, Mary, 287
Kenya, 75
Kerala, 19, 22, 37; emigration, 60; literacy rate, 290-91; migrants in, 67, 71, 267
Khan, Waheeduddin, 227-28, 246-47
Kharia, 152, 186
Kharwar, 152
Khasi, 30, 86, 304

Kol insurrection, 162
Konkani, 27, 29, 51n
Krishna district, 226-27, 229
Krishna, Raj, 280-81, 282
Kumauni, 29, 51n
Kurukh Oraon, 27, 51n
Kuzur, Lalit, 177-81

labor, ethnic division of, 4-12,
  47-49, 284, 351
labor force: and local population,
  351-56; growth, 281, 367;
  skilled, 4-6, 283-84, 354, 357;
  unskilled, 4-6, 160-61, 167,
  171, 174-75, 357. *See also* by
  individual state or city
labor markets, 5-6, 90-91, 126-
  30; dual labor market, 4, 5,
  352, 367-68; protected, 335-
  39. *See also* by individual
  state or city
Lachit Sena, 274
land policies, 331, 336; in Chota
  Nagpur, 159, 163-64, 203-204;
  in Telangana, 222. *See also*
  preferential policies
Line System, 1920, 109
linguistic dispersal index, 278-79
linguistic minorities: and preferential policies, 335-36, 364-66;
  constitutional protection, 330-
  32; preservation of 306-307
Linguistic Minorities Commission, 134
"local" populations: ethnic identification of, 299-324, 342;
  hypothesis, 321-24; political
  identification of, 302, 307;
  terminology, 300-307; territorial identification of, 299-
  324, 342

Madhya Pradesh, 29, 37, 243;

migrant population, 69, 71;
  tribal population, 152, 361
Madras, 24, 36, 225, 309; linguistic composition, 19, 56;
  migrant population, 60, 68,
  221; presidency, 48, 70
Maharashtra, 12, 30, 37, 39; and
  separatism, 29, 243; emigration, 60, 225, 278; ethnic tension, 77; literacy rate, 287;
  migrants in, 24, 67-72; preferential policies, 342, 343
Maharashtrians, 313-14; and
  preferential policies, 266, 307,
  361; as migrants, 68-69, 237,
  275, 277, 279; literacy rate,
  286, 287; middle-class, 285,
  287; relations with migrants,
  266, 287
Maithili, 29
Malayalam, 19, 60, 63, 71-72
Malaysia, 73, 75
Marathi, 52-54, 58, 60. *See also*
  Maharashtrians
Marwaris: as migrants, 9, 45, 46,
  52, 69-70; in Assam, 86, 102-
  106, 128-29; in Chota Nagpur,
  180, 193
Meghalaya, 30, 83, 152, 267;
  creation, 86-87, 304
members of parliament, 308-24
Mikir, 86, 87, 304
millennarian and messianic movements, 150, 177, 201, 202, 265
Mina, 152
Ministry of Labour, Employment
  and Rehabilitation, 340-41,
  342
Minz, Reverend Nirmal, 197-200,
  201
missionaries: and education, 123,
  185-88, 193; relations with
  tribals, 156, 190, 195
Mizo, 30, 86, 304

379

Mizoram, 30, 87, 152, 304
moneylenders, 156, 160, 171, 173, 331
Montagu-Chelmsford reforms, 335
Morley-Minto reforms of 1909, 335
Mughal rule: in Assam, 84, 91, 102; in Chota Nagpur, 146-47, 150, 158, 200; in Telangana, 223
Mukherjee, Dilip, 243n
mulki rules, 222, 233, 248-51; and constitutional amendment, 253-55; and five-point formula, 251-53; justification of, 238, 250, 313. *See also* Gentlemen's Agreement; preferential admissions; preferential recruitment
Mulki Rules Act, 253
mulkis, 217, 222, 223, 312; agitations, 218-19, 234; competition with migrants, 228, 239, 289-90; cultural identity, 220, 236-43, 247, 255, 277; employment, 223, 228, 235-36; members of parliament, 311-13; middle-class, 235, 243, 246, 247, 265-66, 289-90. *See also mulki* rules; Telugus
Mundas, 180, 186; and Birsa Munda, 164, 178; in Assam, 86, 160; in Chota Nagpur, 146, 148n, 152-58, 165, 202
Muslim League, 85, 97-98, 101, 108-110
Muslims, 49-50, 84; as students, 254-58; in Assam, 102, 124; in Chota Nagpur, 157-58, 185; in Hyderabad, 223-24, 237n, 240-43, 274. *See also* Bengali Muslims

Mymensingh, 86, 98, 100-101, 113n
Mymensinghias, 86, 96-100, 304. *See also* Bengali Muslims
Mysore, 22, 37; education in, 53, 290-92; emigration, 60, 225, 278; migrants in 67-72; preferential policies, 292-93, 341, 343

Nagaland, 30, 86, 152, 304
National Commission on Labour, 282
national identity, 325-26
National Integration Council, 340, 342-44
nativism, 14-16, 24, 275, 277-79; and cultural identity, 272-73; and preferential policies, 356-58, 364-66; and social mobility, 8, 293-94, 352; and unemployment, 280-85; conditions for development, 274-94; contrasted with regional movements, 294-98; impacts, 361-63, 366-71; theories, 269-73, 356
nativist political parties, *see* Birsa Munda; Birsa Seva Dal; Jharkhand party; Kannada Chaluvaligars; Lachit Sena; Shiv Sena; Telangana Praja Samiti
NEFA, *see* Arunachal Pradesh
Nehru, Jawaharlal, 110n, 121n
Nepalis: as migrants in India, 21, 27, 32, 35, 50, 51n; in Assam, 86, 104, 134
N.G.O., *see* nongazetted officers
Nigeria, 75
Niligiri hills, 152
Nizam College, 218
Nizam of Hyderabad, 222-23, 240

non-Christian tribals, 204, 206-207; conflict with Christians, 191-92, 195, 209; education and employment, 184-88, 193, 196; urbanization, 187n
nongazetted officers (N.G.O.s), 218, 232, 234, 290
Non-gazetted Officers' Central Union, 289
nontribals in Chota Nagpur: and conflicts, 162-65; and development, 148-50; and land problem, 157-59. See also dikus
North East Frontier Agency, see Arunachal Pradesh
Nowgong, 96, 97, 98, 119

Oraon, Kartik, 184-86, 192-93
Oraons, 180, 186; employment in Chota Nagpur, 148n, 168-69; in Assam, 86; in Chota Nagpur, 146, 152, 154-55, 165
Orissa: emigration, 47, 61, 137, 152, 158; migrants in, 66, 69
Oriya, 52, 60, 69, 73-74
Osmania University, 218, 290

Pahari, 27, 51n
Pakistan: creation of, 85-86, 108-109; East Pakistan, 98, 109; emigration, 21, 32, 35, 85; immigration, 23, 55, 351
Parliament, 252, 308-24, 339
People's Democratic Party (PDP), 127
plains tribes, 86-87, 120-24. See also Bodo, Kachari
Plantations Labour Act, 1951, 91
political parties, see Birsa Munda; Birsa Seva Dal; Congress party; Jana Sangh; Jharkhand party; Kannada Chaluvaligars;

Lachit Sena; millennarian and messianic movements; Shiv Sena; Tana Bhagat; Telangana Praja Samiti
Prasad, Rajendra, 337-39, 342
preferential admissions, 319-20, 336, 342-44, 361-63, 366-71; in Assam, 108, 111-12, 131, 186; in Chota Nagpur, 185-86, 199-200, 204-207; in Telangana, 222, 253-55, 356-57. See also Gentlemen's Agreement; mulki rules
preferential policies, 136, 327, 335-37, 361-63, 327, 364, 366-371. See also domicile rules; preferential admissions; preferential recruitment; reserved constituencies
preferential recruitment, 48, 267, 282, 315-18, 336, 340-44, 356-57, 361-63, 366-71; in Chota Nagpur, 183, 185-86, 193, 199-200, 203-207; in Telangana, 218, 222-23, 238, 253-55, 289, 356. See also Gentlemen's Agreement; mulki rules
Presidential powers, 253-55, 330, 331
Public Employment Act of 1957, 248, 249, 251, 290
Punjab, 29, 37, 62; migrants in, 65, 66, 68, 79n, 280. See also Akali Dal
Punjabis: as migrants, 46, 68, 134; in Assam, 86, 104, 129

Rajasthan (formerly Rajputana), 37, 52, 69-70, 102-103, 152
Rajputana, see Rajasthan
Rajputs, 158, 180
Ranchi, 147; development, 165-67; nativist movement, 271;

Ranchi (*cont.*)
tribal population, 153-54, 171,
186, 275, 361
Ranchi University, 147, 148, 154,
207
Rayalaseema, 221, 226
Reddy, Brahmananda, 246
religion, *see* Bengali Hindus;
Bengali Muslims; Christian
tribals; Hinduism; missionaries;
Muslims; *Sarna*
reserved constituencies: in Chota
Nagpur, 185-86, 191, 203-207,
222

Saadulla, Mohammad, 85
Sadani, 155
safeguards, *see* Gentlemen's
Agreement; *mulki* rules; pref-
erential policies
Samyukta Maharashta Samiti,
295, 296
Santal Parganas, 148n, 154, 160,
162
Santals, 27, 51n, 86, 152; in
Chota Nagpur, 148n, 154, 165
Sardar movement, 163
Sarna, 156, 163, 195
scheduled castes, 185; constitu-
tional provisions for, 331-32,
335-36
scheduled tribes, 331-32, 335-36.
see also Chota Nagpuri tribals
Separate Telangana Convention,
218
Shiv Sena, 266, 274, 287, 354,
358, 361
Sikhs, 29, 45
Sindhi, 27, 50, 51n
Singbhum district: development,
165-67; tribals in, 154, 171,
186, 275
Singh, Jaipal, 189
Singh, Suresh, 164

"sons of the soil," 12-14, 151,
255, 272, 311-12, 363
South Africa, 73
Sri Lanka, 73, 75, 351
Statesman, The, 118, 119, 252
student movements: and police,
218; in Telangana, 218-21,
234, 246
Supreme Court of India, 248,
249, 251
Surma valley, 83, 86
Sylhet, 85, 86, 110

Tagore, Rabindranath, 116
Tamil (language), 43, 51n, 54-
60
Tamil Nadu, 37, 61; government,
267-68; literacy rate, 290-91;
migrants in, 67, 70, 71
Tamils, 9, 48, 49, 361; as migrants, 63, 71-74
Tana Bhagat, 164-65, 202
Tata, Jamshedji, 147
Tata Iron and Steel Company
(Tisco), 147
Tea District Labor Agency, 182
tea plantations: creation, 88-90;
ethnic preference in employment, 47, 80, 83, 86, 90, 91,
104, 149, 160-62, 182, 279;
in Assam, 80, 83, 86, 88-91;
in Bengal, 149, 160-62
Telangana, 30, 217, 231, 246,
312; development, 221-22, 229,
238, 244; education, 218, 229,
232-33, 237, 244-45, 266;
employment, 244-46, 290;
ethnic conflict, 218, 220, 248,
253; government, 218-19, 228,
238; Islamic influence, 223,
240, 242, 247, 273; literacy
rate, 222, 237-38, 288; members of parliament from, 311-
13, 318; merged with Andhra,

228, 289; migrants in, 226, 244; political elite of, 246, 247, 253-54; political movements, 220, 246, 265-66, 274; Regional Council of, 222; support for separatism, 218-21, 230-31, 234-35, 236, 242-48, 254-57, 313; under feudal rule, 238, 240, 244, 250-51. *See also* Congress party; Gentlemen's Agreement; *mulki* rules; *mulkis;* preferential policies; Telangana Praja Samiti

Telangana Praja Samiti (T.P.S.), 218-19, 221-23, 249, 254, 274; social base, 220-21, 231-36, 258

Telugus: as a migratory population, 70-72, 279; as migrants, 52-56, 61; bilingualism in, 58; in Telangana, 221, 222, 236-37, 241

territorial ethnicity, 4

Tiga, Julius, 189

Times of India, The, 243n, 292

T.P.S., *see* Telangana Praja Samiti

trade unions, 91, 148, 290

Tripura, 37, 66

Uganda, 75, 351

United States, 72, 268-70

U.P.: *see* Uttar Pradesh

urban growth, 24, 358-60; and development, 77-78, 366; in Ahmadabad, 22, 366. *See also* Bangalore; Bombay; Calcutta; Chota Nagpur; Delhi; Gauhati; Hyderabad; Ranchi

Urdu, 19, 27, 49-50, 51n

Uttar Pradesh (U.P.), 37, 19, 243; emigration, 60, 104; migrants in, 66, 68

Vaghaiwalla, Mr., 98, 99-100

Visalandhra, 221, 222

West Bengal, 37, 66, 85, 305-306; emigration, 60, 280, 267; migrants in, 65-67, 71, 79n, 280

West Godavari, 226-27, 229

LIBRARY OF CONGRESS CATALOGING
IN PUBLICATION DATA

Weiner, Myron.
  Sons of the soil.

  1. Migration, Internal—India.   2. India—Popu-
lation.   3. Social mobility—India.   4. Ethnology—
India.   I. Title.
HB2099.W44   301.32'6'0954   78-51202
ISBN 0-691-09379-2